International Communism and the Cult of the Individual

Kevin Morgan

International Communism and the Cult of the Individual

Leaders, Tribunes and Martyrs under Lenin and Stalin

palgrave
macmillan

Kevin Morgan
Sch of Social Sci Politics
University of Manchester
Manchester, United Kingdom

ISBN 978-1-349-95337-0 ISBN 978-1-137-55667-7 (eBook)
DOI 10.1057/978-1-137-55667-7

Library of Congress Control Number: 2016957363

Printed on acid-free paper

This Palgrave Macmillan imprint is published by Springer Nature
The registered company is Macmillan Publishers Ltd.
The registered company address is: The Campus, 4 Crinan Street, London, N1 9XW, United Kingdom

Acknowledgements

This book draws on research into communist history going back over many years and it is impossible to register all the debts I have accumulated here. Nevertheless, a number of these must be recorded dating from the period I spent working specifically on this project in 2013–2015. For this opportunity I must first acknowledge the support of the Arts and Humanities Research Council (award AH/J005975/1: 'Communism and the cult of the leader') supported by sabbatical leave from the University of Manchester and the cover provided by my colleagues in Politics. I was very fortunate to have the assistance of Francis King while researching in the Moscow archives and for guidance on diverse translation issues. Unless otherwise stated, translations from Russian sources are by Dr King. I am also grateful to Julie Johnson and Norman LaPorte for help with translations from the German and diverse other matters, to José Neves and Stephen Parker for help with original texts which I had read in French and to Gavin Bowd and Gareth Price-Thomas for their comments on other translation issues. I must also thank Lynda Morris for assistance in locating the Picasso images, and owe special thanks to Aldo Agosti for the translation of the letter of Togliatti cited in Chaps 2 and 3, and for assistance with a number of other queries.

The immediate idea for writing the book came from editing the inaugural issue of *Twentieth Century Communism* on 'Communism and the leader cult' in 2009. I must therefore record my debt to those who contributed to that issue and to my fellow journal editors. I also derived much benefit from the Manchester seminar on the cult of the individual in December 2013, and would like to thank Balázs Apor, John Bulaitis,

Sarah Davies, Mario Kessler, Norman LaPorte, Marietta Stankova and all who contributed to a stimulating day. I also appreciated the opportunity to present parts of this research at events organised by the Society for the Study of Labour History and the Communism Group of the Political Studies Association, and at the ESSHC and Historical Materialism conferences held respectively in Vienna and London in 2014. A final presentation at the University of Bern provided the occasion for comments on the introduction from Brigitte Studer which I found particularly helpful.

The broader treatment offered here would have been impossible without the stimulus and intellectual generosity of colleagues working on communism and left movements internationally. In addition to those already mentioned, those who helped through discussion, feedback, sources or advice on specific points include Kasper Braskén, John Callaghan, Madeleine Davis, Jean-François Fayet, Mike Jones, Anastasia Koukouna, Carl Levy, Adriá Llacuna, Stuart Macintyre, John Manley, Emmet O'Connor, Bernard Pudal, Ole Martin Rønning, James G. Ryan, Andrew Thorpe, Stephen White, Serge Wolikow and Matthew Worley. I am particularly grateful to those who read over sections of the text dealing with matters in which they have particular expertise, namely John Bulaitis, Romain Ducolombier, José Gotovitch, Norman LaPorte, Lars T. Lih, Silvio Pons, Tim Rees and Tauno Saarela. Given our published collaborations in the field, I owe it to Norry LaPorte in particular to point out that I alone am responsible for the interpretations presented here.

On many occasions in the past I have already had to record my thanks to colleagues at the Working Class Movement Library, the Labour History Archive and Study Centre and other research libraries in Britain. As well as further research at RGASPI in Moscow, I must now also acknowledge the assistance I received from libraries and archives in Paris including the departmental archives of Seine-Saint-Denis; the Bibliothèque de documentation internationale contemporaine at Nanterre; the archives of the PCF; the Archives nationales; and the Centre d'Histoire Sociale du XXe siècle. I must also thank the Centre des Archives Communistes en Belgique for assistance with visual materials; and for permission to consult sections of the Thorez deposit in the Archives nationales in Paris I must thank the Thorez family. My special thanks as always to Julie, Sam and Jane.

The usual caveats apply, and for both the judgements offered here and any errors or misunderstandings I am alone responsible.

December 2015

Contents

Abbreviations

ARAC	Association Républican des Anciens Combattants
CGT	Confédération générale du travail
CGTU	Confédération générale du travail unitaire
CPGB	Communist Party of Great Britain
CPUSA	Communist Party of the United States of America
ECCI	Executive Committee of the Communist International
IMEL	Marx-Engels-Lenin Institute
KPD	Kommunist Partei Deutschlands (German communist party)
MOPR	Mezhdunarodnaya Organizatsiya Pomoshchi Bor'tsam Revolyutsii (International Red Aid)
PCB	Parti communiste de Belgique (Belgian communist party) / Partido Comunista do Brasil (Brazilian communist party)
PCE	Partido Comunista de España (Spanish communist party)
PCF	Parti communiste français / Parti communiste de France / Section française de l'Internationale communiste (French communist party)
PCI	Partito comunista italiano (Italian communist party)
POB	Parti ouvrier belge (Belgian workers' party)
PUWP	Polish United Workers' Party
RCP	Russian Communist Party
SED	Sozialistische Einheitspartei Deutschlands (Socialist Unity Party of Germany)
SPD	Sozialdemokratische Partei Deutschlands (German social-democratic party)
UFF	Union des Femmes françaises (Union of French Women)

In Notes

CdB	*Cahiers du bolchevisme*
CdC	*Cahiers du communisme*
CHS	Centre d'Histoire Sociale du XXe siècle (CHS), Paris
CI	*Communist International*
CR	*Communist Review*
DW (L)	*Daily Worker* (London)
DW (NY)	*Daily Worker* (New York)
LM	*Labour Monthly*
MQ	*Modern Quarterly*
NA	National Archives, London
NC	*La Nouvelle Critique*
Pens.	*La Pensée*
SSD	Archives Départmentales de Seine-Saint-Denis
TCC	*Twentieth Century Communism: a journal of international history*
WD	*Workers' Dreadnought*

A Note on Terminology

Over the period covered here, several of the parties discussed went through at least one change of name. Where there was basic organisational continuity, the most familiar of these names is used here for simplicity's sake. Thus, although the Communist Party of Great Britain became the British Communist Party in the 1940s, the more familiar acronym CPGB is used throughout; and similarly the most familiar acronyms for other parties with a continuous history are also employed generically here, e.g. PCF and PCI. The nomenclature of party offices and committees has also to some extent been standardised, for example referring to the German *Zentrum* as central committee. In the case of widely transliterated names and terms, I have tended to follow the conventions of contemporary English-language sources, except, at the obvious risk of some inconsistency, where commonsense or familiarity suggested otherwise.

List of Figures

CHAPTER 1

Introduction: Wherever a Communist Party is at Work...

(i)

In December 1949, millions across the world took part in one of the defining public rituals of the twentieth century. Cold War tensions were reaching their height. Germany's division had been sealed, NATO formed, and the first of a new wave of show trials held in eastern Europe. In China, communism's second great revolution had prevailed, while on the Korean peninsula tensions would soon break out in open warfare. Overseeing all from the Kremlin, on 21 December the Soviet leader Stalin marked his 70th birthday with a demonstration of personal power that arguably had had no historical parallel. In the sky above Red Square, searchlights picked out his giant profile, suspended from balloons. In the Soviet daily *Pravda*, every line of every page was given over to Stalin's accomplishments. Plays were staged, films released, songs composed and presents received—so many presents that a special museum was needed to display them. The 'stream of greetings' would feature in *Pravda* for more than a year; if any quality was mentioned more than the others, it was Stalin's modesty.

Stalin was not the only dictator to relish such performances. What was of a different order was the promotion and reproduction of his cult on an international scale. Not only from Stalin's newly extended eastern bloc, but from both sides of the iron curtain offerings arrived in truckloads. In Paris alone, some four thousand gifts were assembled. These included not only the products of diverse handicrafts, trades and professions, but also the revolver of resistance hero Colonel Fabien; a baby's bootees kept

K. Morgan, *International Communism and the Cult of the Individual*, DOI 10.1057/978-1-137-55667-7_1

as a memento of a daughter killed by the Nazis; a widow's wedding ring from a husband shot dead by French police; a 20-minute film, 'The Man We Love the Most', sonorously narrated by the poet, Paul Éluard. Picasso contributed a drawing, Éluard himself a poem, and a birthday anthem *Camarade, Bonjour!* thanked Stalin for having done away with winter. In *La Pensée*, the communists' 'journal of modern rationalism', *hommages* were contributed by a linguist, psychologist, soldier, chemist, biologist, musician, lawyer and designer—most of them acclaiming some quality of excellence or inspiration in their own field. Watched over by a huge illuminated portrait, and surrounded by panels of scenes from Stalin's life, 40,000 Parisians viewed the offerings before they were packed into trunks—116 of them—and dispatched to the Soviet capital.[1]

Communists sometimes claimed that no man had had such world-wide popularity as Lenin. Certainly, no man's birthday, excepting only Christ's, can have been celebrated on so wide a scale as Stalin's. Internationalists according to their guiding precepts, it was as if the communists of all lands were now to unite, not even in allegiance to a particular state, but in the veneration of an individual. When Stalin died in 1953, the British communist R. Palme Dutt evoked the scenes of mourning in just these terms: 'Hitherto the recognition of greatness across the barriers of countries and continents, of nations and language, of race and colour, has had to await the verdict of generations and of centuries. Communism has changed this. Already through Communism the human race begins to become one kin.'[2] (Fig. 1.1)

Though Stalin at the apex had no rival, the party he headed served as a model as well as inspiration. The quality of 'greatness' did not therefore only emanate from the Kremlin; it was also reproduced at national level in sometimes strikingly imitative forms. France in 1949 had the world's strongest non-ruling communist party, the *Parti communiste français* (PCF), enjoying nearly 30 per cent of the popular vote and the cultural and intellectual prestige epitomised by the recruitment of Éluard and Picasso. The week immediately following Stalin's birthday celebrations, the PCF's secretariat began planning for the 50th birthday the following spring of the party's own general secretary, Maurice Thorez. The same party worker, Jean Chaintron, was put in charge. If anything, the preparations were even more painstaking. There were 40,000 posters instead of 30,000, a Maurice Thorez stamp and postcards, the decking out of the Ivry town hall in Paris's red belt, the gifts, the songs, the poems, the relics of resistance martyrs, a handkerchief soaked in the blood of an injured demonstrator—all

Fig. 1.1 Homage to Stalin, Salle de la Madeleine, Brussels, 10 March 1953 (Centre des Archives Communistes en Belgique)

culminating after several days in a firework display and the releasing of carrier pigeons.[3] In the journal of modern rationalism, Thorez was equated with the century that bore his imprint, while a popular anthem added the note of his ubiquity: 'for everywhere that we are, he is'.[4]

The French are sometimes said to have a penchant for the providential or otherwise exalted leader.[5] Thorez's biographers ponder the significance in this connection of the country's Catholic traditions, or of the legacy of absolutism.[6] The PCF itself is held to have conformed particularly closely to the stalinist canons of the time, and had resources with which to do so far exceeding those of most other oppositional communist parties. Even so, it is the international character of the cult phenomenon that stands out during the Cold War. Not only did every communist party of sufficient size or standing boast a Stalin-figure of its own. These individuals were also clearly signalled as part of an interdependent and mutually reinforcing order of party paragons through which both the indivisibility and the authentic national character of the world's communist parties were expressed. Everywhere these parties had grown in stature, ran one Stalin tribute; 'everywhere have shot up the likes of Thorez and Duclos, Togliatti, Markos, Carlos Prestes, Mao-Tse Tung, Gottwald and William Foster'. If the names as yet are unfamiliar, they will become less so in the chapters that follow. In Europe, East and West, in Asia and the Americas, communism was a school of struggle in which at every level the best of its leaders were found in the place befitting them. '*Wherever a communist party or central committee is at work, Stalin is alive.*'[7]

(ii)

This is a book about the meaning of such claims and how they came to be made. It explores the communist cult phenomenon from its earliest manifestations under Lenin to its condemnation in 1956 by Stalin's successor Nikita Khrushchev. It draws on what is already an extensive literature, including accomplished studies of the Lenin, Stalin and other ruling party cults. The focus here, however, is on communism as an international movement embracing parties of every conceivable legal status, from the monopoly of power to outright persecution. Respectively in Europe, Latin America and Asia, figures like Togliatti, Gottwald, Prestes and Mao were the focus of cultlike practices that were clearly interlinked and shared common features, but according to varying political imperatives and the most disparate political circumstances. Having originated in the USSR, the internationalisation of the cult phenomenon can be traced from the first continuous promulgation of Stalin's own cult in the early 1930s. Nevertheless, it was a complex, spasmodic and in some respects uncertain process which was properly formalised only in the period of 'high stalinism' in which Stalin's 70th birthday fell. It is this uneven and often contradictory development that the present study charts through both different national cases and the interconnections between them.

Its primary focus is on the oppositional parties of Europe and to a lesser extent America. Nevertheless, it is impossible to make sense of these national-level cults without also considering the projection internationally of the Soviet cult figures which served as exemplar and inspiration, and to which the lesser party cults were, by 1949, overtly subordinated. Lenin and Stalin therefore figure prominently here, as they did in the political imaginations of the communists themselves. There was never, on the other hand, just a transposition from one environment to another. In considering the different ways in which communists used the politics of personality, scholarly interpretations developed within a purely Soviet context will therefore also require adaptation.

These interpretations vary widely, and divisions evident in the wider field of Soviet studies may equally be found in writings on the Soviet cult of leaders.[8] One important reading, albeit less influential in recent years, emphasises the singularity of Stalin's cult and the role of his personal cravings and insecurity.[9] Another gives primacy to specifically Russian contingencies and cultural structures, and to the persistence through successive epochs of Russian history of traditional or neo-traditional practices conducive to the cult of the ruler.[10] A third reading, which we might describe as a modernist or comparativist one, looks beyond Russia's borders to a notion of the modern personality cult as a characteristic if not ubiquitous feature of an age of mass politics.[11] Divergent as these readings clearly are, there is a common point of reference which is the sacralisation of some centre of sovereign power. It was the Chicago sociologist Edward Shils who argued that every society has an 'ultimate and irreducible' symbolic centre sustained by sentiments of sacredness and an 'affirmative attitude' towards established authority.[12] From a neo-traditionalist or exceptionalist perspective, this may be linked, as it is by J. Arch Getty, with 'deep structures' in Russian culture concerning the sacralised person of the ruler.[13] Should a broader context be allowed, as it certainly was by Shils, this may suggest affinities with a political religions approach grouping bolshevism with fascism as 'religiously charged symbolic universes'.[14] Getty, while insisting on the specificity of the Russian case, cites Shils in postulating a universal human tendency to anthropomorphise power.[15] The cult of personality, in all these cases, is therefore in some basic sense the cult of power.

Another common feature is that communism as an international movement barely figures in these accounts. Nevertheless, the opportunities to make the connections between these fields of study have in some ways never been greater. Where just a decade ago the historiographies of Soviet and international communism appeared to have 'hardly taken proper notice of each other', there has since then emerged a flourishing literature seeking in different ways to overcome this divide.[16] Major publishing projects draw on specialists in both these fields, or seek to synthesise their work, in addressing the need for a truly global history of communism.[17] A vigorous recent trend in Soviet historiography also seeks to break down what Katerina Clark refers to as an 'intellectual iron curtain' and the denuding of Soviet history of its transnational interactions.[18] From the other side of this curtain, the predominance in international communist historiography of the single-party monograph has also been giving way to a broader concern with transnational agencies and forms of interaction.[19] Nevertheless, the international literature has so far dealt only in passing with the discourses and rituals of the leader cult, while conversely, accounts approaching the cults as the sacralised centre of some or other communist state have largely disregarded their transnational aspect. Within the Soviet historiography, it is not only exceptionalists who play down external factors in their narratives of Russian history, for even comparativists have worked within a typology which in some cases is explicitly confined to 'closed' societies and to comparators in practice of the authoritarian right.[20] Within the recent global histories of communism, leading authorities deal cogently with the cult of personality, but as a feature of the communist polity whose international aspect remains in many respects elusive.[21]

Where these communist polities may themselves accommodate a transnational dimension is in respect of the hierarchy of interlocking cults that assisted in the sovietisation of eastern Europe after 1945. Here too there is an important literature, including the introduction by Alexey Tikhomorov of the helpful notion of an international cult community.[22] Recalling Weber's idea of the charismatic community, identification with a common sacral centre could be seen here as an instrument of discipline and exclusion, and it is within the wider perspective of the eastern bloc that E.A. Rees has characterised the leader cult as a 'deliberately constructed and managed mechanism' aimed at integrating some polity around the leader's persona. On the other hand, the recognition of a cultic bloc may merely reinforce the binary pairing of closed and open systems, with communist systems that were doubly closed, as Rees puts it, 'both domestically and in their relations to the outside world'.[23] Intriguingly, it is not in Stalin's case but Mao's that a global history of the *Little Red Book* has been produced by scholars from a wide range of areas and subject specialisms.[24] Considering the ever-burgeoning literature on Stalin, it is symptomatic of the iron curtain which Clark alluded to that works of similar scope have not so far been devoted to either his or Lenin's cult.

In approaching the subject as a historian of international communism, the differences to be accommodated are in part ones of periodisation. Disregarding minor discrepancies as to their dating, every authoritative account of the Soviet cult of Stalin identifies two distinct phases culminating respectively in the pre-war period of the Moscow trials and the post-war period of high stalinism. Internationally speaking, the same distinction broadly holds, with a 'turn to the individual' that is clearly traceable from 1934 and becomes more emphatically projected onto the figure of the leader with the onset of the Cold War. In France, for example, Annie Kriegel's periodisation of the Thorez cult corresponds closely to Stalin's own, with a first phase in 1936–1938 and a second in 1947–1953.[25] Though both Kriegel and Stéphane Sirot note that there was an intensification of the cult in the second of these periods, no significant distinction is drawn between them, as if there were the same basic continuity of purpose and effect that is evident in the USSR itself.[26]

The premises of the present account are different. In respect of the communists' envisaged cult community the differences are very simple. In the first of these phases of cult-building, as it recovered from the shock of Hitler's victory in Germany, international communism was a movement whose effectiveness and even survival depended on reaching out to new constituencies and mobilising them under the banner of anti-fascism. In the second of these phases, on the other hand, communism was a movement far more firmly established even in the West, but subject as if under siege to the intense external pressures of the Cold War. Despite the obvious elements of synchronicity between national and international developments, the relevance to these situations of a system of exclusive sacral rites was clearly not the same. The Soviet cult of Stalin, according to those who allowed it some functionality, had gained traction as a device to draw together a heterogeneous population around the 'concrete living figure' at its centre.[27] Though the rationale in this case was that of a party already holding power, there was at least a basic congruence between these esoteric practices of a formalised cultic hierarchy and the turning in upon themselves of western communist parties, as notoriously happened during the Cold War. What is far less clear is how gathering round a venerated ruling figure served the object of the popular-front mobilisations and reaching out to a liberal public that coincided with communism's first phase of cult-building.

Writing of this period, Silvio Pons has noted the difficulties that existed in exporting a Soviet conception of the nation that was more akin to fascism itself than to the anti-fascist discourse with which communism became associated in the West.[28] There was certainly no less a predicament in seeking to export a leader cult that within the USSR bordered on deification. For just this reason, however, it was not initially this that was principally exported. Within a specifically Soviet context, historians observe that Stalin's personal cult cannot be properly grasped in isolation, but has to be located within the wider turn to the heroic that was so much a feature of the stalinist culture of the 1930s.[29] It was this wider heroisation of communist discourse, rather than the single symbolic centre of Stalin himself, that in the first of these cult-building phases was generalised throughout the parties of the Comintern. Already one can speak of the cult of the individual, in a way one could not have in the 1920s. Nevertheless, this was represented through conceptions of the leader and the communist hero that varied considerably according to changing political imperatives and the disparate conditions in which these were or could be made effective.

No single notion of the personality cult will encompass these differences. In the attempt to bring them within a common field of vision, the key distinction is therefore made here between an integrating cult figure and an enkindling one. An integrating figure may be thought of as activating, controlling and meshing together more closely a population already in some sense won for communism. This might be a society subject to communist rule, like Russia's, or an oppositional microsociety, as most famously delineated by Kriegel in the case of France.[30] An enkindling figure, on the other hand, served to draw into communism or communist-sponsored campaigns a larger population neither subject to the party's authority nor yet freely accepting it. This distinction is more fully elaborated in Chapter 3. It will be seen there that it offers a way of distinguishing particular features of the cult phenomenon as these were variously grouped together over time rather than a crude device for classifying individual cases. Stalin's cult was for many years sui generis as that of a ruler already established in power. Nevertheless, even Stalin had designs of his own upon an international public, albeit with just the aforementioned difficulties of translation from one political environment to another. As subsequently sometime martyrs and party tribunes were also installed in power, the singularity and complexity of international communism was not just the interlocking of such figures within a movement of unprecedented cohesion, but the encompassing over time of multiple transitions from one such figure to another. In seeking to acknowledge these complexities, the devices of the integrating and enkindling figure allow the rubric of the cult to be extended both to those monopolising symbolic capital and to those engaged as communists in political battles waged through competing personalities.

Within the wider literature on which the present account draws, there now exist studies of several key individuals addressing these different facets of the cult phenomenon. Though Mao's cult in the period considered here was of no such global reach as Stalin's, it was in some ways more characteristic of the wider communist movement in being shaped and reshaped for ends which were not confined to the exercise of power. Daniel Leese thus describes the cult's origins prior to the Chinese revolution, in many respects as a mirror image of that of Mao's rival Chiang Kai-shek, and in doing so brings to the fore transitions both over time and internationally that resonate directly with issues arising in a broader context.[31] Other state cults originating in the Comintern period include those of Mátyás Rákosi, the post-war leader of communist Hungary, and the German Ernst Thälmann, whose cult as party leader segued into phases of martyrdom and then state memorialisation following his murder by the Nazis in 1944.[32] Mention should finally be made of the Thorez cult in France, which has occasioned an extensive critical literature that addresses head-on its relation to that of Stalin, and which figures prominently here as arguably the most conspicuous example of such practices among all the western parties.[33]

There is as yet no such study of this type devoted to the Bulgarian Georgi Dimitrov.[34] Nevertheless, if any single figure can encapsulate the interaction between the national and international in dramatically changing contexts, it is Dimitrov. Hitherto a shadowy Comintern functionary, he achieved an instant international celebrity through his defiance of the Nazis at the 1933 Reichstag fire trial and was then installed by Stalin as the Comintern's secretary and chief figurehead. Acclaimed beyond its ranks as the Comintern's first indisputable hero, Dimitrov went on to head Bulgaria's post-war communist government; when he died in 1949 he was the first communist since Lenin to be installed in his own mausoleum. Both morally and politically he was nevertheless a hugely diminished figure, enjoying the spoils of office thanks only to Stalin's continuing preferment.

Communism's distinctiveness as a movement was not just that it comprised both authority and anti-authority figures, sometimes as here within a single career history, but that it was the tribune and the martyr and not the symbol of the communist state who provoked the more spontaneous and deep-seated impulses of veneration. Communist cult practices were linked at once with resistance to tyranny, its maintenance in power and the transformation of one into the other. One of the objects of this study is to investigate how these connected together within a movement whose guiding principle, even internationally, was one of monolithic integration.

(iii)

It is the leader far more than the tribune or the martyr who figures in the literature to date. Shils in his 'Center and periphery' essay invoked a basic human need for incorporation into something transcending and transfiguring the individual and resulting in the sense of sacredness which he held to inhere in authority. Nevertheless, Shils did also recognise the existence of individuals whose connection with the central value system was not affirmative but passionately negative. Not numerous but often of great importance, these were the source or focal point of opposition to established institutions, and of those forms of transcendence that perhaps lay in the very act of denial, or in the affirmation of some alternative value system. This, moreover, was also to be found embodied in the individual, and according to Shils was the breeding ground of prophets, of revolutionaries and of 'doctrinaire ideologists'.[35]

It is with figures of this type that the earliest usages of the personality cult may be identified. The term's introduction into common parlance is usually dated from the immediate post-Stalin period, and in particular from Khrushchev's repudiation of Stalin at the 20th congress of the Soviet communist party (CPSU) in February 1956. Khrushchev's target certainly was the abuse of power; but in seeking some legitimising prop for his iconoclasm the plausible concepts of Bonapartism and Caesarism were ruled out by their Trotskyist associations and the implication of more far-reaching social ills. The cult of the individual, on the other hand, was a more circumscribed notion that allowed the projection onto Stalin of systemic flaws while absolving those who survived him of any real responsibility of their own. The origins of the phrase, perhaps underlining its limitations as critique, had nevertheless had nothing to do with the exercise of power, and predated the Bolshevik regime and even party. On the contrary, the text which Khrushchev cited was Marx's disclaimer of the *Personenkultus* in a private letter of 1877 referring to himself.

Thus freely adapted, the cult of the individual therefore represented the application to Stalin's monocracy of a formulation originally used in relation to an exiled revolutionary whose only real authority lay in the written word. Khrushchev, of course, did not in the least intend suggesting a connection between Marx's prerogatives and Stalin's. Nevertheless, his resorting to such an example does serve as reminder of how in radical political movements it was, in the first place, the contestation of authority that was symbolised or articulated by particular individuals. This indeed was also registered by the social and political thinkers most obviously exercised by the leadership claims to which an age of mass politics was giving rise. Robert Michels and Gustave Le Bon are among the best-known of these. Le Bon in particular is a key point of reference in Yves Cohen's recent study of the preoccupation with the figure of the leader that became so evident in different societies and fields of activity as a result of elite anxieties regarding the new social actor of the masses.[36] Communism is central to Cohen's argument because, as exemplified by Stalin, it demonstrates how strong a force this was even for a movement which had begun by rejecting the principle of hierarchy. Nevertheless, in both Michels and Le Bon there may also be found the paradox whereby the challenge to established authority might equally be represented through the figure of the leader.

Michels in expounding his famous iron law of oligarchy had sought to demonstrate this through the examples of democratic and revolutionary parties. Le Bon in his *Psychology of the Crowd* (1895) had not only reminded those in authority of the need to exercise that authority, but warned of alternative leaders emerging should they fail to do so.[37] More influential in the long run was Max Weber's recovery of the concept of charisma and, in elucidating this shortly before his death in 1920, Weber also gave as one of his contemporary examples the leader of the ill-fated Bavarian socialist republic, Kurt Eisner.[38] Le Bon referred to such figures as *meneurs*, a term familiar from histories of the French revolution which Michels also rendered as 'agitators' or the German *Aufwiegler*.[39] As well as the fomenter of grassroots discontents with which the term is most commonly associated, Le Bon also referred to *grands meneurs* like Mohammed, Luther and Robespierre, through whom the presence of the crowd was made effective in some of the great movements of history. It is sometimes said, without as yet any convincing supporting evidence, that Le Bon's influence can be detected in Lenin's *What Is To Be Done*?

(1902).[40] If that is so, it is the notion of the party as collective *meneur* which can alone be found there.

The figure of the *meneur*, if not the word, was familiar in socialist circles. In Michels's chapter 'The cult of veneration among the masses' it is Marx's rival as socialist founding father, Ferdinand Lassalle, who is described as being greeted in the Rhineland by hymns of welcome, triumphal arches, maids of honour and the 'frenzied applause' of his adorers.[41] Other Lassallean tokens of veneration included portraits, poems, anthems and festivals, to say nothing of pipes, watches, beer-mugs, and a reverence for Lassalle's every written and spoken utterance.[42] Describing this as a 'veritable Lassalle cult', the revisionist marxist Eduard Bernstein would nevertheless recognise its importance for the development of German socialism:

> When all is said and done most persons like to see a cause, which, the more far-reaching its aims at any given moment, must seem the more abstract, embodied in one individual. This craving to personify a cause is the secret of the success of most founders of religions ... and in England and America it is a recognised factor in political party-struggles.[43]

Le Bon might have recognised here the figure of the *grand meneur*. To his followers, Lassalle already in the 1860s carried the promise that he would one day 'enter the capital as president of the German republic, seated in a chariot drawn by six white horses'.[44] For the time being, however, he was scarcely closer to such a prospect than was Marx himself.

In the case of Lenin's cult, like Stalin's, there is clearly a case for considering Russian conditioning factors like the alleged 'cult' predilections of pre-revolutionary study circles and the vanguardist conceptions of *What Is To Be Done?*[45] What Lassalle nevertheless exemplified was a radical tendency to veneration that was pan-European in character and not the product of any particular national environment. Michels thus remarked at various points upon the special susceptibility to leadership claims of the English, the French, the Italians and, in particular, Michels's own fellow Germans. Russians, as it happened, appeared in his analysis mainly in the anti-authoritarian guise of the anarchists Bakunin and Kropotkin. Even anarchism—perhaps, in default of organisation, especially anarchism—was nevertheless projected through leading personalities like the Italian Malatesta.[46] Erik van Ree is therefore surely justified in describing the cult of socialist leaders as a western European and not a specifically Russian invention.[47]

In modernist or comparativist readings, the boundaries that ultimately matter are those of period rather than national ones. Michels was one of the original modernists and his iron law of oligarchy was the product first and foremost of an age of organisation. The 'modern' personality cult, as outlined in this context by Jan Plamper, is also a notion associated with widely varying political systems but inseparable from the idea of new techniques of government and mass communications.[48] Cohen similarly dates the turn to the leader from the 1890s, again as a result of the increasing scale and complexity of organisation, and distinguishes this from the nineteenth-century discourse of the hero.[49] But if a cult like Stalin's is fully intelligible only through the interplay between modernity and tradition, as Balázs Apor has maintained, this may well be truer still of those communist parties which had yet to realise their socialist future, and which laid their claim meanwhile to a longer tradition of protest requiring to be upheld against the modern state.[50]

The intersection of these different temporalities is thus one of the keys to understanding those aspects of the cult phenomenon that also involved the recovery, persistence or simulation of practices long since characteristic of a radical politics of personality. Coming from the other side of the chronological divide, Lucy Riall in her study of the 19th century Risorgimento hero Garibaldi has stressed a radical discontinuity between the democratic tradition of heroism which his cult represented and the more chauvinistic and authoritarian conceptions of the leader that the following century would bring.[51] Even so, what Riall calls Garibaldi's 'radical moment' was also the not-so-radical moment of Bismarck, Louis Napoleon and Thomas Carlyle's *Frederick the Great*, while at the same time its radicalism secured a sort of afterlife through the Garibaldi brigades in which communists later took up arms against fascism. Such forms of appropriation were always contestable and sometimes cynical or self-deluding, as the competing claims to Garibaldi of fascists as well as communists clearly indicate.[52] Nevertheless, it was as *meneur* and not as *chef* that Le Bon had classed him and, as Riall so vividly describes, Garibaldi not only remained undaunted in the face of repeated setbacks, but strove to turn them into symbolic victories through the projection internationally of the cause he incarnated. For communists like Antonio Gramsci who turned even persecution into moral victories, or for those indeed who fought in Spain invoking Garibaldi, this was a radical moment that had not yet entirely passed.

Communism's singularity as an international movement was that it thus combined a common symbolic universe with fundamentally different relations to the state and different degrees of access to the resources and technologies on whose monopolising the statist personality cult depended. If communism of its essence was therefore a movement of tribunes and martyrs as well as ruling functionaries, its binding together in asymmetrical power relationships meant that these distinctions could never be reduced to simple polarities. This was obvious in the case of Lenin, who was both the *chef* (or *vozhd'*) of the Bolshevik dictatorship and the greatest of the *grands meneurs* that his times had known. Even Stalin, who had no such record of revolutionary leadership, was constrained to live up to it. The notorious falsifications of Stalin's personal history did not therefore only demonstrate his capacity to direct such operations. They also reveal the persistence of wider criteria of validation to which Stalin himself was at least initially impelled to conform. There is even a remarkable effusion of Stalin's early cult that linked him with a lineage of international *grands meneurs*—Robespierre, Spartacus, Thomas Münzer, Campanella, Robert Owen, Stenka Razin—whose aspirations he was said to embody at a higher level.[53] As every Eisenstein aficionado knows, even the Russian rebel Stenka Razin had to cede place in the stalinist imaginary to Ivan the Terrible. But if Stalin, as Moshe Lewin put it, sought legitimation in practices and traditions from the tsarist past, it was not on this basis that his cult was ever likely to resonate with communists internationally.[54]

(iv)

The chapters that follow take in a wide range of types and individuals and the ways in which these were represented in the international literature. Chapter 2, immediately following, provides an introductory overview and periodisation focusing first on the Soviet cults and then on the communist movement internationally. Chapter 3 then provides a fuller exposition of the integrating/enkindling distinction, and of the related notions of charisma and political capital. Among the examples discussed at this point are the Brazilian Luis Carlos Prestes, the Spaniard Dolores Ibárruri and the Briton William Gallacher. Chapter 4 focuses on the figure of the party leader, beginning with Stalin, then turning to Thorez, to the Briton Harry Pollitt and to the Belgian Joseph Jacquemotte. Chapter 5 examines how the other varieties of party cult—the tribune, martyr, writer, pioneer and founder—were progressively subordinated to the overriding cult of the leader. Figures discussed in this context include Dimitrov and Thälmann; the writers Henri Barbusse and Aragon; and a variety of veterans and party founders including Clara Zetkin, Tom Mann, Marcel Cachin, W.Z. Foster and Gramsci. Chapter 6, the final substantive chapter, discusses the representation of the cults through different media and genres including film, radio, photography and the indispensable but elusive cult biography. The chapter concludes with the wider phenomenon of communist pantheonisation and the appropriation cults through which claims were made to diverse political and cultural forbears. A short concluding chapter considers the evident survival even after 1956 of the 'craving to personify a cause'.

Focusing on principally European parties in the years before 1956, this is avowedly a culturally, geographically and chronologically delimited narrative. It is nevertheless its relative breadth of the approach that has governed the sources and the research methods used. Archival materials, like the papers of French communists used here, have in some cases been used to document the processes by which these cult figures were constructed. In the case of the more fully documented ruling party cults, it is only on the basis of the archives now accessible that questions may be opened up of cult reception and participation in cult practices of a sort touched upon here only incidentally.[55] Where archival sources do so far appear to have been surprisingly unyielding is in relation to the political rationale for the cults. Even confidentially, the cults were almost never referred to as such, and neither rationalised, projected nor even discussed in such terms except in criticism or dissociation. Such sources have often been crucial in documenting the processes of cult construction but have had less to say about the political meaning of these processes within the context of a wider communist history.

It is this aspect of the cult phenomenon that the chapters here explore through the public representations of such figures. In this respect, communism as an international movement offers unusual opportunities to the researcher to draw connections and make comparisons. As an enterprise among other things for the generation of common texts in different languages, its voluminous print output offers a profusion of cultlike traces whose character and interconnections over time have hitherto been little studied in their own right. If it is feasible now to seek to repair this omission, this is largely because of the rich literature on both Soviet and international communism that have emerged particularly since the 1990s.

More specifically, in 2009 the inaugural issue of the journal *Twentieth Century Communism* demonstrated how effectively such public documents could be used to delineate cult figures from half a dozen different countries never previously juxtaposed in this way. Together these articles suggested multiple themes that might repay comparative evaluation, and this book is in large part the attempt to provide that account.[56]

Just as the Stalin cult has been studied through its representations in *Pravda* and other public media, the internationalisation of the cult phenomenon is traced here through the publications in which these figures were presented to both a communist and a wider public.[57] The use of principally French and English-language sources, often of texts circulating internationally in numerous languages, poses significant issues in itself. Stephen A. Smith has recently noted how even concepts as crucial as state and revolution did 'not pass untransformed through the barrier of language'.[58] So simple a notion as the leader's birthday, like Stalin's in 1949, is packed with hidden complexities. In English, like most other languages, the birthday may be distinguished from the broader notion of the anniversary as the marking of what is typically some sort of public event. On the other hand, there is often no such clarity in translating from the French *anniversaire*, to say nothing of the distinction in some other European languages between ordinary birth dates and more significant markers like the decennial ones which punctuated Stalin's cult.[59] In the case of 'leader', on the other hand, it is the English rendering which flattens out important distinctions in German, Russian and other European languages, and which in a single short passage of French may be found in the three alternative variants of *dirigeant*, *chef* and *leader* itself.[60]

It is partly because of these ambiguities, and partly because its indeterminacy encompasses both the actual and symbolic, that the non-committal expression 'figure' is resorted to so often in these pages. More generally, I have cited contemporary texts as these were publicly represented to the international readerships whose ranks I thereby entered.[61] Like the Comintern itself, I have for the most part reproduced contemporary texts without dwelling on the important matter of their reproduction with different accents in different languages. However, where usages do affect the construction put upon a passage here or by contemporary readers, this has wherever possible been checked against the original-language version, and where appropriate this is noted parenthetically in translations here.

The term 'cult of the individual' is a further case in point. The *kul't lichnosti* which Khrushchev denounced could equally be translated as cult of the individual, as it initially was in English, or of personality, as in French. Historians may also refer to the 'leader cult', which communists avoided because of its fascist connotations, which has both the advantages and disadvantages of precision as a notion usually restricted to political office-holders. To privilege any one of these terms might imply a greater clarity of definition between them than is either necessary or discernible in the existing specialist literature.[62] Nevertheless, the more familiar 'cult of personality' has the drawback of implying some distinctiveness or originality of character which was not a necessary or even allowable feature of many of the communist cults. It is also an emphasis absent in Marx's original usage *Personenkultus*; and when Bernstein did seek to characterise Lassalle's as a cult of personality rather than merely the person, he used a different expression, *Kultus der Persönlichkeit*.[63]

Though in this account too no fine distinction is drawn between these different terms, it is therefore the cult of the individual which is preferred here as an organising concept. This is because it allows the broadest conceptualisation of the theme without the normative complication of personality. Crucially, it also carries the double connotation, both of the cult of a particular individual, as Marx and Khrushchev intended, and of the wider turn to the individual as a category within which these particular cults must be located. In some recent scholarship, the individual has indeed been described as stalinism's 'defining basic entity of human behavior'.[64] As Bernstein saw so clearly, the left was nevertheless well-practised in also representing the plural through the singular, and the cult of the collective, or of some larger cause or campaigning issue, by and through particular individuals.

In what was therefore the interplay between the individual and a narrative of 'anonymous' masses and social forces, the primary focus here is on that smaller group of figures that was accorded some rarefied status, whether as party leaders in the narrow sense, or as founders, heroes, tribunes, scribes or martyrs. Their routine designation as personality cults, in a scholarly literature as well as merely colloquially, cannot in the case of these communist parties be taken to imply the 'godlike' glorification and worship imputed to cults like Stalin's and Mao's.[65] On the other hand, the more minimal definition of a cult as admiration taken to excess is also not quite adequate for our purposes.[66] The cult of the individual is therefore understood here as representing the collective ascription to such figures of a distinctive emblematic quality deriving from their office, from their personal history or from the postulation of extraordinary gifts and capabilities, whether innate or acquired. Often in the case of state cults, the cult relationship is identified with communism's highly ritualised political culture as a ruling system. This in part was what sympathetic westerners like Henri Barbusse had in mind in referring openly to the Stalin cult as practised through such rituals in the USSR.[67] Even so, and as was conceded even by his eulogist and fellow communist Marcel Cachin, Barbusse himself had also devoted a veritable cult to Stalin, but using techniques as a writer and journalist that were long since familiar in radical politics in the West.[68] Barbusse indeed had employed these techniques in a dozen other causes before turning them, as we shall discover, to Stalin's biography, and it is on this broader range of cult representations that the narrative here will draw.

This is a work primarily of political history. It deals with communism as a movement of political activists, and the question of how and why within it particular individuals became freighted with qualities, capacities or achievements by a collectivity that in some sense was also defined by these common symbols. Though insights have been drawn from the rich seams of work on communist biography and subjectivities, or those on Soviet literary and visual culture, the central preoccupation here is with the political uses of text and image, which must finally be regarded as disastrous. Not the Stalin cult alone but what it represented was one of the catastrophes of the twentieth century, and one perpetrated in the name of socialism. At the same time, this was not simply a betrayal or an imposture, though those elements were certainly present, but spoke to instincts that were deeply rooted in an older tradition of the left, and maintained even under Stalin in forms of activism that were also represented in highly personalised ways. One may still recognise the craving to personify that Bernstein noted already in the 1890s. But one can hardly do so now without also recognising the terrible damage that this may inflict on any cause that is represented in this way. It is a point to which we return in our concluding chapter.

Notes

1. See Jean Chaintron, *Le vent soufflait devant ma porte* (Paris: Seuil, 1993), pp. 292–5.
2. R. Palme Dutt, 'Stalin and the future', *LM*, Apr. 1953, 146–7.

3. Chaintron, *Le vent*, pp. 296–8; Jean-Marie Goulemot, *Pour l'amour de Staline. La face oubliée du communisme français* (Paris: CNRS, 2009 edn), ch. 3; also PCF secretariat minutes, 27 Dec. 1949.
4. Léon Moussinac and Roger Desormière, *Fils du peuple* (Paris: Chant du Monde, 1950).
5. Jean Garrigues, *Les hommes providentiels. Histoire d'une fascination française* (Paris: Seuil, 2012); Robert Tombs, 'Was there a French *Sonderweg*?', *European Review of History*, 1 (1984), 169–77.
6. Philippe Robrieux, *Maurice Thorez. Vie secrète et vie publique* (Paris: Fayard, 1975), p. 610; Annette Wieviorka, *Maurice et Jeannette: biographie du couple Thorez* (Paris: Fayard, 2010), p. 442; Annie Kriegel, 'Bureaucratie, culte de personnalité et charisme. Le cas français: Maurice Thorez, secrétaire général du PCF (1900–1964)' in idem, *Communisme au miroir français* (Paris: Gallimard, 1974), pp. 147–9.
7. Georges Mounin, 'Le marxisme et les grands hommes', *NC*, Dec. 1949, 17. In the original, Foster is misspelt.
8. On these divisions, a helpful overview is Michael David-Fox, 'Multiple modernities vs. neo-traditionalism: on recent debates in Russian and Soviet history', *Jahrbücher für Geschichte Osteuropas*, 55 (2006), 535–55.
9. Robert C. Tucker, 'The rise of Stalin's personality cult', *American Historical Review*, 84 (1979); Tucker, *Stalin in Power. The revolution from above 1928–1941* (New York: W.W. Norton, 1992 edn), ch. 7.
10. Nina Tumarkin, *Lenin Lives! The Lenin Cult in Soviet Russia* (Cambridge, MA: Harvard University Press, 1983); J. Arch Getty, *Practicing Stalinism. Bolsheviks, boyars and the persistence of tradition* (New Haven, CT: Yale University Press, 2013).
11. Jan Plamper, *The Stalin Cult. A study in the alchemies of power* (New Haven, CT: Yale University Press, 2012).
12. Edward Shils, 'Center and periphery' (1961) in *Selected Essays* (Chicago, IL: Centre for Social Organization Studies, 1970), pp. 1–14.
13. Getty, *Practicing Stalinism*, p. 86.
14. Emilio Gentile, *The Sacralization of Politics in Fascist Italy* (Cambridge, MA: Harvard University Press, 1996).
15. Getty, *Practicing Stalinism*, p. 77; Plamper, *Stalin Cult*, also refers to Shils as a key point of reference.

16. Brigitte Studer and Heiko Haumann 'Introduction' in idem (eds), *Stalinistische Subjekte. Individuum und System in der Sowjetunion und Der Komintern 1929–1953* (Zurich: Chronos, 2006), p. 40.
17. Silvio Pons and Robert Service (eds), *A Dictionary of 20th-Century Communism* (Princeton, NJ: Princeton University Press, 2010); S.A. Smith (ed.), *The Oxford Handbook of the History of Communism* (Oxford: Oxford University Press, 2014); Archie Brown, *The Rise and Fall of Communism* (London: Bodley Head, 2009); David Priestland, *The Red Flag. Communism and the making of the modern world* (London: Allen Lane, 2009); Silvio Pons, *The Global Revolution. A history of international communism 1917–1991* (Oxford: Oxford University Press, 2014).
18. Katerina Clark, *Moscow, the Fourth Rome. Stalinism, cosmopolitanism, and the evolution of Soviet culture, 1931–1941* (Cambridge, MA: Harvard University Press, 2011), p. 6 and passim; see also e.g. Karl Schlögel, *Moscow, 1937* (Cambridge: Polity, 2012); Michael David-Fox, *Showcasing the Great Experiment. Cultural diplomacy and western visitors to the Soviet Union, 1921–1941* (New York: Oxford University Press, 2012).
19. See for example Studer and Haumann, *Stalinistische Subjekte*; Serge Wolikow, *L'Internationale communiste (1919–1943). Le Komintern ou le rêve déchu du parti mondial de la révolution* (Paris: Éditions de l'Atelier, 2010); Jean-François Fayet, *VOKS: le laboratoire helvétique. Histoire de la diplomatie culturelle soviétique durant l'entre-deux-guerres* (Chêne-Bourg: Georg, 2014); Brigitte Studer, *The Transnational World of the Cominternians* (Basingstoke: Palgrave Macmillan, 2015).
20. Plamper, *Stalin Cult*, pp. xvii–xviii, 5; Plamper, 'Introduction' in Klaus Heller and Jan Plamper (eds), *Personality Cults in Stalinism—Personenkulte im Stalinismus* (Göttingen: V&R Unipress, 2004) proposes a more expansive approach (pp. 19–21) but the comparators discussed in the collection are fascist ones.
21. E. Arfon Rees, 'Cult of personality' in Pons and Service, *Dictionary*, pp. 248–50; Daniel Leese, 'The cult of personality and symbolic politics' in Smith, *Oxford Handbook*, pp. 339–54.
22. Alexey Tikhomorov, 'The Stalin cult between center and periphery: the structures of the cult community in the empire of socialism, 1949–1956—the case of GDR' in Benno Enker and Heidi Hein-Kircher (eds), *Der Führer im Europa des 20. Jahrhunderts*

(Marburg: Herder-Institut, 2010), pp. 297–324; Max Weber, *Economy and Society. An outline of interpretive sociology* (Berkeley, CA: University of California Press, 2 vols, 1978 edn), pp. 243, 245–54. The key collection in this connection is Balázs Apor et al. (eds), *The Leader Cult in Communist Dictatorships. Stalin and the Eastern bloc* (Basingstoke: Palgrave Macmillan, 2004).

23. Rees, 'Leader cults: varieties, preconditions and functions' in Apor, *Leader Cult*, pp. 4, 8, 17.
24. Alexander C. Cook (ed.), *Mao's Little Red Book. A global history* (Cambridge: Cambridge University Press, 2014).
25. Kriegel, 'Bureaucratie, culte de personnalité et charisme', pp. 132–58.
26. Stéphane Sirot, *Maurice Thorez* (Paris: Presses de Sciences Po, 2000), pp. 54–65.
27. Georges Friedmann, *De la Sainte Russie à l'URSS* (Paris: Gallimard, 1938), pp. 217–18.
28. Pons, *Global Revolution*, p. 114.
29. Sarah Davies, *Popular Opinion in Stalin's Russia. Terror, propaganda and dissent, 1934–1941* (Cambridge: Cambridge University Press, 1997), pp. 153–154; David Brandenberger, *Propaganda State in Crisis. Soviet ideology, indoctrination, and terror under Stalin, 1927–1941* (New Haven, CT: Yale University Press, 2011), ch. 4.
30. Annie Kriegel, *The French Communists. Profile of a people* (Chicago, IL: University of Chicago Press, 1972).
31. Daniel Leese, *Mao Cult. Rhetoric and ritual in China's Cultural Revolution* (Cambridge: Cambridge University Press, 2011), p. 18 and passim.
32. Balázs Apor, *The 'Invisible Shining': the cult of Mátyás Rákosi in stalinist Hungary, 1945–1956* (Budapest: Central European University Press, forthcoming 2017); Russel T. Lemmons, *Hitler's Rival. Ernst Thälmann in Myth and Memory* (Lexington, KY: University of Kentucky Press, 2013).
33. See notably Bernard Pudal, *Prendre parti. Pour une sociologie historique du PCF* (Paris: Presses de la Fondation Nationale des Sciences Politiques, 1989); Claude Pennetier and Bernard Pudal, 'Stalinism: workers' cult and cult of leaders, *TCC*, 1 (2009), 20–9; also Goulemot, *Pour l'amour de Staline*.
34. Markus Wien, 'Georgi Dimitrov: three manifestations of his cult' in Apor, *Leader Cult*, pp. 194–207 is a treatment weakest in respect

of the origins of Dimitrov's cult. There is an excellent scholarly biography in English: Marietta Stankova, *Georgi Dimitrov. A biography* (London: Tauris, 2010).

35. Shils, 'Center and periphery', pp. 5–7.
36. Yves Cohen, *Le Siècle des chefs. Une histoire transnationale du commandement et de l'autorité (1890–1940)* (Paris: Éditions Amsterdam, 2013), pp. 9–40.
37. Robert Michels (trans. Eden and Cedar Paul), *Political Parties. A sociological study of the oligarchical tendencies of modern democracy* (1911; New York: Transaction Publishers edn, 1999), pp. 50 and passim; Gustave Le Bon, *Psychologie des foules* (1895; Paris: Félix Alcan, 1930 edn), pp. 98–101.
38. Weber, *Economy and Society*, p. 242; for charisma, see Chap. 3.4 below.
39. Michels, *Political Parties*, p. 90.
40. For conflicting views, see Cohen, *Siècle*, p. 421; Richard Pipes, *Russia under the Bolshevik Regime, 1919–1924* (London: Fontana edn, 1995), p. 270; Robert Service, *Lenin. A biography* (London: Macmillan, 2000), p. 203.
41. Michels, *Political Parties*, p. 94.
42. Andrew G. Bonnell, 'The Lassalle cult in German social democracy', *Australian Journal of Politics and History*, 35 (1989), 50–60.
43. Eduard Bernstein, *Ferdinand Lassalle as a Social Reformer* (London: Swan Sonnenschein & Co, 1893), pp. 188–9.
44. Michels, *Political Parties*, p. 94.
45. Tumarkin, *Lenin Lives!*, pp. 39–42; Plamper, *Stalin Cult*, pp. 19–22.
46. Carl Levy, 'Charisma and social movements: Errico Malatesta and Italian anarchism', *Modern Italy*, 3 (1998), 205–17.
47. Erik van Ree, *The Political Thought of Joseph Stalin. A study in twentieth-century revolutionary patriotism* (London: Routledge Curzon, 2002), pp. 161, 166–7.
48. Plamper, *Stalin Cult*, pp. xvii–xviii.
49. Cohen, *Siècle*, pp. 11–12, 80–2.
50. Apor, *'Invisible Shining'*, ch. 1.
51. Lucy Riall, *Garibaldi; invention of a hero* (New Haven, CT: Yale University Press, 2008 edn), pp. 389–90.
52. Rosario Forlenza and Bjørn Thomassen, 'From myth to reality and back again: the fascist and post-fascist reading of Garibaldi and the Risorgimento', *Bulletin of Italian Politics*, 3 (2011), 263–81.

53. V. Knorin, 'The leader of the world proletarian revolution', *CI*, 1 May 1934, 331–4.
54. Moshe Lewin, 'Stalin in the mirror of the other' in Ian Kershaw and Moshe Lewin (eds), *Stalinism and Nazism: dictatorships in common* (Cambridge: Cambridge University Press, 1997), pp. 110–11.
55. For example Sarah Davies, 'The "cult" of the *Vozhd'*: representations in letters from 1934–41', *Russian History*, 24 (1997), 131–47; Davies, *Popular Opinion in Stalin's Russia. Terror, propaganda and dissent, 1934–1941* (Cambridge: Cambridge University Press, 1997); Plamper, *Stalin Cult*, ch. 6; Apor, *'Invisible Shining'*, chs 5–7.
56. My special thanks therefore to the contributors to that issue: Balázs Apor; José Gotovitch; Sophie Quinn Judge; Claude Pennetier and Bernard Pudal; Tauno Saarela; Marco Aurélio Santana. For their contributions, see Kevin Morgan (ed.), 'Communism and the leader cult', *TCC*, 1 (2009).
57. Plamper, *Stalin Cult*; also Jeffrey Brooks, *Thank You, Comrade Stalin! Soviet public culture from revolution to Cold War* (Princeton, NJ: Princeton University Press, 2000).
58. Alexander Vatlin and Stephen A. Smith, 'The Comintern' in Smith, *Oxford Handbook*, p. 200.
59. On this, see Rennie Yotova, 'Poétique de la commémoration. L'immortalité du personnage communiste. Valko Tchervenkov—entre la culte de la personnalité et l'éviction' in Alain Montandon (ed.), *L'Anniversaire* (Clermont-Ferrand: Presses universitaires Blaise Pascal, 2008), pp. 161–9.
60. For an expert discussion of these issues, see Cohen, *Siècle*, pp. 41–56.
61. As Timothy Cheek points out in a different context, scholarly translations of Mao's original writings are not always to be preferred to the heavily edited official versions in which these were presented to some hundreds of millions of readers; Cheek, 'Mao and Maoism' in Smith, *Oxford Handbook*, p. 98.
62. Two recent summaries thus refer interchangeably to leader and personality cults; see Rees, 'Cult of personality' and Daniel Leese, 'Cult of personality and symbolic politics'.
63. Eduard Bernstein, *Ferdinand Lassalle. Eine Würdigung des Lehres und Kämpfers* (Berlin: Verleft Bein Paul Cassirer, 1919), p. 299.

64. Jochen Hellbeck, *Revolution On My Mind. Writing a diary under Stalin* (Cambridge, MA: Harvard University Press, 2009 edn), p. 28. On this issue, see Chap. 6.3 below.
65. Plamper, 'Introduction', p. 33; Leese, *Mao Cult*, p. 5.
66. Anssi Halmesvirta, 'A foreign benefactor and a domestic liberator: the cults of Lenin and Mannerheim in Finland', *Scandinavian Journal of History*, 34 (2009), 414–32.
67. Barbusse, *Staline. Un monde nouveau vu à travers un homme* (1935; Paris: Flammarion, 1936 edn), p. 86; see also Lion Feuchtwanger, *Moskau 1937. Ein Reisebericht für meine Freunde* (Amsterdam: Querido Verlag, 1937), pp. 76, 83; Friedmann, *De la Sainte Russie*, pp. 213–18.
68. Cachin, preface to Annette Vidal, *Henri Barbusse. Soldat de la paix* (Paris: Éditeurs Français Réunis, 1953), p. 12.

CHAPTER 2

Cult Developments 1917–1956

(i)

By a quirk of fate the historic burying place of the kings of France was also the earliest and staunchest of the municipal fortresses that made up Paris's red belt. Still today, the visitor to Saint-Denis can gaze at royal sepulchres before strolling down the rue Gabriel Péri, named after a communist resistance martyr, or through the displays in the town's museum on the Paris Commune. It was here in Saint-Denis, in the shadow of the famous basilica, that on Lenin's death in 1924 the first of the grandiose obsequies were organised that would become so characteristic of communism in France.[1]

Reports in the PCF daily *L'Humanité* registered the heavy symbolism of the occasion. If 'religious gravity' and an almost sacramental silence befitted the solemnity of the setting, this was not the icy protocol of court or caste and there was also the sense of unity in bereavement with those gathering for the same purpose across the globe. In Berlin, by meeting at the tombs of the murdered revolutionaries Rosa Luxemburg and Karl Liebknecht, mourners for the first time linked the names that would henceforth become associated in an annual campaign of memorialisation. In London's Poplar, the principal speaker was not a communist but the Labour politician George Lansbury. Above all, of course, there was Moscow. 'Separated by so great a distance', Marcel Cachin wrote from Paris, 'the two pious crowds ... were really in communion; their soul was

K. Morgan, *International Communism and the Cult of the Individual*, DOI 10.1057/978-1-137-55667-7_2

as one, and as one their grief at seeing so prematurely brought to nothing the sure guide that led them …'.[2]

The posthumous cult thus initiated is sometimes distinguished rather sharply from the tributes that had been paid to the living Lenin. Boris Souvarine was among the Saint-Denis mourners and later provided a classic exposition of this view in what is still one of the best books ever written on Stalin. This not only emphasised differences of scale between Lenin's time and Stalin's but described how the former was now turned into a kind of deity through practices melding modern advertising methods with the 'grossest artifices of fetichist religions'.[3] The assumed ascription to Lenin of godlike attributes, sometimes seen as integral to the modern personality cult, is in his case centred on the decision to preserve his body for public veneration, in defiance of socialist or any other secular precedent. The canonisation of the leader's body is thus at the heart of Benno Ennker's account of the cult, and Ennker has drawn just this distinction between the adulation accorded the living Lenin and his full-blown posthumous cult as a form of image-worship by decree.[4] Academic judgements differ as to how far this was a matter of cynicism, populism or necessity. As epitomised by Lenin's Red Square mausoleum, or by the shrine-like Lenin corners that now proliferated in Russia, the cult nevertheless appears as one both licensed and promoted by the ruling Bolsheviks through forms of superstitious observance which they had hitherto scorned. Under the fading varnish of marxist theory, Souvarine maintained, there had reappeared the countenance of 'ancient, barbaric Russia'.[5]

The first intimations of such a cult can nevertheless be dated from the earliest months of the revolution.[6] Already in August 1918, the attempt on Lenin's life by the left Socialist Revolutionary Fanny Kaplan brought forth a veritable outpouring of eulogy, lamentation and vengefulness.[7] Lenin's closest acolyte and deputy Grigory Zinoviev delivered a biographical tribute that lifted him clear above his peers and described the revolution itself as largely his personal accomplishment.[8] The sentiments of Leon Trotsky, who alone could rival Lenin in popular esteem, were equally effusive, and circulated in a million copies. Some quality of martyrdom was thus already revealed as a catalyst for forms of veneration that were rooted in the socialist tradition, and not just a specifically Russian one. Superficially their identification with the figure of the ruler may call to mind the martyrising process stimulated by the regicidal attentats of the tsarist era.[9] On the other hand, Lenin's was a revolutionary regime, yet to establish itself like the tsars', and in a context of civil war he was seen as victim of the unsubdued forces of oppression that allegedly moved his assailant's hand. The sense that his life had been cut short by an assassin's bullet was to be a defining motif of Lenin's posthumous cult. But already, as he recovered in time for the revolution's first anniversary, he now became the focal point of the Moscow celebrations which Richard Stites has identified as a landmark in the cult's emergence.[10]

By the time that Lenin's 50th birthday fell in April 1920, the precedent was set of public ceremonial, the issuing of biographies and published 'works', and the filling of newspapers with odes and panegyrics. The more prosaic Russian signifier for the office or function of leader was *rukovoditel'*. In later years, its displacement by the 'charismatic and sacral' *vozhd'* would mark the onset of the Stalin cult and has been equated with the German *Führer* or the Italian neologism *Duce*.[11] *Vozhd'*, however, was already used of Lenin by his closest comrades, and by the hyperbolic laureate of both his and Stalin's cults, Demyan Bedny. What tender names they gave him, Zinoviev wrote of the messages received during Lenin's convalescence, and more than any other the word they chose was *vozhd'*.

> He is really the chosen one of millions. He is the leader by the grace of God. He is the authentic figure of a leader such as is born once in 500 years in the life of mankind.[12]

Though the scale as yet was relatively modest, many of the standard cult features were already prefigured by the time of Lenin's death, from the hagiographies and birthday rituals to the merchandise of Lenin scarves and cigarette boxes.[13] 'We sing "No higher being saves us"—and also "no tribune"', Trotsky admitted; but this was only in 'the last historical sense' that ultimately guaranteed the workers' victory. Lenin in the meantime was an influence on the destiny of his species which history had no standard by which to measure.[14]

In offering such tributes, Bolshevik leaders insisted on the international character of Lenin's appeal. Zinoviev, who headed the Comintern, particularly emphasised this rather more than Lenin's role as leader of the Soviet state.[15] Trotsky in his speech on 'Lenin wounded' also described how Lenin met the need for a new leadership figure that was felt on an international scale. Liberal internationalists had for a time looked to the US president Woodrow Wilson, and it was in his disillusionment with Wilson that Barbusse fastened on Lenin as a 'sort of Messiah'.[16] As a social visionary of comparable stature, there was also perhaps the Indian Gandhi, whose competing claims Barbusse argued out with Romain Rolland.[17] It was within the socialist movement itself, however, that the crisis of authority was possibly sharpest. Ideologically and organisationally, the Bolsheviks identified the breakdown of social democracy with its betrayal of basic internationalist principle in 1914. Fortuitously, this was also symbolised by the passing of those leaders who had best represented the ideals of the pre-war International while enjoying a cultlike status within their own parties.

Trotsky singled out the 'Emperor' of German social democracy August Bebel, whose death in 1913 had been marked by extravagant funeral rites and whom Trotsky described as 'the best figure of an earlier epoch that already belongs to the past'.[18] His only peer, in Trotsky's estimation, was the Frenchman Jean Jaurès, who through his assassination on the eve of war achieved a legendary status which no wartime disillusionment could ever now diminish.[19] Trotsky would not have ranked so highly their nearest British counterpart Keir Hardie. Nevertheless, Hardie's death in 1915 also marked the passing of a figure who had personified his movement's founding ideals both within Britain and in the forums of the International. A further fatal gap was left by Luxemburg's revolutionary martrydom, and the removal thereby of the figure best equipped to counterbalance the Russian influence in the early Comintern. Trotsky had written of the vacuum that followed Jaurès's death; now he maintained that western Europe had 'forgotten, neglected, or failed to bring about the creation of *the* leader' such as Lenin alone now represented.[20] If Lenin appeared precisely as a saviour from the left, it was, paradoxically, not only as the founder of the Third International, but as one of the last great uncompromised figures of the Second.

In Britain, where almost nothing yet was known of those who had led the revolution, Ian Bullock has unearthed a first published dedication to Lenin appearing as early as March 1918. Even Demyan Bedny's 'To the Leader' (*vozhdiu*) did not appear until May, and in its fervour as well as timing this first British exercise in Leniniana was hardly to be outdone by its Russian counterparts:

> *'Tis thine from wrack of empires to create*
> *A Commonwealth of Love, a Federal State,*
> *Not founded on deceit, or gold, or might,*
> *But built by Truth and Justice in despite*
> *Of all the Powers of Moloch and of Hate …*

The sordid cities reared by Lust and Lies,
Are piled as rubble in a marsh of blood;
But at thy word the towers of Peace will rise,
And Wisdom, Brotherhood and Pity bud
In hearts that Death and Sorrow have made wise.[21]

Curiously, the poem's Scottish author had once written no less enthusiastically of Queen Victoria.[22] On the other hand, his Lenin poem may be found in Sylvia Pankhurst's *Workers' Dreadnought*, interspersed with its tributes to Luxemburg, Liebknecht, Hardie and others. One article offers the lineage: 'Marx: De Leon: Lenin'. An address composed by Finnish revolutionaries exudes self-criticism for their own failed revolution while saluting in Lenin the 'firm hand and bright, far-seeing eye' to which the rudder of both workers' state and International could be entrusted.[23] The personalisation of an ancestry beginning with Marx would later become a cliche of Soviet cult production, and the image of the man at the helm would famously be used by Barbusse in his Stalin cult biography.

'Don't create a cult', the poet Mayakovsky wrote on Lenin's death, 'in the name of the man, who all his life fought against all and every cult'.[24] Even so, when Khruschchev in 1956 also insisted on Lenin's revulsion for such practices, he did not produce a single supporting citation and had to go back to Marx. Completely sincere in his personal modesty, Lenin blocked some of the grosser hagiographical initiatives such as a proposed cult film.[25] Nevertheless, his absolute commitment to safeguarding the revolution meant that he was adaptable on almost any secondary point that assisted in this. As Getty notes, he understood the practical advantages that came of being photographed, filmed and otherwise marketed.[26] He also did not underestimate the importance of making himself available to visiting dignitaries and delegations, notably including those who could assist in promoting his cause in the West. London in particular was a fulcrum of communications as well as commerce and diplomacy, and Lenin's image internationally derived as much from his encounters with journalists like Lansbury and Arthur Ransome as it did from the Bolsheviks themselves. When the writer H.G. Wells called upon him, Lenin took it seriously enough to brush up beforehand on Wells's science fiction.[27] He was even among the several Bolshevik leaders who sat for the sculptor Clare Sheridan, whom no special artistic or political distinction recommended, but who was a cousin of Winston Churchill and whose impressions were publicised through organs like *The Times* and a frisson-exciting travelogue *From Mayfair to Moscow* (1921).

Ransome described a Lenin so unburdened by the sense of personal destiny that he was continuously breaking out in laughter.[28] Lansbury, a Christian pacifist, evoked a spirit of absolute self-abnegation, like 'one of the saints of old … a father of his people … who toils for them, thinks for them, acts for them, suffers with them'.[29] However disparate these impressions, or the face that Lenin revealed in such encounters, what all agreed on was Lenin's utter disregard of self. In this respect, a persona was established in which some of the key motifs of the Stalin cult—modesty, austerity, self-discipline and dedication to a larger cause—were already clearly signalled. One wonders if any living Russian had ever been so widely depicted outside of their own country, or any other living socialist outside of theirs. Already in 1919, there appeared the first book-length profiles, both hostile and eulogistic.[30] By the time of Lenin's death, the figure was well-established of an almost legendary being in whom the hopes of all the world's workers were made incarnate and 'the spirit of internationalism and universal brotherhood … made flesh'.[31]

There is therefore no mystery as to how such crowds could be got together so quickly on the news of Lenin's death. One can to this extent speak of spontaneity, but on the part of an international left-wing public rather more than of ordinary Russians. Within Russia, security reports suggest that Lenin's passing met with considerable scepticism and negativity except among those closest to the Bolsheviks.[32] Though scholarly judgements differ widely, the new cult instruments of the mausoleum and mummified corpse are also said to have answered no significant public demand that can be documented archivally.[33] Souvarine himself, from his movements between Moscow and Paris, was to record that the only apparent emotion displayed on Lenin's death was that of the communists themselves.[34] He might also have remembered that there were forms of veneration long established on the secular left, that these conventionally were allowed the fullest licence only posthumously, and that Paris itself had a Panthéon that more than counterbalanced the royal Valhalla at Saint-Denis. Souvarine himself, indeed, was among the Paris mourners, and in contributing to *L'Humanité*'s saturation coverage depicted a flawless figure, 'Ilyich, dear Ilyich', who, if not exactly godlike, exercised a sort of 'omnipotence' through his superhuman labours and the confidence reposed in him by his followers.[35] At Saint-Denis the tears were seen to flow; in London, Dutt wrote in a private letter of 'the hardest blow of all, leaving the world so sad and empty and the International somehow not meaning the same. … It makes the whole fight feel very much lonelier.'[36]

It was known to all that Lenin's widow Krupskaya had spoken out in *Pravda* against empty commemoration, and had not approved the ceremonialisation of his body.[37] Mayakovsky was also disgusted by the mausoleum and chocolate-box approach, and the 'cloying unction' of memorialisation by decree.[38] Some of the rituals of the new state cult were therefore tolerated at best by many Bolsheviks, and even at the height of stalinism western communists could refer to the reverence extended Lenin's body as a peculiar adaptation to the Russian 'peasant mind'.[39] What this should not obscure is how far the impulse to commemorate Lenin's life, and not its casing, was shared across an international cult community defined by socialist ideals rather than the bounds of statehood. Both Trotsky and Krupskaya contributed personal memoirs to the posthumous explosion in Leniniana. Though Mayakovsky celebrated Lenin's simplicity, it was in the form of an epic poem that proved one of the cult's most popular and durable expressions. In Paris, Jean Guéhenno, not even a communist, so felt the loss that he set about learning Russian and for two years worked at an abortive Lenin biography.[40] In the militant English coalfield village of Chopwell, Lenin's image was set alongside Hardie's on the miners' banner and thus assimilated into a much older tradition of labour movement heroes.[41] It is difficult to see that any prominent communist dissented from such treatment; and Souvarine was certainly justified when later he reminded Trotsky that 'pseudo-Leninist conformism' and the biblification of Lenin's writings were common to all those who now fought for Lenin's legacy.[42]

Maxim Gorky's eulogy of Lenin was not only one of those most widely circulated but encapsulated many of the complexities of the cult phenomenon. Politically, Gorky was at once an unattached fellow-traveller and a personal and political intimate of Lenin's. Intellectually, he linked the Nietzschean and god-building tendencies within pre-revolutionary Bolshevism with the 'revolutionary romanticism' that in Stalin's time would cross-pollinate with the cult of the individual.[43] As Russia's best-known living writer, with a seer-like conception of the writer's role, Gorky would himself become the focus of a cult as well as cult practitioner.[44] Most of all, he was caught squarely between the national and transnational as a writer in Russian employing Russian themes, but as a European literary celebrity who for most of the 1920s lived in Capri.

Gorky had returned there from Russia in 1921. Briefly after the revolution, he had seen in Lenin's rule the coming of a strict and pitiless *vozhd'* imposing his ideals upon a hapless people.[45] By the time that he left Russia, he had come to celebrate the very same qualities, and precisely in the name of these socialist ideals. Saint-like in his private life and a genius in his powers of intuition, the Lenin he portrayed had shaken up Russia's 'desultory, misbuilt, slothful semi-human ant-hill' and used it as a battering ram against the old world order.[46] Originally published in the *Communist International*, the article was regarded by Lenin as un-communist and even anti-communist. Gorky, unrepentant, nevertheless grouped him on his death with Tolstoy and Peter the Great as the sort of 'monstrous, fairy-like and unexpected' personality that Russia alone produced, and the perfect incarnation of 'the will directed at an aim'.[47] When later Gorky returned to Russia, the re-editing of his Lenin tribute was among the first political tasks he undertook. Its dilations upon Russia's peculiar genius were excised; so was the too candid avowal that no leader was possible who was not in some degree a tyrant.[48] Nevertheless, the doctored text retained its currency, for the Lenin cult at this stage was indispensable to the shadowy successor whose initial claim to power was that of being his best disciple.

(ii)

The apogee of Lenin's cult, as Tumarkin relates, was in the two years immediately following his death.[49] It would be absurd to see this only as an instrument of the factional conflict then being fought out by his successors. Nevertheless, its character as the legitimation of living rulers by a dead one is only really comprehensible if this is taken into account. Lenin's passing did not in itself imperil Soviet rule; this had never derived its legitimacy from a single ruler, and it is to underestimate Lenin's legacy of the ruling party to overstate the importance of his personal authority. Where this did really matter was within the party itself; and what might have destabilised the regime was the inner-party succession crisis that was already prefigured during Lenin's final illness. In other circumstances, the ritualising of Lenin's political remains might have been the means of maintaining party unity through the one point of reference that none dared call into question. In the circumstances that actually existed, what it principally provided was a means of neutralising and then effacing the real or imagined threat posed by Trotsky.

Except among old Bolsheviks, Trotsky's was the name which was most of all coupled with Lenin's, and few even among old Bolsheviks questioned that his was the revolution's outstanding personality now that Lenin was no more. In his mastery of the written and spoken word Trotsky had ceded nothing even to Lenin; and when the fate of the revolution hung in the balance, he had acquired the further dashing persona of the successful military leader. 'Little father Lenin will save us', declaimed the muzhik of the communist imagination, 'and Trotsky with his Red Army'.[50] Intellectuals, Gorky among them, saw Trotsky as one of their own; Souvarine described the welling of support following Lenin's death as like a plebiscite in Trotsky's favour.[51] An American follower, Max Eastman, had had Trotsky's co-operation in producing a hagiography suffused with hero-worship of 'the most universally gifted man in the world of today'.[52] Another American, later a Stalin devotee, drew the comparison with Leonardo da Vinci.[53] Stalin was not alone in regarding this with apprehension, and Trotsky himself recalled the politburo member Kamenev also warning: 'Are we to allow Trotsky to become the one person empowered to direct the party and the state?'[54] Comintern loyalists alluded darkly to the dangers of Caesarism; Gorky's revised Lenin tribute would have Lenin musing sadly on the echo in Trotsky of the self-regarding Lassalle. As initially Trotsky's politburo colleagues joined forces against him, Eastman in 1925 characterised them as the 'anti-Bonaparte fraction'.[55]

The Lenin cult therefore served as anti-cult in a double sense: first, of its inimitability at any personal level; and secondly, of its dependency for a quasi-immortality, not on Lenin's physical remains, but on the collective Lenin of the party. Long before Lenin's death, Bolsheviks had sought to capture in the romantic ascription of genius some quality of acuity, profundity or decisiveness in their leader. For Trotsky such a figure appeared once a century; for Zinoviev, Bukharin and Stalin not even so often.[56] While embalmers worked on Lenin's body, his brain reposed in a laboratory, later the quintessential cult emplacement of the Institute of the Brain, where science and superstition combined in awe of an organ apparently unconstrained by ordinary human limitations.

Of greater immediate practicality was the notion of leninism. First employed in a positive sense by Zinoviev, this allowed the codification of Lenin's legacy as a corpus of teaching and example that would henceforth be embodied in the party that he left behind him. Emelyan Yaroslavsky was a leading Bolshevik historian and the biographer in turn of Lenin and Stalin. Nevertheless, he had at first anticipated no such individual succession but urged instead that Lenin's place be taken by '*collective strength, collective work, collective will*'.[57] Gustav Klutsis, who through photomontage would provide some of the most striking visual images of Stalin's cult, similarly at this stage depicted Lenin and the masses with the motto

Millions Have Risen In Place of One.[58] Even as a Stalin cult did later make its appearance, the ascription of genius was for the time being confined to Lenin himself, and Stalin represented precisely as the incarnation of collective strength and will.[59]

For still unexplained reasons, Stalin from the early 1920s had begun to post-date his birth from December 1879, and it is from the 50th anniversary of this earliest of his falsifications that the beginnings of his cult are usually dated.[60] There are suggestions of a sort of proto-cult. When in December 1925 Kamenev denounced the idea of 'a "leader" theory' and the concentration of powers in the secretariat, delegates at the 14th party congress rose in ovation to the party and central committee as identified with Stalin.[61] In Stalin's native Georgia, the *New Masses* correspondent Joseph Freeman had already in 1926 witnessed ovations of several minutes' duration that seemed like a foretaste of what was to come.[62] The following year one of the earliest exposés of the emerging cult was issued by the oppositionist Ter-Vaganyan, and at that year's tenth party congress the Soviet premier Rykov felt impelled to challenge the allegations of Stalin's dictatorship. Nevertheless, Stalin's Georgian appearances had not been published for a national audience, and the delegations that in 1927 arrived in Russia to celebrate the revolution's tenth anniversary would not as yet have taken him for anything more than primus inter pares.[63] Notoriously, Sergei Eisenstein's anniversary film *October* had favourable depictions of Trotsky edited out. There was, however, no insertion yet of Stalin in Trotsky's place.[64] Crucially, his cult was not the instrument by which he prevailed over his rivals and cemented his grip on power. On the contrary, it was the silencing, co-optation or exclusion of all such figures that was the precondition of a Stalin myth whose basic premises were otherwise plainly refutable.

The significance of Stalin's half-centenary was not therefore just the implicit parallel with Lenin. 1929 had also been the year of Trotsky's physical banishment, removing the figure whose claim to Lenin's legacy stood most in Stalin's way, and of the expulsion from the politburo of Nikolai Bukharin, who latterly had represented the dominant figure of the party right. This not only confirmed the rout of Bukharin's supporters but brought under Stalin's control the key party organs like *Pravda* which would henceforth provide the principal vehicles of his cult. It was in *Pravda*, expanded to twice its normal size, that the parallel with Lenin was subliminally evoked by the diversion to Stalin's achievements of the entire contents of his birthday issue. In the context of the party, the revolution and even the Red Army, the challenging of 'Trotskyist' narratives was at once explicit and quite unscrupulous as to factual accuracy.[65]

The Comintern at this stage also remained a crucial sphere of legitimation and cult projection. Though successively Zinoviev and Bukharin had been its recognised leaders, articles by the Comintern secretaries Kuusinen and Manuilsky now detailed Stalin's ostensible oversight of its activities. Manuilsky's, originally entitled 'Comintern and Stalin', even carried the corrected version 'Stalin, leader of the Comintern', with possibly the first use in this context of the expressive variant *vozhd'*.[66] Greetings from the Comintern and its sections also featured prominently, and subsequent translations of this material into the main Comintern languages strongly emphasised this international dimension. It was a sign therefore of the last-minute character of the operation that the occasion had gone unmentioned in party organs like *L'Humanité* and the CPGB's *Workers' Life*.[67]

Even more than in Lenin's which was also Trotsky's day, the Bolsheviks now had a single pre-eminent leader. To assuage the curiosity of an international public, a flurry of mostly hostile Stalin biographies appeared.[68] Stalin himself now granted his first interviews with western press correspondents; like a modern catch-all party leader, he thereby cut out the party and its activists, and the atrophy of the Comintern as communication channel would be symbolised in due course by the intimation in this way of everything from shifts in policy to ruminations on philosophy.[69] Interviews with leading public intellectuals were crucial to Stalin's cultivation of a sage-like image internationally. The first of them, with the unpredictable Bernard Shaw in July 1931, was conducted on terms of confidentiality.[70] That with the French writer Romain Rolland in 1935 turned to critical issues of Soviet policy and was also embargoed.[71] On the other hand, interviews with Emil Ludwig (December 1931) and H.G. Wells (July 1934) were among the most widely circulated of Stalin's pronouncements. The Ludwig interview, in occasioning Stalin's reflections on the individual's role in history, became one of the most citable of his texts and a staple of future cult productions. Entertaining Wells, meanwhile, not only recalled Lenin's similar encounter, but carried Wells's agreeable assurance that Stalin's voice alone, along with that of US president Roosevelt, was now heeded right across a troubled world.

Even so, there was as yet no sustained promotion of Stalin's cult as there had been of Lenin's. Both visually and textually, Stalin's was a surprisingly low profile even in *Pravda*. When later his *Works* were collected a single volume sufficed for the three-and-a-half years spanning the party congresses of 1930 and 1934. In Britain and the USA a 'Stalin Pocket Series' had been launched but promptly abandoned, presumably for lack of material. It was only in mid-1933 that Stalin's image began to figure more in *Pravda*, and his name to appear more frequently in lead editorials.[72] The 'real explosion of the cult' occurred the following January with the 17th party congress, the so-called Congress of Victors.[73] The opening of the congress marked the tenth anniversary, not of Lenin's death itself, but of the memorial speech by Stalin which had come to symbolise his succession. Erstwhile oppositionist Karl Radek marked the occasion with probably the first substantial article devoted exclusively to Stalin's adulation. Two-and-a-half years earlier the renowned documentarist Dziga Vertov had been commissioned to produce the anniversary film *Three Songs of Lenin*. Now its release was delayed, as with Eisenstein's *October*, but this time to rectify the inadequacy of its treatment of Stalin.[74] By the time that Ludwig pulled together his impressions of the latter for his *Leaders of Europe* (1934), he depicted him as the principal though not the only object of an 'over-powering craze for public hero-worship'.[75]

Domestically, this might be seen as the moment that Stalin's power became unassailable, or that of the pulling clear from the traumas of collectivisation which he might have thought twice about personifying in the public mind. What was clearly also a motivating force was the transformation of the international situation following Hitler's installation in power in January 1933. Yves Cohen has hypothesised that Stalin's preoccupation with Hitler's example was a catalyst for the resurgence of his own cult, and that each in fact learnt from the other.[76] This still leaves the question of why Hitler's example should have registered so much more quickly than Mussolini's, whose cult has also been proposed as Stalin's model, and whose regime's tenth anniversary celebrations had offered a symbiosis of leader and vaunted revolution offering more obvious analogies with bolshevism.[77] What Hitler did represent more than Mussolini was threat rather more perhaps than exemplar. Not only was this a likely stimulus to Stalin's own projection of a counter-cult; through Dimitrov and the Reichstag fire trial it also produced the first example since Lenin of a communist to whom a significant international public rallied as if spontaneously. Though a Soviet biography of Stalin had to wait until 1939, it was in the summer of 1933 that Barbusse, who more than any other communist had the ear of this public, was commissioned to produce for it Stalin's own authorised life.

The high point of the pre-war cult was in 1936–1937.[78] On the 20th anniversary of the revolution, resolution after resolution singled Stalin out as architect and executant of socialist construction.[79] At the Paris international exhibition, where the Soviet pavilion was famously surmounted by Vera Mukhina's *Worker and Collective Farm Girl*, all within exuded the cult of the individual, and in murals, canvases and statues Stalin now assumed his rightful place alongside Lenin.[80] In Mikhail Romm's film *Lenin in October*, he was for the first time depicted by an actor: statuesque and commanding, Graham Greene's review wryly noted, while Lenin by comparison seemed nervous, small and gesticulating—this last a feature which even Soviet commentators thought unsatisfactory.[81] Posters not only carried more Stalin images, in larger editions, but where the two leaders were depicted together he usually had primacy: 'he was foregrounded, he alone gazed directly at the viewer, or his image was larger'.[82]

Even within a Soviet context, one must be careful not to predate the eclipsing of Lenin's cult. Not all representations were as responsive to the moment as film screenings or the daily *Pravda*. Texts of and about Lenin were dispersed in huge editions and remained an indispensable quarry. There was also a 'Lenin Statue Population' which Theodore Dreiser had in 1927 irreverently calculated as 'at least 80,000,000'.[83] Even the unrealisable Palace of the Soviets, symbol of Stalin's hubris, was to have been crowned by Sergei Merkurov's gesturing Lenin, which by the final design of 1934 had attained the colossal prospective height of 80 metres. Though the project never got much beyond the foundations, it was not until much later put finally into abeyance, and still in 1938 a Comintern publication evoked the sight awaiting the future traveller.

> When still many miles from his destination he will see in the far distance, as if suspended in mid-air, a huge figure, the characteristic attitude of which is known to every worker in the world. Like a vision the figure of Lenin will appear on the horizon, with arm outstretched, as if pointing the way … leading from capitalist misery and oppression.[84]

This seems very different from a Soviet-centred reading in which the statue is imagined pointing to Stalin and the patristic centre of the Kremlin.[85] This only confirms, of course, that no single reading need be assumed. Though there were before the war clear indications of the winding down of Lenin's cult, publications like the lavish *Stalin on Lenin* continued to appear in new editions as if to reaffirm the exclusive rights that Stalin had in the Lenin franchise.[86]

By the time of Stalin's 60th birthday in 1939, there was an abundance of cult materials available for communist parties still legally functioning. At the same time, this more than ever was like the rippling out from Moscow of a state-centred leader cult. The dominant motif of leader of the peoples thus signified the peoples of the USSR and the refashioning of older formulae as a form of internationalism in one country. This, for example, was a feature of the 'stellar' birthday exhibition 'J.V. Stalin and the people of the Soviet land of fine arts', while Prokofiev's Stalin cantata *Toast* (Zdravitsa) provided settings of poems in several of the USSR's national languages extracted from the 20th anniversary publication *Works of the People of the USSR*.[87] As Stalin's Soviet biographies at last materialised, this again was an important emphasis, reinforced by the publishing of new materials on Stalin's early years in Transcaucasia.[88] Even Dimitrov in his *Pravda* tribute focused less on the Comintern than on the Soviet leader who embodied his country's achievements.[89] If Stalin, according to the New York *Daily Worker*, led the teeming millions of every continent, he did so as 'captain of the Socialist society' that was now their vanguard state.[90] As Khrushchev later observed, Stalin now surpassed even the tsars in establishing in his own lifetime prizes bearing his own name.[91] At this stage these were confined exclusively to Soviet citizens, and the statist frame of reference, like the caste recognition of an earlier age of kings, was summed up by Stalin's exchange of birthday greetings with his fellow leader Hitler.[92]

Arguing the persistence into the twentieth century of a transcendent political charisma, the anthropologist Clifford Geertz fixed on the five national war leaders Stalin, Hitler, Churchill, Roosevelt and de Gaulle.[93] For Stalin, more than any of them, the period of the Great Patriotic War (1941–1945) was once more one of paradox. On the one hand, he alone of the five, until Hitler confronted certain defeat, temporarily retreated from the domestic spotlight.[94] On the other hand, he simultaneously acquired a standing with an international public that stretched across the political spectrum and was based for the first time on his own presumed achievements as mastermind of the Soviet war effort. As the Nazi offensive was turned back at enormous human cost, the cult of the civil war was sidelined, and Stalin now came forward in the soldierly guise of 'Marshal' or 'Generalissimo'. Kliment Voroshilov, who on Stalin's 50th birthday had concocted the legend of his civil war exploits, would on his 70th salute him as the 'commander of genius' to whom the vanquishing of a second wave of invaders was principally attributable.[95]

Jeffrey Brooks called it Stalin's theft of the war.[96] By extension, it also meant his projection internationally as the liberator of occupied Europe. This contributed to the particular resonance of Stalin's cult in France, where claim and counterclaim of complicity and resistance were central to the Cold War battlefield of collective memory. There were thus still differences of emphasis within the communist cult community: Stalin was for all of them the man of socialism, victory and peace, but for the French perhaps more than other communists it was the man of victory they saluted first.[97] Even so, as Europe now formed itself into blocs, Stalin's cult more than ever was beamed out internationally, without those elements of asymmetrical interaction that still did exist in the time of Barbusse. One might deposit a gift; one could not ask a question. The once so favoured Walter Duranty of the *New York Times* could not even get into Russia, and a Stalin interview now meant a statement scripted in dialogue form with *Pravda* correspondents.[98] On notable occasions, the interviews with Wells and Ludwig continued to do service, and already while still living Stalin was beginning to resemble El Cid propped up on his horse.[99]

Alone of the period's dictators, he was by this time best known to mass audiences as performed by some or other actor. Film, indeed, provides a useful gauge of Stalin's appropriation of symbolic capital, and of the edging aside by his own decennial birthday markers of the anniversary of the revolution itself. In 1929, with so little notice, no films had been made for Stalin's birthday. Instead, the cream of Soviet directors had two years earlier received prestigious commissions for the revolution's tenth anniversary.[100] In 1939, there were still no films for Stalin's birthday, but in the 20th-anniversary production *Lenin in October*, and more surely in its sequel *Lenin in 1918*, his role was now brought forward even at the expense of Lenin's own.[101] Already the Georgian director Mikhail Chiaureli was developing projects like *The Vow*, eventually released in 1946, which moved on from the Lenin years to those whose lustre Stalin needed share with no one.[102] By 1947, there was seemingly no major commission for the revolution's 30th anniversary; instead it was Stalin's birthday two years later that saw the making of the quintessential cult production, Chiaureli's *Fall of Berlin*.[103]

Between the *Lenin* films and *The Fall of Berlin* one may trace the projection onto Stalin of the myths of Soviet statehood, and the edging aside of the civil war by the defeat of fascism.[104] What *The Fall of Berlin* also captures is the further reconfiguration of the national and the international in the politics of high stalinism. The victory depicted in film is one decided on the eastern front alone, and not only Hitler but Churchill and an ailing Roosevelt are produced as counterfoils to the imperturbable maestro of the Soviet war effort. Unlike his rivals, moreover, Stalin is both the pre-eminent national leader and one in whom, in Thorez's words, the living International of the workers was also reaffirmed.[105] As fancifully the film climaxes with Stalin alighting from a plane in liberated Berlin, British and American flags wave among the welcoming crowds and voices are heard in their separate languages: *Salut, Staline! Vivat Stalin! Long Live Stalin!*

In just this spirit, the Stalin prizes were at this point supplemented by the Stalin Peace Prize. They thus brought within the reach of a stalinist system of honours what now, as in Lenin's day, was clearly conceived of as an international cult community. Where Lenin, however, had appeared as himself the founder and acknowledged head of an international movement, Stalin's authority was that of the vanguard state to which humanity's better future was to be entrusted. And just as such a claim presupposed a manifest hierarchy of parties and states, with the USSR unassailable at its centre, so too Stalin's paramountcy was still further enhanced by the lesser cults beneath him which in Lenin's day had had no counterpart.

(iii)

Ousted as his party's secretary in 1948, the Polish communist Wladyslaw Gomulka had years in prison to ponder the meaning of the cult phenomenon. As he told his party following Stalin's death, this was not confined to the USSR, but had been transplanted to the great majority of communist parties whether or not they exercised power. A hierarchy was thus established in which those beneath Stalin also 'donned the robes of infallibility', but only on their own home territory, and with a merely reflective brilliance like the moon's.[106] Doubtless Gomulka had in mind his rival Boleslaw Bierut, whose advancement, like that of so many of his counterparts, had been possible only as the candidate and political instrument of Stalin himself.[107]

What Gomulka described as a system of cults was exemplified by the celebration of the leader's birthday. The minimum age was usually 50, the symbol of what by now was an ageing leadership cohort. The practice was also confined to mainly decade or sometimes half-decade markers, and not every smaller party had an appropriate figure even for these. Even so, what followed Stalin's 70th birthday was a virtual contagion of such commemorations. Already in 1946 the Czechoslovakian Klement Gottwald had provided the first post-war example on a large scale. With variations of scale as resources allowed, commemorations that followed included those in 1950 of the Frenchman Thorez, the Vietnamese Ho Chi Minh, the Bulgarian Chervenkov and the Briton Pollitt; those in 1951 of the Romanian Gheorghiu-Dej and the Finn Kuusinen; and those in 1952 of Bierut and the Hungarian Rákosi. Even the pariah Tito followed the practice, while in Italy Palmiro Togliatti's 60th birthday coincided with Stalin's death and galvanised a cult that has been seen as partly compensating for it.[108] (Fig. 2.1) Even now, as the Stalin cult began to be dismantled, there were the birthdays of the Belgian Lalmand (1954), the Spaniard Ibárruri (1955) and the American Foster as late as 1956. Only in China, it seems, did a resolution of March 1949 actually prohibit the celebration of leaders' birthdays, which in Mao's case had to await the Cultural Revolution of the 1960s.[109] The cult of the leader had in this period become an all-but generic feature of communist parties, and with the early deaths of Dimitrov and Gottwald even had its first mimetic embalmments.

Fig. 2.1 Cover image from the Togliatti pictorial biography *Vita di un italiano* (Life of an Italian), 1953 (Courtesy Editori Riuniti)

Just as destalinisation, within its limits, saw the relinquishing of these practices, stalinisation is often regarded as the condition of their emergence.[110] Most famously expounded in Hermann Weber's work on German communism, the stalinisation concept was there identified with a process of homogenisation and tightening central control that began in the year of Lenin's death and was carried through in all essentials by 1929.[111] The leader cult itself was peripheral to Weber's analysis, as was doubtless consistent with its weak development in Russia in the period in which he located the decisive transformation. Nevertheless, the example of the KPD leader Ernst Thälmann lent support to the view that the emergence in the stalinised parties of a single dominant leading figure was at very least a possible by-product of the process that Weber described.[112] Already during the Weimar years, Thälmann presented arguably the first major example of such a cult outside of Russia, and the first such national party figure to be routinely described as leader.[113] Following his imprisonment by the Nazis in 1933, Thälmann's case gave rise to a sustained international protest, and his 50th birthday in 1936 was the first such occasion to provide communists internationally with a major campaigning focus.[114]

If stalinisation is limited to the installation in each party of a compliant central leadership, this was certainly achieved by the early 1930s, and increasingly identified with the authority of a single individual. In a Comintern overview appearing immediately following the Congress of Victors, the consolidation of a 'monolithic world party' was particularly identified with the period 1928–1930 and the establishment in each national section of a leadership demonstrating 'implicit allegiance' to the International. Already in the cases of Thälmann, Gottwald and Pollitt this was represented by a single-named figure, and similarly in Poland the achievement of a 'consolidated and monolithic party' was identified with the ill-fated Julian Lenski.[115]

While elsewhere no individual was yet singled out, the same basic story was told of recalcitrant elements excluded and fractional activities surmounted. When in February 1934 Dimitrov was released following the Leipzig trial, the Comintern itself now acquired a 'leader' who was universally recognised as such. It was around this time that Pollitt in Britain was first described in such terms. In France, where the veteran Cachin was as yet the one recognised pretender to such a role, his 65th birthday that September was possibly the first after Lenin's and Stalin's to occasion festivities and accolades directed at one who was still exercising significant party responsibilities.[116] In Ireland too, it was at this point that a 'tentative personality cult' of party secretary Sean Murray briefly surfaced.[117]

At the Comintern's seventh and final congress in July–August 1935, Dimitrov's report was now the centrepiece. It was Thorez who followed him at the podium, and whose party led the way with the popular front, and as the model now for the Comintern's other sections. Pollitt, Gottwald and the American Earl Browder, in that order, also made prominent contributions. So too did Lenski, who together with his party was to be wiped out in the purges, while the mention of the absent Thälmann drew an ovation rivalling Stalin's own. With their very different destinies, it seems reasonable to think of these as the 'Stalin generation' of communist party leaders.[118]

In his contemporaneous Comintern history, Franz Borkenau wrote that leaders of this type—he also mentioned the Spaniard José Díaz—wielded an 'absolute power' within their parties, whose 'worship of the leader-superman' was akin to fascism.[119] Annie Kriegel, while emphasising the phenomenon's bureaucratic nature, described it as the transposition of a form of normative authority that was characteristic of all communist parties, and which in Thorez's case followed the periodisation of the Stalin cult, with peaks in the late 1930s and during the Cold War.[120] Also writing on Thorez, Stéphane Sirot has expressly linked the imposition of such a figure with the Comintern's stalinisation.[121]

Rather than a superman, the party leader was at once the symbol and encapsulation of a centralised leadership and an incarnation of the political qualities for which the communist parties purportedly stood. Until Stalin showed the way, it had been difficult in most of them even to make out any single figure of the leader. By the late 1930s when Borkenau was writing, it was evident in everything from congress arrangements to the authorship of binding pronouncements and the portraits with which both text and platform were adorned. At the seventh world congress, the mere 'applause' accorded to some established figures was notched up in the published proceedings to warm applause for Pollitt, warm and prolonged applause for Thorez, and 'tumultuous and prolonged applause, cheers and ovations' for Stalin and Thälmann.[122] In a movement defined by 'implicit allegiance', ceremonial as a form of bonding was now manifestly more the function of such gatherings than was collective deliberation or debate. Trotsky had described how in the Russian party a 'special small science' had been devoted to the honorary presidium, with displacements and juxtapositions that provided a measure of factional manoeuvring.[123]

For the stalinised parties that had eradicated factionalism, the same fine-tuned gradations expressed the palpable sense of a leadership hierarchy. The PCF in 1937 thus apostrophised Díaz as his party's general secretary, Thälmann as his heroic party's leader and Stalin as his glorious party's beloved leader.[124] Even in death five years later, Díaz was described as one formed by Stalin, and his personal courage as no mere 'spontaneous manifestation' of character but a demonstration of how he had steeled himself by study of Stalin's works.[125]

Following the seventh world congress, transcripts of proceedings were at least published in *Inprecorr* according to the well-established conventions of labour movement bodies. On the other hand, published proceedings of national party congresses were increasingly orientated to the utterances of the leader or small group of leaders in a spirit of implicit approbation. Already in 1932, the CPGB's comprised a report and reply to discussion, but no discussion. By 1935, it bore the title *Harry Pollitt Speaks*; by 1937, there was comment on the domination of proceedings by the platform, and delegates were required to remain in their seats for the duration of Pollitt's report.[126] Topical presentations of communist policy appeared as pamphlets bearing Pollitt's name and portrait, the latter now in self-consciously statesmanlike dress and pose. Pollitt's workman's cap was last sighted in such a context in 1936; Thorez's had been abandoned the previous November, to avoid, he said, any suspicion of demagoguery.[127] Browder, according to his biographer, looked like a midwestern college professor, or possibly, with his double-breasted suit and cigar, like a realtor out of a Sinclair Lewis novel.[128] More than just a pamphleteer, Browder had pretensions as a strategic thinker and by 1940 his more substantial expositions were being marketed by his party as the 'Browder Library'.[129]

In a period of sudden policy shifts, when the shibboleths of one year were not infrequently inadmissible by the next, their personalisation in this way served to complicate the relationship of leader and party to be found in more stable or predictable bureaucracies. In 1939, Pollitt's identification with the CPGB's initial support for Britain's war effort meant his temporary demotion as party leader. Also during the war, Browder's increasingly self-assured adaptations of international positions culminated in 1945 in the anathematisation of 'Browderism' as he took the step too far of replacing his party with a 'Communist Political Association'. Thorez's position was particularly invidious, for having deserted his regiment on the Comintern's instructions he was stranded in Moscow for the entire resistance period which proved so formative in his party's post-war identity.[130]

Any discrepancy between personal history and collective memory now had to be reconciled with the symbolic role vested in the person of the leader. This was not just a matter of centralised direction, but assumed the encapsulation in this figure of the narrative of struggle and future deliverance for which the party stood. Biography was for this reason at the heart of the cult phenomenon, not merely or even necessarily as a literary genre, but as the representation through the individual of exemplary qualities, associations and experiences. It was in just this fashion that Pollitt was introduced to delegates in 1937 as one who through a lifetime of struggle had come to represent the flower of his class.[131]

Among the earliest of the published biographies through which such qualities were represented were Peter Maslowski's *Thälmann* and the Canadian pamphlet *Tim Buck—Dauntless Leader of the Canadian Working Class*, both published in 1932.[132] In 1934 there followed at least two further biographical pamphlets as part of the international Thälmann campaign, and in due course Togliatti, Foster and Prestes were all among those receiving some extended treatment either at their own hand or that of some faithful follower.[133] Thorez's *Son of the People* (Fils du peuple), first published in September 1937 and twice reissued in revised editions, aimed precisely at maintaining the identity between Thorez's personal history and the collective history which he supposedly incarnated. Bernard Pudal has described it as a model of the communist leader's biography, and it is commonly located within the wider generation of such texts conjecturally deriving from a Comintern directive in 1935. As Michelle Perrot has put it, Stalin as 'father of the peoples' wanted sons in his own image, and the exemplary lives that would demonstrate the irresistible momentum of their cause.[134]

The evidence of a co-ordinated campaign is nevertheless still to be produced. The system identified by Gomulka was at this stage embryonic, and it is probably more helpful to think instead of a repertoire of cult practices producing certain common features. International communism in the 1930s was a movement in flux. Most parties by the end of the decade were illegal. Others, primarily in the liberal democracies, experienced rapid gains in membership, influence and sometimes electoral support. The challenges communist parties confronted, and their resources with which to do so, consequently varied enormously, and were subject to dramatic transitions. Anti-fascism and pro-Sovietism were powerful unifying themes, and each was embodied in individuals, notably Dimitrov and Stalin, whose appeal transcended the specificities of national context.

On the other hand, there was explicit recognition of the need to find new ways to connect with the diverse political constituencies required to stem the tide of fascism. With the implicit allegiance of the 'Stalin generation' now largely secured, and to some degree having to compensate for the paring, purging and eventual dissolution of the Comintern, the scope and even necessity for adaptability in the application of a common strategy was for the time being widened.

It was thus that the seventh world congress combined an induction into the cult as live performance with the urging by Dimitrov of a strategic reorientation of communist parties towards national traditions and forms of struggle. According to Pollitt two years later, communists had to demonstrate their roots in their own native labour movement. 'If we are going seriously ... to convince the British people that we are a British Party, we should not always be appealing to them to join it because we are the Party of Stalin, Dimitrov and Thaelmann.'[135] Although the popular front in the narrow sense was everywhere either still-born or short-lived, this adaptation to national political cultures transformed the public face of communism and was often taken to the point of outright opportunism. Though in one aspect it clearly borrowed from the Bolsheviks' example and the stalinist culture of the heroic, in its timing and evident political rationale the projection of communism in more personalised ways was also one of its most characteristic adaptations of the popular-front era.

The very fact of designating a leader serves to illustrate this. In Germany, Thälmann's styling as 'Unser Führer' (Our leader) has been regarded as a direct imitation of Soviet practices and the evidence of a plagiarised cult of Thälmann himself.[136] In just this way, the CPGB's first academic historian also referred to Pollitt emerging as his party's leader 'just as Stalin was the leader of the Comintern as a whole and Hitler the leader of the Nazis'.[137] Attlee, Baldwin and Lloyd George, however, were also the recognised leaders of Britain's mainstream parties, and Pollitt was to this extent assuming a role directly analogous to theirs. Both in 1928 and again in 1937 the CPGB promoted what in effect were socialist unity campaigns. On the first occasion, it took its name from two non-party figureheads, A.J. Cook and James Maxton; on the second, it was Pollitt himself who now stole the show with an oratorical bravura owing nothing to Stalin and a good deal to local traditions of the radical platform. The Brazilian Luis Carlos Prestes was a very different figure, who as a soldier by profession had had no involvement at all in the Comintern's formative years. He had however led the famous Prestes Column, and as the legendary 'Cavalier of Hope' revived the tradition of the radical military leader so powerfully resonant in Latin America. It was to draw the maximum advantage from this that following his embrace of communism Prestes became the focus of one of the most remarkable of the Stalin-era party cults.[138]

Taking only these two cases, it is evident that this was not a simple transposition of the Stalin-type cult but also an adaptation to diverse environments in which the role of political leaders was already strongly accentuated. Homogenising pressures became much stronger during the Cold War, and offered a means of managing and consolidating the advances made by communism in the 1940s. In the meantime, one must not only register the phenomenon's uneven development from country to country, and what was often the ambiguous marking out of a cultic hierarchy. In contrast to his ubiquity within the USSR, there was also the surprisingly intermittent visibility of Stalin himself as cultic archetype and incarnation of the communist ideal. The following section deals with both these points in turn.

(iv)

Uneven development was partly conditional on variations in the opportunity or even requirement for some overt personalisation of the cause for which the communists stood. For a legally functioning party like the CPGB, almost the only individual profiles routinely appearing in the early communist press were those marking either electoral candidacies, prosecutions by the state or deaths. Leaving aside contingencies of personnel and deeper cultural differences, these in general were the main external prompts to collective practices that could become focused on a much smaller number of individuals. Even ruling parties could seek legitimation in this way through the state elections that were subject to their authority. Sometimes there was the accentuation of a single figure among a party leading group.[139] Beyond these ruling parties, it was the office of elected national president, as for example in Brazil, the USA and Germany, that was most obviously conducive to the singling out of a figurehead. In Brazil, the PCB considered Prestes as a presidential candidate even before he had fully accepted its programme. In the USA, the salience of presidential elections reflected a culture of political celebrity to which radical groups were also susceptible, and which for socialists was exemplified by their three times presidential candidate Eugene Debs. No precursor was more often invoked by the communists, and the candidacies successively of Foster (1924–1932) and Browder (1936–1940) similarly meant a focus on the party's standard-bearer, backed up in 1936 by records, films and coast-to-coast radio broadcasts.[140] In Germany too, Thälmann's preferment as presidential candidate in 1925 was a crucial moment in his establishment as party leader. It is from this point that his mystique as epitome of the German revolutionary worker can be traced, and by the 1932 election it was inconceivable that the KPD might have put forward any other candidate.[141]

Authoritarian regimes were not alone in imprisoning communists on political grounds. Particularly in the Comintern period, this was even a generic feature of communist politics, albeit with such variations as provided the rationale for the communists eventually rallying to the defence of the bourgeois democracies. Where a leading figure either was or could be singled out, this targeting by the state provided a campaigning issue, source of moral capital and possible courtroom platform that lent itself almost irresistibly to exploitation through the individual. Where communist parties functioned legally, campaigning was primarily at a national level. An early example was the Canadian Buck, whose prosecution was the catalyst for what has been described as a typical personality cult beginning with the *Dauntless Leader* pamphlet.[142] Eight years later Browder's similar predicament was also answered biographically, through a *Daily Worker* serial 'The man they want to get' and a hagiographical pamphlet issued by the 'citizens' committee' established on Browder's behalf.[143] Where no such activity was feasible, campaigns were organised internationally. This was one of the functions of the MOPR, or International Red Aid, which already in the 1920s played a prominent part in the campaign around the Italian-American anarchists Sacco and Vanzetti. What changed by the 1930s was not so much the preference for communist victims as the singling out of leadership figures as if emblematic of wider persecutions. Thälmann was the most prominent example; others were Prestes and the Hungarian Mátyás Rákosi, whose later claims to authority would be bolstered by these earlier privations. The Italian Antonio Gramsci, though with Rákosi the earliest of these prisoners and his party's recognised 'founder and leader', secured a comparable publicity only posthumously.[144]

The precedent for such posthumous commemorations was set by the annual Luxemburg-Liebknecht campaign which from the late 1920s was combined with the Lenin anniversary to provide one of the centrepieces of the communist calendar. In all of these cases, assassination, attempted assassination or brutal incarceration gave sufficient grounds for the martyr's aura so marked in, though not peculiar to, the communist movement. The last Soviet figure to have something of this allure was the Leningrad party boss Sergei Kirov. Kirov's assassination in December 1934 provided a catalyst and pretext for the Stalinist terror, but it also required his depiction as a martyr like the '3 Ls' and was capable of moving idealists in the West to similar forms of empathy and identification.[145]

As Jean-Pierre Bernard notes, in France the passing of almost any major figure tended to be marked by a 'promotion', or enrolment campaign, after the fashion of the Lenin enrolment of 1924.[146] With the bureaucratisation of the communist exemplar, almost any leader could be described as having 'fallen in the struggle', as Kirov's successor Andrei Zhdanov was when he died almost literally in office in 1948.[147] Even so, the quality of martyrdom where Stalin ruled was now monopolised by Stalin's victims; rather, it was in Europe's partisan and resistance movements that communism gave rise to a new generation of combatants who symbolised their cause and helped cement its establishment on a much extended popular basis. In the words of E.P. Thompson, himself a communist recruit of just this vintage, between the mid-1930s and mid-1940s the communists' vocabulary took on the 'active verbs' of individual initiative, resistance, heroism and sacrifice: 'It was a decade of heroes, and there were Guevaras in every street and every wood.'[148] Among them, Thompson's own brother Frank died fighting with Bulgarian partisans and was afterwards commemorated there as a national hero.

Doubtless Thompson romanticised the period; just as the details of his brother's death were among those which in the interests of propaganda were embroidered to the point of distortion.[149] Nevertheless, the evocation of a wider cast of heroes was faithful to the atmosphere of the times, and there was certainly not at this stage that overshadowing of these Guevaras by a single commanding figure that was so characteristic of the Cold War. There were, it is true, already the impulses to delineate such a figure. If *Son of the People* was an archetype, it is not just because Thorez, even in 1937, identified himself so closely with his party, but because the role of any other figure in its history passed almost without mention. In later years, the epithet 'Maurice Thorez's party' was to become notorious as a symbol of his cult. In Canada, nevertheless, there had appeared as early as 1939 an official CP history *The Story of Tim Buck's Party*, named after the general secretary as already some local party branches were.[150] When a CPGB history was swiftly withdrawn in 1937, one of the complaints made in Moscow was that Pollitt's role had been lost in a crowd of lesser figures, not even excluding renegades.[151]

It was Pollitt, even so, who had approved the history's publication. In Britain, the production of exemplary leaders' lives had not even begun with Pollitt, but with the MP William Gallacher.[152] In the USA too, it was not Browder as general secretary but the party chairman Foster who followed suit. James G. Ryan refers to Browder's 'cultlike following', and justifiably so.[153] At one New York rally a crowd of 16,000 accorded him an 'ear-splitting ten-minute ovation' before starting up again on the announcement that it was his birthday.[154] In 1938, on the occasion of the CPUSA's national convention, Browder achieved the ultimate accolade of a land of celebrity, his portrait on the cover of *Time* magazine.[155] Though privately subjected to petty humiliations, publicly Foster's image too was nevertheless displayed alongside Browder's, and as the figure best representing the party's working-class base he was indulged in theatrically delayed entrances at rallies with 'triumphant music' playing.[156] In Spain the general secretary Díaz was all but overshadowed by Dolores Ibárruri, the famous Pasionaria, whom one verse tribute apostrophised, not as helmsman, but as 'the great figurehead / At the prow of the ship: Spain'.[157] While Ibárruri did eventually succeed Díaz following his suicide in 1942, in Belgium the passing of Joseph Jacquemotte six years earlier left a gap which as yet only Jacquemotte's own posthumous cult really filled.[158] Even in France, as we shall see, the extent to which Thorez had at this stage imposed himself on his party should not be overstated.[159]

As to Stalin's as the cult of cults, there was not yet even a biography for the party reading lists. Barbusse's, published in 1935, had been placed on the Kremlin index in rather less time than it took him to write it.[160] Panegyrists were not found wanting when required, and the anniversary of the revolution itself might now occasion greetings addressed to Stalin personally as its embodiment.[161] What the fate of Barbusse's text did nevertheless indicate was how difficult it was to incorporate the veneration of so fugitive a figure into the quotidian routines of party life. Writers on the Soviet 1930s stress that Stalin's cult was not an isolated phenomenon but belonged within a wider culture teeming with heroes, role models and popular icons.[162] Rather than Stalin's particular personality, it is this that one finds reflected in the western communist press. In March 1936, there was complaint of the neglect of Stalin's 'historic role' in the Belgian party press.[163] In the British *Daily Worker* in the first half of that year there were just a handful of passing references to Stalin and a single major item, his interview with the US press correspondent Roy Howard. What was abundantly evident was the wider turn to the individual signalled in articles on historical anniversaries (Paine, Burns, Marx, James Watt), past and present martyrs (Thälmann, Prestes, Liebknecht) and veterans to be honoured (Tom Mann and the American Mother Bloor).

Above all, and as yet surmounting any cultic pyramid, there was Lenin. Whatever may have been the case within the USSR, it was in the early 1930s that the wider European vogue for Lenin biographies reached its height. The commonest impression, in contrast to that of Stalin, was of an admirable and disinterested if somewhat forbidding personality.[164] Communists themselves were prolific in what the Russians had called Leniniana. Lenin editions and commentaries remained staple party reading. There were also new biographies, the reissuing of works by Gorky and Clara Zetkin, and in France a new series, *To Know Lenin Better* (Pour mieux connaître Lénine) launched in 1934.[165] As these parties began to give rise to their own cult biographies, encounters with Lenin had pride of place, while Stalin featured incidentally if at all.[166] This was even true of *Son of the People*, despite the fact that Thorez privately inscribed a copy to Stalin in 'absolute fidelity and … filial love'.[167] Within the communist calendar, the most important dates from year to year were the anniversaries of the revolution in November and of Lenin's death in January. In the *Daily Worker*, in that same quarter of 1936, none could have complained of the underestimation of Lenin's role as they might have of Stalin's. Following a screening of Vertov's *Three Songs of Lenin*, Pollitt in an atmosphere of 'reasoned but unbounded enthusiasm' paid his accolade to the 'greatest revolutionary of all time' and it was several minutes before the cheering subsided.[168] A few, like Cachin, depicted Stalin as both the master architect and the disciple who now clearly overshadowed his master.[169] But at least until the war years, it was Lenin internationally who continued to personify the communist ideal.

The obvious explanation is that communism as an oppositional movement turned most readily to oppositional figures as the symbols of its struggle. The Yugoslav leader Tito, who was shortly to lead the successful struggle of his country's partisans, suggested in notes of 1940 that Stalin and his ideas mattered more to Soviet workers than to those in countries still to achieve their emancipation, who were principally guided by 'Lenin's thought, the thought of revolution'.[170] It was Lenin who personified the idea of revolution; it was as the 'Spanish Lenin', for example, that the socialist Largo Caballero rallied support on seemingly embracing the idea of revolution in 1933.[171] Following the example of Lenin's widow Krupskaya, whose published memoirs terminated at just this point, communist biographies of Lenin focused overwhelmingly on the revolutionary years that culminated in the taking of power.[172] Ralph Fox, in producing such a life for British readers, dealt with the post-revolutionary period in just one of his 19 chapters, and even this derived substantially from Lenin's *State and Revolution*. This was a Lenin with 'the burning faith of a man and a leader', and if the commitments this inspired recall the great popular religions, it was Lenin, not Stalin, who embodied them.[173]

When Fox outlined the new conception of the hero so central to socialist realism, it was Dimitrov whom he presented as its archetype.[174] In the 1930s cultural organ the *Left Review*, poems also celebrate Thälmann, Rákosi and Pasionaria, but never Stalin.[175] Hugh MacDiarmid, one of Britain's finest poets of this generation, published the first of his three 'hymns' to Lenin with an appropriately Christ-like note in 1931. MacDiarmid did also manage a wartime dedication to Stalin, hinging on a generic reference to his Georgian origins which appealed to MacDiarmid's Scottish nationalism.[176] There was, however, no similar hymn to Stalin, by MacDiarmid or by anybody else in Britain. A poem MacDiarmid published at the height of Stalin's wartime popularity gives some indication why:

> … you might talk to a woman who had been
> A young girl in 1917 and find
> That the name of Stalin lit no fires,
> But when you asked her if she had seen Lenin
> Her eyes lighted up and her reply
> Was the Russian word which means
> Both beautiful and red.
> Lenin, she said, was '*krassivy, krassivy*'.[177]

MacDiarmid had not even been to Russia, and the unlit fires were his own. Moving in and out of the CPGB, he was a heterodox and even wilful figure, a Bolshevik before the revolution, he wrote, 'but I'll cease to be one quick / When Communism comes to rule the roost'.[178] MacDiarmid was not alone, however, in being a Bolshevik before the revolution, and in respect of the politics of personality it is remarkable how little as yet was made of those communists who ruled the roost.

(v)

The obvious point about the Cold War was the division of the world into two blocs or camps. A second feature, somewhat cutting across the first, was that communism was politically strengthened on both sides of the divide. Though the Cold War in the West saw communists ostracised and the politics of red scare normalised, communism's legal proscription was mostly avoided, and in some parts of western Europe it maintained a higher level of support than at any time between the wars. West Germany was an obvious exception, and in much of southern Europe this remained an age of dictatorships of the right. But in France and, not quite so dramatically in Italy and Finland, communist parties were now established as a dominant force on the political left.

It is in this period that Gomulka's system of cults is most clearly discernible. To countries liberated from fascism, both East and West, there returned from what was usually a Moscow exile some communist figurehead unmistakably bearing Stalin's favour. Some were already known locally, through an earlier phase of open activity or through propaganda conducted in exile. None, except for Tito, had played any significant role in their country's liberation. Nevertheless, it was on the kudos of the communists' contribution to the defeat of fascism that they now sought to capitalise. When Thorez returned to France in November 1944, he took the stage to a tumult of *Vive Thorez!* and the immersion of the platform in flowers.[179] Already some addressed him, not only as their party's leading personality, but as the undisputed mastermind of the resistance itself.[180] Even so, this was a political capital that at this stage could only be realised collectively.[181] Footage of the PCF congress of June 1945 shows images of Thorez as well as Stalin prominently displayed, but along with others representing a clearly identified leading group that also featured in poster images and sound recordings.[182] In Italy, where Togliatti was more decidedly his party's dominant personality, some twenty short biographies were nevertheless issued to popularise the returning party leadership.[183] The communist parties that made such striking gains in the first post-war elections did not do so through the projection of a single figurehead.

Instead, it was in the new 'eastern' democracies that leaders acquiring a semblance of Stalin's powers began to assume for themselves also a semblance of his grandiosity. Dimitrov by now was sufficiently Stalin's client that he had to wait a year in Moscow to be allowed to return to Bulgaria. In the meantime, his reputation already loomed the largest, quite literally in the form of the 15-foot statue that on May Day 1945 was unveiled in front of Sofia's royal palace.[184] In Czechoslovakia Gottwald led a party which, like Thorez's, headed the lists in free elections, but with the presence of the Red Army as an ultimately more decisive political guarantor. Already in April 1946, Pollitt wrote of ovations in Czechoslovakia such as he had hitherto witnessed only in the USSR, and with Gottwald's installation as the country's premier his 50th birthday that September was the first in this period to be celebrated in defiance of all canons of modesty.[185] There was also a genuine liberation hero in the shape of Tito, who, as Geoffrey Swain writes, had some claim to have led the world's 'second successful socialist revolution' through a partisan struggle conducted largely independently of the Russians.[186] By repute at least a veteran of both the Russian and Spanish civil wars, Tito, like Stalin, had taken the designation Marshal; he was, wrote the Slavist R.W. Seton-Watson, a warrior-leader like the Serbian Karadjordje more than a century earlier, 'but possessed of certain qualities of organisation ... which are essential in our more mechanical age'.[187] It was as the one such European of this independent stature that Tito, like Trotsky before him, was from 1948 anathematised as diabolic counterpart to a second wave of cult-building.

Every orthodox communist party denounced him; every one of them celebrated Stalin. If variation persisted, it was in the extent and pervasiveness of a supererogatory cultism that went beyond these basic requirements. The PCF in this respect went furthest of the western parties. Symptomatic of this was the common usage *stalinien*, the rendering of 'stalinist' by the communists' detractors, which Thorez now reclaimed as a title of honour.[188] Victor Joannès, a member of Thorez's secretariat, even put the same positive construction on the concept 'stalinism', a usage that was clearly discountenanced in the USSR.[189] 'Yes, as Lenin and Jules Guesde were *marxistes*, as Stalin, Zhdanov and Vaillant-Couturier were *léninistes*, I, like Rákosi and Maurice Thorez, am *stalinien*', ran one Stalin tribute, without suggesting any clear distinction as between the approved Russian *stalinski* (in the Stalin manner) and the unallowable *stalinist*.[190]

If Thorez was the 'best French stalinist', it is not surprising that the PCF in turn could be described as bearing the 'thorézien imprint'.[191] It was not only the earliest of the western parties in initiating a full-blown leader cult, but more than any other placed this at the centre of party life through the continuous generation of new occasions by which to mark it in ever more ritualised ways. It was not therefore just the usual decade markers that called forth such observances; so did Thorez's other birthdays, the reissuing of his autobiography, the instalments of his *Works* and the real and imagined attacks of his political enemies. Even during his second long absence in the USSR, terminating only in the wake of Stalin's death, Thorez's cult was privileged over a wider cast of communist heroes, and the degrading epithet *parti de Maurice Thorez* at the expense of the honourable one *parti des fusillés*—the party of those shot by the Nazis. The French case will figure extensively in this book, and these developments are discussed more fully in Chapter 4.

When the PCF greeted its Italian counterpart as 'Palmiro Togliatti's party', the latter—the Partito comunista italiano, or PCI—neither took this up nor reciprocated.[192] Donald Sassoon has also commented on the occasional nature of the PCI's glorification of Stalin.[193] Distinctions therefore remained even between these two most obviously comparable of mass parties. Smaller-scale parties had smaller-scale cults, and if no obvious candidate was available—as in Switzerland, Norway, Ireland and Australia—usually did without one of their own. Within the PCF itself, there were also differences. There was certainly at first less than unanimous approval of the 'purely platonic and sentimental gesture' of sending Thorez gifts.[194] Even as this became enshrined as a party duty, such instincts persisted in the dedication to Thorez of campaigning and recruiting activities rather than physical objects, and the secretariat itself intimated that celebrations of his half-centenary should remain simple, 'normal' and fraternal.[195] As Togliatti's 60th birthday approached, he also set out guidelines enjoining '*sobriety* and *moderation*', and with the same ambiguous emphasis co-operated in a cult biography while disclaiming any responsibility for the idea. Nevertheless, Togliatti's specification of undesirable practices, notably the exhibiting or even offering of gifts beyond a 'few personal items', did suggest differentiation both explicitly from the ruling parties and implicitly from the PCF. On Lenin's death, Krupskaya had publicly urged that he be honoured only in some socially useful way and through the observance of his teachings. The sentiments were known to all communists of Togliatti's generation, and he too now asked that some other occasion be found to display popular handicraft, and that his birthday be commemorated by contributions to some appropriate campaign or party institution.[196]

There was, however, no simply opting out of the cult system and remaining a communist party. Togliatti himself did not object to appropriate forms of commemoration. Despite his misgivings there was even a lavish pictorial biography, like that produced the following year on Rákosi's birthday, whose final page showed Togliatti's image being borne aloft in

Fig. 2.2 Palmiro Togliatti, images from 60th birthday, 1953, from the pictorial biography *Vita di un italiano* (Life of an Italian), 1953 (Courtesy Editori Riuniti)

Berlin, Beijing and Moscow.[197](Fig. 2.2) In Berlin, though Thälmann's posthumous cult overshadowed that of any successor, the ubiquity of Stalin's more than compensated for any local tentativeness.[198] In Beijing alone there was at this stage a toning down of Mao's earlier cult, though this would later be taken to extremes exceeding even Stalin's.[199] As Stalin's birthday followed swiftly on the victory of the Chinese revolution, the relative parsimony of the Chinese party's rhetoric and offerings does now appear as a possible augury of later hostilities.[200] Nevertheless, Mao did not withhold his personal presence from the festivities and for Stalin's supporters in the West the accomplishment of the Chinese revolution was but a further demonstration of Stalin's greatness.[201] When Stalin followed Lenin into the mausoleum in March 1953, there was as yet no hint of the retractions to come.

When Thorez in 1949 updated his *Son of the People*, he put right the omission of the now-obligatory encounter with Stalin. When Pollitt in 1950 reissued his own autobiography *Serving My Time*, there were no such alterations. Pollitt nevertheless made handsome amends on Stalin's death, recalling an implausible first meeting in 1921, and a Stalin 'so kindly and considerate … so obviously actuated by the desire to help' as Pollitt had never encountered in any other individual. 'Never the dictator: never to lay the law down, always eager … to understand another's point of view …'[202] In appending to such sentiments a lesser tribute to Gottwald, who had died on returning from Stalin's funeral, Pollitt reaffirmed the hierarchy of cults, and in twice citing Mao he also underlined its universal character.[203]

When three years later Khrushchev acknowledged the terrible history that lay behind these claims, Pollitt's leadership, like Rákosi's, was one of the casualties, while Ibárruri was one of those who continued with a hugely diminished authority.[204] Though Thorez and Togliatti remained in post until their deaths in 1964, this was also at the cost of the willing or begrudging disavowal of cultic practices, at least in the forms that these had lately taken. The story of the cults does not end there, but it was certainly the beginning of a new chapter, and the closing of the one on which the present account now focuses in greater detail.

Notes

1. Jean-Pierre A. Bernard, 'La liturgie funèbre des communistes (1924–1983)' in *Vingtième Siècle. Revue d'histoire*, 9 (1986), 37–52.
2. Reports and citations from *L'Humanité*, 28 Jan. 1924 including Cachin, 'Le prolétariat à Saint-Denis'.
3. Boris Souvarine, *Stalin. A critical survey of Bolshevism* (London: Secker & Warburg, 1939), pp. 349–51.
4. Benno Ennker, *Die Anfänge des Leninkults in der Sowjetunion* (Cologne: Bohlau Verlag, 1997); Ennker, 'The origins and intentions of the Lenin cult' in Ian D. Thatcher (ed.), *Regime and Society in Twentieth-Century Russia. Selected papers from the Fifth World Congress of Central and East European Studies, Warsaw, 1995* (Basingstoke: Macmillan, 1995), pp. 118–29.

5. Souvarine, *Stalin*, p. 351.
6. Nina Tumarkin, *Lenin Lives! The Lenin Cult in Soviet Russia* (Cambridge, MA: Harvard University Press, 1983), pp. 79–80.
7. Tumarkin, *Lenin Lives!*, pp. 80–90.
8. G. Zinovieff, *Nicolai Lenin. His life and work* (London: CPGB, 1920), pp. 41–3.
9. See Tumarkin, *Lenin Lives!*, pp. 10, 17; Richard S. Wortman, *Scenarios of Power: myth and ceremony in Russian monarchy. Volume two: from Alexander II to the abdication of Nicholas II* (Princeton, NJ: Princeton University Press, 2000), pp. 196–203.
10. Richard Stites, *Revolutionary Dreams. Utopian visions and experimental life in the Russian revolution* (New York: Oxford University Press, 1991 edn), pp. 91–2.
11. Jan Plamper, *The Stalin Cult. A study in the alchemies of power* (New Haven, CT: Yale University Press, 2012), p. 35; Victoria E. Bonnell, *Iconography of Power. Soviet political posters under Lenin and Stalin* (Berkeley, CA: University of California Press, 1993), 140; Yves Cohen, *Le Siècle des chefs. Une histoire transnationale du commandement et de l'autorité (1890–1940)* (Paris: Éditions Amsterdam, 2013), pp. 422, 683.
12. Tumarkin, *Lenin lives!*, p. 82; Olga Velikanova, *Making of an Idol. On uses of Lenin* (Göttingen: Muster-Schmidt Verlag, 1996), p. 32; for similar usages see Trotsky, 'Lenin wounded' (speech to All Russian General Executive Committee, 2 Sept. 1918) in Leon Trotsky, *Lenin* (London: Harrap, 1925), pp. 227, 231 (pp. 152, 157 in original Russian edition); Lars T. Lih, *Lenin* (London: Reaktion Books, 2011), pp. 210–11, citing Bukharin.
13. Velikanova, *Making*, pp. 30–1.
14. 'Lenin ill' (Apr. 1923) in Trotsky, *Lenin*, pp. 237–8. Trotsky was citing the line in the *Internationale* normally translated as 'No saviour from on high delivers'.
15. Zinovieff, *Nicolai Lenin*, pp. 3–4, 36; Tumarkin, *Lenin Lives!*, p. 212.
16. Barbusse, *La Lueur dans l'Abîme. Ce que veut le groupe Clarté* (Paris: Éditions Clarté, 1920), p. 43.
17. See Evelyn Roy, 'Mahatma Gandhi: revolutionary or counter-revolutionary?', *LM*, Sept. 1923, 158–67.
18. Trotsky, 'Lenin wounded', p. 228; also William Harvey Maehl, *August Bebel. Shadow emperor of the German workers* (Philadelphia, PA: American Philosophical Society, 1980), p. 40.

19. Vincent Duclert, *Jaurès 1859–1914. La politique et la légende* (Paris: Autrement, 2012), p. 111.
20. Trotsky, 'Lenin wounded', pp. 229, 231.
21. Ronald Campbell Macfie, 'To Lenin', *WD*, 9 Mar. 1918; also Ian Bullock, *Romancing the Revolution. The myth of Soviet democracy and the British left* (Edmonton, Alberta: AU Press, 2011), p. 354, and Tumarkin, *Lenin Lives!*, pp. 79–80 for Demyan Bedny.
22. Macfie, 'To the Queen of England' in his *New Poems* (London: John Lane, 1904).
23. 'An open letter to Lenin' (3 Sept. 1918), *WD*, 19 Jul. 1919; also Margaret P. Watt, 'Marx: De Leon: Lenin', *WD*, 15 Jun. 1918.
24. Mayakovsky, 'Notes to the poem "Lenin"' cited Herbert Marshall (trans. and ed.), *Mayakovsky* (London: Denis Dobson, 1965), p. 41.
25. See Chap. 6.1 below.
26. J. Arch Getty, *Practicing Stalinism. Bolsheviks, boyars and the persistence of tradition* (New Haven, CT: Yale University Press, 2013), p. 85.
27. Stites, *Revolutionary Dreams*, p. 263, n. 13.
28. Arthur Ransome, *Six Weeks in Russia 1919* (1919) (London: Redwords edn, 1992), pp. 120–1.
29. George Lansbury, *What I Saw in Russia* (London: Leonard Parsons, 1920), pp. 27–8.
30. Respectively M.A. Landau-Aldanov, *Lénine* (Paris: J. Povolozky, 1919); Albert Rhys Williams, *Lenin: the man and his work* (New York: Scott & Seltzer, 1919).
31. Henri Guilbeaux, *Le portrait authentique de Vladimir Ilitch Lénine* (Paris: Librairie de l'Humanité, 1924), pp. 11–12, 65 (account first published in German translation in July 1923).
32. Velikanova, *Making*, pp. 77, 94–6, 102–6.
33. Velikanova, *Making*, pp. 58–9; Ennker, 'Origins and intentions'; Getty on the other hand (*Practicing Stalinism*, p. 308 n. 33) refers to unsolicited letters and telegrams filling nearly a hundred archival folders.
34. Souvarine, *Stalin*, pp. 349–51.
35. *L'Humanité*, 27 Jan. 1924.
36. Dutt papers (Working Class Movement Library, Salford), R. Palme Dutt to Salme Dutt, 21 Jan. 1924.

37. Robert H. McNeal, *Bride of the Revolution. Krupskaya and Lenin* (Ann Arbor, MI: University of Michigan Press, 1972), pp. 241–2.
38. Mayakovsky, 'Vladimir Ilyich Lenin. *Dedicated to the Russian Communist Party*' (1924) in Marshall, *Mayakovsky*, pp. 250–1.
39. Christopher Hill, *Lenin and the Russian Revolution* (London: Hodder & Stoughton, 1947), ch. 8.
40. Jean Guéhenno, *La Foi Difficile* (Paris: Bernard Grasset, 1957), pp. 58–71.
41. See John Gorman, *Banner Bright. An illustrated history of the banners of the trade union movement* (London: Allen Lane, 1973), p. 103.
42. Cited Pierre Daix, *Les hérétiques du PCF* (Paris: Robert Laffont, 1980), p. 89.
43. See Mary Louise Roe, 'Gorky and Nietzsche: the quest for a Russian superman' in Bernice Glatzer Rosenthal (ed.), *Nietzsche in Russia* (Princeton, NJ: Princeton University Press, 1986), pp. 251–73.
44. Roe, 'Gorky and Nietzsche', pp. 270–1; on this see also Chap. 5 below.
45. 'For the attention of the workers' (23 Nov. 1917) in Maxim Gorky, *Untimely Thoughts. Essays on revolution, culture and the Bolsheviks 1917–1918* (London: Garnstone Press, 1968), pp. 87–9.
46. Gorky, 'In praise of Lenin', *WD*, 11 Dec. 1920.
47. Gorky, *Nicolai Lenin: the man* (London: Daily Herald, n.d. but 1924), p. 2; also Tumarkin, *Lenin Lives!*, p. 106.
48. See Gorky, *Days with Lenin* (London: Martin Lawrence, n.d. but 1932); Tovah Yedlin, *Maxim Gorky. A political biography* (Westport, CT: Praeger, 1999), p. 94.
49. Tumarkin, *Lenin Lives!*, p. 207.
50. Clara Zetkin, *Reminiscences of Lenin* (New York: International Publishers, 1934), p. 8.
51. Gorky to Romain Rolland, 3 Mar. 1924, in Jean Pérus (intr.), *Correspondance Romain Rolland Maxime Gorki* (Paris: Albin Michel, 1991), p. 127; Souvarine, *Stalin*, p. 352.
52. Max Eastman, *Leon Trotsky: the portrait of a youth* (1924) (London: Faber & Gwyer, 1926).

53. Mike Gold (Oct. 1926) cited Theodore Draper, *American Communism and Soviet Russia* (New York: Vintage Books, 1986 edn), p. 388.
54. Trotsky, *My Life. An attempt at autobiography* (Harmondsworth: Penguin, 1975 edn), pp. 509–10, citing Lev Kamenev.
55. Max Eastman, *Since Lenin Died* (New York: Boni & Liveright, 1925), ch. 2; W.N. Ewer, 'Trotsky and his "friends"', *LM*, Jun. 1925, 373–5; Albert Treint cited Philippe Robrieux, *Maurice Thorez. Vie secrète et vie publique* (Paris: Fayard, 1975), p. 86; Gorky, *Days with Lenin*, pp. 56–7.
56. Trotsky, 'Lenin ill', report to RCP seventh conference, 5 Apr. 1923 in Trotsky, *Lenin*, p. 241; Zinoviev (1918) cited Tumarkin, *Lenin Lives!*, p. 82; Bukharin, *Lenin as a Marxist* (London: CPGB, 1925), pp. 5–6; Stalin, *Works*, vol. 6, p. 52.
57. Cited Tumarkin, *Lenin Lives!*, p. 166.
58. Alexander Shklyaruk and Sergei Larkov, *Gustav Klutsis—Valentina Kulagina: posters, book graphic arts, magazine graphic arts, newsphotomontage 1922–1937* (Moscow: Contact-Cultura, 2010), p. 56.
59. See 'Stalin' in *The Life of Stalin: a symposium* (London: Modern Books, 1930), pp. 12–16.
60. Stalin's actual birthdate was 6 Dec. 1878.
61. Stephen Kotkin, *Stalin: paradoxes of power 1897–1928* (London: Penguin, 2015 edn), pp. 579–85.
62. Freeman, *An American Testament* (London: Gollancz, 1938), pp. 400–3.
63. Miklós Kun, *Stalin. An unknown portrait* (Budapest: Central European University Press, 2003), pp. 234–5; Kotkin, *Stalin*, pp. 600, 650–2.
64. Ian Christie, 'Canons and careers: the director in Soviet cinema' in Richard Taylor and Derek Spring (eds), *Stalinism and Soviet Cinema* (London: Routledge, 1993), p. 151.
65. L. Kaganovich, 'Stalin and the Party', S. Ordzhonikidze, 'The "Diehard" Bolshevik' and K. Voroshilov, 'Stalin and the Red Army', all in *Life of Stalin*.
66. Manuilsky, 'Staline, chef de l'Internationale communiste' and O.V. Kuusinen, 'Staline et le bolchévisation des sections de l'Internationale communiste' in *Staline* (Paris: Bureau d'Éditions: 1930), pp. 78–105; Souria Sadekova, 'Dmitri Manouilski',

Communisme, 40–1 (1995), 60–1; Manuilsky's article first appeared as 'Stalin kak vozhd Kominterna', *Pravda*, 21 Dec. 1929.

67. On the last-minute character see Benno Enkker, 'The Stalin cult, Bolshevik rule and Kremlin interaction in the 1930s' in Balázs Apor et al. (eds), *The Leader Cult in Communist Dictatorships. Stalin and the Eastern bloc* (Basingstoke: Palgrave Macmillan, 2004), p. 84.
68. For example those by Isaac Don Levine (1931), Essad-Bey (English edition, 1932) and the more sympathetic Stephen Graham (1931).
69. For the first Stalin interviews see Eugene Lyons, *Assignment in Utopia* (London: Harrap, 1938), pp. 262–6; S. J. Taylor, *Stalin's Apologist. Walter Duranty: the New York Times's man in Moscow* (New York: Oxford University Press, 1990), p. 169.
70. Dan H. Laurence (ed.), *Bernard Shaw: collected letters 1926–1950* (London: Viking, 1988), p. 258.
71. See Chap. 4.1 below.
72. Plamper, *Stalin Cult*, pp. 36–7, 227–9; Jeffrey Brooks, *Thank You, Comrade Stalin! Soviet public culture from revolution to Cold War* (Princeton, NJ: Princeton University Press, 2000), p. 65.
73. Sarah Davies, *Popular Opinion in Stalin's Russia. Terror, propaganda and dissent, 1934–1941* (Cambridge: Cambridge University Press, 1997), p. 148.
74. Jeremy Hicks, *Dziga Vertov. Defining documentary film* (London: Tauris, 2007), pp. 91–2.
75. Emil Ludwig, *Leaders of Europe* (London: Ivor Nicholson & Watson, 1934), pp. 349, 356.
76. See Cohen, *Siècle*, pp. 727–8.
77. Emilio Gentile, *The Sacralization of Politics in Fascist Italy* (Cambridge, MA: Harvard University Press, 1996), p. 159.
78. Davies, *Popular Opinion*, p. 150.
79. See inter alia the greetings of ECCI, Marcel Cachin and the French and British communist parties in *The World Hails Twentieth Anniversary of the Soviet Union* (Moscow: Foreign Languages Publishing House, 1938).
80. Sarah Wilson, 'The Soviet Pavilion in Paris' in Matthew Cullerne Bown and Brandon Taylor (eds), *Art of the Soviets. Painting, sculpture and architecture in a one-party state, 1917–1992* (Manchester: Manchester University Press, 1993), pp. 111–14.

81. Including Lenin's widow Krupskaya: see Timofei Rokotov, 'Recent Soviet historical films', *International Literature*, Apr. 1938, 98–104; also Greene, 'Lenin in October' (*Spectator*, 25 Nov. 1938) in Graham Greene, *The Pleasure-Dome. The collected film criticism 1935–40* (London: Secker & Warburg, 1972), pp. 206–7.
82. Bonnell, *Iconography*, pp. 159–60.
83. Cited Michael David-Fox, *Showcasing the Great Experiment. Cultural diplomacy and western visitors to the Soviet Union, 1921–1941* (New York: Oxford University Press, 2012), p. 133.
84. C. Kramer, 'The Soviet palace—a monument to Lenin', *Inprecorr*, 3 Dec. 1938, 1308; also Timothy J. Colton, *Moscow. Governing the Socialist Metropolis* (Cambridge, MA: Harvard University Press, 1995), pp. 331–4.
85. Plamper, *Stalin Cult*, pp. 99–102.
86. *Stalin on Lenin* (Moscow: Foreign Languages Publishing House, 1939); also Robert H. McNeal, 'Krupskaya: the feminine subcult' in Bernard W. Eissenstat (ed.), *Lenin and Leninism. State, law, and society* (Lexington, KY: Lexington Books, 1971), pp. 222–4; Tumarkin, *Lenin Lives!*, pp. 244–51.
87. Plamper, *Stalin Cult*, pp. 175–80; Vladimir Orlov, 'Prokoviev and the myth of the father of the nations: the cantata *Zdravitsa*', *Journal of Musicology*, 30, 4 (2013), 577–620.
88. Alfred J. Rieber, 'Stalin, man of the borderlands', *American Historical Review*, 106 (2001), 1657–68.
89. *Pravda*, 21 Dec. 1939.
90. 'Stalin's birthday', *DW* (NY), 22 Dec.
91. *The Dethronement of Stalin. Full text of the Khrushchev speech* (Manchester: Manchester Guardian, 1956), p. 28.
92. Robert C. Tucker, *Stalin in Power. The revolution from above 1928–1941* (New York: W.W. Norton, 1992 edn), p. 609; Brooks, *Thank You*, pp. 221–2 notes the paucity of foreign greetings.
93. Clifford Geertz, 'Centers, kings and charisma: reflections on the symbolics of power' in Joseph Ben-David and Terry Nichols Clark (eds), *Culture and its Creators. Essays in honor of Edward Shils* (Chicago, IL: University of Chicago Press, 1977), p. 168. The others Geertz mentioned were Sukarno, Nkrumah, Mao and Nasser, all leaders of successful national or social liberation struggles.

94. Brooks, *Thank You*, pp. 164–7, 184–8; on Hitler, see Ian Kershaw, *The 'Hitler Myth'. Image and reality in the Third Reich* (Oxford: Oxford University Press, 1989 edn), p. 219.
95. K.E. Voroshilov, 'Military commander of the Great Patriotic War' in *'Pravda' Articles on the Occasion of the 70th Birthday of Joseph Vissarionovich Stalin December 21, 1949* (London: Soviet News, 1950), pp. 44–5.
96. Brooks, *Thank You*, ch. 8.
97. Thorez, 'Hommage à Staline', *CdC*, Jan. 1950, 12–34; Thorez, 'Vive Staline', *CdC*, Dec. 1949, 1451–7; 'Longue vie et bonne santé au camarade Staline', greetings of PCF central committee, *CdC*, Jan. 1950, 5–6; Fernand Demany, *Staline, l'homme du socialisme, l'homme de la victoire, l'homme de la paix* (Brussels: SPE, 1949); 'Viva il compagno Stalin!', greetings of PCI central committee, *l'Unità*, 21. Dec. 1949.
98. Taylor, *Stalin's Apologist*, pp. 321–2.
99. See for example *DW* (L), 23 Dec. 1949.
100. Jay Leyda, *Kino. A history of the Russian and the Soviet film* (London: Allen and Unwin, 1960), ch. 11.
101. Judith Devlin, '"Recreating history on film". Stalin and the Russian revolution in feature film, 1937–1939', *Media History*, 13 (2007), 149.
102. Devlin, '"Recreating"', 161–3.
103. Richard Taylor, *Film Propaganda. Soviet Russia and Nazi Germany* (London: Tauris, 1998 edn), pp. 99–124 and 239–41 for a discussion and a filmography.
104. However, two years later Chiaureli's *Unforgettable Year 1919* returned to the civil war for a still more fanciful presentation of Stalin's successful defiance of the Allied intervention.
105. Thorez, 'Hommage', 12.
106. Cited Mancin Zaremba, 'The second step of a ladder: the cult of the first secretaries in Poland' in Apor, *Leader Cult*, pp. 262–3.
107. Izabella Main, 'President of Poland or "Stalin's most faithful pupil?" The cult of Boleslaw Bierut in Stalinist Poland' in Apor, *Leader Cult*, pp. 179–93.
108. David Forgacs and Stephen Gundle, *Mass Culture and Italian Society from Fascism to the Cold War* (Bloomington, IN: Indiana University Press, 2007), p. 264.

109. Daniel Leese, *Mao Cult. Rhetoric and ritual in China's Cultural Revolution* (Cambridge: Cambridge University Press, 2011), pp. 4, 45, 145.
110. For the limits of destalinisation, see Polly Jones, *Myth, Memory and Trauma. Rethinking the stalinist past in the Soviet Union, 1953–70* (New Haven, CT: Yale University Press, 2013).
111. For the stalinisation concept, see Norman LaPorte et al. (eds), *Bolshevism, Stalinism and the Comintern: perspectives on stalinization* (Basingstoke: Palgrave Macmillan, 2008).
112. See Norman Laporte and Kevin Morgan, '"Kings among their subjects?" Ernst Thälmann, Harry Pollitt and the leadership cult as stalinization' in LaPorte, *Bolshevism*, pp. 124–45.
113. See Hermann Weber, 'Ernst Thälmann (1886–1944)' in idem and Bernhard H. Bayerlein (eds), *Der Thälmann-Skandal. Geheime Korrespondenz mit Stalin* (Berlin: Aufbau, 2003), pp. 12–20. Kasper Braskén informs me that there were also signs in 1931 of an incipient cult of Willi Münzenberg, the *Führer* of the Berlin-based Workers' International Relief. My thanks also to Norry LaPorte for advice on these points.
114. See Chap. 5.1 below.
115. 'The world proletarian revolution of the new type', *CI*, 15 Mar. 1934, 195–203.
116. See the coverage in *L'Humanité*, 11–16 Sept. 1934.
117. Emmet O'Connor, *Reds and the Green. Ireland, Russia and the Communist Internationals 1919–43* (Dublin: University College Dublin Press, 2004), pp. 199–200.
118. Kevin Morgan, *Harry Pollitt* (Manchester: Manchester University Press, 1993), pp. 60–1.
119. Franz Borkenau, *The Communist International* (London: Faber & Faber, 1938), p. 394.
120. Annie Kriegel, 'Bureaucratie, culte de personnalité et charisme. Le cas français: Maurice Thorez, secrétaire général du PCF (1900–1964)' in idem, *Communisme au miroir français* (Paris: Gallimard, 1974), pp. 144–9.
121. Stéphane Sirot, *Maurice Thorez* (Paris: Presses de Sciences Po, 2000), pp. 23–4, 242–4.
122. Wolikow, 'Préface' to 'Année 1935: Le VIIe congrès de l'Internationale communiste' in Denis Peschanski (ed.), *Marcel*

Cachin. Carnets 1906–1947 (Paris: CNRS Éditions, vol 4, 1997), pp. 56–7.
123. Trotsky, *My Life*, pp. 519–20.
124. Resolutions of PCF Montreuil conference, Jan. 1937, *CdB*, 20 Feb. 1937, 244–7.
125. Marty papers (PCF archives) 281 J box 39, draft tribute by Marty, 24 Mar. 1942 and 'À la memoire de Jose Diaz', tribute from PCE and Comintern leaders, 21 Mar. 1942.
126. RGASPI 495/100/1025, CPGB 14th party congress, May 1937, contribution of Rose Smith.
127. Annette Wieviorka, *Maurice et Jeannette: biographie du couple Thorez* (Paris: Fayard, 2010), pp. 217–18.
128. James G. Ryan, *Earl Browder. The failure of American communism* (Tuscaloose, AL: University of Alabama Press, 1997), pp. 104, 254.
129. See regular features and advertisement in *DW* (NY), Jan. 1940.
130. See Chap. 4.2 below.
131. RGASPI 495/100/1025, contribution of Rose Smith.
132. John Manley, '"Audacity, audacity, still more audacity": Tim Buck, the party, and the people, 1932–1939', *Labour/Le Travail*, 49 (2002), 12–13.
133. See Chap. 6.2 below.
134. Bernard Pudal, *Prendre parti. Pour une sociologie historique du PCF* (Paris: Presses de la Fondation Nationale des Sciences Politiques, 1989), pp. 222–7; Michelle Perrot, 'Les vies ouvrières' in Pierre Nora (ed.), *Les Lieux de mémoire* (Paris: Gallimard, 1997 edn), pp. 3937–3969.
135. CPGB archives, central committee proceedings, 10 Sept. 1937 (microfilm).
136. Russel Lemmons, *Hitler's Rival. Ernst Thälmann in Myth and Memory* (Lexington, KY: University of Kentucky Press, 2013), pp. 100–1.
137. Henry Pelling, *The British Communist Party. A historical profile* (London: A. & C. Black, 1975 edn), p. 89.
138. See Chap. 3.3 below.
139. Balázs Apor, 'Leader in the making: the role of biographies in constructing the cult of Mátyás Rákosi' in Apor, *Leader Cult*, pp. 67–8.
140. *DW* (NY), 21 Jul. 1936.

141. Ruth Fischer, *Stalin and German Communism. A study in the origins of the state party* (Oxford: Oxford University Press, 1948), p. 219; Lemmons, *Hitler's Rival*, pp. 38–43.
142. Manley, '"Audacity"', 12–15.
143. Elizabeth Gurley Flynn, *The Man from Kansas* (New York: Workers' Library, 1941). The *DW* serial, by Robert Minor, ran from 19 Jan. to 7 Feb. 1940.
144. See Chap. 5.2 below.
145. See for example John Cornford's poem 'Sergei Mironovitch Kirov' in Pat Sloan (ed.), *John Cornford. A memoir* (London: Cape, 1938), pp. 176–7. For the martyr theme, see Manuilsky's funeral address, *CI*, 5 Jan. 1935, 46–7; also Matthew E. Lenoe, *The Kirov Murder and Soviet History* (New Haven, CT: Yale University Press, 2010), ch. 12.
146. Bernard, 'Liturgie funèbre', 41.
147. Laurent Casanova, 'Jdanov et le mouvement ouvrier internationale', *CdC*, Oct. 1948, 1081–92; Aragon, 'Jdanov et nous', *Les Lettres françaises*, 9 Sept. 1948.
148. E.P. Thompson, 'The poverty of theory: or an orrery of errors' in *The Poverty of Theory and other essays* (London: Merlin, 1978), p. 264.
149. Peter J. Conradi, *A Very English Hero. The making of Frank Thompson* (London: Bloomsbury, 2013 edn), chs 12–14.
150. Manley, '"Audacity"', 34.
151. RGASPI 495/100/1041, 'Review of Comrade Tom Bell's Short "History" of the British CP' by Max Raylock.
152. See Chap. 3.3 below.
153. Ryan, *Earl Browder*, pp. 137, 146–7.
154. Alan Max, 'Browder Tells CP Position On Fall Elections and War', *DW* (NY), 22 May 1936.
155. *Time*, 30 May 1938
156. Ryan, *Earl Browder*, p. 147.
157. Charlotte Haldane, 'Passionaria', *Left Review*, Apr. 1938, 926.
158. See Chap. 4.3 below.
159. See Chap. 4.2 below.
160. See Chap. 6.2 below.
161. 'Greetings from the Executive Committee of the Communist International to Comrade Stalin' in *World Hails*, pp. 31–5; 'À

l'occasion du XIXe anniversaire de la Révolution russe: le Parti communiste français adresse son salut au camarade Stalin', *CdB*, 1 Dec. 1936, 1410–11.

162. David Brandenberger, *Propaganda State in Crisis. Soviet ideology, indoctrination, and terror under Stalin, 1927–1941* (New Haven, CT: Yale University Press, 2011), ch. 4; Davies, *Popular Opinion*, pp. 153–4.
163. RGASPI 495/93/257, report on work of Belgian party leadership, 4 Mar. 1936.
164. Lenin biographies appearing in English or French included those of Valeriu Marcu (English trans., Gollancz, 1928), Pierre Chasles (Plon, 1929), D.S. Mirsky (Holme Press, 1931), James Maxton (Nelson, 1932), F.J.P. Veale (Constable, 1932), Curzio Malaparte (French trans., Bernard Grasset, 1932), Marc Vichniac (A. Colin, 1932), Ferdinand-Antoine Ossendowski (Albin Michel, 1932), Jean Jacoby (Flammarion, 1933).
165. Marie-Cécile Bouju, *Lire en communiste. Les Maisons d'édition du Parti communiste français 1920–1968* (Rennes: Presses universitaires de Rennes, 2010), p. 61.
166. William Gallacher, *Revolt on the Clyde* (1936) (London: Lawrence & Wishart, 1940 edn), ch. 11; Harry Pollitt, *Serving My Time. An apprenticeship to politics* (1940) (London: Lawrence & Wishart, 1941 edn), pp. 138–9, 189–94; William Z. Foster, *From Bryan to Stalin* (New York: International Publishers, 1937), pp. 150–6.
167. Philippe Buton, 'Le Parti communiste français et le stalinisme au lendemain de la Seconde Guerre mondiale', *Journal of Modern European History*, 2, 1 (2004), 70.
168. 'Lenin Needs No Monument', *DW* (L), 27 Jan. 1934.
169. Cachin, 'Long Live Stalin!' in *The World Hails*, pp. 137–40.
170. G. R. Swain, 'Tito: the formation of a disloyal Bolshevik', *International Review of Social History*, 34 (1989), 262.
171. Paul Preston, *The Last Stalinist. The life of Santiago Carrillo* (London: Collins, 2015 edn), pp. 27–8.
172. Nadezhda K. Krupskaya, *Memories of Lenin (1893–1917)* (London: Lawrence & Wishart, 1942 edn).
173. Ralph Fox, *Lenin. A biography* (London: Gollancz, 1933), p. 129 and passim.
174. See Chap. 5.1 below.

175. *Left Review*, Jan. 1935, 123–4, Mar. 1935, 233, Apr. 1938, 926.
176. MacDiarmid, 'Lamh Dearg Aboo (To Stalin)' in Maurice Lindsay (ed.), *Poetry Scotland*, II (Glasgow: William Maclellan, 1945), pp. 45–7.
177. First published in Hugh MacDiarmid, *Lucky Poet. A self-study in literature and political ideas* (London: Methuen, 1943), p. 113.
178. MacDiarmid, 'Talking with Five Thousand People in Edinburgh' in Lindsay, *Poetry Scotland*, II, pp. 47–50.
179. *L'accueil enthousiaste de Paris au grand patriote Maurice Thorez de retour en France* (Paris: Éditions du PCF, 1944 or 1945), pp. 1–2.
180. See Chap. 4.2 below.
181. See Chap. 4.3 below.
182. 'Fragments du 10ème congrès du Parti Communiste Français', Jun. 1945, also 'Trois discours' by Thorez, Marty, Duclos, also 1945 all at http://cinearchives.org (accessed Jun. 2015); PCF archives 89 FI 26–9 (1946) for poster images.
183. Bruno Groppo, 'Entre autobiographie et histoire. Les récits autobiographiques de communistes italiens publiés après 1945' in Claude Pennetier and Bernard Pudal (eds), *Autobiographies, autocritiques, aveux dans le monde communiste* (Paris: Belin, 2002), p. 251.
184. Marietta Stankova, *Georgi Dimitrov. A biography* (London: Tauris, 2010), p. 189.
185. Harry Pollitt, *Impressions of Czechoslovakia* (London: CPGB, 1946), p. 9.
186. Geoffrey Swain, *Tito. A biography* (London: Tauris, 2011), p. 83.
187. Seton-Watson, preface in *The Story of the Partisans of Free Yugoslavia* (London: Yugoslav Emergency Committee (British), 1944), pp. 1–2.
188. Jacques Duclos, 'Être stalinien', *CdC*, Jun. 1952, 585–6.
189. Victor Joannès, editorial, *NC*, May 1950, 12; Joannès, '"Fils du peuple" et la lutte pour les principes du léninisme', *CdC*, Oct. 1949, 1202–11.
190. André Wurmser, 'D'un amour lucide …', *NC*, Dec. 1949, 7; also Georges Mounin, 'Le marxisme et les grands hommes', *NC*, Nov. 1949, 14. My thanks to Francis King for advice on Russian usages.
191. Duclos, 'Être stalinien', 585; Serge Zeyons, 'Le parti de Maurice Thorez à 30 ans', *Regards*, 15 Dec. 1950, 2.

192. Cachin papers 290 J 36, 'En Italie', Jan. or Feb. 1949.
193. Donald Sassoon, 'Italian images of Russia, 1945–56' in Christopher Duggan and Christopher Wagstaff (eds), *Italy in the Cold War. Politics, culture and society 1948–58* (Oxford: Berg, 1995), 199–200.
194. Thorez papers 626 AP/231, PCF Aix-en-Provence section to Thorez, 15 Apr. 1945.
195. PCF secretariat minutes, 3 Jan. and 11 Apr. 1950.
196. Togliatti to Luigi Longo, 11 Feb. 1953 in Togliatti, *La guerra di posizione in Italia. Epistolario 1944–1964* (Turin: Einaudi, 2014), pp. 182–5. My special thanks to Aldo Agosti for this reference and its translation.
197. Togliatti to Longo, 11 Feb. 1953; S. Scuderi (ed.), *Vita di un italiano* (Rome: Edizione di Cultura Sociale, 1953); Balázs Apor, *The 'Invisible Shining': the cult of Mátyás Rákosi in stalinist Hungary, 1945–1956* (Budapest: Central European University Press, forthcoming 2016), ch. 4.
198. See Tikhomorov, 'Stalin cult'; Jan C. Behrends, 'Exporting the leader: the Stalin cult in Poland and East Germany (1944/5–1956) in Apor, *Leader Cult*, pp. 161–78.
199. Leese, *Mao Cult*, pp. 4, 254.
200. Brooks, *Thank You*, p. 223.
201. See for example Marius Magnien, 'La victoire de la politique stalinienne en Chine', *CdC*, Mar. 1950, 48–61; Thorez, 'Hommage', 28–9.
202. *DW* (L), 6 Mar. 1953.
203. Pollitt, *In Memory of Joseph Stalin and Klement Gottwald* (London: CPGB, 1953).
204. Preston, *Last Stalinist*, pp. 198–200, 211.

CHAPTER 3

Cult Variations

3.1 Integrating and Enkindling

(i)

When Henri Barbusse announced his intention of writing Stalin's biography, Stalin is said to have responded with a gesture of helplessness.[1] Lion Feuchtwanger, another western interlocutor, wrote that the immoderate worship of Stalin's person was 'manifestly irksome' to him. Of course this was wrong, Stalin added, but 'what can one person do—they see in me a unifying concept, and create foolish raptures around me'.[2]

The notion that Stalin could do nothing need not detain us. On the other hand, the idea that the encouragement of such raptures could serve a unifying purpose has the support of many of those writing on the wider cult phenomenon. There are accounts which trace the origins of Stalin's cult to his personal neuroses and cravings, or which identify it as a 'Leadership regime' whose elevation of the leader was itself the object and not the means of achieving it.[3] Nevertheless, wherever leadership regimes are allowed a measure of functionality, almost always it is as the unifying concept to which Stalin referred. Both Lenin and Mao, for example, have been described as providing a stable symbolic centre in societies in a state of flux.[4] Mussolini is likewise described as a 'focal point for the integration of the Italian population into a system of regimented consensus', while the 'Hitler myth' is seen as performing a 'vitally important integratory function' in providing the Nazi regime with a mass base of

K. Morgan, *International Communism and the Cult of the Individual*, DOI 10.1057/978-1-137-55667-7_3

support.[5] Ranging further over time, Getty has identified functional similarities between tsarist and Bolshevik practices, and Peter Burke a whole series of parallels with the 'cult of royal personality' which assisted the rise of the centralising state in France.[6] Tim Mason spoke of Hitler transforming himself into the function of Führer, and in all these cases a similar process might reasonably be inferred.[7]

More particularly, these may be thought of as the attributes of an integrating cult. In a closed-society context, like all of those just mentioned, integration was effected at a societal level, and a cult community constructed by a sort of universal conscription into its practices. In modern examples, mass communications allow saturation coverage of a discrete population concomitant with the state, where the expression of an indivisible sovereignty is neither politically contested, nor the subject of meaningful collective deliberation, but appropriated by an all-reaching authority centred on or articulated through a person. There are conflicting views as to how far this must be distinguished from those pre-modern cults, whether in Russia or in France, whose claims were neither rooted in the subject of the people, nor addressed to that people in its entirety, nor even technically communicable to them in the form of standardised cult products.[8] What is more important in the present context is that an integrating function may also be conceived of at the level of the movement or the party rather than the polity as a whole. There were basically two types of situation that offered a particular rationale for such integrating practices. The first was that of controlling and holding together a movement exposed to strong centripetal or disintegrative pressures, whether of factionalism, localism, ideological discord or political disengagement. The second was that of consolidating newly won or precariously held attachments in the face of either internal dissension or external threat. Both conditions held in Russia, where bolshevism's cults emerged as the instrument at once of faction and regime, and the focus on Lenin assisted both the unification of the 'organised minority' and the overt promotion of his personality to the 'less articulate masses'.[9]

In the communist movement more broadly, the primary use of the integration figure was as a loyalty test and control mechanism that served to simplify and concretise the disciplines and authority structures of democratic centralism. This might, for example, help explain the inflexion towards the International of the embryonic Stalin cult of the late 1920s. It might also account for the paradox whereby the full effect of Stalin's cult was felt, not when the communist parties' material and organisational ties with Moscow were strongest, but if anything when these had in many respects been somewhat curtailed. In other words, this might be seen as one of the cultural, ideological and even personal bonds that helped to make up for or even make possible the attenuation from the mid-1930s of organisational-structural ones.[10]

Most of all, it would help explain why it was the attempt to consolidate communist advances in a hostile world environment that brought the Cold War cult system into being. Believing that Stalin's own urgings alone could satisfactorily explain his cult, Robert C. Tucker maintained that no political rationale could account for its continuation once Stalin's grip on power was secure.[11] It is certainly true that the cult was played down in just those periods of forced collectivisation (1930–1933) and German military advance (1941–1943) in which its political utility might in theory have been demonstrated in mobilising the Soviet people behind their regime. Should an international perspective also be allowed, however, the emergence of a full-blown stalinist cult system may be seen to reflect both the adversarial logic of the Cold War and the brittleness of communism's political and territorial gains. It is thus that Tikhomorov evokes Stalin's Cold War cult as a transnational integration cult which simultaneously personified the unity of his socialist 'empire' and marked its symbolic boundaries with the other world of capitalism. The formation of this imagined community, Tikhomorov continues, was thus an overarching symbolic project for the integration of the elements of the Soviet periphery into a single unified political body.[12]

There is no reason why such an insight should be confined to the Soviet sphere of influence. Communism was never just a bounded empire, and its values, codes and allegiances cut across the hermetic construction of a symbolic as well as physical bloc. Thorez in 1948 summed up what for communists was the axiomatic truth that the 'two great camps' into which the world was divided should 'not be considered merely horizontally (in terms of geography) but vertically (in terms of the organization of society in all countries)'.[13] For 30 years, the camps had existed in a continuously volatile relationship with each other, with ever-changing configurations, vertical as well as horizontal, and episodes of encroachment and fraternisation as well as the bipolar opposition of the Cold War. Even so, it is specifically in this latter period that one can trace the wide and systematic employment of the practices that are here identified with the integration cult. Stalin did not only seek to consolidate his East European empire. There were also communist parties in the West whose legal basis, organisation and mass support were in several cases better established than at any time between the wars, but which were nevertheless subjected to the intense polarising logic of which they were both instrument and potential victim.

This was nowhere truer than in France. All commentators agree that the boundaries between the PCF and the rest of French society in this period became more rigid and clearly defined, and the allegiance required of party members, in Ronald Tiersky's words, 'more dogmatic and absolutist'. It is also primarily in this period that Tiersky located the Thorez cult as a defining party ritual that provided focal point and compliance mechanism for a counter-community beset by severe external pressures.[14] Though with possibly less chronological precision, Kriegel similarly described it as a 'party affair' and a point of convergence for the procedures already put in place to 'constitute the party as a closed microsociety and prevent it from being penetrated by the other society which surrounded it'.[15]

This, however, was a strong variant of a general trend. In Italy and Belgium as well as France, communists in the spring of 1947 were indefinitely excluded from a role in government. It is also from 1947 that the Italian communists are said to have used Stalin's name and image 'to integrate their party … and render it ideologically compact'.[16] Both Italy and Belgium, though not France, were also among the countries—Japan was another—in which the assassination or attempted assassination of leading communists further contributed to the febrile atmosphere in which these cults could flourish as the symbols of a defiant apartness. Indeed, in the case of the PCI leader Togliatti, the attempt on his life in 1948 was arguably the decisive event in the emergence of his own personal cult, as was vividly attested in the documentary films, *14 July* (14 Iuglio) and *Togliatti Has Returned* (Togliatti è ritornato), and in the culminating chapter of his later cult biography.[17]

Luciano Cavalli has written of the tendency of 'large movements formed around a charismatic leader' to shape a 'closed universe of social relationships which the leader himself (or herself) defines'.[18] Putting to one side the vexed question of charisma, it is in the culture of Cold War stalinism that Cavalli's contention is most clearly demonstrated in the history of the communist movement. Communism in effect had become its own cult community, and if nothing else there was a basic congruence between these esoteric practices of a formalised cultic hierarchy and the turning of communist parties in upon themselves.

(ii)

While the integrating cult can to this extent be traced across the wider communist movement, at an international level it is clearly only part of the story. In particular, this is true if account is taken of stalinism's two distinct phases of cult-building. Despite its unevenness over time, accounts of Stalin's domestic cult reveal a basic linearity exhibiting many common features across the two discrete periods of pre-war and post-war.[19] There are few discussions of the wider cult phenomenon across this basic divide, and in the literature on international communism, the war years and Comintern dissolution provide a basic if often implicit watershed delimiting many of the most important contributions.[20] For Annie Kriegel, who did write about the Thorez cult across this divide, the popular-front phase of cult-building nevertheless corresponded to Stalin's pre-war cult just as surely as the second phase corresponded to its Cold War revival.[21] This is not the view adopted here, and the integrating cult alone cannot sufficiently account for the wider communist turn to the individual from the early 1930s.

In both these phases, the communist parties were detachments of a revolution which had now become a state to be defended. The vanguardist ethos and fortress mentality of the Soviet hegemon thus generated a fixation on discipline, ideological rectitude and the purging of impurities which the cult of the leader did manifestly assist. But it is also clear that communism as a universe had first of all to be established before it could turn in on itself. As the self-proclaimed party of the future, it came into being with ambitions that far outstripped its capacities. It was also exposed to existential threats, most obviously fascism, that also threatened other groups and movements and could in due course pose immediate issues of alliance-building, recruitment and campaigning effectiveness.

The charisma of the revolution, which was also that of Lenin, had had a compelling force of attraction for communism's founding cohorts.[22] Stalin's unifying concept, on the other hand, was one pitched at the level of the Soviet state itself. To the extent that his supporters internationally subscribed to its tenets, these were also brought within the wider ambit of this state and the attachments it sought to inculcate. But neither Stalin's cult itself nor the leader function that it represented lent themselves to the broadening of communist influence or the drawing into its ranks of new post-Lenin enrolments. Indeed, the very opposite was true: unification around such a symbol, where this by definition was a fiercely partisan symbol, had the moral force of integration by exclusion and withdrawal lacking only the material sanctions of the party-state. Fortuitously but entirely aptly, each of Stalin's key decennial markers coincided with and epitomised a phase of extreme introversion and sectarianism in the communist movement, namely Class Against Class, the Nazi-Soviet pact and the Cold War.

For communist parties in the West, there was therefore an inherent tension between communism's obsession with control and the aspiration to the broadening rather than deepening of its support and public influence. Even within a Cold War environment, this tension can shed light on such variations as the PCI's avoidance of the full logic of ghettoisation as experienced by the PCF. It was certainly relevant in this connection that Togliatti, even in approving his own party cult, warned against activities not conforming to his country's current political customs: 'We are not in power and unfortunately we have to submit to these customs if we wish to avoid obvious damage (exposing ourselves to caricature and public mockery, in which any rubbish in the popular press is promptly directed at us).'[23]

Without disregarding these differences, the primary emphasis here is on how this tension may be traced diachronically through strongly contrasting phases of communist policy. The transitions were nowhere more abrupt than in France, and in writings on the PCF they are usually represented in terms of alternating phases of relative openness and communist 'counter-community'. Tiersky, following Kriegel, adopts such a periodisation, and the Cold War Thorez cult may be readily identified with the third of Tiersky's phases of counter-community (1947–1962). The paradox remaining to be explained is why, on the other hand, the cult should have made its initial appearance in the popular-front phase of relative openness (1934–1939) when the PCF succeeded in reaching out well beyond the shrivelled communist counter-community of the early 1930s.

This earlier phase of cult-building not only resembled the extolling of political leaders in 'more open political systems', but was precisely that.[24] Historians have thus adapted the cult designation to figures like Garibaldi as well as France's Louis Quatorze, and it is just this sense of reaching out to wider constituencies that one finds in the term's very earliest usages. As Eduard Bernstein put it, the 'cult for the personality of Lassalle did, for a long time, greatly help on the movement':

> The name Lassalle became a standard which created more and more enthusiasm among the masses the more Lassalle's works spread among the people. ... The strength of conviction that breathes in [his] writings has enkindled hundreds of thousands to struggle for the rights of labour ... in those places where, amongst the workers, the traditions of the Lassallean agitation were strongest, as a rule, most was accomplished in the way of organisation.[25]

Though the passage has figured prominently in discussions of the communist cults, the lines reproduced here have not previously registered in the way they so obviously do in this broader context.[26] Personality here was not the human face of organisation, or of the state, but a force in its own right through which Bernstein described the organisation itself developing. Here too there were foolish raptures, as Bernstein and others carefully detailed; but these did not just serve to unify but to enkindle.

In its recovery from the political nadir of the early 1930s, the communist movement also had names like Lassalle's that became a standard and were consciously deployed as such. It is this enkindling figure that therefore needs to be set alongside Stalin's unifying concept in tracing what in practice were the cults and not simply cult of the individual. The broader distinction, if not the particular application, is a familiar one. Written at the height of the Cold War, Hannah Arendt's account of totalitarianism clearly identified the basic duality of a movement that sought not only to control but to influence and attract. 'Since totalitarian movements exist in a world which itself is nontotalitarian', Arendt argued, 'they are forced to resort to what we commonly regard as propaganda. But such propaganda always makes its appeal to an external sphere—be it the nontotalitarian strata of the population at home or the nontotalitarian countries abroad.' It was thus Arendt distinguished between this propagating activity, which she believed the more necessary the smaller the movement or the greater the external pressure upon it, and the indoctrination which she held to be the very essence of totalitarianism.[27]

It was intrinsic to Arendt's intuitive teleologism that the duality was merely on the surface and that no real tension was possible between the indoctrination that helped to define the totalitarian movement and the merely secondary and external necessity of propaganda. Even non-ruling parties, Arendt asserted rather than demonstrated, did not seriously compete with other parties or attract the same sorts of people as members. The rather different premise of the present study is that interaction with the 'non-totalitarian world', whether competitive, conflictual or claiming common interest, is one of the keys to these parties' history and the only way their development over time and place can be properly understood. In Francophone writings, the distinction is sometimes drawn between a politics of *rassemblement*, employed in just the sense of reaching beyond a core constituency, and that of the 'fortress party' that sought to stop the outside world from reaching in.[28] The distinction is formulated here as that between an enkindling or propagating figure and an integrating or unifying one. Like the propaganda which initially was an instrument of the Catholic Church, the former assumed a faith or cause that must be propagated but through the particular instrument of the individual who personified it, or some aspect of it. The integrating figure, on the other hand, was concerned with the binding and control of some existing communist polity through an emblematic individual symbolising its monolithicity and a manifest principle of hierarchy.

The grouping of these features is perhaps most evident in the more premeditated form of the integrating cult. This may be identified with an unambiguous symbolic hierarchy culminating in a single individual. Typically that individual represented either some pre-eminent social type or else, rather than some subaltern or peripheral identity, an encompassing protean quality in which diverse associations and accomplishments were united. There was also a symbiosis of leader and movement. This tended to mean the downplaying of any purely personal history, and a process of manufacturing or refashioning to meet these requirements, not only in respect of the central cult figure, but in the observances that their elevation to cultic status demanded. Nothing could be less spontaneous than Stalin's affectations of cultic impotence. If sometimes Stalin expressed diffidence and even disapproval of cultic practices, one effect was to create a radical uncertainty as to how to gauge his pleasure and how to deflect his unpredictable wrath. These are the sorts of feature one can recognise in E.A. Rees's description of the leader cult as a 'deliberately constructed and managed mechanism' aimed at integrating some polity around the leader's persona.[29]

The heuristic device of the enkindling cult allows the recognition of a number of features which such a definition excludes. The cult of the individual could thus extend to multiple figures, whether of similar or contrasting type, existing in ambiguous relations of hierarchy. These individuals might not only represent distinct proficiencies and social environments, but do so through public identities and biographical histories that in some key aspects were individualised, inalienable and, at least in theory, detachable from the party to which they belonged. Addressed at least in part to an audience still to be won over, both practices and representations were exoteric in character. Biography was a basic form of cult production in the case of both integrating and enkindling figures. Nevertheless, the construction of a narrative that could both indoctrinate and propagate proved particularly difficult to achieve. Biography, as we shall see, was therefore best used to wider effect where a biographical persona was achievable that was not primarily a function of office-holding, but was generated in some way independently of the party itself.

These distinctions are not offered as a checklist or a scheme of classification. The object rather is to bring within a common field of vision interconnected cases which may otherwise be sealed from each other or reduced to somewhat mechanical relations of reproduction in different settings. Integrating and enkindling features will therefore be encountered here in variants and combinations that not only altered over time but help account for the advancement, displacement or refashioning of particular individuals.

There is however an underlying pattern that the grouping of these features helps bring out more clearly. It is striking in a longer perspective that the principal growth periods of western communism, in the mid-1930s and early-to-mid-1940s, were not only characterised by anti-fascism but by a heroisation of communist discourse that was adapted from Soviet practices but not as yet consistently centred on the Kremlin. Even Stalin brushed himself up for a wider public, and the pseudo-democratic constitution to which he gave his name was intended to assist his supporters internationally as a bulwark against dictatorship.[30] That Stalin simultaneously launched the Moscow trials, and even licensed the production of full published transcripts for perusal by this same western public, reveals the tension between impulses of effectiveness and control in its most acute form. Nevertheless, it was in periods of contraction or consolidation that the Stalin cult registered most. Following the hiatus of the Nazi–Soviet pact (1939–1941), conditions of urgent political necessity had for a time combined with mass recruitment, enforced extemporisation and the disruption of the minutiae of control to tilt the balance once again towards a more diffuse and politically extrovert projection of the individual. But with the late 1940s and the Cold War, a second wave of show trials followed, and with them the closed and processed leader cults that were their mirror-image and corollary. It is in this period that the notion of stalinisation can be applied with the sense of apparent finality which its earliest proponents intended. But even this was to prove only temporary, for when Stalin died in 1953, he was so much the single integrating figure that no real provision for a successor had yet been possible.

The chapters that follow are not organised chronologically, but through particular themes as exemplified in individual cases. Nevertheless, the distinction will be made throughout between these different phases of cult-building as notably evidenced in the adjustment over time between integrating and enkindling features. The rest of the current chapter therefore seeks first to elaborate the unifying–enkindling theme, as illustrated by appropriate examples, concluding with a discussion of charisma and political capital as the commonest alternative ways of conceptualising what cult practices might have represented.

3.2 A Unifying Concept

(i)

Pierre Bourdieu described as the 'mystery of ministry' the process by which a person becomes 'something other than what that person is', whether that something be a people, a nation, a state or a party.[31] The singularity, literally, of the integration figure was that this identification had to be complete and all-encompassing. Stalin as a unifying symbol could allow no rival. With the sole exception of Lenin, he could also allow neither peer nor mentor at any stage of his biography. If the unity of the party were to be encapsulated in a single figure, this therefore required an absolute symbiosis between that individual and the party. The cult of personal modesty did not from this perspective imply self-depreciation; it meant an uncompromised claim to wider prerogatives that were those of the party alone. According to his acolyte Lazar Kaganovich, Stalin's most characteristic attribute was never to have diverged from Lenin, never to have vacillated to right or self-styled left, and to have made incarnate in himself 'all of the chief features of the Bolshevik Party'.[32] If this was the mystery of ministry Bolshevik party-style, the significance of the integration cult was that 'all its chief features' were corporealised in this way.

This figure therefore had to bear an enormous symbolic weight. If Stalin encapsulated the unity of the party, the party itself encapsulated both the unity of theory and practice, which was the key to its vanguard role, and the coming together under its leadership of the diverse social groupings whose interests lay in socialism. Both intellectually and socially the integration cult therefore demanded either some particular profile of recognised pre-eminence, as classically identified for example with the leading role of the working class, or else a more protean quality through which the disparate features of the cult community were encompassed in a higher synthesis. More precisely, to the extent that the ideal of the integration figure was fully accomplished, there was a shift from the first to the second of these as projections of the leader took on progressively more fantastical and all-embracing forms. This will be clearly demonstrated if we consider in turn first the intellectual and then the social characteristics of the integrating figure.

Intellectually, the critical notion of genius was already established in Lenin's time to signal mastery at once of marxist theory and revolutionary practice, and, even more than that, the conjoining of the two. This vaunted unity of theory and practice, and the expression of one through the other, was equally a feature of the derivative Stalin cult. Kaganovich and others strongly emphasised it in *Pravda*'s 50th birthday tributes, and in presenting these to a French audience Cachin described Stalin as the very definition of the 'modern, authentic and complete' revolutionary leader.[33] The designation of Stalin himself as a genius, according to Dmitri Volkogonov, came with the Congress of Victors.[34]

Two further attributes of his genius were those of infallibility and omnicompetence. Implicitly, infallibility was also familiar through Lenin's example, which Bolsheviks had not made a habit of subjecting to critique. Nevertheless, it was Stalin who in 1931 aggressively reaffirmed this position in a much-publicised intervention in the journal *Proletarskaya Revolyutsiya* which denounced the notion that Lenin's political judgement may ever in any aspect have been found wanting.[35] The target at this point was 'Luxemburgism', whose rebuttal was the signal that marxism contained within it no scope for alternatives.[36] Through Marx's commemoration on the half-centenary of his death in 1933, and that of Engels on the 40th anniversary of his in 1935, a longer succession was depicted in which at every stage the unity of theory and practice was personified in some towering figure whom none could match unless it was their successor. A characteristic contemporary practice, adopted in the pages that follow, was to refer to them as the 'Four Giants'.[37]

Though Lenin was beyond meaningful criticism, Tumarkin notes that his cult did not at first involve a claim to authority in other fields than politics.[38] Stalin too did not initially pretend to omnicompetence. In attempted negation of Trotsky's better-founded credentials, his 50th birthday tributes did bring to light Stalin's hitherto unsuspected brilliance as civil-war military leader.[39] Theoretical accomplishments were also stressed, and Tucker refers to a 'mono-authority regime' being established in philosophy, though still in the early 1930s this was through Lenin rather than directly through Stalin.[40] In any case, it required the subjection to party control of ever wider fields of activity for Stalin's genius itself to be conceived of in truly polymathic terms. With the famous exposition he provided of dialectical materialism, the *Short Course* party history of

1938 already melded teleology, ideology and personality into one of the truly defining stalinist texts. By the time of his 70th birthday, Stalin was hailed a genius as a matter of course, and more particularly now through the 'Stalinist military science' which during the war he had demonstrated with 'magnificent singleness of purpose through co-ordinated operations on several fronts … through one strategic plan and the single guiding will of the Supreme Commander-in-Chief'.[41]

If the figure of the Generalissimo was the militarised version of the integration cult, Stalin also in this period came to be venerated as the 'coryphaeus of science', and of human knowledge in general.[42] In France, a commission of philosophers, scientists and historians expounded the principles, not of the party of a new type, but of the new type of savant that was to head it. Rigorous, universal and encyclopaedic, stalinist science was the 'fundamental science of our times', and the Four Giants 'universal thinkers' who acted as the leaders, guides and educators of the working class.[43] Concluding the 'hommages' with which *La Pensée* marked Stalin's anniversary, the child psychologist Henri Wallon evoked the strategists, thinkers, popular leaders and statesmen whose greatness was already known to history. 'But does one know of anyone who has combined in himself all these forms of genius, and can one deny this Stalin?'[44]

The logic of the integration cult did not only lie in its tapering to a single point. There was also its dependence upon claims that few or none could entertain who did not already subscribe to its basic postulates. This was obviously true of Stalin's 'penetrating many-sidedness', and the very notion of a multiform genius carried diminishing conviction in an age that was self-consciously one of professionalisation and functional specialisation. Like the diversion of internationalism into the marking of Stalin's birthday, there was therefore an older ideal buried in the reaction against this 'narrow specialisation' and the celebration through Stalin of the 'very breadth of … wisdom and experience' that supposedly informed his writings. For the British crystallographer J.D. Bernal, himself a thinker of polymathic ambitions, it conjured up the many-sided prodigies of the Renaissance which capitalism had whittled down through the division of labour.[45] In France, a commission of communist historians conceded that their academic colleagues might demur from their championship of Thorez as a 'historian of a new type'. Their rationale in nevertheless doing so was not merely the unity of theory and practice, through Thorez's role in actually making history, but the breaching of the compartmentalisation of the bourgeois academy.[46] None but a communist could have entertained such claims. The manufactured character of the integration cult, and of the qualities ascribed to the object of the cult, were thus intrinsically linked with the bounded character of the imagined cult community.

(ii)

Socially, the assumption by the cult object of the same encompassing character was more ambiguous. A real or purported identification with different class environments might in theory assist the enkindling of the broadest possible political constituency; but equally it could help to cement the socially disparate ranks of the monolithic state or party in the manner of the integration cult. Moreover, while the achievement of a polymorphous social identity might in certain cases capture the idea of working-class advancement within a single exemplary career narrative, as notably in respect of Thorez, this had to be set against a notion of incorruptibility as expressed in the inalienability of one's social roots. There were in any case limits to the manufacturing of identity. While the massaging of social credentials was to varying degrees a routine feature of communist politics, it was also subject to diverse forms of verification. These ranged from documented work and associational experiences to the very accents in which one spoke, to say nothing of one's sex, race or ethnicity. For all these reasons there remained considerable variation in the assumed social character of the cult figures heading each communist party by the late 1940s. Indeed, the initial importance of a proletarian social identity was to some extent subsumed within the more indeterminate figure that on the one hand transcended it, and on the other could be made to accommodate whichever individual had Stalin's preferment.

The pre-eminent social type was nevertheless initially the worker.[47] During the power struggles of the 1920s, it was Stalin's plebeian identity that set him apart within a Bolshevik leadership predominantly comprising intellectuals, and at least until the 1940s his dress, speech and public demeanour remained those of the putative worker.[48] At the same time, he was uneasy with the peasant origins recorded on his passport, and this was a point on which Barbusse was asked to amend the draft of his Stalin biography.[49]

The bolshevisation of the Comintern that coincided with Stalin's emergence as its dominant personality was also a process of aggressive proletarianisation, both symbolically and in respect of the composition of leading party bodies. For a decade from 1926, the Comintern's International Lenin School turned out hundreds of cadres for leadership positions according to clear and explicit class criteria. Though advancement from this cohort to the very highest positions did not usually occur until a later period, similar criteria operated in respect of those already installed as their parties' leaders. The 'Stalin generation' was thus one essentially comprising workers by origin, and in each case this was central to their political persona. Thorez's *Son of the People* was an archetypal representation; beginning with scenes of France's northern coalfields, its opening declaration, 'son and grandson of miners', would become familiar to every French communist.[50] Pollitt, a boilermaker, was a worker to the core; the Australian Jack Miles an unassuming stonemason whom a budding cult transformed into 'inspiring proletarian patriarch'.[51] José Díaz first worked as a baker, which certainly counted for less, but with a precocious advancement to union and other labour movement responsibilities in his native Seville.[52]

First of them all was the former Hamburg dockworker Thälmann. Within a party initially dominated by intellectuals, Thälmann had entered the leadership as embodiment of its 'healthy proletarian elements' and as such had enjoyed Stalin's direct protection when scandal threatened his party career in 1928.[53] Powerfully built with 'two strong fists', he stood for a combative and somewhat militarised conception of workers' struggle that clearly differentiated his party from the reformist labour bureaucracy of the Weimar years. Barbusse in a biographical pamphlet would describe him as 'moulded and constructed' by the crowd which Thälmann truly did personify, theatrically ripping off his collar and virtually haranguing them in his Hamburg dialect. There were no pretensions at this stage to the claims of the theoretician, and the liberties Thälmann took with conventional grammar merely reinforced the close rapport between speaker and audience. It seemed, wrote Barbusse, 'as if they spoke with his voice', and already contemporary reports refer to protracted ovations and 'the proletarian love of the masses for their revolutionary Führer'. With the turn to the figure of the leader in 1934, it was Thälmann whose example Dutt in Britain urged on Pollitt, as he envisaged for him the 'full Thaelmann position' as 'visible leader' of a mass opposition movement who at the same time would bind the 'scattered strands' of party organisation in the manner of the integration cult.[54]

Thorez would not have ripped off his collar, nor was he much enamoured of the clenched-fist rituals of Thälmann's party.[55] His roots in class as lived experience were certainly no less central to his public persona, but in a popular-front inflexion in which the workers held not just the future in their hands but every past and present legacy worth preserving. Thorez's faithful scribe and panegyrist Jean Fréville located him in a lineage of outstanding French workers' leaders of whom Thorez alone, nevertheless, was himself also a worker. 'With you we go into the country of slag-heaps', Fréville began his poem 'After a reading of *Son of the People*'—the autobiography which Fréville had himself also written for Thorez—and in one of his cultlike character sketches he evoked Thorez's immediate rapport with his own people as he ventured down a mine.[56] It was 'Maurice' whose first name alone identified him, as likewise 'Teddy' Thälmann and 'Pepe' Díaz, with a familiarity recalling both the 'Ilyich' of the Lenin cult and the camaraderie of the workshop. Nevertheless, in Thorez's case, recognition of his humble origins was progressively combined with pride in what he had since achieved without betraying those origins. To be born a son of the people was simple, one admirer wrote; what traitors like Tito showed was how difficult it was to remain one.[57] Combining both rootedness and attainment, Thorez was thus addressed by supporters as variously the 'Statesman of a new type, faithful to your origins', the 'teenage miner who became … the revered and beloved leader of our Great Party', the son of the people who was also the 'living exemplar of the ascent of the working class, which in its own breast forges … the genuine elites of today and tomorrow'.[58]

With the tempering by the 1940s of the Stalin generation's proletarian ethos, a cultic status was extended to certain survivors of an earlier formation whose parties had hitherto been proscribed and who had therefore operated either clandestinely or in exile until the end of the war. Otto Wille Kuusinen did not return to his native Finland even then. Graduating from Helsinki University in the revolutionary year of 1905, Kuusinen became a revolutionary social democrat and was one of the leaders of the short-lived Finnish workers' republic of 1918 before subsequently assuming high office for the Comintern.[59] As notional head of the puppet 'people's government', established as an instrument of the Soviet–Finnish war in 1939, Kuusinen personified his party's Soviet links and from 1941 was even a member of the CPSU central committee. To celebrate his 70th birthday, as his party did in 1951, was therefore an embattled and almost gratuitous gesture of identification with a figure whom many Finns regarded as a national traitor.[60] Kuusinen's was now portrayed as the leading role throughout his party's history, to the exclusion of those other figures, like Kullervo Manner, whose ousting and subsequent persecution were the counterpart and condition of his own aggrandisement. Kuusinen's cult, even so, was very much the cult of the theoretician or party intellectual, overshadowing the activist mentality and impatience with 'academic science' which had been foregrounded when he was still primarily a Comintern leader.[61]

In terms of background, career and mindset, Kimmo Rentola notes the resemblance between Kuusinen and the Italian Togliatti, leader of the one western communist party whose membership and electoral base was consolidated and even enhanced during the Cold War.[62] Born in 1893, Togliatti's 60th-birthday commemorations centred on the substantial biographical productions that he had previously lacked. There was no dissimulation in this case of how Togliatti came to the workers' struggle from without, or of the sharpness of the break this required with his family environment.[63] On the contrary, an aspirational story was told in which Togliatti and his siblings all achieved for themselves positions of some professional standing. Perhaps this betrayed the sensitivity to Italy's 'numerically so important' middle classes that so distinguished Togliatti and his party.[64] There is even an admission of physical frailty as a factor extenuating Togliatti's unfamiliarity with manual labour and his initial hesitation in definitively committing to communism.[65] While a similar fragility had also figured in the image of Díaz, who died so prematurely, it was conspicuously absent in the invocations of Thälmann's iron constitution, or of the rock-like Thorez whose stroke in 1950 so dumbfounded his supporters. Both apt and indispensable in Togliatti's case was the legitimising foundation cult of Gramsci as the consummate intellectual in politics.[66]

Togliatti could never have been described as 'son of the people'. Nevertheless, the designation of one of his cult biographies as the 'life of an Italian' was not just a personal idiosyncrasy but represented a wider turn to nationality and ethnicity as key defining features of the integration cult.[67] In the Soviet context, Olga Velikanova notes how already circumspection regarding Lenin's family origins had shifted over time from the issue of class and Lenin's noble status to that of nationality and the 'non-Russian' elements in his background.[68] Internationally, one sees a similar shift in the case of another of the pre-Stalin generation, Mátyás Rákosi. The food commissar in the Hungarian soviet government of March–August 1919, Rákosi then spent 15 years in the prisons of the dictator Horthy following a spell of activity in the early Comintern apparatus. Hailed as the 'Hungarian Dimitrov', he was already one of the Comintern's best-known personalities through the international publicity given his trials in 1925–1926 and 1934–1935.[69] Less fortunate, ironically, was Béla Kun, Hungary's most senior communist and a Comintern colleague of Kuusinen's and Togliatti's who perished in Stalin's purges. Released through an agreement with the Soviets in 1940, it was, conversely, Rákosi the class-war prisoner who survived to enjoy one of the most extravagant of the post-war leader cults.

Both Rákosi and Kun, a former law student, were Jewish. In campaigning material from the popular front years this was not necessarily regarded as a liability. Rákosi was 'not a worker, like Thaelmann', but his educational strivings were sympathetically invoked as characteristic of the Jewish petty bourgeoisie.[70] His prison experiences remained a crucial aspect of his biography, and in the heavy use of national symbols his post-war cult did not so much emphasise statesmen and state-builders as Rákosi's role as the last in a line of Hungarian freedom-fighters.[71] Nevertheless, there was no further mention of his Jewishness and a proletarianisation of his biography took place that was also a form of de-judaisation.[72]

Jewishness posed particular sensitivities given the simultaneous deployment of anti-Semitism both as an instrument of anti-communism and in the guise of anti-cosmopolitanism by communists themselves. Already in Lenin's case, concerns with popular anti-Semitism had lent their particular edge to the preservation of his image as an ethnic Russian, and Trotsky described his own Jewishness as a possible obstacle to his occupying the foremost role in the Soviet state.[73] The preferment as the Czechoslovakian party's general secretary of Klement Gottwald, another of the Stalin generation, has similarly been ascribed by Kriegel to his having neither the Jewish, the petty-bourgeois nor the minority national background that, already in 1929, disqualified his major rivals.[74]

In Hungary, where Rákosi was vilified as 'king of the Jews', both leader and party did more to accommodate such attitudes than to challenge them.[75] In neighbouring Romania, the issue was compounded in the case of Ana Pauker by the fact of her also being a woman. Like Rákosi, Pauker had come to international prominence through a pre-war political trial in which she symbolised not only her party's struggles but the persecution of Romania's Jews.[76] Returning from Moscow exile in 1944, she occupied successive government posts and in some accounts appears as the country's dominant leader behind the scenes. Nevertheless, Pauker claimed afterwards to have ruled herself out as party leader, reminding Dimitrov: 'I'm a woman, a Jew, and an intellectual.'[77] Just as Gottwald continued to enjoy Stalin's favour, the same preferment fell in any case on the railwayman and ethnic Romanian Gheorghe Gheorghiu-Dej. Arrested in February 1953, Pauker was spared a show trial only by the good fortune of Stalin's death.

Stalin himself, of course, was not an ethnic Russian but known to all as a Georgian—if only because Lenin had once referred to him as the 'wonderful Georgian'. Through art works and historical materials assembled in the late 1930s this Georgian component of Stalin's identity was actively publicised; and, while in some instances his representation in films was Russianised, the defining performances in *The Vow* (1946) and *The Fall of Berlin* (1949) were by the heavily Georgian-accented Mikhail Gelovani.[78] As Alfred J. Rieber has argued, in both class and ethnic terms Stalin nevertheless constructed a multiple identity conceived as appealing across his party and neutralising the threat posed by wider divisions in Soviet society.[79] Ethnic particularism was thus at no stage to detract from the state or federation as primary identity through what Plamper refers to as Soviet universalism.[80] Prokofiev's Stalin cantata, despite its use of texts of diverse purported origins, has thus been linked with a form of Russification through a 'musical language ... represent[ing] a unified whole which models itself exclusively on the Russian classics'.[81]

The same basic logic might certainly apply in other heterogeneous societies. Nevertheless, it was not usually Rieber's 'man of the borderlands' who served as a vehicle for some common identifier, but a figure conforming to some implicit norm or counter-norm. Browder, for example, was presented as 'the champion of America's foreign-born' who revelled in the epithet of the 'Negro party'. Nevertheless, he did so as one who advertised his deep ancestral roots in the white settler experience as 'just about the most thoroughly American figure' in the country's political life.[82] There is certainly a parallel between Rákosi's grandfather, said to have taken part in the national struggle of 1848–1849, and the Littleberry Browder who reputedly had fought with Thomas Jefferson in 1776.[83] James B. Ford was a Fisk University graduate of considerable personal and physical presence, but he stood out among the CPUSA's leading black organisers because of his unreserved commitment to Browder and the party's predominantly white leadership. Three times in presidential elections, Ford stood as running mate in turn to Foster and to Browder, but the CPUSA was not so much a Negro party as to have reversed the roles.[84]

In Brazil, it was to an imagined black lover that Jorge Amado addressed his Prestes biography. Nevertheless, it was Prestes himself who represented the Brazilian people in all its diversity, and whom Amado likened to the nineteenth-century 'poet of the slaves' Castro Alves as the voice through which Brazil's black population expressed itself.[85] In Switzerland, cantonisation may have been a factor in the failure to emerge of any single dominant figure.[86] In Australia, Miles's obvious Scottish origins may have detracted from the 'patriotic status' enjoyed by a Pollitt or a Thorez.[87] In South Africa and divided Ireland, leadership figures from respectively the white and Ulster protestant minorities could also not be elevated in this way. There was therefore no real sequel to the briefly flickering Irish cult of Sean Murray, whose main popularity was in Dublin; while in South Africa it was the black communist Moses Kotane who from the mid-1930s was unambiguously his party's figurehead.[88]

The fully developed integration figure was therefore both socially and ethnically an encompassing one. In venturing with Thorez among the slag-heaps, Fréville's poem, as we saw, began with the bedrock of Thorez's political identity. Nevertheless, in the stanzas that followed Fréville also went with Thorez among metalworkers, dockers, the aged, students, peasants and Catholics. With all such groups Thorez was said to speak a common language, and on being asked to identify his outstanding quality, each of a dozen respondents answered differently.[89] Even before the war, Thorez was described by one party intellectual as the 'prototype of the new man' who as worker and intellectual harmoniously incorporated 'all of the ancestral qualities of the French people'.[90] After the war, such tributes became almost formulaic. One described him as a militant worker, statesman, economist and philosopher; while Fréville characteristically linked his 'continuous ascent' with the ability to discourse freely with the epoch's greatest minds without relinquishing his ties to the common people.[91]

Elsewhere too, this was now a stock motif. Gottwald's career was thus also described as a progression through different milieux connecting him with peasants, artisans and factory proletariat, and finally the administrators and intellectuals who marvelled at his cultural range and technical competence.[92] Even Pollitt in Britain, the least likely such figure, was fitfully acclaimed as theoretician. The one aspect in which Thorez's cult was nevertheless taken further than any contemporary's was its extension to his second wife and political co-worker Jeannette Vermeersch. The collaboration of Lenin and Krupskaya had already been offered as the virtually perfect example of a union combining love, equality and shared political purpose.[93] Nevertheless, stability in personal relations, idealised even in Lenin's case, was not in general easy to reconcile with the exacting demands of the Comintern period. Cult biographies did not much dwell on marital histories and these were sometimes sufficiently compromised as to be passed over or actively dissimulated—as most brutally in the case of Stalin's wife Nadezhda Alliluyeva, who committed suicide in

1932. For Dimitrov, Pollitt and even Stalin himself, an exemplary history might be humanised and authenticated in the figure of the leader's mother. Much rarer was a figure like Olga Prestes, German wife of Luis Carlos Prestes, who as prisoner and victim of the Nazis was allowed a sort of companionate role in her husband's cult.[94]

Thorez too did not advertise the break-up of his first marriage. On the other hand, Vermeersch even before the war was brought forward as connubial helpmate, notably in an unshown publicity film for *Son of the People*: as if substantiating in scenes of domesticity the embrace of the traditional roles and values represented by the PCF's 'outstretched hand' (*main tendue*) to Catholic France.[95] Active in this period in the communist youth organisation, the *Union des jeunes filles de France*, Vermeersch shared Thorez's wartime exile in Moscow, and on her return assumed a high political profile as a deputy, a central committee member and a leading figure in the women's organisation, the *Union des femmes françaises* (UFF). As Thorez's cult reached its height, images with wife and children frequently predominated over more conventional political scenes, presumably in recognition of France's new female electorate and as a demonstration by example of the PCF's pro-natalism.[96] Inseparable from Thorez in the public mind, Vermeersch herself was elected to the politburo in May 1950. When five months later Thorez on suffering a stroke took up a further extended residence in the USSR, Vermeersch became unmistakably established as custodian and joint beneficiary of the Thorez cult itself.

Not surprisingly, this comes across most strongly in the messages and resolutions of communist women's organisations. Trade unionists addressed their 'sister in struggle' as their leader, standard-bearer and model 'in all domains', alluding, as in many such communications, to the responsibilities for family and ailing husband that Vermeersch combined with her diverse political roles.[97] A Paris women's meeting evoked the 'consummate harmony' of the Thorez menage, and the feelings of indebtedness as well as cordiality that marked the authentic cult relationship:

> INDEFECTIBLE FRIENDSHIP because they feel in you the sister, the sensitive, humane woman, the mother with a noble heart who understands their troubles, their anxieties, their sufferings …
>
> INFINITE GRATITUDE because you are at the forefront of all the women of France, the greatest Fighter for Peace who has shown them the path to follow …[98]

Despite the later notoriety of Romania's Ceauşescu family cult, the standing accorded Vermeersch was in this period a PCF peculiarity, and it would add its own distinctive edge to the party's leadership rivalries.[99]

No practice better captures the logic of the integration cult than the celebration of the leader's birthday. Cohen describes this as stalinism's central cultic practice and one that marked the collapsing of the distinction between the public and private spheres.[100] Precedents for the practice can be traced within the socialist movement. In Stalin's particular case, it could also signal the passing from the dead to the living leader, for Lenin until the Khrushchev years was always commemorated on the anniversary of his death. Nevertheless, as the practice was generalised through whichever chosen vessel Stalin favoured, the dignification of the non-event of the birthday signalled the elevation of office over achievement, and an arbitrary preferment that need not depend on any particular personal history or capacity.

In dynastic systems where power and prerogative were a matter of birthright, it is not surprising that royal birthdays should be celebrated. In Hitler's case too, the extreme personalisation of authority was reflected in the annual celebration of his birthday as a focal point of the Nazi calendar.[101] In France, the Victor Hugo birthday celebrations of 1881 marked the transition to a laic cult of greatness in which the republic was apotheosised in the shape of its leading personality.[102] Similar practices were also adopted by radical movements focused on some dominant leading figure, as for example Garveyism; or as a way of subverting and appropriating establishment rituals, as in the case of older English radical movements.[103] Nevertheless, even Mussolini was sufficiently a radical in his own perception, or self-conscious enough about his age, that his regime did not commemorate his birthday but the symbolic breakthrough of the March on Rome.[104] Though in this case it was more overtly personalised, the same was essentially true of Atatürk Commemoration Day in Turkey.[105] Not every communist leader could celebrate a successful workers' revolution or the defiance of the Nazis from the dock. On the other hand, any functionary spared the hazards of the struggle, or of Stalin's terror, could have some hope of reaching 50.

This therefore was not a mark of distinction but its negation, which at the same time implicitly defined the cult community in purely party terms. In this respect the wonted intimacy of the birthday ritual was reproduced as a sort of collective turning inwards, with a difference principally of scale. Of all the western parties, this again was particularly a feature of the PCF, and may be seen in part as a borrowing back of practices originating in France's own republican tradition. It was with just this reference to indigenous custom that already in 1936 *L'Humanité* announced the marking of respectively the 50th and 40th birthdays of André Marty and Jacques Duclos.[106] Nevertheless, it was not just the turn from the event to the person, but the association of the person with the most banal of human landmarks, that in due course became the hallmark of the stalinist politics of commemoration.

Even in Stalin's case, the practice was principally confined to the decennial markers. There was thus a reining in of early efforts on his 55th birthday in 1934, most likely because of the dramatic shift in the political atmosphere following Kirov's murder in the weeks immediately before.[107] With the exception of imprisoned leaders whose predicament was thereby publicised, the same limitation was mostly observed by other communist parties. The PCF however was an exception.[108] Already during the war, Thorez's April birthday was marked by clandestine party organs.[109] In 1944, with attention turning to his impending return, there were clear signs of co-ordinated activities.[110] Even so, it is in 1947, as Cold War tensions mounted, that the first large files of greetings appear representing what was henceforth a systematic campaign of commemoration. Already there are typed lists of these communications; by 1950, there are printed forms and postcards, and the messages have been individually numbered and sorted into categories.[111]

Thanks to their collation by Thorez's secretariat, it is immediately obvious that virtually every communication emanates from within the world of the communists themselves. In both form and content, these were the esoteric practices that marked out the boundaries of the fortress party. As epitomised again by the role fictitiously accorded Thorez in the resistance, the leadership claims thus advanced demanded of the celebrants an active suspension of disbelief whether out of solidarity, faith or party discipline.[112] Numerous resolutions spelt out the underlying logic: that the more violently Thorez was attacked, the more fervently his supporters would rally round him, forming, according to one such resolution, 'but a single bloc behind our central committee and its leader'.[113] The logic of the integration cult was of an outwardly sealed political formation, not at all resembling the atomised mass that Arendt imagined, but nevertheless uniting around the single, clearly identified individual at its head.

3.3 'By Desert and Accident': The Enkindling Figure

(i)

In his biography of Thorez, Philippe Robrieux grouped the Scotsman Willie Gallacher with Thälmann and Togliatti as part of a cohort of cult figures elevated at Stalin's instigation in the mid-1930s.[114] Though Robrieux rightly described the claim as speculative, it has since reappeared in a number of other accounts, still in the absence of any real supporting evidence.[115] In Gallacher's case, the supposition of a cult of personality rests upon the publication in the summer of 1936 of his autobiography *Revolt on the Clyde*: harbinger as it appears of the new genre of leaders' lives which the following year would include Thorez's own *Son of the People*. Gallacher, even so, was not his party's general secretary, nor had he any pretensions to the topmost position in its leadership hierarchy. Instead, the immediate occasion for his autobiography was his being returned to parliament as the CPGB's sole MP in the general election of November 1935.

In proportion to his party's capacities, one can certainly see why Gallacher might be identified with the personality cult. As well as a platform aura that drew large crowds, there were birthday commemorations, tributes in prose and verse, above all the personal history on which Gallacher drew prolifically in several volumes of autobiography.[116] When the CPGB in 1936 campaigned around 'The March of English History', it was with Gallacher's return to parliament that the chronology culminated.[117] When three years later it published the *Handbook of Freedom*—'a record of English democracy through twelve centuries'—it was *Revolt on the Clyde* which provided concluding extracts.[118] When in 1945 the CPGB experimented with a free congress vote for the party's executive committee, it was Gallacher and not Pollitt who topped the poll.[119] Through translation of one or other of his autobiographies into the languages of most of the major communist parties, Gallacher also stood as a symbol of the militant British worker for the wider communist world. In contrast to Thorez or Togliatti, however, Gallacher's was at no point the cult of the party leader singular. Its rationale, at the time of his election as MP, was not that of holding the party as a cult community together. Its principal forms of expression and its political character were also rather different.

The integration cult implied a single overriding unifying symbol. Its construction required both the projection through this individual of generic claims and attributes, and the exclusion, diminution or subordination through some manifest hierarchy of alternative claimants to some or other aspect of pre-eminence. If *Revolt on the Clyde* stood for something rather different from this, it was through the exploitation of resources and opportunities that arose, and to some extent were even sustained, independently of the process of party cult-building. This was not primarily the projection onto Gallacher of the institutional identity he was meant to translate into flesh and blood. Rather, it was the exploitation for party ends of political assets which were distinctly and even inimitably Gallacher's own.

These opportunities did not arise solely from circumstances of the party's own making, nor was there any inherent reason why the ascription of exceptional qualities should be confined to a single individual or social type. Usually the individual's marking out did result in or coincide with the holding of some key party office. Nevertheless, the enkindling figure was never simply derived from that office and the bureaucratic procedures by which it was filled. By the late 1940s, these bureaucratic procedures, as personified in the figure of the general secretary, were becoming ever more pervasive. One result was the rendering innocuous of such figures through incorporation, subordination or the anathematisation of exclusion or the show trial. The enkindling figure, by contrast, had implied the eschewal of a language and ritual accessible only to devotees, and its promotion instead in forms and genres both familiar and acceptable to some wider population, however this was defined. As such, this was a phenomenon far more of the pre-war phase of cult-building than of the fortress mentality of the Cold War.

That Gallacher represented the CPGB in parliament was not something the party itself entirely controlled. In the 1935 election it had fielded just two candidates, partly as a gesture towards unity, but also as a way of concentrating resources on its two most credible public figures. The priority was the provision with a parliamentary platform of Pollitt as the party's general secretary. Pollitt accordingly was airlifted into the South Wales constituency in which the CPGB's support was strongest.[120] Wherever he stood, Pollitt would have had to reconcile national campaigning commitments with the necessary attendance to his prospective constituency.[121] In Britain's system of mainly single-member constituencies, the further unpredictability was introduced of the uncertainty in any single case as to which other parties would put up candidates. When unexpectedly the Liberals withdrew locally, Pollitt was faced with a straight fight against the sitting Labour MP and his success now depended on securing an absolute majority of the votes. No communist candidate in Britain ever attained this threshold. Although polling slightly worse than Pollitt, it was Gallacher, already long since rooted in his coalfield constituency of West Fife, who took up his parliamentary seat on a plurality of the votes.

Such an opportunity brought its own claims to precedence. Three months later Gallacher was said to be continuously on the move and capitalising on his drawing power 'practically every day and night'.[122] His credentials for his parliamentary nomination included a matchless record of activity in the west of Scotland, and he had planned a book about this even before he became an MP.[123] Possibly it was discussed in Moscow; but there is no particular mystery in Gallacher's now rushing through the project. If one thing came more easily to Scottish labour leaders than to Stalin, it was writing autobiographies. The very month that Gallacher entered parliament, one of them, the Clydeside MP David Kirkwood, had published his own account of the wartime struggles in which both he and Gallacher had made their reputations.[124] Politically and personally they were close; Gallacher began sitting next to Kirkwood in the Commons and would refer to him as a 'revered and never-failing pal'.[125] But at the same time, he and his party had their own claims to the Clydeside legacy, and Gallacher in his very title echoed Kirkwood's *My Life of Revolt*.

Nothing could have spoken more directly to the traditions of the British labour movement than *Revolt on the Clyde*. As the protocols of his party required, Gallacher rejected the notion that the vote he received in Fife was a personal one.[126] In recording his election as the crowning denouement of an autobiography, he did nevertheless represent it as the culmination of a personal history of struggle. The explicit object of Stalin's biographies was to depict a life inseparable from that of the party which he led.[127] Gallacher, conversely, told of chapters mostly predating the party's existence, and if anything tending to stamp the party with his own image. 'Certainly Gallacher is an egotist', wrote a communist reviewer, 'a healthy and vibrant egotist. … The main lesson to be drawn from the book is that however courageous and militant the workers may be, they are almost certainly doomed to failure without an equally courageous, trained and level-headed leadership—and an organisation built around this leadership.'[128]

The text was not primarily intended for internal party use. Pollitt likened Gallacher's lone parliamentary role to Dimitrov's stance at Leipzig, with the party outside providing support.[129] Gallacher, however, also aspired to the closest relations with his Labour colleagues. His advocacy of unity through the CPGB's affiliation to the Labour Party went further than any other communist leader's, even if necessary at the expense of Comintern disaffiliation.[130] It was in just this spirit that Gallacher through his autobiography rehearsed a story of workshop struggles and political battles in which a generation of Labour veterans had also played their part. The Comintern itself would barely have registered had it not been for the much-recounted meeting with Lenin that was so much part of the Gallacher legend.

According to E.H. Carr, not yet the historian of Soviet Russia, Gallacher was 'by desert and accident' the CPGB's most representative figure, displaying not the 'esoteric side of party life', but its public face as 'an extreme Left wing within the British parliamentary system'.[131] Where the Thorez of *Son of the People* was a 'bureaucratic' and 'impersonal' construction unimaginable without his party, the strength of Gallacher's biographical persona lay in the framing of a personal quality or experience that he brought to the party rather than derived from it.[132] The young Michael Foot, a future Labour Party leader, ascribed the wider support Gallacher attracted to his 'fine sense of humour, a colourful taste in platform epithets, huge powers of endurance, and … unflinching and almost ascetic devotion to a cause'.[133] A later communist reviewer even had him standing out against the 'regimentation of parties' as the 'very antithesis of the political and party bureaucrat'. Freely indulging in humour and invective, he so entertained the reader with 'loops of reminiscence, sidelines of anecdote, outbursts of indignation or affirmation' that one almost failed to notice the importance of the social issues he gave voice to.[134]

(ii)

Spontaneity in the abstract is a hazardous notion. Its usefulness in the marxist tradition is nevertheless in signifying external contingencies arising independently of the conscious political direction of the marxists themselves. The disposition of candidates and votes in a parliamentary election is one example. Experience and kudos accruing to the party through the individual is another. Gallacher was already nearly 40 when he became a communist. Born in 1892, Luis Carlos Prestes was a decade younger, but by the age of 30 had achieved an almost mythical status hardly imaginable in prosaic Britain. A young army officer influenced by the reforming *tenentista* movement, Prestes had between 1925 and 1927 led a paramilitary faction known as the Prestes Column some 15,000 miles across Brazil. Stirring up revolt as he went, Prestes—the Cavalier of Hope (*Cavaleiro da Esperança*)—has been likened to a latter-day Robin Hood, defying and eluding his pursuers through what some described as a gift of second sight.[135]

Prestes at this time had no knowledge of marxism nor any significant contact with the communist movement. When in 1930–1931 he did first move into the ambit of the Brazilian communist party (PCB), there was scepticism as to *Prestismo*'s petty-bourgeois character and what leading communist Fernando Lacerda referred to as the 'belief in "elites", "heroes", or "cavaliers of hope" '.[136] Four years spent in Moscow brought a closer understanding, and when Prestes returned to Brazil in 1935 he was advanced to the PCB politburo. Doubts nevertheless remained, which Dimitrov apparently shared, and the explicit rationale was therefore spelt out of establishing a 'complete, firm, and indivisible bond between the proletarian leadership of the Party, and the national popular hero'.[137]

In March 1936 Prestes was arrested following the failed insurrection of the 'National Liberation Alliance' (*Aliança Nacional Libertadora*). Sentenced to 16 years' imprisonment, he now became the focus of an international campaigning effort as symbol of the struggle against the Vargas dictatorship. Though imprisonment alone was not sufficient to generate such activity, it does once more emerge as a key component of communist cult-building, particularly at the international level. In Brazil itself the party maintained a tenuous and somewhat disunited existence. Still in prison, it was Prestes who at its provisional conference of August 1943 was elected general secretary. On being amnestied in April 1945, he assumed his public role as leader during a two-year period in which the PCB enjoyed both full legal rights and a much expanded membership and electoral base. Older party cadres remained divided as to his leadership credentials.[138] Nevertheless, a well-informed observer described the PCB as now 'a Prestista party almost more than … a Communist Party', with a popularity deriving in large measure from Prestes's personal following.[139]

Even more than with Gallacher, the centrepiece of the Prestes cult was a book. In the late 1930s, Jorge Amado was emerging as one of Brazil's brightest young literary talents as well as a fervent communist. In critical evaluations, *The Cavalier of Hope* does not usually rate among his more memorable achievements. Devotees of the cult biography, on the other hand, will rarely encounter a more highly coloured one. Written in 1941, it was initially published in Spanish translation and its circulation in Brazil required a clandestine campaigning effort which Amado described as itself a crucial weapon in the agitation for Prestes's release.[140]

Though Amado as a novelist broadly adhered to the canons of socialist realism, the demands of actuality drew him into a syncretistic variant of revolutionary romanticism in which the popular ascription of magical properties was so faithfully recorded as might easily be taken for their endorsement. This was very much akin to the use of folkloric or pseudo-folkloric elements to provide a measure of Stalin's greatness in the simple faith and credulity of the common people. In the Brazilian case too, hyperbole was rendered through the images and fetishes of the vernacular. Prestes was not just the son of the people, like his European counterparts, but a 'miracle of the people'. In humble dwellings his image stood with candles lit, like the effigies of saints that were frequently to be found alongside it. Objects he had touched were also preserved as relics; soldiers of his column wished in their final moments only to die in his presence. For these he was a god of battle; others thought him a forest deity whom beasts could not resist, and who read into mortals' inner thoughts.[141]

No cut-and-dried distinction is possible between the integrating and enkindling function. Prestes was in many ways the archetypal integrating figure for a party at once fragmented, disabled by state repression and thinly spread over a vast and heterogeneous country. He certainly represented a pre-eminent social type, though in the Latin American tradition of the radical soldier-hero and through the one profession which, according to Amado, his modest family circumstances allowed.[142] This retained the prestige epitomised in earlier times by the liberator Simón Bolívar, by Benjamin Constant, founder of the Brazilian republic, and by a dozen other such heroes listed both by Amado and by Pablo Neruda in his Prestes cult poem *Hard Elegy*. To Neruda, Prestes was 'our Captain'; to Amado he was the greatest of soldiers in a country of soldiers. In *The Cavalier of Hope* it is the Prestes Column that provides the centrepiece and longest section.[143]

This was quite a contrast with the party-centred narrative of *Son of the People*. The Prestes legend, more perhaps than any other of his leading counterparts', neither derived from nor coincided with the holding of office, nor even, in its principal chapters, with party membership. What it did have in common with that of Stalin was the encompassing character of its vaunted accomplishments. Amado described him as the people itself 'synthesised in the figure of a man'. A general, engineer, geographer, doctor, judge, entrepreneur, worker, administrator and gifted mathematician—as Prestes turned from military exploits to the reclamation of the virgin forest, hardly a field of human endeavour seemed beyond him. To this extent, one may again trace the survival of a polymathic ideal, in this case in a military inflexion which in much of Europe had lost or never had this sort of credibility. As Amado asked ingenuously, what was there indeed that eluded Prestes? 'What detail of human knowledge escapes his prodigious genius?'[144]

(iii)

Though neither Gallacher nor Pollitt seemed singled out by history in this way, both were cut from the same proletarian cloth, and with their skill and masculinity they did also represent a pre-eminent social type. In the CPGB more than most parties, this authenticity of class was indeed an indispensable requirement which Pollitt explicitly privileged in designating his successor as general secretary. 'He is the Worker as Leader', the same communist reviewer wrote of Gallacher. 'Were the platform a mile long he would still dominate it.'[145] Despite this, the attempt to mobilise a wider public through the politics of personality did not have to mean a single domineering social type. On the contrary, its diversification in the image of the popular front might seem to promise a greater effectiveness, exactly as the proletarianisation of leading party bodies gave way to a more socially representative conception of their role.

Even Amado, while hardly setting a limit to Prestes's accomplishments, repeatedly evoked the complementary figure of the Poet through whom the people's aspirations also found expression.[146] Mátyás Rákosi could never have been described in these terms. Nevertheless, for a public of intellectuals he too was presented as a 'revolutionary intellectual' and as a champion of the cause on which their free expression depended.[147] Though his plight was less well-publicised, Gramsci was also presented by the writer Romain Rolland as the intellectual as leader, with a thirst for learning and an intolerance of those who did not share it.[148] The CPGB itself was not so tied to its proletarian origins as to overlook the example of the intellectuals who fought in Spain, and there was a specifically youth or student cult of the dashing and gifted John Cornford, who was killed at Córdoba at the age of 21.[149]

In France the experience of the resistance provided a whole number of such figures. Some survived to take up post-war political roles; others through their sacrifice provided the PCF with an immense reserve of human legitimation. The most widely commemorated of the latter, in poems and in Paris street names, was the *L'Humanité* foreign editor Gabriel Péri, imprisoned by the Nazis in May 1941 and shot the following December. Anything but the worker in his easy social intercourse with his fellow deputies and diplomatic contacts, Péri's projection as an archetype of the intellectual convert to communism was positively accentuated in his post-war memorialisation.[150] Even the monument planned for him eschewed socialist realism for the modernist stylings of the Swiss sculptor Alberto Giacometti.[151] Another *L'Humanité* journalist, Paul Vaillant-Couturier, had until his death in 1937 symbolised the broadening cultural horizons of the popular front. Vaillant-Couturier was to have had his monument designed by the cynosure of architectural modernism, Le Corbusier, representing a book as well as the head and hand of the orator.[152] Neither monument was actually constructed. Like Picasso later on, both Giacometti and Le Corbusier hence discovered that the communists' artistic pluralism did not extend to the representation or commemoration of figures intended as exemplars.[153]

Discrepancy of cult projection and party office was perhaps most strongly marked in Spain. Here too, the civil war period saw the emergence of a distinct youth cult focusing on the future party secretary Santiago Carrillo, at this time the 'rudder and great guide' of the 'great Youth Federation' formed by the merger of the socialist and communist youth movements.[154] More distinctively, there was at the very head of the Spanish party (Partido Comunista de España or PCE) a sort of dual leadership represented by José Díaz and Dolores Ibárruri. It was Díaz who figured on Borkenau's list of spurious supermen 'instituted by orders from above'.[155] 'Likeable but deeply uncharismatic', as Tim Rees describes him, he had been the PCE's general secretary since 1932, and as such enjoyed the usual formal precedence.[156] According to André Marty, reporting on the PCE to the Comintern in 1936, Díaz was head and shoulders above his politburo colleagues, above all in respect of his practical capabilities.[157] In a tribute to another Spanish communist four years later, Marty initially described him as 'along with José Díaz, best-loved by the portworkers', but in the approved cult fashion the formula is corrected to 'after José Diaz'.[158] Though allegations have been made that Díaz was not only murdered but posthumously slighted in 1942, there is no serious evidence for the former claim, and Ibárruri and others paid lavish tribute to Díaz as inspirer of his party and his people.[159]

In Marty's report on the PCE, Ibárruri herself was summed up last and with terse condescension: 'carries out propaganda and work among women'.[160] A politburo member since 1931, Ibárruri had indeed been involved in campaigns like those around the children displaced by the brutal suppression of the Asturias miners' strike in 1934. Attitudes like Marty's do not seem conducive to women emerging in some wider leadership role, and the state personality cults have been described as inherently requiring male protagonists.[161] As Gina Herrmann writes, Ibárruri's use of maternal symbols and an asexual femininity was nevertheless a model of performative leadership that also influenced later figures like Indira Gandhi, who witnessed the 'Dolores effect' in person in 1938.[162] Because of the debilitating health problems that would eventually contribute to Díaz's suicide, Ibárruri was increasingly called upon to share his political responsibilities. But in any case it was also she, better known by the cognomen Pasionaria, who for the public at large had the presence, persona and powers of expression to galvanise opinion and render the Spanish conflict in the compelling accents that its urgency demanded.

Already at the seventh world congress, Ibárruri's eloquence and authenticity had attracted notice—'very plebeian, very Spanish', noted Cachin—and from the early days of the war she and Díaz were noticed internationally as co-leaders of their party.[163] Even Borkenau described her as the one communist loved by the masses, and Paul Preston has noted how she eschewed a narrow party appeal while yet bringing her party huge political benefit as the republic's 'single most representative figure'.[164] It was Pasionaria whom supporters of the Spanish cause apostrophised in verse. It was Pasionaria to whom the CPGB in 1937 devoted one of its first biographical pamphlets. It was Pasionaria who, alone of western communist leaders, also had her speeches, writings and radio broadcasts collected together and distributed internationally.[165] There was at this time no more effective cult figure, not through the playing down of Ibárruri's gender, but through its harnessing and idealisation as the 'widow, mother, sister' who symbolised a people forced into struggle to defend the most basic human values.[166]

The CPGB pamphlet *Pasionaria, the story of a miner's daughter* may perhaps be grouped with *Revolt on the Clyde* and *The Cavalier of Hope*. All were products of Thompson's age of heroes; none depicted a figure who as yet was leader in the formal sense of general secretary. By 1945, both

Prestes and Ibárurri had become so, the latter after a power struggle in which a woman's suitability for such a position was reputedly among the possible objections raised by the Soviets.[167] Both also found their place within the more formalised cult system that centred on the ritual of the leader's birthday. Every Prestes birthday, it was claimed, had since 1947 been a 'political event'; in both cases these were certainly cultural happenings marked by outpourings of verse and song.[168] Both Prestes and Ibárurri also remained figures familiar to communists internationally, though conditions respectively of clandestinity and exile meant that effective political direction was increasingly being exercised by others. By the time the cults were brought into question in 1956, even Ibárurri, now her party's 'grand arbiter', was functioning essentially as a focal point of integration and control in an atmosphere of bitter political in-fighting.[169]

The CPGB by comparison remained as durable in its inner core as a well-established family firm. Living in his town of birth and unmolested by the authorities, Gallacher died in 1965, still writing autobiographies. Nevertheless, the transition to something more like the integration cult was also evident in the British party's case. The declension from a public figure to an essentially party one was symbolised for Gallacher by the loss of his parliamentary platform in 1950, and his compensation instead with the honorific office of party chairman. That his light among comrades remained undimmed was evidenced by the 70th birthday celebrations that followed two years after Stalin's in 1951. Even so, Pollitt's primacy as general secretary was in a double sense subtly confirmed.

The first was that of Gallacher's dignification as a sort of party elder, addressed now as the party's 'Grand Old Man', like the octogenarian Cachin in France.[170] The second was that of his localising as a Scot, who on his 70th birthday was celebrated in Glasgow with Burns renditions, birthday toasts in dialect and a dedicatory poem set to *The Road to the Isles*.[171] Notably, it was also Hugh MacDiarmid, a staunch Scottish nationalist but not at this point a CPGB member, who was asked to write the cult poem 'Scottish Universal'. Scots were anything but peripheral to the CPGB leadership, and Pollitt indeed was grooming one as his successor. That Gallacher's Scottishness was brought to the fore was nevertheless at once an affirmation of the spirit of self-government to which the CPGB had lately become committed, and a form of demarcation that implicitly confirmed Pollitt's pre-eminence for the party as a whole. 'There in the front of the March he goes', Gallacher himself wrote of Pollitt in a verse tribute for his 60th birthday.[172] Exactly like Cachin's in France, what was now the clearly secondary Gallacher cult confirmed the hierarchical principle on which the integrating cults of the Cold War were founded.

3.4 Capital and Charisma

According to Díaz, when Ibárruri entered a worker's home they would place their hands upon her 'to make sure that she is really and truly of flesh and blood, just like anyone else'.[173] Invariably she appeared dressed in black, and according to Borkenau she was like a medieval ascetic or a religious personality: 'The masses worship her, not for her intellect, but as a sort of saint who is to lead them in the days of trial and temptation.' Though Borkenau was a seasoned and even cynical observer of the communists, he did not dismiss such attitudes. On the contrary, he was in no doubt as to Pasionaria's 'simple, self-sacrificing faith' and aloofness from any hint of political intrigue or even calculation.[174]

The word most commonly used to describe this nowadays is charisma. Following its recovery earlier in the century by Max Weber, the term entered into wider parlance in just this period, initially as a way of understanding Hitler's mass appeal.[175] Weber had held that charisma in its pure form represented the treatment of the charismatic individual as one endowed with 'supernatural, superhuman, or at least specifically exceptional powers or qualities'.[176] As with his other ideal types, he also laid stress on the myriad impure forms in which charisma was to be encountered historically. Even so, charisma has often seemed a difficult concept to employ without entering into what Bourdieu referred to as the charismatic illusion of some 'mysterious objective property' that might or might not inhere in the fetishised individual.[177] In Weber's own initial exposition, this was certainly implicit in the beguiling notion of a 'genuine' charisma which, as Weber intimated, alone properly merited the epithet, and which existed 'simply by virtue of natural endowment'.[178]

Gifts from nature figure relatively little in the literature on communist cults. Instead, identification of a charismatic force within communism tends to signify party, ideology or revolution rather than the individual, and the vesting in the latter of a form of institutional charisma. Charisma is not therefore congenital but constructed, and conferred upon the individual through a complex social process involving multiple actors.[179] Such a usage is clearly congruent with the social ascription of exceptionality as here identified with the cult of the individual, and notions like the charismatic community or coterie can be profitably adapted to the political relationships that the cults involved.[180] Weber himself referred to the 'mechanisation' or manufacturing of charisma, and it is with this sort of emphasis that communism's state cults have been identified with a 'historically unique attempt to mass manufacture charisma of institutions, ideas and personalities, and to impose cultic veneration on their populations'.[181] If Stalin, as Richard Stites writes, saw clearly how to use charisma to political effect, it was not as a natural endowment but through his school of falsification and what might as well be called the charismatic apparatus.[182]

Descriptively, charisma thus indicates that a quality of exceptionality is imparted to some person, cohort, concept, institution or event. Where its meaning is elusive, causing many careful scholars to steer clear of using it, is in how this 'mysterious objective property' came to be constituted. Le Bon, preceding Weber, had already advanced the notion of 'prestige' as an inexplicable aura attaching to person, work or doctrine. This, Le Bon wrote, might either inhere in an individual, and a 'truly magnetic fascination' be revealed already in the pre-leadership stages of a career, or else be accrued as through an office.[183] Within a specifically communist context, a similar distinction has been held to mark out the genuine charismatic personality, for example the charisma of the returning Lenin of 1917 as distinguished from the cult that was subsequently constructed around him.[184] The problem, of course, is that it is so difficult to get at this charisma except through the sources by which it was constructed, and that the very notion of an 'artificial' or manufactured charisma suggests some implicit benchmark of a truly charismatic quality that can be abstracted from the particular social relations through which it is produced.

For communists, these social relations were both central and indispensable to the exercising of the role of the individual in history.[185] For this reason, they did not so much invoke a notion of charisma, with its seeming obfuscation of this point, as that of the political capital that was accrued historically through just this interaction between the individual and the collective. There were two distinct senses in which communists used this notion of human capital. The first was known to all of them through the address to Red Army graduates in May 1935 that became one of the most widely cited of Stalin's dicta, in particular, in its referring to 'man', or people, as the world's most precious capital.[186] Six months later Gallacher was already being described as one of the 'old militant workers' who constituted the CPGB's 'most precious capital'.[187] When subsequently Gallacher's French contemporary Pierre Semard was killed under the Nazis, this similarly was described as depriving both party and people of their capital.[188] Stalin had been referring to the larger body of cadres who, he said, decided everything. For Trotsky, this 'notorious slogan' above all signified the cult of officialdom.[189] Nevertheless, the further cultic variation was also possible that identified the communists' most precious capital more particularly with the figure of the leader.[190]

If the individual could be thought of as the capital of the collective, a second inflexion represented some accrual of capital to the individual through a personal history of associations or activities that served to distinguish them within the collective, though in ways that again were always socially constituted. Gallacher and Semard provide conspicuous examples of this. Semard had been a railworkers' leader and sometime PCF general secretary, and in his posthumous memorialisation a life history was evoked in which for 30 years he shirked no trial or responsibility, and died not only as a leader (*dirigeant*) in the administrative sense but as the capitalised *Chef* who 'all his life knew how to be a leader [and] died as a great leader knows how to die'.[191] Though Semard's personal qualities and agitational skills were also invoked, it was always in the sense of their being developed as an asset at once embodied in the individual and made over to the party. This again was a familiar usage: as with the deported militant of Polish origin who wrote to Thorez seeking to return to France, having earned there what he described precisely as his political capital, which he would have to build up again in his native Poland.[192]

One advantage of this notion is thus that communists themselves employed it to distinguish one individual from another. A second advantage is that it does avoid the mystification of the innate or otherwise unfathomable as ostensible key to the ascription of exceptionality. Political capital also depended on social and cultural capital. It could be inherited, through family and social environment; it might be earned or accumulated, through activities undertaken or responsibilities held; it might be appropriated, either by one individual from another, or by the individual on behalf of the collective; and it was therefore also a matter of claim, counter-claim and sometimes the most bitter contestation. Biographical capital was key, and it is for this reason that the cult biography is central to the understanding of the whole cult phenomenon.[193]

Within the context of a highly centralised communist movement, the idea of personal political capital, and of the individualisation of biography, could also pose the threat of the individual's advancement at the expense of the all-embracing collective. That is why the politics of personality was always for the communists a matter of profound ambivalence. It was not often that party authorities warned explicitly of the amassing of 'personal political capital', as they did during China's Cultural Revolution.[194] Strictures against 'petty-bourgeois individualism' were nevertheless routine, and Pennetier and Pudal describe the intense suspicion in the French case of those who amassed their own 'cultural and political capital' through participation in some or other form of mass activity.[195] This was precisely the issue between the integrating cult and a more fragmented politics of the individual, and it was a characteristic feature of the former that all other forms of biographical capital were subordinated to that projected through the leader.

Charisma itself remains fugitive in its meaning except as embodied in these claims and the individual and collective agencies through which they were made effective. Lenin, for example, certainly exercised what Le Bon would have called a magnetic fascination. Attending the Comintern's fourth world congress in 1922, Souvarine would later recall that when Lenin made his address the delegates pressed towards the platform as if 'an elemental force had with a single movement carried the auditorium forward'.[196] Other accounts describe prolonged ovations on Lenin's simply entering the hall, and Benno Ennker provides several examples of the impact he made upon speaking.[197]

Few, however, refer to Lenin as an orator in the classic mould. Admirers speak of an irresistible logic and the avoidance of unnecessary gestures or flights of rhetoric. Reed even refers to a monotonous effect, as of 'being able to go on for ever', and Trotsky's more dazzling platform skills were recognised by all.[198] What nevertheless drew them to Lenin before he even spoke, and in a language which they might or might not understand, was the incomparable political capital of having led the first successful workers' revolution. A Bolshevik émigré in London wrote of him as 'endowed with no special grace of either exterior or of popular talent … but rich in thought, initiative, courage, devotion, and goodness of heart; the leader of the first Socialist Republic in history … the incarnation of the age-long dreams of the best of mankind'.[199] Primed by such articles, Pollitt on first visiting Moscow wrote of his anticipatory excitement to see in person the 'greatest revolutionary figure that had ever lived', and on merely shaking Lenin's hand he walked away 'literally on air'.[200]

What Lenin by common consent had earned, Stalin's cult appropriated and then monopolised. It was thus that Ibárruri in rather similar fashion described how the 'ardent desire and dream' to see Stalin had prevailed over every other feeling on her own first visit to the USSR, and how it was nevertheless 'not Joseph Stalin but the leader of the world proletariat' whom she saw, and who by his steely will had rallied his people with such overpowering force.[201] This is not so different in its way from the touching of Ibárruri's own garments, and as recounted on Stalin's 60th birthday represented the making over of Ibárurri's own reputation and political capital to the symbolic edifice which Stalin crowned. It is telling in this respect that the only international voices in Pravda's birthday tributes were Ibárurri's and Dimitrov's: the two leaders whom even Borkenau allowed had regained for their movement some of the prestige which it had otherwise squandered.[202]

It was Dimitrov himself who described his achievement at the Leipzig trial as 'political capital for the Communist International' which ought to be comprehensively exploited.[203] At the same time, in his trial defence he had demonstrated as never before the political effect to be obtained by deployment of the personal political capital that was embodied in his own life history. The cadre autobiography was in just this period being established as one of stalinism's key control mechanisms and a sort of cleansing ritual through which alien elements would unwittingly expose themselves. 'Oh precious grey files', the Hungarian novelist Tibor Méray later wrote. 'How your truths, often as sharp as swords, help us to cut many a Gordian knot! A trifling contradiction among the several *curricula vitae*, some single material detail in the subject's past, a pertinent remark made by his concierge …'.[204] It is uncanny, however, how close the resemblance was between these autobiographies and Dimitrov's notes for his first speech in court, differing only in the proudly affirmative note that the occasion required.[205]

As subsequently the Comintern extracted the maximum advantage from Dimitrov's bearing and political courage, it was precisely the idea of political capital that was preferred to that already beginning to be referred to as charisma. So astounding were his dignity and fearless defiance, commented the 'Brown Book' of the Leipzig trial, that some sought to explain it in terms of a miracle:

> but in truth there was nothing miraculous about Dimitrov's conduct, nothing of inspiration in his words. Dimitrov's intelligence, his courage and his personality were all the fruits of a long experience in the Bulgarian working-class movement, they were the product of his lifelong practical and theoretical study of the working-class movement.[206]

It was the same long experience that taught Dimitrov to feel the solidarity of the world's masses whose tribune he had become; and as their focus subsequently shifted to the imprisoned Thälmann, the point was this time explicitly made that there was nothing of the 'mystical quality of the charismatic summons' attaching to the personality of the true proletarian leader.[207]

Communists did not always thus disdain that language of the miraculous in which Weber held that charismatic claims originated and had their validation.[208] With its profusion of religious imagery, we have seen already that Amado's *Cavalier of Hope* was a text suffused with what Weber understood by charisma.[209] Doubtless in Brazil, prevalent religious discourses meant both susceptibility to such usages and pragmatic justification for them. Commentary on the Thorez cult has also made these connections; but it was above all Pasionaria, with her 'collapsing of Catholic values into proletarian politics', who stands out in Catholic Spain as the most striking example of a communist charisma.[210] Both Jorge Semprún, who had broken with communism, and Carrillo, who had not, used the language of charisma to ascribe to her some quality of fascination that was specific and unique.[211] 'Her beautifully chiselled face exposes an unconquerable personality', wrote a contemporary journalist:

> she radiates warmth and confidence; there is nothing artificial about her. … What innate quality does she possess that makes a roomful of people suddenly halt what they're doing and stare at her with awe, admiration, and affection?[212]

Borkenau also emphasised the lack of any self-regard or ostentation, and instanced the pathos of Ibárruri's Valencia address as eventually her voice gave way in a gesture whose palpable sincerity he found irresistible.

One can gauge something of the effect from its rendering in the PCE newspaper *Mundo Obrero*. Having arrived directly from the battlefront, Ibárruri begins by warning lest she be overwhelmed by her feelings in telling of the savagery and destruction wreaked on her country by the fascists:

> *Pasionaria's voice grows weaker. It is with great effort that she can continue. The audience perceives her condition and calls to her to stop.*
>
> *However, Pasionaria continues her speech. She is listened to with strained attention although her voice is scarcely audible. Profound silence reigns in the stadium. One hundred thousand people listen with bated breath.*
>
> *Pasionaria says that the chief thing is to maintain and still further consolidate unity, to strengthen the People's Front and to give greater assistance to the government, so as to enable it to crush the criminal revolt.*

> We shall very soon achieve victory and return to our children …
>
> *These last words are heard only by the platform. A storm of applause. The audience of one hundred thousand Valencia workers cheer and applaud Pasionaria for several minutes.*[213]

Ibárruri was not a political ingénue, and was here doing her very utmost to galvanise support for the cause to which she was so deeply committed. That Borkenau could write of her absolute disregard for theatrical effect merely underlines how consummately skilled a performance this was, and how compelling the public presence that Pasionaria exercised.

As to what seemingly innate quality this represented, one might propose a threefold answer. First there was that combination of native aptitude and its cultivation through practice that made for Ibárruri's command of the arts of communication both on the platform and in her radio broadcasts. That it was a woman who achieved this celebrity was not just down to her ability to link a maternalist imagery with the promise of resistance. There were of course other Stalin generation leaders who owed a good deal to their platform skills and easy rapport with mass audiences.[214] Nevertheless, insofar as charisma was exercised through the arts of performance, it was associated with Kerensky rather than Lenin, and within the communist movement itself by Trotsky rather than the undemonstrative Stalin.[215] Pasionaria was the best-known communist orator of her day and it is possible that the command of an audience through the spoken word raised fewer misgivings in one whom sex seemed to relegate to a secondary political role, and whom the uncharacteristically credulous Borkenau placed somewhere beyond the mundane world of politicking. In contrast to the shadowy domesticities of most cult figures, Ibárruri further emphasised the 'profound motherliness' which so impressed Borkenau by having her daughter alongside her as she spoke. Elements of theatricality were also in her case less transgressive of Bolshevik ideas of masculinity. Kerensky, whose platforms skills similarly included fainting fits at once sincere and perfectly timed for his peroration, came under ridicule for his unmanly qualities, and a barb aimed at Trotsky was that in his vanity and self-absorption he resembled him.[216] The Pasionaria phenomenon thus represented the licensing of a form of visceral display whose joining with the role of party tribune—Díaz's characterisation—was crucially bound up with Ibárruri's gender.[217]

The second observation is that this was a collective endeavour. Nothing seemed to come between Pasionaria and her audience, and for the larger cult community the congress or public platform was the nearest there was to a face-to-face encounter with the leader. Even so, it involved elaborate organisation, staging and the observance of well-practised conventions for the interaction between speaker and audience. Dissemination beyond those immediately in attendance brought in a further cast of cult co-workers; *Mundo Obrero*'s correspondent was also a skilled practitioner, and there were also the actors and oil-painters who depicted Stalin better than he could himself, the ghost-writers of speeches and biographies, the sculptors who froze Lenin in the gestures that outlived him.

The basically social nature of cult construction also highlights the role of what Roger Eatwell describes as coterie-charisma.[218] Lenin exercised as few others this fascination for those who fell within his immediate orbit, and this played its part in the unanimity with which his colleagues observed his posthumous cult.[219] That Ibárruri prevailed in the battle for Díaz's succession was also said to rest upon a 'tightly knit clique of unconditional supporters', while Thorez's post-war cult required that a cohort of devoted *thoréziens* contribute the communications and other skills which no single individual could have possessed.[220] One would not in these cases want to isolate the force of personality from the command of machinery and patronage, and the enjoyment in turn of Moscow's favour. Indeed, the obvious example of coterie charisma would be Stalin himself, through that hold on both immediate associates and the wider apparatus which recent scholarship has been at pains to document.[221] Trotsky referred in Stalin's case to the 'hypocritically religious kowtowing' to 'the Leader' who embodied the power and privileges of those who exalted him.[222] One may certainly agree that coterie-charisma presupposed a conception of the world, which in this case was the world of the party, in which leader and coterie alike had a stake.

The third and critical consideration is that of the political capital whose embodiment in individual, group or cohort itself constituted a source and possible form of charisma. There was, of course, no more precious capital than that of the Bolshevik revolution. In describing the 'anti-Bonaparte fraction' that mobilised against Trotsky after Lenin's death, Max Eastman conjured up a sort of collective charisma in 'the idea of the sacredness of "Old Bolsheviks" and friends of "Old Bolsheviks", and friends of the friends of "Old Bolsheviks", and people who have acquired an odour of sanctity from the laying-on of hands of "Old Bolsheviks"'.[223] In a later context, Catherine Epstein describes precisely as charisma the role which a personal history of anti-fascism was to play in legitimising leadership in the post-war GDR.[224] Nevertheless, the source of this charisma was in both cases the historical capital which Eastman described as a surrogate for the economic power which older ruling groups had exercised, and which meant that 'the present value of the heroic past is accordingly defended with exaggerated violence'.

It was through the projection of this capital onto the individual that the earliest communist cults were instituted: some, of course, with better foundation than others. In Pasionaria's case, it is to the Spanish people's struggle, now rivalling October and eclipsing it in urgency, that the source of her charisma must be traced. A Paris audience is described as being reduced to tears by a characteristic performance delivered in Spanish. 'She stretches forth her hands and pleads by gesture and voice, which at moments of wrath and disgust becomes almost hoarse', runs *L'Humanité*'s report. 'Thousands of eyes are transfixed by this inspiring figure, bathed in the white beams of the spotlights.' It was a face, the paper said, 'expressive of suffering and struggling Spain herself', and of the 'fiery courage and militant spirit' by which she personified it.[225] As to the 'social magic' by which, according to Bourdieu, the person became identified with a collectivity or social entity, the necessary alchemistic ingredient was social or biographical capital.[226] The 'miner's daughter' as an epithet exemplified this, and within Spain and beyond Ibárurri had the aura of her deep roots in the coalfields and in coalfield struggles. 'And La Pasionaria, the Passion Flower, is the wife of a miner and the daughter of a miner', a laundry worker was quoted in the communist press. 'She is a woman and she is the Luxemburg of Spain.'[227] If Thorez was the son and grandson of miners, Ibárruri in her own autobiography went two better, as the granddaughter, daughter, wife and sister of miners whose proletarian roots were fundamental to her political persona.

With its generalisation across the communist movement, the ambivalence of the personality cult was that it required both the exploitation of political capital like Dimitrov's and its subordination to the higher collective interest of the party. It is here that the competing logics of integration and enkindling were most conspicuously in tension. As Borkenau rightly noted, Dimitrov had done more than almost anybody to advance the communist cause, but Stalin had no intention that either he or any other communist leader acquire a personal prestige which would make them independent of him.[228] Critical commentary on leaders like Browder and Thorez suggested that it was precisely the lack of such prestige or political capital which commended them to Stalin, while at the same time it necessitated the neutralisation of those within their own parties who could call upon such independent resources.[229] The paradox of the cult of the individual was that it always in the end came up against the cult of the collective, on which latter basis alone Stalin had overcome his more conspicuously gifted rivals. It is to the demonstration of this paradox that we now turn.

Notes

1. Annette Vidal, *Henri Barbusse. Soldat de la paix* (Paris: Éditeurs Français Réunis, 1953), p. 327.
2. Cited Sarah Davies, 'Stalin and the making of the leader cult in the 1930s' in Balázs Apor et al. (eds), *The Leader Cult in Communist Dictatorships. Stalin and the Eastern bloc* (Basingstoke: Palgrave Macmillan, 2004), p. 37; also Feuchtwanger, *Moscow 1937* (London: Gollancz, 1937), pp. 85–95.
3. Robert C. Tucker, *Stalin in Power. The revolution from above 1928–1941* (New York: W.W. Norton, 1992 edn), ch. 7; Leonard Schapiro, *Totalitarianism* (London: Macmillan, 1978 edn), pp. 38–43 and passim.
4. Nina Tumarkin, *Lenin Lives! The Lenin cult in Soviet Russia* (Cambridge, MA: Harvard University Press, 1983), p. 2; Chang-tai Hung, *Mao's New World. Political culture in the early People's Republic* (Ithaca, NY: Cornell University Press, 2011), p. 84.
5. Stephen Gundle, Christopher Duggan and Giuliana Peri, 'Introduction' in Stephen Gundle et al. (eds), *The Cult of the Duce. Mussolini and the Italians* (Manchester: Manchester University Press, 2013), p. 1; Ian Kershaw, *The 'Hitler Myth'. Image and reality in the Third Reich* (Oxford: Oxford University Press, 1989 edn), pp. 2–3.
6. J. Arch Getty, *Practicing Stalinism. Bolsheviks, boyars and the persistence of tradition* (New Haven, CT: Yale University Press, 2013), p. 20; Peter Burke, *The Fabrication of Louis XIV* (Cambridge, MA: Yale University Press, 1992), pp. 198–203.
7. Mason cited Kershaw, *'Hitler Myth'*, p. 3.
8. Compare Jan Plamper, *The Stalin Cult. A study in the alchemies of power* (New Haven, CT: Yale University Press, 2012), pp. xvii–xviii and Getty, *Practicing Stalinism*, ch. 2.

9. Samuel Northrop Harper, *Civic Training in Soviet Russia* (Chicago, IL: University of Chicago Press, 1929), p. 40.
10. See Brigitte Studer, 'More autonomy for the national sections? The organisation of the ECCI after the Seventh World Congress' in Mikhail Narinsky and Jürgen Rojahn (eds), *Centre and Periphery. The history of the Comintern in the light of new documents* (Amsterdam: International Institute of Social History, 1996), pp. 102–13.
11. Tucker, 'Rise', 347–8.
12. Alexey Tikhomorov, 'The Stalin cult between center and periphery: the structures of the cult community in the empire of socialism, 1949–1956—the case of GDR' in Benno Ennker and Heidi Hein-Kircher (eds), *Der Führer im Europa des 20. Jahrhunderts* (Marburg: Herder-Institut, 2010), pp. 313, 320–1.
13. Thorez papers 626 AP/273, press interview with Thorez by Sulzberger, Paris, 3 Feb. 1948.
14. Ronald Tiersky, *French Communism 1920–1972* (New York: Columbia University Press, 1974), pp. 322–3.
15. Annie Kriegel, 'Bureaucratie, culte de personnalité et charisme. Le cas français: Maurice Thorez, secrétaire général du PCF (1900–1964)' in idem, *Communisme au miroir français* (Paris: Gallimard, 1974), pp. 144–5.
16. David Forgacs and Stephen Gundle, *Mass Culture and Italian Society from Fascism to the Cold War* (Bloomington, IN: Indiana University Press, 2007), p. 264.
17. Marcella and Maurizio Ferrara, *Palmiro Togliatti. Essai biographique* (Paris: Éditions Sociales, 1954), ch. 29. The Belgian party president Lahaut was killed in October 1950; the Japanese party secretary Tokuda was said to have survived a similar attentat two months earlier.
18. Cavalli, 'Considerations on charisma and the cult of charismatic leadership', *Modern Italy*, 3 (1998), 161.
19. Plamper, *Stalin Cult*, ch. 2 and passim.
20. The principal exception is Russel Lemmons, *Hitler's Rival. Ernst Thälmann in Myth and Memory* (Lexington, KY: University of Kentucky Press, 2013).
21. Kriegel, 'Bureaucratie', pp. 132–58.

22. On the former see Gleb J. Albert, ' "Esteemed Comintern!" The Communist International and world-revolutionary charisma in early Soviet society', *TCC*, 8, 2015, 10–39.
23. Togliatti to Luigi Longo, 11 Feb. 1953 in Togliatti, *La guerra di posizione in Italia. Epistolario 1944–1964* (Turin: Einaudi, 2014), pp. 182–5.
24. See Chap. 1 above for this distinction.
25. Bernstein, *Ferdinand Lassalle as a Social Reformer* (London: Swan Sonnenschein & Co, 1893), pp. 188–9.
26. Jan Plamper, 'Introduction' in Klaus Heller and Jan Plamper (eds), *Personality Cults in Stalinism—Personenkulte im Stalinismus* (Göttingen: V&R Unipress, 2004), pp. 25–6; Daniel Leese, *Mao Cult. Rhetoric and ritual in China's Cultural Revolution* (Cambridge: Cambridge University Press, 2011), pp. 16–17.
27. Hannah Arendt, *The Origins of Totalitarianism* (1951) (New York: Schocken Books, 2004 edn), pp. 451–3.
28. See for example José Gotovitch, *Du communisme et des communistes en Belgique. Approches critiques* (Brussels: Editions Aden, n.d.), pp. 142–3; Jean-Pierre A. Bernard, *Le Parti communiste français et la question littéraire* (Grenoble: Presses Universitaires de Grenoble, 1972), pp. 12–13.
29. E.A. Rees, 'Leader cults: varieties, preconditions and functions' in Apor, *Leader Cult*, p. 4.
30. David Priestland, *Stalinism and the Politics of Mass Mobilization. Ideas, power and terror in inter-war Russia* (Oxford: Oxford University Press, 2007), p. 280.
31. Pierre Bourdieu, 'The social space and the genesis of groups', *Theory and Society*, 14 (1985), 723–44.
32. Kaganovich, 'Staline et le parti' in *Staline* (Paris: Bureau d'Éditions: 1930), pp. 37–47.
33. Contributions of Cachin (preface), Kaganovich and G. Krumin in *Staline*, pp. 5–9, 37–47 and 106–13.
34. Dmitri Volkogonov, *Stalin: triumph and tragedy* (London: Weidenfeld & Nicolson, 1995 edn), ch. 20.
35. John Barber, *Soviet Historians in Crisis, 1928–1932* (London: Macmillan, 1981), ch. 10.
36. See Chap. 6.3 below.
37. For example, Dutt, 'Homage to Stalin', *LM*, Dec. 1949, 354–5; Browder, 'Joseph Stalin's 60th Birthday', *DW* (NY), 21 Dec. 1939.

38. Tumarkin, *Lenin Lives!*, p. 60.
39. See K. Voroshilov in *The Life of Stalin: a symposium* (London: Modern Books, 1930), pp. 48–84.
40. Tucker, *Stalin in Power*, pp. 148–51; Barber, *Soviet Historians*, p. 96.
41. K.E. Voroshilov, 'Military commander of the Great Patriotic War' in *'Pravda' Articles on the Occasion of the 70th Birthday of Joseph Vissarionovich Stalin December 21, 1949* (London: Soviet News, 1950), pp. 43–58.
42. Ethan Pollock, 'Stalin as the coryphaeus of science: ideology and knowledge in the post-war years' in Sarah Davies and James Harris (eds), *Stalin: a new history* (Cambridge: Cambridge University Press, 2005), pp. 271–2, n. 2.
43. Jean T. Desanti, 'Staline, savant d'un type nouveau', *NC*, Dec. 1949, 33–61.
44. 'Hommages', *Pens.*, Nov.–Dec. 1949, 14–20.
45. Bernal, 'Leonardo da Vinci', *LM*, Apr. 1952, 170–6; also John Eaton, 'Stalin's contribution to economic theory', *CR*, Apr. 1953, 120; Ronald L. Meek and George Houston, 'Some aspects of Stalin's "Economic Problems" ', *MQ*, summer 1953, 143–58.
46. Jean Bruhat, 'L'apport de Maurice Thorez à l'histoire', *CdC*, Apr. 1950, 33–4.
47. Claude Pennetier and Bernard Pudal, 'Stalinism: workers' cult and cult of leaders', *TCC*, 1 (2009), 20–9.
48. Alfred J. Rieber, 'Stalin, man of the borderlands', *American Historical Review*, 106 (2001), 1669–70.
49. Barbusse papers, Alexei Stetsky to Barbusse, 15 Sept. 1934.
50. Maurice Thorez, *Fils du peuple* (Paris: Éditions Sociales, 1950 edn), p. 11.
51. Stuart Macintyre, *The Reds. The Communist Party of Australia from origins to illegality* (Sydney: Allen & Unwin, 1998), pp. 69, 360.
52. 'Jose Diaz, general secretary of the CP of Spain', *Inprecorr*, 17 May 1938, 591–4.
53. Norman LaPorte and Kevin Morgan, '"Kings among their subjects?" Ernst Thälmann, Harry Pollitt and the leadership cult as stalinization' in LaPorte et al. (eds), *Bolshevism, Stalinism and the Comintern. Perspectives on stalinization, 1917–53* (Basingstoke: Palgrave Macmillan, 2008) pp. 129, 135–7. The following paragraph also draws on Henri Barbusse, *Connais-tu Thaelmann?*

(Paris: Comité pour la Libération de Thaelmann et des Antifascistes Allemands emprisonnés), 1934, pp. 5–6; *Thaelmann* (Paris: Éditions La Défense, 1934), pp. 11–15; Ruth Fischer, *Stalin and German Communism. A study in the origins of the state party* (Oxford: Oxford University Press, 1948), p. 423.

54. Cited Kevin Morgan, *Harry Pollitt* (Manchester: Manchester University Press, 1993), p. 85.
55. Paul Vaillant-Couturier, *Au Service de l'esprit* (Paris: Éditions Sociales Internationales, 1936), pp. 21–2.
56. Fréville, 'L'homme qui veut une France libre, forte et heureuse', 'Une déscente dans la mine' and 'Après une lecture de "Fils du peuple"', all in idem, *Avec Maurice Thorez* (Paris: Éditions Sociales, 1950), pp. 9–10, 63–89, 91–3.
57. André Parreaux, 'Maurice Thorez', *Pens.*, Mar—Apr. 1950, 73.
58. Thorez papers 626AP/243, PCF 1757 cell resolution, n.d. but 1947; Cantonniers workplace cell, resolution, 28 Apr. 1947, Paris XIe Arr. section resolution, 28 Apr. 1947.
59. Kimmo Rentola, 'Finnish communism, O.W. Kuusinen, and their two native countries' in Tauno Saarela and Kimmo Rentola (eds), *Communism: national and international* (Helsinki: Finnish Historical Society, 1998), pp. 159–81.
60. Rentola, 'Finnish communism', p. 181.
61. Tauno Saarela, 'Dead martyrs and living leaders: the cult of the individual within Finnish communism', *TCC*, 1 (2009), 37–41; 'Fiftieth birthday of Kuusinen', *CI*, 15 Oct. 1931, 562–3.
62. Rentola, 'Finnish communism', p. 170.
63. Ferrara, *Palmiro Togliatti* , pp. 42–4.
64. Ferrara, *Palmiro Togliatti*, p. 132.
65. Ferrara, *Palmiro Togliatti*, pp. 10, 127; also Aldo Agosti, *Palmiro Togliatti. A biography* (London: Tauris, 2008), p. 10.
66. See Chap. 5.3 below.
67. S. Scuderi (ed.), *Vita di un italiano* (Rome: Edizione di Cultura Sociale, 1953).
68. Olga Velikanova, *Making of an Idol. On uses of Lenin* (Göttingen: Muster-Schmidt Verlag, 1996), p. 132.
69. *Libérez Rakosi* (Paris: Éditions de Secours Rouge Internationale), n.d., c. 1934.
70. Stefan Priacel, *Au nom de la loi! … Les grands procès politiques de notre temps* (Paris: Éditions Sociales Internationales, 1936), pp. 87–90.

71. Balázs Apor, 'National traditions and the leader cult in communist Hungary in the early cold war years', *TCC*, 1 (2009), 50–71.
72. Béla Illés, *Mátyás Rákosi* (Rome: Edizioni di Cultura Sociale, 1952); Balázs Apor, *The 'Invisible Shining': the cult of Mátyás Rákosi in stalinist Hungary, 1945–1956* (Budapest: Central European University Press, forthcoming 2017), ch. 2; Árpád von Klimó, '"A very modest man": Béla Illés, or how to make a career through the leader cult' in Apor, *Leader Cult*, p. 52.
73. Velikanova, *Making*, pp. 98–100; Robert Service, *Trotsky. A biography* (London: Pan edn, 2010), p. 309; Stephen Kotkin, *Stalin: paradoxes of power 1897–1928* (London: Penguin, 2015 edn), pp. 349–50.
74. Annie Kriegel and Stéphane Courtois, *Eugen Fried. Le grand secret du PCF* (Paris: Seuil, 1997), p. 76.
75. Martin Mevius, *Agents of Moscow. The Hungarian Communist Party and the origins of socialist patriotism 1941–1953* (Oxford: Oxford University Press, 2005), pp. 94–7; Paul Kelemen, 'The Hungarian Communist Party, ethno-nationalism and antisemitism', *TCC*, 4 (2012), 210–12.
76. Marcel Willard, *La défense accuse ... De Babeuf à Dimitrov* (Paris: Éditions Sociales Internationales, 1938), pp. 279–85.
77. Robert Levy, *Ana Pauker. The rise and fall of a Jewish communist* (Berkeley, CA: University of California Press, 2001), pp. 71–4.
78. Aldred J. Rieber, 'Stalin, man of the borderlands', 1652; Jan Plamper, 'Georgian Koba or Soviet "Father of Peoples"? The Stalin cult and ethnicity' in Apor, *Leader Cult*, pp. 126–7.
79. Rieber, 'Stalin', 1690–1.
80. Plamper, 'Georgian Koba', p. 124.
81. Vladimir Orlov, 'Prokoviev and the myth of the father of the nations: the cantata *Zdravitsa*', *Journal of Musicology*, 30, 4 (2013), 593–9. For the cantata's commissioning for Stalin's 60th birthday, see Chap. 2 above.
82. Minor, 'Browder—the man they want to get', *DW* (NY), 19 and 20 Jan., 6 and 7 Feb. 1940.
83. *Mátyás Rákosi: On the Occasion of his Sixtieth Birthday* (London: Hungarian News and Information Service, 1952), p. 3; Minor, 'Browder—the man they want to get', 20 Jan. 1940.
84. Mark Naison, *Communists in Harlem During the Depression* (New York: Grove Press edn, 1985), pp. 98–9.

85. Jorge Amado, *Le Chevalier de l'Espèrance* (Paris: Éditeurs Français Réunis, 1949), pp. 27–30 ; citations here and elsewhere checked against Amado, *O Cavaleiro de Esperança. Vida de Luiz Carlos Prestes* (Rio de Janeiro: Colecção Novos horizontes, 1956), with thanks to José Neves. Amado's *ABC de Castro Alves* had been published in 1941.
86. With thanks to Brigitte Studer for this suggestion.
87. Macintyre, *The Reds*, pp. 285–6.
88. Emmet O'Connor, *Reds and the Green. Ireland, Russia and the Communist Internationals 1919–43* (Dublin: University College Dublin Press, 2004), pp. 225–6.
89. André Wurmser cited Philippe Robrieux, *Maurice Thorez. Vie secrète et vie publique* (Paris: Fayard, 1975), p. 377.
90. Thorez papers 626 AP/212, F. Armand, 'Le livre de Maurice Thorez', *La Champagne*, Reims, 3 Dec. 1937.
91. Thorez papers 626 AP/233, communists of Paris 1er arr. to Thorez, 27 Apr. 1949; Fréville, 'L'homme qui veut', pp. 14–15.
92. Frantisek Necasek, *Klement Gottwald. Communist Premier of Czechoslovakia* (London: CPGB, 1947), pp. 31–2.
93. Henri Barbusse (ed., with Alfred Kurella), *Lettres de Lénine à sa famille* (Paris: Rieder, 1936), pp. 15–16.
94. Amado, *Chevalier*, pp. 258–62, 320–8; see also above Chap. 1.
95. Film accessible at http://cinearchives.org.
96. See for example *La Provence Nouvelle*, Oct. 1949 and *Regards*, 28 Apr. 1950 (both in Marty papers CHS AM 42); *Travailleur*, weekly journal of Ivry Canton, Apr. 1950 (Thorez papers 626AP/243).
97. Thorez papers 626AP/251, CGT Commission Féminine Confédérale to Thorez, 27 Apr. 1951.
98. Thorez papers 626AP/252, address of meeting of women and mothers of Ivry to Vermeersch, n.d.
99. See also Chap. 4.2 below.
100. Yves Cohen, *Le Siècle des chefs. Une histoire transnationale du commandement et de l'autorité* (Paris: Éditions Amsterdam, 2013), pp. 454–5.
101. Kershaw, *'Hitler Myth'*, pp. 27–8, 57, 79, 140–1, 159.
102. Maurice Agulhon, *La République. De Jules Ferry à François Mitterand (1880 à nos jours)* (Paris: Hachette, 1990), p. 24; Claude Grimmer, 'Histoire de l'anniversaire: une fête laïque qui

s'impose à tous' in Alain Montandon (ed.), *L'Anniversaire* (Clermont-Ferrand: Presses universitaires Blaise Pascal, 2008), pp. 150–1.
103. Rupert Lewis, *Marcus Garvey. Anti-colonial champion* (London: Karia Press, 1987), p. 89; James Epstein, *Radical Expression. Political language, ritual and symbol in England, 1790–1850* (London: Breviary Stuff, 2014 edn), ch. 5.
104. R.J.B. Bosworth, *Mussolini* (London: Arnold, 2002), pp. 257 ff.
105. M. Şükrü Hanioğlu, *Atatürk. An intellectual biography* (Princeton, NJ: Princeton University Press, 2011), p. 97.
106. 'Hommage à André Marty et Jacques Duclos militants dévoués, lutteurs infatigables!', *L'Humanité*, 6 Sept. 1936.
107. See Chap. 2.1 above; also Plamper, *Stalin Cult*, p. 253 n. 81.
108. 'I picture ... weary postmen carrying sacks of letters to your house', Angela Tuckett wrote on Gallacher's 70th birthday, 'as though it were the birthday of a class war prisoner in gaol!' (CPGB archives, CP/Ind/Gall/7/1, Tuckett to Gallacher, 23 Dec. 1951).
109. Stéphane Sirot, *Maurice Thorez* (Paris: Presses de Sciences Po, 2000), p. 56; A. Rossi, *Les Communistes français pendant la drôle de guerre* (Paris: Iles d'or, 1951), p. 77.
110. Thorez papers 626 AP/231.
111. See respectively Thorez papers 626 AP/232 and 626 AP/233.
112. See Chap. 4.2 below.
113. Thorez papers 626AP/243, PCF Villejuif section to Thorez, 27 Apr. 1947.
114. Robrieux, *Maurice Thorez*, pp. 201–2.
115. Michelle Perrot, 'Les vies ouvrières' in Pierre Nora (ed.), *Les Lieux de mémoire* (Paris: Gallimard, 1997 edn), pp. 3937–3969; Sirot, *Maurice Thorez*, p. 23; Marie-Cécile Bouju, *Lire en communiste. Les Maisons d'édition du Parti communiste français 1920–1968* (Rennes: Presses Universitaires de Rennes, 2010), p. 124.
116. On Gallacher see Andrew Thorpe, 'Communist MP: Willie Gallacher and British communism' in Kevin Morgan et al. (eds), *Agents of the Revolution. New biographical approaches to the history of international communism in the age of Lenin and Stalin* (Bern: Peter Lang, 2005), pp. 133–58.

117. *The March of English History* (London: CPGB, 1936), pp. 4–10.
118. Jack Lindsay and Edgell Rickword (eds), *A Handbook of Freedom* (London: Lawrence & Wishart, 1939).
119. Dick Etheridge papers (Warwick University Modern Records Centre) MSS 202/CP/30, notes on CPGB 18th congress, 1945.
120. For Pollitt's efforts, see Kevin Morgan, 'Harry Pollitt, Rhondda East and the Cold War collapse of the British communist electorate', *Llafur*, 10, 4 (2011), 16–31.
121. RGASPI 495/100/990. meeting with Comrade Marty, 29 Oct. 1935, contribution of Raylock.
122. RGASPI 495/24/17, Marty secretariat, 20 Feb. 1936, contribution of Arnot.
123. William Gallacher, *The Clyde in War Time. Snapshots of a stormy period* (Glasgow: Collets Bookshop, n.d., c. 1935), p. 22; also Gallacher, 'May Day in Wartime', *DW* (L), 30 Apr. 1932.
124. David Kirkwood, *My Life of Revolt* (London: Harrap, 1935).
125. See Gallacher, *The Rolling of the Thunder* (London: Lawrence & Wishart, 1947), pp. 89, 153; R. Bishop, 'Gallacher and the new parliament', *Inprecorr*, 30 Nov. 1935, 1583.
126. Bishop, 'Gallacher', 1582–3; Bishop, 'Foreword' to Gallacher, *The Chosen Few. A sketch of men and events in parliament* (London: Lawrence & Wishart, 1940), p. 11.
127. *Joseph Stalin. A short biography* (London: Lawrence & Wishart, 1940), p. 93.
128. J.B., 'A forceful record of leadership', *LM*, Sept. 1936, 579–80.
129. 'Huge meeting greets Gallacher', *DW* (L), 22 Dec. 1935.
130. RGASPI 495/14/241/43-8, 'Memorandum by Comrade Gallacher on policy of CPGB', 17 Aug. 1937.
131. Carr, 'Mr Gallacher and the CPGB' in his *Studies in Revolution* (London: Macmillan, 1950), pp. 166–80.
132. Pennetier and Pudal, 'Stalinism', pp. 26–7.
133. *New Statesman and Nation*, 13 Jun. 1936, 938–9.
134. Randall Swingler, 'The Red Flag at Westminster', *Public Opinion*, 22 Jun. 1951, cutting in Gallacher papers CP/Ind/Gall/2/3.
135. Robert J. Alexander, *Communism in Latin America* (New Brunswick, NJ: Rutgers University Press, 1957), pp. 100–1.
136. Cited Alexander, *Communism in Latin America*, pp. 107–8; also Prestes, 'Meeting with Georgi Dimitrov' in *Memories of Georgi Dimitrov* (Sofia: Sofia Press, 1972), pp. 211–12.

137. Cited Alexander, *Communism in Latin America*, p. 108.
138. John W. F. Dulles, *Brazilian Communism. Repression during world upheaval 1935–1945* (Austin, TX: University of Texas Press, 1983), pp. 198–9.
139. Alexander, *Communism in Latin America*, pp. 101, 115; Marco Aurélio Santana, 'Re-imagining the Cavalier of Hope: the Brazilian Communist Party and the images of Luiz Carlos Prestes', *TCC*, 1 (2009), 120–2, 125.
140. Amado, *Chevalier*, preface to French edn, pp. 9–25.
141. Amado, *Chevalier*, pp. 132, 172–6, 216–17, 250, 314, 349.
142. Amado, *Chevalier*, pp. 40–6, 68, 78–81.
143. Neruda, 'Dura Elegia. En la tumba de la Senõra Leocadia Prestes'; Amado, *Chevalier*, pp. 132, 373.
144. Amado, *Chevalier*, pp. 30–1, 152, 229–30.
145. J.B., 'Forceful record', 579–80.
146. E.g. Amado, *Chevalier*, pp. 30–2.
147. Istvan Fekete, 'Mathias Rakosi. Tragédie et héroisme d'une vie', *Monde*, 11 Jan. 1935.
148. Romain Rolland, *Antonio Gramsci. Ceux qui meurent dans les prisons de Mussolini* (Paris: no publisher, n.d. but 1934), pp. 9–15.
149. See Pat Sloan (ed.), *John Cornford: a memoir* (London: Cape, 1938).
150. For example Jean Fréville, 'L'homme communiste: Gabriel Péri', *NC*, Dec. 1949, 64; Alexander Courban, *Gabriel Péri: un homme politique, un député, un journaliste* (Paris: La Dispute, 2011), pp. 16–17.
151. Courban, *Gabriel Péri*, ch. 7.
152. Jean-Louis Cohen, *Le Corbusier and the Mystique of the USSR. Theories and projects for Moscow 1928–1936* (Princeton, NJ: Princeton University Press, 1992), pp. 226–7.
153. For Picasso see Chap. 6.1.
154. Paul Preston, *The Last Stalinist. The life of Santiago Carrillo* (London: Collins, 2015 edn), pp. 94–5.
155. Franz Borkenau, *The Communist International* (London: Faber & Faber, 1938), p. 395; see also Chap. 2 above.
156. Tim Rees, 'The "Good Bolsheviks". The Spanish Communist Party and the Third Period' in Matthew Worley (ed.), *In Search of Revolution. International communist parties in the Third Period* (London: Tauris, 2004), p. 190.

157. Voroshilov to Manuilsky 17 Oct. 1936 enclosing Marty's report on Spain to the ECCI secretariat, 10 Oct. 1936, in Ronald Radosh et al. (eds), *Spain Betrayed. The Soviet Union in the Spanish Civil War* (New Haven, CT: Yale University Press, 2001), pp. 50–1.
158. Marty papers (SSD) 281 J box 39, 'Saturnino Barneto Atienza: enfant du peuple espagnol, exemple d'hier et de demain', 13 Jun. 1940.
159. David Wingeate Pike, *In the Service of Stalin. The Spanish communists in exile, 1939–1945* (Oxford: Oxford University Press, 1993), pp. 156–7 and 337 n. 43; Dolores Ibárruri, 'Jose Diaz', *LM*, May 1942, 158–9; Marty papers 281 J for tributes including 'À la memoire de Jose Diaz', 21 Mar. 1942, signed by PCE and Comintern leaders.
160. Voroshilov to Manuilsky 17 Oct. 1936.
161. Plamper, *Stalin Cult*, p. xviii.
162. Gina Herrmann, *Written in Red: the communist memoir in Spain*, 2010 (Urbana, IL: University of Illinois Press, 2010), pp. 25–53, also citing Vásquez Montalbán.
163. Denis Peschanski (ed.), *Marcel Cachin. Carnets 1906–1947* (Paris: CNRS Éditions, vol. 4, 1997), p. 110, entry for 25 Jul. 1935.
164. Franz Borkenau, *The Spanish Cockpit* (London: Faber & Faber, 1937), pp. 120–1; Paul Preston, *Comrades! Portraits from the Spanish Civil War* (London: HarperCollins, 1999), pp. 289–90.
165. *Dolores Ibarruri. Speeches and articles 1936–1938* (Moscow: Foreign Languages Publishing House, 1938).
166. Paul Lebar, *Pasionaria* (Paris: ER, 1937).
167. Pike, *In the Service*, pp. 157–9.
168. Santana, 'Re-imagining', 123; Preston, *Comrades!*, p. 277. Anastasia Koukouna informs me that the Greek leader Zachariadis was not celebrated in this fashion, perhaps because in Greece birthdays were marked far less than name days, but also because of the far greater focus on martyrs and hence on the Greek resistance struggle.
169. Preston, *Last Stalinist*, pp. 148, 172.
170. Gallacher papers CP/Ind/Gall/7/1, Dutt to Gallacher, 21 Dec. 1951 and CPGB London district committee to Gallacher, 14 Dec. 1951.

171. Gallacher papers CP/Ind/Gall/2/3, printed programme for seventieth birthday celebrations, 23 Dec. 1951.
172. Gallacher, 'To Harry Pollitt' in idem, *Relaxation* (London: Daily Worker Bazaar Committee), p. 16.
173. Cited *Pasionaria. The story of a miner's daughter* (London: CPGB, 1937), p. 22.
174. Borkenau, *Spanish Cockpit*, pp. 120–1.
175. Theodore Abel, *Why Hitler Came To Power. An answer based on the original life stories of six hundred of his followers* (New York: Prentice-Hall, 1938), pp. 64–7, 180–3.
176. Max Weber, *Economy and Society. An outline of interpretive sociology* (Berkeley, CA: University of California Press, 2 vols, 1978 edn), pp. 241–54 and 1111–57, citation here at p. 241.
177. Bourdieu, 'Social space', 740.
178. Weber, *Economy and Society*, p. 400.
179. Cohen, *Siècle*, pp. 152–4.
180. For the former, Weber, *Economy and Society*, p. 243; for the latter, Roger Eatwell, 'The concept and theory of charismatic leadership' in António Costa Pinto, Roger Eatwell and Stein Ugelvik Larsen (eds), *Charisma and Fascism in Interwar Europe* (London: Routledge, 2007), pp. 3–18.
181. Weber, *Economy and Society*, p. 1121; Rees, 'Leader cults', p. 22.
182. Richard Stites, *Revolutionary Dreams. Utopian visions and experimental life in the Russian revolution* (New York: Oxford University Press, 1991 edn), pp. 246–50.
183. Gustave Le Bon, *Psychologie des foules* (1895) (Paris: Félix Alcan, 1930 edn), pp. 108–18.
184. Annie Kriegel, 'Bureaucratie', pp. 132–3; Benno Ennker, 'The origins and intentions of the Lenin cult' in Ian D. Thatcher (ed.), *Regime and Society in Twentieth-Century Russia. Selected papers from the Fifth World Congress of Central and East European Studies, Warsaw, 1995* (Basingstoke: Macmillan, 1995), p. 119.
185. See Chap. 6.3 below.
186. Stalin, 'Address to the graduates from the Red Army academies' in idem, *Problems of Leninism* (Moscow: Foreign Languages Publishing House, 1940 edn), p. 544.
187. RGASPI 495/100/990, 'Gallacher. The first MP for the British parliament elected upon a communist programme', n.d. but 1935.

188. Gaston Monmousseau, 'Hommage à Pierre Semard', *CdC*, Mar. 1946, 62.
189. Trotsky (trans. Max Eastman), *The Revolution Betrayed* (1937) (New York: Pioneer Publishers, 1945 edn), p. 238.
190. See various examples in Thorez papers 626AP/251 e.g. Union de la Jeunesse Républicaine de France, Seine federation, to Thorez, 5 Sept. 1951.
191. Monmousseau, 'Hommage', 61–2.
192. Thorez papers 626AP/271, Thomas Olszanski to Thorez, 23 Mar. 1945.
193. See Chap. 6.2 below.
194. Leese, *Mao Cult*, p. 228.
195. Claude Pennetier and Bernard Pudal, 'Deux générations de militants communistes français (1931–1951) en proie à des procès d'épurations internes' in José Gotovitch and Anne Morelli (eds), *Militantisme et militants* (Brussels, 2000), pp. 128–33.
196. Souvarine, 'Illitch, cher Illitch', *L'Humanité*, 27 Jan. 1924.
197. Sen Katayama, 'Mes rencontres avec Lénine' in *Nos Rencontres avec Lénine* (Moscow: Éditions en Langues Étrangères, 1939), pp. 9–10; Lunacharsky cited Henri Guilbeaux, *Le portrait authentique de Vladimir Ilitch Lénine* (Paris: Librairie de l'Humanité, 1924), p. 61.
198. Katayama, 'Mes rencontres'; Clara Zetkin, *Reminiscences of Lenin* (New York: International Publishers, 1934), p. 31; Reed, *Ten Days That Shook the World* (London: Martin Lawrence, 1932 edn), pp. 104–7; Guilbeaux, *Portrait*, pp. 63–4.
199. W.A.M.M., 'Lenin: a birthday sketch', *The Call*, 8 Apr. 1920; Ian Bullock, *Romancing the Revolution. The myth of Soviet democracy and the British left* (Edmonton, Alberta: AU Press, 2011), p. 356 notes the authorship by Theodore Rothstein.
200. Harry Pollitt, *Serving My Time* (London: Lawrence & Wishart, 1941 edn), pp. 138–9.
201. 'Pasionaria tells of first meeting people's leader', *DW* (NY), 21 Dec. 1939.
202. Borkenau, *Communist International*, p. 405; Borkenau, *Spanish Cockpit*, p. 193.
203. Ivo Banac (ed.), *The Diary of Georgi Dimitrov 1933–1949* (New Haven, Conn.: Yale University Press, 2003), p. 11, entry for 3 Apr. 1934.

204. Tibor Meray, *The Enemy* (London: Secker & Warburg, 1958), p. 71; see also Claude Pennetier and Bernard Pudal, 'La vérification (l'encadrement biographique communiste dans l'entre-deux-guerres)', *Genèses*, 23 (1996).
205. 'Dimitroff's notes for his first speech in court, 23rd September 1933' in Alfred Kurella (ed.), *Dimitroff's Letters from Prison* (London: Gollancz, 1935), pp. 68–76.
206. *The Reichstag Fire Trial. The Second Brown Book of the Hitler Terror* (London: Bodley Head, 1934), p. 134.
207. Pierre Merin in Anna Seghers et al, *Ernst Thaelmann. What he stands for* (London: Workers' Bookshop, 1934), pp. 13–21; on this see also Chap. 6.3 below.
208. Weber, *Economy and Society*, pp. 242, 1114.
209. Amado, *Chevalier de l'Espèrance*, pp. 29–30.
210. Herrmann, *Written*, p. 26.
211. Semprún cited Herrmann, *Written*, p. 30; Santiago Carrillo with Régis Debray, *Dialogue on Spain*, (London: Lawrence & Wishart, 1976), p. 103.
212. Cited Preston, *Comrades!*, p. 303.
213. 'Fascism shall not pass' (23 Aug. 1936) in *Dolores Ibarruri. Speeches and articles*, pp. 15–17 (ellipses in original).
214. For examples see Chap. 4.1 below.
215. For the latter comparison see Chap. 4.1 below.
216. Orlando Figes and Boris Kolonitskii, *Interpreting the Russian Revolution. The language and symbols of 1917* (New Haven, CT: Yale University Press, 1999), pp. 81, 91; M.N. Pokrovsky, 'About a certain "experiment in autobiography"', *LM*, Sept. 1930, 569, 572–3.
217. Díaz cited *Pasionaria. The story of a miner's daughter*, p. 22.
218. Eatwell, 'Concept and theory', pp. 15–16.
219. For this fascination, see Anatoly Lunacharsky, *Revolutionary Silhouettes* (London: Allen Lane, 1967 edn), p. 43.
220. Preston, *Last Stalinist*, p. 111; for Thorez, see Chap. 4.2 below.
221. Sheila Fitzpatrick, *On Stalin's Team. The years of living dangerously in Soviet politics* (Princeton, NJ: Princeton University Press, 2015); Kotkin, *Stalin*, ch. 10.
222. Trotsky, *Revolution Betrayed*, p. 139.

223. Max Eastman, *Since Lenin Died* (New York: Boni & Liveright, 1925), ch. 11.
224. Catherine Epstein, *The Last Revolutionaries. German communists and their century* (Cambridge, MA: Harvard University Press, 2003), pp. 154, 232.
225. 'Better die standing, than live kneeling!' (*L'Humanité*, 13 Sept. 1936) in *Dolores Ibarruri*, pp. 18–21.
226. Bourdieu, 'Social space', 740.
227. Ann Rivington, 'A Message from la Pasionaria', *DW* (NY), 23 July 1936.
228. Borkenau, *Communist International*, p. 395.
229. For Browder see Chap. 5.3 below.

CHAPTER 4

Leader Cults

4.1 A Leader Made of Filth

(i)

According to Trotsky, Stalin used to quote a Russian proverb *Iz gryazi delayut Knyazia*—a Prince can be made out of filth.[1] This was certainly how Stalin's rise to power was perceived by Trotsky himself. At the time that Stalin had him killed, he was engaged on a Stalin biography in which scorn and a sort of incredulity spilled over from virtually every page. None could have written as Trotsky did of Lenin had he had a fundamental objection to the glorification of the leader. What Trotsky was determined to demonstrate was Stalin's utter unworthiness for the laurels of the revolution. Unlike even the fascist dictators, he had no capacity or attribute that in Trotsky's estimation either fitted him for leadership or even assisted him in achieving it. Neither a thinker, a writer nor an orator, it was through an impersonal machine alone that Stalin could have acceded to power, and 'it was not he who created the machine, but the machine which created him'.[2] Stalin had prevailed as 'the supreme expression of the mediocrity of the apparatus'.[3]

However damning the characterisation, it is strangely congruent with the image that Stalin constructed of himself.[4] In the issue of Lenin's succession, Stalin had had no illusions that he might have been favoured by his personal history or the quality of his public persona. Instead, it was precisely as the expression of the higher interests of the party, which he

K. Morgan, *International Communism and the Cult of the Individual*, DOI 10.1057/978-1-137-55667-7_4

would only have forborne from calling a machine, that he rose to his dominant position among Trotsky's antagonists. Questioned on the differences between them in 1927, Stalin declined to explain his own position, insisting that the issues were not personal ones and that it was against the party's principles for individuals to 'thrust themselves forward'.[5] Even when his full-blown cult surfaced two years later, he set down the accolades he received as 'addressed to the great Party of the working class, which bore me and reared me in its own image and likeness'.[6] Two years later, it was Trotsky's example which he cited to Emil Ludwig to demonstrate the limits of the role of the individual, and to show how even a reputation like Trotsky's counted for nothing should the link with the masses be severed.[7]

What Trotsky dubbed Stalin's school of falsification showed every ingenuity in embedding him within a party history which in reality he had so little claim upon. There was, on the other hand, no attempt to delineate a political persona or career trajectory which in any way set Stalin apart from the party. Researchers in Soviet archives have uncovered numerous examples of Stalin's apparent ambivalence regarding his own cult. This has plausibly been attributed both to the circumscription of the role of the individual within the marxist tradition and to the cultlike properties attaching to the quality of modesty itself.[8] What also mattered was that modesty and impersonality were among the few points on which Stalin could not only outdo more conspicuously gifted rivals but turn his limitations into positive assets.

When Stalin spoke of modesty, and Trotsky of mediocrity, it is therefore hard to avoid the impression that they were referring to the same thing. Surrounded by his acolytes, Stalin would recall in 1937 how not only Trotsky but Bukharin, Zinoviev and others had at one time exceeded him in popularity. He, however, had had the support of the 'middle cadres', which certainly did mean the apparatus. '*They're the ones who choose the leader*', Stalin saluted them. '*They don't try to climb above their station; you don't even notice them.*'[9] Dimitrov recorded the encounter, which also included the pledge to destroy all those who erred even in their thoughts; and as the Comintern's most popular personality the moral would certainly not have been lost on him. The peculiarities of Stalin's cult are impossible to grasp fully without this sense of how it originated as an anti-cult. Above all, at least to begin with, it was the anti-cult of Trotsky himself.

This is an aspect of the phenomenon that perhaps stands out most clearly in an international setting. Domestically, the sending of Trotsky into exile signified his removal as a political rival. Internationally, it not only marked him out as Stalin's chief antagonist; it also gave him the opportunity, and financially the necessity, of publicising his alternative claims to Lenin's legacy through works like his autobiography *My Life* (Moya Zhizn) and its serialisation in popular newspapers. News coverage of Trotsky's activities had been eliminated from the Soviet press; the trickle of copies of the *Byulleten' oppozitsii* that filtered through the censorship had dwindled rapidly. Through *My Life* and his monumental *History of the Russian Revolution* (1932–1933), Trotsky nevertheless fashioned a biographical persona and narrative of Bolshevik history whose brilliancy, fluency and rapidity of execution made the efforts of the apparatus appear positively lumbering. The immediate contraction of Stalin's cult over the course of 1930 has been explained in various ways. These include residual opposition to Stalin within the party and his desire not to be identified with the traumas of collectivisation.[10] But there was also the humiliating reminder that this was not a terrain necessarily favourable to him, and that a usable political capital could no more be manufactured overnight than could a socialist economy that was also starting out from a position of relative backwardness.

Whatever the reason, the appearance of *My Life* provoked a forthright rebuttal of its foregrounding of a personality which in this case was Trotsky's own. M.N. Pokrovsky was the doyen of Bolshevik historians, and one who a few years later would become the target of a campaign of posthumous vilification. There were various reasons for this, among them Pokrovsky's alleged depreciation of the historical role of the individual.[11] Until his death in 1932, Pokrovsky nevertheless retained his preeminence, and Stalin himself was a pall-bearer at his funeral. His review of *My Life* was therefore authoritative. Appearing in the central committee journal *Bol'shevik*, it characterised Trotsky as Trotsky himself depicted Kerensky: as an idol of the passing moment who was blinded by the glare of his own publicity. The party in any case was not a feudal fief; it could not delegate power over itself to 'any single person', least of all to one who had conclusively revealed himself a 'philistinish individualist'.[12]

According to Pokrovsky's biographer George M. Enteen, this might have been an aesopian swipe at Stalin himself. The persistence of anti-Stalin sentiment should certainly not be underestimated; but it was not as yet in these terms that even those hostile to Stalin tended to refer to him. On the contrary, it was Trotsky's 'subjectivism', or that by extension of his supporters, that had been a staple of the 'anti-Bonaparte fraction' since its first coalescing in the months of Lenin's final illness. Already five years earlier, Dutt in Britain had complained of '*the old familiar bourgeois recipe of the personal struggle for power*' and of the Trotsky debate being 'degraded into a cheap film-drama for Western European and American readers'.[13] The British party more than most was congenitally averse to the extension of any special prerogatives, either to Trotsky as an individual or to the intellectuals with whom he was identified. In reaffirming this position at the Comintern, the dour Scottish ironmoulder Tom Bell thus stressed that not only were romanticism and 'valiant service' now required, but 'real discipline and above all centralised direction'.[14]

When simultaneously with Pokrovsky the future CPUSA leader Earl Browder expressed very similar views of Trotsky's autobiography, he would have been horrified at the suggestion that he might have had Stalin in mind. Browder too objected to Trotsky's allegedly presuming to something like a divine right of kingship which could be transmitted from Lenin to himself, and the entire party and its leadership thereby subordinated to his 'individual will'. If, as Enteen inferred, there was 'an indisposition on Pokrovskii's part to laud the party's leader', Browder apparently shared it. What he focused on instead was the alleged absence in Trotsky's account of almost 'any hint of the existence of the *working class*', whose shadowy presence served only to throw into higher relief Trotsky's own dazzling exploits, and the desirability of loyal service to him. The party, Browder continued, fared even worse, and the Red Army was completely obscured by Trotsky's strutting figure, as if it existed 'only as an extension of his own personality'. In future years it might certainly have seemed intrepid to suggest that the party could have 'no more dangerous or insidious enemy than a leader inside its apparatus who thinks in terms of personal power'.[15] But there is no doubt whatsoever that Browder believed he was justifying Stalin's authority rather than undermining it.

The lavishing on Trotsky of such attentions, however critical, may have seemed like taking him far too much at his own self-estimation. Possibly it was on this line of reasoning that in its English translation the second instalment of Pokrovsky's review never appeared. Certainly, one should not exaggerate the extent to which communists internationally polemicised with Trotsky, as if he were a contender still for Lenin's legacy. The circulation internationally of Osip Piatnitsky's *Memoirs of a Bolshevik* did provide an implicit counter-narrative in which the 'personal element' merged into the collective and a life of devotion to the party.[16] But when Trotsky's erstwhile follower Karl Radek removed the original essay on him from his *Portraits and Pamphlets*, it was not to replace it with a denunciation, but to make way for one of the first truly sycophantic eulogies of Stalin, initially appearing in *Pravda* in the run-up to the Congress of Victors.[17]

As Stalin edged his way onto the international stage, it was nevertheless the drama of his personal battle with Trotsky that held the attention of a wider public. Ludwig, though given so little encouragement, was typical. In his published Stalin profile, also appearing in 1934, he offered an extended juxtaposition of the Trotsky who inspired the masses, and who was versatile, brilliant and alert, and the cautious, ponderous Stalin who preferred to organise them. Trotsky was like a 'high-powered motor car' taking every gradient at speed, while Stalin's was the 'slow plodding movement' of a tractor as silently and inexorably it broke through the soil.[18] In every such depiction one has a glimpse already of the Napoleon—'not much of a talker, but with a reputation for getting his own way'—and the vivacious Snowball of Orwell's *Animal Farm*.[19]

The linking of their names seemed impossible to get away from. When Barbusse took on the commission of Stalin's biography, he described how his anticipated American reading public 'hardly knew the USSR except through Trotsky'.[20] Barbusse was the one European writer who combined a communist party commitment with an international literary reputation. Though his casting in the role of biographer must in part have seemed to Stalin the answer to the charge of mediocrity, he clearly also had in mind Barbusse's particular credentials for reaching this wider public. This had been the rationale for Barbusse's cultural review *Monde*, discussed with Stalin at its inception, and Barbusse himself envisaged the Stalin volume as one 'capable of getting everywhere and being understood by all and influencing what is called "public opinion" or "the general public"'.[21] To achieve this, Barbusse also held that the popular impression of a personal power struggle required an unbiased portrait of Stalin's defeated rival confirming Trotsky's incapacity to lead the USSR even in spite of his 'brilliant qualities'. As Barbusse rightly anticipated, this was the aspect of his treatment that most provoked his sponsors' misgivings.[22]

The draft was overseen by Alexei Stetsky, the CPSU's head of Kultprop, and it was Barbusse's 'extreme indulgence' towards Trotsky that most concerned him: 'I cannot understand why in a book about Stalin, who is leading the construction of socialism, there is so much about Trotsky's "spiritual tribulations", and why it is so tolerant towards him.'[23] Specific objections were detailed in Stetsky's comments on the manuscript. Their basic premise was that Trotsky, having gone over to the counter-revolution, need not therefore be cited in any positive context whatever the period this related to. Barbusse accordingly made certain cosmetic adjustments; and on revisiting Moscow he was provided with specific leads on these issues by the Hungarian Béla Kun, with whom his principal Moscow contact Alfred Kurella had at one time collaborated in Comintern agitprop.

Intended as a summation of Stalin's better qualities, Barbusse's published text consequently revealed a model and exemplar very different from the image which French or American readers had of Lenin. When famously Barbusse characterised Stalin as the 'Lenin of today', he did not merely imply an equivalence of stature and an identity of basic outlook; he also allowed for the different qualities which their different times required. It was Kun whose lead he followed in thus describing Lenin as an agitator 'by force of circumstances' which no longer existed. In Lenin's day, Kun explained, the system was not yet organised, and to have a connection it was necessary to go among the masses. 'Now the whole system is so organised that by talking with the cadres one can know of everything that happens in the country and thus be very close to the masses.' It was thus, he maintained, that Stalin preferred not to address the masses directly. Where Lenin was a sort of directing head (*chef dirigeant*), Stalin was the figure of the manager (*gérant*) and the teacher. Faithfully reproduced in Barbusse's text, one therefore finds the distinction between Lenin as himself the 'Director' and Stalin working through what was now a 'vast directive system' and the intermediary of the organisation. Stalin had pointed out to Ludwig that the great man was not himself the maker of history in the Carlylean sense. Barbusse, in returning to Carlyle, described him instead as the indispensable figure called forth by history, 'like a centralising machine'—exactly as the party through which Lenin reproduced himself was a 'machine for the production of leadership' (*une machine productrice de direction*).[24]

It is easy to see why this should be regarded as a cult of the collective reproduced in the individual rather than originating there.[25] Crucially, it was a cult of the party; as fashioned by Barbusse, it was also a cult of the new workers' state with whose symbolic centre in the Kremlin his narrative both started and concluded. When Barbusse, addressing the western reader, referred to Stalin as if watching over them, and holding the better part of their destinies in his own hands, it was like the vesting of the interests of a wider cult community in his paternalist embrace. But at the same time, the cult of the collective combined with Stalin's particular limitations to demand a form of anti-charisma through the discrediting of the particular accomplishments that were Trotsky's.

In an extended juxtaposition, Barbusse thus conjured up an anti-Stalin who not only nurtured bonapartist ambitions but was bereft of the constructive and statesmanlike qualities which the new Soviet state required. Barbusse conceded Trotsky's qualities, in particular his mastery of the written and spoken word. Nevertheless, in describing him as simply the reverse of Stalin, it was as if these as much as Trotsky's defects were to be regarded as in some way suspect. This was especially true of Trotsky's reputation as one of the foremost public speakers of his times. In accents reminiscent of Le Bon, Pokrovsky had depicted a figure intoxicated by his own oratorical powers and the command this gave him of the public platform.[26] According to Kun, Trotsky had never understood what the party represented, but sought to seize hold of the 'amorphous mass'. He was still not at this stage accused of conspiracy or actual treachery, but it was as if this were how the disciplines of the machine were circumvented: like an incitement to the spontaneity for which 'Luxemburgism' was in just this period also anathematised.[27]

(ii)

It was only in the USSR that communism was a directing system whose leaders did not sometimes have to put themselves before the masses. Where communist parties sought not to exercise power, but to contest it through movements of protest or resistance, it is not surprising that Lenin still spoke more to their imaginations. Sarah Davies refers in the Soviet context to a 'feudal-like pyramid' of cults and mini-cults, with Stalin at the head embodying an order that was static, conservative, self-contained and 'the antithesis of revolution'.[28] There was of course another narrative, according to which the Soviet state embodied the revolutionary hopes of millions, and justified the exercising of a form of leadership that was accountable only to the movement of history itself.[29] It is far from clear, however, that this was the figure that Stalin presented to those drawn to communism, or the conception of the leader by which as yet the commitments they freely made to it were principally impelled.

In a world of great uncertainty, there is no doubt that the image of the 'man at the helm', and of the Soviet state itself as a force in world affairs, could resonate beyond the communists' ranks. Romain Rolland was a close collaborator of Barbusse whose attraction towards Soviet Russia was inseparable from his revulsion from the experience and impending threat of war. Reading Stalin's interview with H.G. Wells, Rolland singled out his 'perfect self-mastery' and granite-like solidity of mind among the qualities that led him to hope for a similar meeting.[30] When this was duly arranged, Rolland even referred to the USSR having something akin to an 'imperial' responsibility to watch over the interests of other peoples. Nevertheless, Rolland also posed Stalin such pointed questions regarding the more controversial aspects of Soviet policy that the interview was never authorised for publication. Rolland, moreover, was deeply troubled by the news of arrests, and wrote privately of his revulsion for the 'idolatry of individuals', whether under fascism or communism. Beatrice Webb described the 'idolisation of the leader, past and present' as a cause of 'disastrous developments in the USSR … insecurity, hypocrisy, lack of initiative, the selection of individuals for important posts, who are stupid or selfish or deceitful'. Despite the preference in each of these cases for Stalin over Trotsky, it is clear that the USSR held their loyalty in spite of the form of leadership he represented, not because of it.[31]

There was one final audience, with the German Lion Feuchtwanger. Held as the show trials had already begun, its importance lay in counteracting the much-publicised disillusionment in Stalin and his dictatorship of the quondam fellow-traveller André Gide.[32] Widely circulated in the West, Feuchtwanger's impressions included a further extended rumination on the two contrasting revolutionary leaders, the one able to rouse the masses in times of strife, the other once more the figure of 'unyielding solidity' able to organise them. Though the Soviet system as described by Feuchtwanger was anything but static, he did dismiss concerns like Gide's with its material inequalities as 'an atavistic derivative of primitive Christian views'; and he did describe the one basic division in Soviet society as that between the 'fighters' who had made the revolution and the 'workers' whose rather different qualities were needed for reconstruction. He even justified the show trials of these fighters now turned traitors by analogy with the unlamented Warren Hastings, whom he had earlier written a play about, and who was one of the most brutal, cruel and notorious of the Britons who had 'introduced Western civilisation into India' using similarly salutary methods. With its extended discussion of the 'antithesis of character as of opinion' which Stalin and Trotsky represented, Feuchtwanger's account appeared in a substantial Soviet edition as well as the other main European languages.[33]

Even at their most benign, the constructions of Stalin as statesman and administrator were not easy to adapt to circumstances which for most communist parties were more akin to Lenin's times than Stalin's managerial revolution. There were of course innumerable such discrepancies, and from strikes to civil liberties the paradox but not the oxymoron of popular-front stalinism was founded on these difficulties of translation. The journalist W.H. Chamberlin paraphrased Trotsky in describing how the extension of Stalin's regime to the International tended to 'eliminate vigorous personalities and ... bring to positions of leadership in Communist parties throughout the world colorless bureaucratic mediocrities'. Unlike Trotsky, Chamberlin recognised a certain functionality to such a system within a 'going concern' like the USSR. 'But this is emphatically not the type of man who can lead a successful revolution ... for which independence, daring, and initiative are required.'[34]

Trotsky would have pointed out that this was why the Comintern led no successful revolutions. Despite some initial uncertainty, Stalin was no longer to be compared to revolutionary heroes like Spartacus or Stenka Razin. The figure Barbusse depicted was the symbol of a 'new world' that was also the Soviet state. It was on this that his account centred at every stage; it was as the leader of this state that Stalin's example extended even beyond its borders, with the Comintern intruding only momentarily as a breeding-ground for deviations.[35] The replication internationally of a pyramid-like hierarchy of cults did therefore signify both the bureaucratisation of the communist movement and its overt subordination to the higher state interest of the USSR. This, nevertheless, was realised in any systematic way only during the Cold War. The communist parties of the 1930s–1940s might not have led any revolutions. They did however engage in struggles and achieve political advances requiring something more than the projection of colourless mediocrities. Thälmann, Pollitt, Ibárruri: all were described precisely as fighters, just as Dimitrov extolled the leadership of 'real Bolshevik fighters' that the experience of irreconcilable class struggle could alone produce.[36] Collective disciplines were always reasserted in the end, and figures excluded who demonstrated a genuine initiative and independence. Nevertheless, both as inspiration and as model the reproduction of the Stalin cult internationally was far less central to this first phase of cult-building than one might have imagined.

What it did provide was an integrating cult for the more select population connecting Moscow and the Comintern's national sections. To extrapolate from Kun's distinction, Stalin's cult at this stage was not so much linked with the wider body of communist activists as with the organisational intermediaries which an originally Francophone literature characterises as 'Cominternians'. Extending beyond the upper tier of party leaders, this was the larger population which, through some longer or shorter period spent in the USSR, was exposed at first hand to such characteristic Bolshevik practices as self-criticism and the purge.[37] The Stalin cult was one of these practices. For those inducted into it in or by the early 1930s, it mattered less as public symbol of their cause than as an integrating force demanding the overt conformism of the middle cadres who on an international scale included the leaders of the national communist parties themselves.

Few could illustrate better than Marcel Cachin how exposure to this environment could socialise the functionary into a culture of disciplined allegiance that eventually extended from party and party-state to the individual who symbolised its authority. In Cachin's case, exceptionally, the process is documented in his private journals. A fervent supporter of the 1914–1918 war, Cachin had already in 1920 shown his susceptibility to such influences when he returned from Moscow as a socialist party delegate now committed to his party's unconditional affiliation to the Comintern. Though in subsequent accounts Cachin's interview with Lenin was given pride of place, his journals evoke the general impression made by the staging of a genuine world congress, and the grandiose mass spectacles in which scenes of the revolution were re-enacted for the delegates. Lenin's ovations were interminable, Trotsky's only a little less so, and Stalin of course was the shadowiest of figures. Even when Cachin did first notice him in 1925, there was no intimation that the sober gestures and colourless voice would ever prove a source of fascination.[38]

If Stalin did nevertheless come to exercise a sort of charisma, it was not the source of his power but a way of demonstrating it. In Cachin's case, it was not until the CPSU central committee plenum of January 1933 that for the first time he depicted the organiser of tenacious will and leninist faith in whom the party's homogeneity had become embodied. Attentive now to his every movement, Cachin lingered on Stalin's mode of address:

> Stalin speaks. Black hair and moustache, solidly built, reads slowly, very few gestures, brief and simple; his hand sometimes cuts through the air as if to slice it, but often the two hands are crossed and pulled up over his stomach. The tone is that of ordinary conversation, silences, hesitations, repetitions; he speaks with a detached and distant air, as if to himself. He allows the end of each phrase to fall away, instead of shouting it forth; he never gets excited, the tone is monotonous, without the slightest flourish. It's an absolute contempt for eloquence, form, emphasis. The emotion is in the figures, in the findings of the victory bulletin, in the simple, clear dialectic, in the feeling of

> self-assurance, in the results announced. Every now and then a voice comes from the floor: 'we can't hear you'. He replies, 'it's this devil of a microphone. I'm not used to it, I don't know where to put myself in front of it.' And everybody laughs.[39]

Like the gunslinger in an American western, Stalin turned inarticulacy itself into a sort of mystique. In Georgia some years earlier, the *New Masses* correspondent Joseph Freeman had witnessed him stoke up a frenetic clamour by bowing slowly, declining to speak and exuding 'reserve, dignity and power'. Freeman too described an initially inaudible Stalin addressing the Comintern in 1926, again provoking complaisant hilarity on explaining that he had been eating herring.[40]

Far more than Ibárruri, Stalin could use such techniques knowing that all would strain to hear and none would dare speak over. Attending as a delegate from her party, Ibárruri herself described how at the Congress of Victors, she drew inspiration from merely seeing Stalin, 'seeing his firmness', seeing the calmness with which he weathered all storms. A cadre of long standing, she knew that it was more important to learn from Stalin than to set eyes upon him. 'None the less I must admit frankly that I arrived in the Soviet Union precisely with the desire to see Stalin … a desire which completely enveloped my feelings and thoughts.'[41] The Briton Maggie Jordan, one of hundreds who attended the International Lenin School, had afterwards stayed on in the USSR to work in a Soviet enterprise. Unlike the great majority of her fellow British communists, she consequently had a glimpse of Stalin in the flesh during the May Day procession in Red Square:

> We do not march, we dance, singing and cheering, waving to the well-loved figures on the tribune.
>
> Did you see, Stalin pointed out our contingent, waved to us!
>
> *To each it seems that Stalin's smile, Kalinin's greeting, the attention of the great leaders of the people, was directed specially to THEIR contingent.*[42]

The one sometime British communist to attempt Stalin's biography was another Cominternian, J.T. Murphy, whom the CPGB had expelled as early as 1932, but who had personally witnessed Stalin's rise to power and even moved the resolution of Trotsky's expulsion from the Comintern executive. Browder in the USA was another who would come to speak out against his party and finally even the USSR, but not, as long as he lived, against 'his idol, Joseph Stalin'.[43]

Accounts like Ibárruri's were for public consumption. Nevertheless, there was no 'We meet Stalin' collection to collate these impressions like the ones devoted to Lenin.[44] The paradox of Stalin's cult internationally was that in a culture of the written word it was verbally impoverished, and that in a world of mass communications it privileged rites of participation from which western communists were generally excluded. The paradox is encapsulated by the Comintern's seventh world congress in 1935. In cultic terms, this was a Comintern counterpart to the Congress of Victors, with a new departure in congress arrangements when Togliatti saluted Stalin on the delegates' behalf. 'Military music with trumpets', Cachin's journal records.

> Impeccable and powerful processions. Warm and enthusiastic atmosphere. The homage to Stalin, unanimous, vibrant.

Stalin knew better than to ruin the effect by replying. Even the *Pravda* photo apparently showing him with delegates was a political contrivance.[45] Cachin himself succumbed completely to these influences, and it was Stalin whom by now he credited with an epoch of transformation stretching back even into Lenin's time.[46] Nevertheless, in its published record and collective memory, the seventh congress was Dimitrov's moment, not Stalin's, and it was Dimitrov who in articulating its leitmotiv of anti-fascist unity became as if synonymous with it. 'Here what the Seventh Congress said, / If true, if false, is live or dead', John Cornford wrote just before his death in Spain. What the Seventh Congress said was what Dimitrov said, and Stalin, who said nothing, seemed at times a figure not dead but nor fully living either.[47]

'Watch Stalin make a speech', wrote another of the few who had done. 'Note the simplicity. Not a single platform gesture. He speaks rather as an ordinary comrade, to comrades.'[48] In fact, his hand, if sometimes raised, was usually seen in regal wave, or thrust into his coat like Napoleon. Through emulation or a form of natural selection, this did over time become a *stalinski* style that a number of communist party leaders seem to have adopted. Prestes and Togliatti, both lacking any formative experience of the mass platform, were two such leaders whose manner was explicitly distinguished from the more expressive forms of political oratory. Prestes was 'calm, affable, tranquil, simple', Togliatti also calm and measured, and Gottwald in his 'dry, matter-of-fact manner' would pile up words like bricks, soberly, calmly and without gesticulation or a single oratorical flight. Browder according to one profile was 'addicted to dry, pedestrian prose, and … orates in a relentless monotone, using gestures sparingly'. There was even a well-intentioned Browder song, *The Quiet Man from Kansas*.[49]

Nevertheless, what Souvarine acidly referred to as Stalin's 'precious gift of dumbness' was not the obvious way to mobilise a public for political struggle.[50] Pollitt was an old-school orator whose perorations brought audiences to their feet.[51] Thälmann, in Barbusse's words, was the 'man of crowds', who personified the mass before him and could move it to scenes of indescribable enthusiasm.[52] Even Thorez, often described in *stalinski* terms, had studied the orators of the French revolution, and in this respect was commended by his normally so critical biographer Philippe Robrieux.[53] Barbusse contrasted Stalin both with the big mouths like Hitler and with the bleatings of a Gandhi. He not only described how Stalin dispensed with the usual platform arts, but also claimed that Lenin's gesturing statues gave a misleading impression of the Bolshevik leader.[54] Even so, when a publication was planned about Barbusse himself, he expressly requested that he be shown in just this classic pose, with 'arm raised in the course of giving a speech'. Although events in Germany prevented the publication's appearance, it was in this way that Barbusse was depicted in the volume of tributes published after his death.[55]

If ever a Bolshevik was summed up by a visual prop, it was Stalin and his pipe. In the French cult collection *Stalin in Images* (1950), it replaces the cigarette in the mid-1920s, and with the wartime appearance of the Generalissimo is again relinquished for the cigarette, though it by no means disappeared from Soviet graphic art. In the meantime, like the simple clothes he wore, it told you that Stalin was not of the old ruling establishment. 'The pipe is ordinary, and so is the jacket', wrote Mikhail Koltsov in his 50th-birthday *Pravda* sketch.[56] In Britain they would even carol to a local folk air: 'Your Uncle Joe's a worker / And a very decent chap / Because he smokes a pipe and wears / A taxi-driver's cap'.[57] It was a crucial part of Stalin's image, and in Britain at least helps to explain his wartime popularity. '"Just like us" is the commonest phrase', claimed one party eulogist. His quiet and unassuming manner was a positive advantage, and in his refusal for the time being of gold braid and orders, '"Joe" in his cap and "Denims"' embodied 'all the virtues of the common man'.[58]

The pipe, even so, was not just a social signifier. If to Britons it suggested avuncularity, it was as the hallmark of a Stalin who in an age of commotion was never flustered, never provoked, never to be hurried and always in control. 'His speeches develop in strict order', Koltsov's piece continued; 'first, second, fifth, sixth'. Barbusse's Stalin says nonchalantly, 'it's nothing', and, though in this case it is a cigarette, carries on smoking as the tsar's secret police surround him.[59] Manuilsky also had him 'calmly smoking his pipe' while opponents screamed hysterically at Lenin: just the scene depicted by their screen doubles in *Lenin in October*.[60] Manuilsky, like Dimitrov, was one of those who also took to being photographed with a pipe, and wearing one of the 'leaders' suits' (*vozhdevki*) which latterly were referred to as Stalin suits.[61]

In the context of Bolshevik iconography, the binary opposition of plebeian pipe and plutocrats' cigar is certainly suggestive.[62] Nevertheless, when Graham Greene observed Stalin's pipe and headmasterly manner in *Lenin in October*, the analogy that struck him was with that other plain, unhurried, faux-naïf countryman on the other side of Europe, Stanley Baldwin.[63] Both cultivated assurance and stability as the rest of Europe tore itself apart; and while we need not agree with Greene that Stalin played his part 'on Worcestershire lines', it is fascinating to learn of him being sent good solid pipes of British manufacture.[64] What distinguished him as much as Baldwin from the agitator and the malcontent was a persona exuding authority more than the challenge to authority, mastery of time instead of a sense of urgency, and command of self rather than possession by the spirit of revolt. 'Whoever you are', Barbusse concluded, 'the better part of your destiny is in the hands of this other man, who also watches over all, and who labours – the man with the head of a scholar, the face of a worker, and the dress of a simple soldier'.[65]

4.2 Maurice Thorez's Party

(i)

Souvarine visualised the Stalin cult as a diptych. One side depicted Stalin's glorification; the other, the ruin and degradation of those he vanquished through the trials that synchronised with his pre-war cult.[66] The marginalisation or subordination of rivals was also possible. But Stalin's weakness in personal political capital necessitated not just the fabrication of his own accomplishments but the negation or obliteration of alternative claims. Anticipating his physical assassination in 1940, Trotsky's symbolic liquidation was effected through the show trials; and though Stalin's scripted role as plotters' target was initially somewhat understated, by the time of the third trial in March 1938 he was brought forward more decisively as 'the people's defender and hope'.[67] With the Cold War systematisation of cult production, the pattern was repeated in a series of further show trials that only Stalin's death brought to a close. In every case, there was the same hunting out of heresy. In every western communist party, the effect produced was of a closer bonding of the party faithful, through the credence given proceedings eliciting general disbelief and centring on an esoteric and deeply disturbing ritual of self-incrimination.

The PCF alone of the major western parties went as far as outright imitation.[68] The expulsion in 1952 of two of the party's most experienced leaders, André Marty and Charles Tillon, could not have resulted in their physical elimination. Tillon, whose role in the affair was a supporting one, did not even lose his party membership. Marty, on the other hand, was subjected to a vicious campaign of defamation, including the allegation of being a police spy, and was henceforth expunged from the party's collective memory except in the guise of traitor. Tillon's later account of the affair aptly described it as a Moscow trial staged in Paris.[69]

Thorez's was a cult more exaggerated, pervasive and tenuously documented than that of any other western communist leader's. Marty did not in other respects resemble Trotsky, but he did possess the personal political capital which Thorez lacked, and a deep conviction as to what such a record represented in terms of entitlement and identity. Marty's name was synonymous with the famous Black Sea mutiny in support of the infant Soviet republic, and he was already one of communism's most celebrated figures when he redoubled his political capital as organiser for the Comintern of the International Brigades. Who else, as Cachin put it, had played such a part in the two decisive movements of his generation?[70] The only possible answer in France would be Tillon, who was also a Black Sea mutiny veteran, and who subsequently headed the communist resistance movement and assumed the high responsibilities in party and briefly government that his wartime record seemed to justify. Whatever the precise origins of the Marty–Tillon affair, its framing as a diptych was understood by all. In the charges brought against the accused, a final section, 'With Maurice Thorez', reaffirmed Thorez's 'stalinist political leadership' against their attempts to undermine it.[71] When Marty three years later published his counter-indictment, it centred on what already, without waiting for the Khrushchev speech, he called the cult of the individual.[72]

The rivalry of Thorez and Marty had deep roots and many causes.[73] Marty by his own admission was a difficult man, and his combative manner and political outlook sat uncomfortably with the more accommodating phases of communist policy. Though he had a base in Paris as an elected representative, Marty could not have reached out to a wider national public; and if Tillon, according to Denis Peschanski, was the least Cominternian of Cominternians, Marty's distinction was to have achieved the highest standing within the international apparatus of any member of a fully legal party.[74] What both in their different ways did nevertheless represent was a presence within the PCF that implicitly detracted from the Thorez cult, and underlined its bureaucratic character as one, like Stalin's, requiring the annulment of alternative narratives of party history and the willing or enforced compliance of those whose personal histories embodied them. If an integrating cult meant the centring on the leader of a Manichean conception of the party citadel, no oppositional party represented this better than the Cold War PCF. It is on this aspect of Thorez's leadership that the discussion here will focus.

When in 1935 he followed Dimitrov onto the podium at the seventh world congress, Thorez was aged just 35. Two years later there appeared his autobiography *Son of the People*, which was drafted on his behalf, and commanded a third of its communist publishers' annual publicity budget.[75] As Thorez himself acknowledged, one did not as a rule produce an autobiography at this age. This did therefore represent the deliberate construction of a public persona rather different in character from a superficially similar production like Gallacher's *Revolt on the Clyde*.

Most of all, Thorez's account bore the promise of the chapters that were still to be written. For the bolshevising Comintern, the first attraction of youth was as a biographical tabula rasa that minimised the exposure to contaminating influences like social democracy. For the PCF's popular-front enrolment, on the other hand, what Thorez's youth conveyed was a positive quality presaging a radical break with an ailing political establishment and a better future still to be realised. If youth, as Julian Jackson writes, was a watchword of the popular front, it could hardly now be captured by the sexagenarian Cachin.[76] Léon Blum, Thorez's socialist counterpart, was also nearly 30 years his elder: a man of letters and reputed wealth easily caricatured as a decrepit figure whom the so much younger Thorez had taken in hand.[77] Communism, Vaillant-Couturier wrote, was 'the youth of the world', and Thorez as the youngest of the Stalin generation was the proof. The popular front would remain his principal source of political capital, and its aura would for many years remain attached to him, like the Dorian Gray of the passing moment when everything had seemed achievable. A message on Thorez's 44th birthday thus recalled the younger figure who had carried such assurance and described him even now as personifying the 'youthfulness of our ideal'.[78] The communist mayor of Choisy, himself aged nearly 70, addressed him simply as 'the light, the future, the youth of the world', and the promise, again in much-cited words of Vaillant-Couturier, of 'tomorrows that sing'.[79]

At the PCF's Villeurbanne congress of January 1936, Cachin was still acclaimed as the party's 'venerated leader', and he alone had been singled out as exemplar in a resolution commemorating the PCF's foundation. It was Thorez, even so, who delivered the main congress report to prolonged ovations.[80] He was also now publicly identified as general secretary, and in the spring elections that marked the communists' electoral breakthrough he headed the campaign and delivered the PCF's first ever election broadcast.[81] A first *L'Humanité* profile also appeared, styling Thorez the party's leader, but with youth as his credential rather than venerability. 'He's one of those lads from the Nord', wrote its female author with disconcerting relish, 'with an athlete's body, straight as a pillar, broad-shouldered, all of it solid muscle'—and the rosy cheeks of a child running in from the wind. Everybody, she continued, addressed him as Maurice, or by the familiar 'tu'; like Thorez's age, its informality marked him out from Cachin as well as Blum.[82] In the recordings of speeches issued for the election, Cachin handled the traditional themes of communism and the soviets, but it was Thorez who expounded the new ideas of the popular front and union of the nation.[83] As the slogan 'Soviets everywhere!' gave way to 'Thorez into power!', it was the party's younger supporters, according to Angelo Tasca, who most of all tended to personalise their cause in this way.[84] Stalin's evident approval was in Thorez's case both expressed and reinforced by his close personal and working relations with the Comintern's secret delegate in France, the Slovakian Eugen Fried.[85]

Nevertheless, in the public manifestations of his leadership Thorez did not as yet exercise the exclusive prerogatives of the integration figure. When Jacques Solomon reviewed *Son of the People* in the PCF journal *Cahiers du bolchevisme*, it was still Barbusse whom he recognised as the champion of unity, and a posthumous collection of Barbusse tributes was one of the communist best-sellers of the period.[86] Cachin's enduring popularity, meanwhile, was sustained by his high visibility in *L'Humanité*. The same was true of Vaillant-Couturier, the paper's editor-in-chief, whose sudden death in October 1937 occasioned Paris's largest ever communist funeral and reputedly the biggest mass turnout of the popular front.

Still short of his 46th birthday, and an enthusiast at once for aviation, blood-sports and the arts, Vaillant-Couturier himself conveyed as well as expressed the image of 'eternal youth'.[87] As mayor of the red-belt Villejuif municipality, he had also promoted initiatives in housing, public health and education that perfectly symbolised the spirit of enlightenment and modernity so crucial to the appeal of 1930s communism.

Above all there was Marty. When Marty addressed the Villeurbanne congress, there were also scenes of 'indescribable enthusiasm' and the strains broke forth of the 'Hymn to the Black Sea sailors'—an adaptation of the older 'Hymn to the Seventeenth Regiment', which had refused to fire on striking workers.[88] Marty through his role in the mutiny had indeed acquired an almost legendary status. According to Jean-Richard Bloch, not a patch of Soviet water was without a ship bearing his name, while Ernest Hemingway in *For Whom the Bell Tolls* (1940) had the Russian Karkov wonder prophetically about the future renaming of factories and collective farms should Marty fall from favour.[89] When the Comintern in 1935 introduced secretariats named after their responsible secretary in the spirit of the turn to the individual, Marty was one of those charged with this responsibility, and it was in this capacity that he played the role that earned him notoriety at the head of the International Brigades. Even the jaundiced depiction of him to be found in Hemingway's novel did confirm his identification in the public mind with one of the defining conflicts of the age.[90]

As Thorez meanwhile assumed a leading position in France, he began to gather round him the cult coterie which in due course would provide him with a personal entourage quite distinct from the party's political secretariat.[91] In the loyalty he commanded from a layer of intellectual recruits there was perhaps already a foretaste of the synthetic quality of the integrating cult. Much as Thorez exploited the mystique of his coalfield origins, he never underestimated the contribution that communists of bourgeois origin and education could make to the PCF's establishment as a cultural as well as political force. Paradoxically, it was actually Marty, though he did not advertise the fact, who held a bachelor of sciences from the prestigious school of marine mechanics. A native of a Perpignan whose father was a veteran of the Narbonne Commune, Marty nevertheless adopted an abrasively proletarian world-view and identity and would account for its rough edges by invoking the imprint of Catalonia and the syndicalism of the naval dockyards.[92] Not the least of Thorez's attractions to the emerging body of thorézians was that he was free of any such taint. Already in 1934–1935, when Marty had oversight of *L'Humanité*, there were clear signs of the differences between them, and Marty ascribed to Thorez's active or tacit assent the undermining of his own authority by journalists like Vaillant-Couturier and Gabriel Péri.[93]

It was Marty's personal history rather than his temper that made him a figure to be reckoned with. When *L'Humanité* profiled Thorez, there was no mention of labour movement responsibilities nor of his leading any major political action. Apart from his imprisonment for agitation against the Rif war in Algeria, his biographical capital thus appeared as a series of party offices listed and dated in ascending order, like one's movement through any other bureaucracy.[94] In greeting Marty on his 50th birthday a few months earlier, the Comintern had emphasised instead the antecedents and personal history that marked him out as the incarnation of a class in struggle.[95] Rémi Skoutelsky refers at this point to a veritable Marty cult, and the messages and greetings in Marty's papers are certainly as fulsome as any yet addressed to Thorez.[96]

Nobody had a stronger sense of political capital as an accrual both by and through the individual.[97] Marty's two-volume account of the Black Sea mutiny was revised and reissued as a single volume in 1939 and again in 1949, and there was also a shorter pamphlet version. Marty also mapped out a similar history of the International Brigades which but for the outbreak of war would have been serialised in the *Communist International*.[98] Rosa Michel, who worked with him in the Comintern's Marty secretariat, even conveyed a sense of the miraculous in the story of the paralysed Spanish volunteer, unable to communicate in any way, who on receiving Marty's friendly note recovered powers of speech and began to recuperate.[99] Michel also invoked Marty's involvement in the two great events of his times, and it was on these anniversaries, not merely the brute fact of his birth, that revolutionary salutations might be sent him. 'If twice, twenty years apart, one finds André Marty there', wrote Michel, 'it is simply because Marty is *always* in the first line of the struggle, always in the most advanced and dangerous post, the post of honour'.[100]

(ii)

It would be hard on Thorez to say that the reverse was true. Nevertheless, even within the long span of his party leadership, the outstanding event in its history was that of the wartime resistance in which almost everybody had a greater part than he. It was Louis Aragon who coined the phrase the party of *fusillés*. The number killed was usually given as 75,000; the actual figure, excluding deaths in combat or concentration camps, was probably between 15,000 and 20,000, of which something over a third were communists.[101] Many were well-known party figures, at local, regional or national level, and they secured for the PCF an immense moral and political capital in which numbers mattered less than identifiable examples constituting an authentic martyrology. Foremost among them were Péri, whom Aragon celebrated in the self-consciously mythologising 'Passion of Gabriel Péri'; and Danielle Casanova, whose heroism was at the centre of the 'cult of remembering' propounded by the communist women's movement, the UFF.[102] The PCF had been particularly badly damaged by the Nazi–Soviet pact, and no western communist party enjoyed so spectacular a revival of fortunes as the French one did through the resistance. If this indeed was Thorez's party, the challenge for Thorez was that he had relocated to Soviet soil for the duration of this struggle. It was as if Stalin had slipped away to Paris during the Great Patriotic War; and one doubts whether even communist history can reveal any wider divergence between the personal and collective histories which according to the conventions of the leader cult were supposedly indivisible.

From the start this meant the embroiling of Thorez's party in a pact of dissimulation shading into outright falsification. The official legend had it that Thorez left France in the spring of 1943 to approve the dissolution of the Comintern. He was even described as having commanded his 'great anti-fascist army' from Paris.[103] Even as fictitious alibi, one wonders what order of priorities could have suggested so perfunctory a pretext for forsaking so weighty a responsibility. In fact, the primary emphasis initially was on the collective projection of a leadership from whose accomplishments in the resistance Thorez was implicitly held inseparable. The illustrated brochure *Frenchmen in whom France can have confidence* provided thumbnail sketches of those at the party's head whose continuous record of leadership had in several cases been tested to the point of death. One edition shows them in a cloud of heads with Thorez's slightly magnified and rising highest. In the text, he is nevertheless assimilated into the collective narrative as the 'organiser and educator' of the thousands who followed his lead. Repeatedly the formula is invoked of the five leading figures—Thorez, Duclos, Marty, Cachin and Benoît Frachon—whose names, it seemed, were not at this stage to be picked out individually.[104]

The difference with Moscow was that in Paris any such contrivances were a matter of public contention. Thorez had already become invested as a partisan cause when de Gaulle initially blocked his return to France.[105] Few of his supporters could have been much troubled by his having taken evasive action as his party was suppressed at the beginning of the war. Nor did this remain an obstacle to Thorez's acceptance by de Gaulle or his entrustment with high ministerial office. What Thorez lacked was any plausible account of the intervening years spent in the USSR. Much was made of a party appeal issued but not signed 'on French soil' in the summer of 1940.[106] There was however no real attempt to fill in the detail of Thorez's wartime activities, nor even, until the very summer of the liberation, a leaflet or a Moscow radio broadcast. Unsupported by any utterance, sighting or documentation, Thorez's wartime leadership could be credited only as a matter of implicit party faith.

That he was the face of a party in whose principal moral and political capital he had no share was one obvious incongruity. A second was that he was a deeply polarising figure whose credo for the moment was one of national unity. Thorez was never an especially militant figure. De Gaulle had sanctioned his return as one who could lend his authority to the disbandment of the partisan militias, and as minister Thorez did not so much demonstrate radical fervour as a statesmanlike demeanour backed up by obvious administrative competence. It was not therefore the adoption of extreme political stances that provoked controversy, but the question of Thorez's fitness or otherwise as vehicle of his party's claims as first party of the resistance.

Popular as he was among communists, beyond their ranks Thorez was already as much a liability as an asset. According to figures provided by Robrieux, his post-war vote in the red-belt municipality of Ivry showed an immediate falling back as compared with that of 1936.[107] This was in signal contrast with his party's general electoral advance, like an echo of Thälmann's failure to realise his party's full support as a Weimar presidential candidate. Through repudiation as well as belonging, the appellation *tu* now marked the boundaries of a distinct political community, as in the leaflet cited by Wieviorka which pointedly avoids it: '*Maurice Thorez, vous êtes un salaud*' (Maurice Thorez, you're a bastard).[108] With the further wartime diptych of resistance and collaboration, no party insisted more than the PCF on the accountability for past actions of both individual and collective actors. It was therefore hardly surprising that Thorez should receive the same sorts of scrutiny from political competitors. It was thus with every appearance of entitlement that in May 1946 the socialist interior minister André Le Troquer, who like Blum had played his own part in the resistance, accused Thorez of having abandoned those whom ostensibly he led.[109]

Cachin's reputation had also taken a heavy blow, due to a wartime disavowal of acts of violence that the authorities had exploited as an implied repudiation of his party's role in the resistance.[110] A loyal correspondent wrote that he and Thorez had come to appear like two balls dragging at the party's feet.[111] Nowhere else had a communist party promised so much in the way of a wider cultural and political renaissance, and seen the prospect so quickly recede. Celebrity recruits like Picasso and Éluard were part of a formidable intellectual enrolment that demonstrated the potency of the PCF's drawing power. Thorez's every political instinct was to cultivate such links; that was why Aragon, that other sometime surrealist who was so central to this mobilisation, identified himself so strongly as a *thorézien*. Almost in spite of himself, the polarising logic of Thorez's leadership was nevertheless like a premonition of the Cold War isolation that his full-blown cult came to epitomise.

With every attack upon him, communists insisted that Thorez was only the more precious to them.[112] With every questionable accolade to the 'first artisan' of the resistance, they also closed their ranks against the world beyond.[113] Just because of Thorez's biographical deficit, the vindication of his leadership required the quintessentially cultic device of the gifting or attribution to him of activities actually carried out by others, as symbolised by the prominence of resistance relics among his 50th-birthday gifts.[114] Gustave Vergneau was a former International Brigader who had also been active in the resistance. 'Everywhere and at every moment, it is your example of firmness, courage and loyalty which guided me', he wrote to Thorez following Le Troquer's attack. 'You my dear Maurice have been for me the star projecting through the darkness of 1939–44 the powerful rays of hope which allowed me to overcome all difficulties and afflictions.' Not only had the attacks of 'vile calumniators' enhanced rather than diminished Thorez's greatness, but Vergneau undertook to redouble his efforts at party-building as his response to the slanders of those were, after all, the other major component of any past or future politics of *rassemblement*.[115]

Given Thorez's lack of utterance during France's years of darkness, there was something almost mystical about the influence that was here acknowledged. At the same time, it was like the validation if not yet the cult of the office in which the party's achievements were now invested. Responding to Le Troquer's 'unspeakable aggression', Thorez's faithful number two Duclos insisted that the communists' role in the liberation was not just one of heroic sacrifices but required the 'guide and brain' that made them effective.[116] Thorez and his secretariat thus combined the outright untruth that he had been called to Moscow only in 1943 with the thrice-repeated evasion, slipping impenitently between first-person singular and plural, that he had played his part in the struggle as and at his party's head. 'During all those years of illegality, at the head of the party, I continued to do my duty and you know well enough the results obtained by the communists' struggle in France to know that we spared neither our pains nor our blood.'[117]

Immediately following Le Troquer's attack, Cachin summed up the PCF's predicament: 'We are strong, but we are alone!!!'[118] In France, as elsewhere, the decisive turn to militant isolationism came a year later, in the spring of 1947. It was no coincidence that Thorez's birthday that year saw a campaign of messages and resolutions running for the first time into hundreds.[119] Parliamentary exchanges had reached new heights of verbal violence, and de Gaulle that month launched his *Rassemblement du peuple français* as his contribution to the communists' isolation. Just the week following Thorez's birthday, the government was then reconstituted with the communists excluded. Once more the attacks on Thorez were cited as the token of his steadfastness, and the same refrain was henceforth heard with every new affront.[120] When Thorez in October 1950 suffered a stroke, his mysterious confinement in the Soviet Union prompted renewed political battles over his ability to discharge his responsibilities as an elected politician. Thorez was also now endowed with an aura of martyrdom that by his own actions he had scarcely merited. In resolution after resolution, communists expressed a sense of responsibility and even shame for not having worked harder to spare their leader the toil and anxiety that had had such devastating consequences. 'For we know very well', wrote one party group, 'that if you have fallen ill, it is because you have overworked yourself, and if you have overworked yourself, it's in large part because of our inadequacies…'[121]

Already at this point, the project of Thorez's *Works* had been launched. The previous year, 1949, had seen the reissuing of his *Son of the People* with a promotional campaign exceeding even that of 1937. As long as Thorez remained in the USSR, resolutions of support were routinely passed at party gatherings, with a bonding effect reinforced by the ritual of collective signatures amounting in some cases to several hundred.[122] Through the medical cares he was held to owe to Stalin's solicitude, the notion of a hierarchy of cults was also reaffirmed, and the principle of 'proletarian internationalism' further personalised as the contract between one leader and another.[123] Birthdays remained a focus; in 1951, those attending the annual Fête de l'Humanité could send a pre-addressed printed card from the 'Maurice Thorez stand'.[124] Both real and symbolic lines of democratic accountability were inverted as Thorez's party rendered account to him for activities carried out, or not sufficiently carried out, and undertook to remain always worthy of his leadership. 'Dear comrade', runs a typical address, 'we give you heartfelt thanks for the precious assistance you brought us in the course of a tough electoral campaign, in which each of us, notwithstanding the distance, felt your kindly presence close by, so true is it that one cannot speak of the PCF without evoking the face, smiling with tranquil confidence, of he who has made it so great and so fine.'[125] Once more, as during the war, several months had passed at this point since Thorez's last appearance or communication. Other general secretaries enjoyed the formulaic rituals which Thorez's 50th birthday merely took to extremes. What was here more distinctive was the continually renewed campaign of veneration that really did merit the epithet of Maurice Thorez's party.

The 30th anniversary of the PCF's formation fell as Thorez's second Russian sojourn was beginning. The marking of these institutional anniversaries was itself symptomatic of the more inward-looking mentality that had already been expressed in 1947 in the establishment of a party history commission.[126] In the PCF's case, there was also the notion that the establishment of a mass communist party was itself a history vindicated, and the realisation merely by its existing of the 'future victories' presaged at its foundation.[127] If the party had thus itself become a surrogate for revolution, the anniversary was also the opportunity to propound a thorézian party narrative that cast the leader brought forth by history as the decisive element in its becoming so. Of the three key themes indicated for the anniversary, one was that of the party of Maurice Thorez who had forged the instrument that 'simple folk' now gave his name.[128] The underlying assumption, already spelled out on Thorez's 50th birthday, was that of a first step taken with the PCF's formation, but of a party still to be constructed that above all bore Thorez's personal imprint.[129] In Britain with its older leadership cohort, the 1920s and the 1926 General Strike remained central to the communists' collective memory. In France, there was a veritable leap from the founding Tours congress to Thorez, as the PCF's history was itself reconfigured in its leader's image.

(iii)

Though Thorez was not the story's only hero, this did imply the management, evisceration or depersonalisation of any such history as threatened to detract from his dominant presence within it. In a positive sense, the popular front was strongly emphasised as representing the only real political capital that Thorez had. A particular focus was the mobilisation against the fascist leagues in 1934, which demonstrated the PCF's pioneering role in anti-fascism while counteracting narratives hinging on its temporary dereliction from the struggle in 1939.[130] This, more than anything, made it Thorez's party, and it did not unduly stretch credulity that the popular front should be described as the incarnation of the man and the moment each in the other. The resistance itself could thus be presented as but the popular front's continuation, and the vindication of the hopes which inscribed Thorez's name 'at the head of one of the most glorious chapters of our history'.[131] Following Thorez's return to the head of his party, his political reports from 1936, 1937, 1939 and 1945 were issued together as if to personalise the connection and demonstrate the underlying continuity of political direction.[132]

It was in this spirit that Vaillant-Couturier was posthumously confirmed as one of the PCF's foremost heroes. Dying in a hunting accident in 1937, Vaillant-Couturier presented no complicating factor of Spain or the resistance. He was a foundation party member and a long-time associate of Barbusse; but if he gave his name to so many post-war party cells, it was as a figure whose emergence from the political wilderness in the early 1930s coincided with both the chronology and the political dynamic of 'Thorez's party'.[133] In this account of the popular front, Barbusse and even Dimitrov were either written out of the story, or else described as taking up Thorez's lead.[134] Fréville had Vaillant-Couturier hailing Thorez as 'the one who will lead the French proletariat to victory' as early as 1924.[135] At the same time, the updated *Son of the People* paid Vaillant-Couturier a tribute remarkably generous by that volume's standards, even employing the first-name terms that were otherwise reserved for Thorez himself.[136]

More generally, there was a playing down of any episode or personality tending to deflect from Thorez's leadership. Of the PCF's founding generation, Cachin was the indispensable survivor who publicly deferred to Thorez as the leader needed for the fulfilment of the PCF's mission.[137] The experience of Spain, according to Skoutelsky, was in any case overshadowed by the resistance in a way that had no counterpart in Britain or the USA.[138] Nevertheless, on the part of both French volunteers in Spain and Spanish anti-fascists exiled in France, there was a continuity between one armed struggle and another that got buried somewhere in the focus on the popular front within France itself.[139] Notoriously, the political capital of the resistance itself was also rendered innocuous. By

1950, Thorez's accreditation with its leading role had become a mandatory fiction to which the individuals and organisations that did rightly bear these credentials seemed most of all impelled to contribute.[140] Also in 1950, the PCF's central committee was renewed in such fashion as seemed actively directed at those who had fought in Spain or in the resistance.[141] A closer statistical analysis suggests that this perception was much exaggerated.[142] The plausibility of the contention nevertheless lay both in the general tenor of the party's propaganda and in the individual cases that appeared to support it, most notably that of former resistance leader Charles Tillon.

André Marty had not fought in the resistance. He did, however, have a record of continuous wartime activity, culminating in his heading the PCF delegation to de Gaulle's committee for national liberation in Algiers. Even his remaining in Moscow could be presented, as in Togliatti's case, as the positive asset of having learnt in the school of socialism and under the incomparable teacher that was Stalin.[143] In Marty's papers are carefully preserved the resolutions on his 59th birthday in 1945, mainly from his local base in Paris, that salute him on a personal record that none could surpass.[144] Marty did, however, also have a wider conception of historical legitimation, and no other leading party member was so ready to write or speak in solidarity or commemoration. It was Marty who in 1944 had taken charge of the history component of the central party school, and of the relevant title in the PCF's 'Doctrine and History' series of publications.[145] It was also Marty who on Dimitrov's death in 1949 drove a campaign of commemoration that brought out the international character of the anti-fascist mobilisation of the 1930s.[146] Spain was an abiding concern, as Marty pressed for greater coverage in *L'Humanité* and the inclusion of the International Brigades in a proposed book series on 'Heroic Youth'.[147] He was active on behalf of the rights as ex-combatants of the Spanish volunteers, but he also showed this commitment to the resistance legacy in which he had no personal part, and as president of the ex-combatants' organisation ARAC reacted fiercely against any tendency to marginalise those who had fought in the resistance.[148]

Pierre Semard was not precisely a resistance hero. He was however accorded a sort of honorific status as one following his shooting as a hostage by the Nazis in 1941. When Semard's funeral obsequies were organised in 1945, Gaston Monmousseau, like Semard a railworker and trade union militant, described him as the greatest of those who had fallen and as the 'first proletarian general secretary' of what Monmousseau even described as 'Pierre Semard's party'.[149] With his years of experience as a railworkers' leader and what Frédérick Genevée calls a rich curriculum vitae in the matter of repression, Semard's was another light that needed dampening if Thorez's was to reign as if effulgent.[150]

As Serge Wolikow puts it, he thus became the PCF's forgotten general secretary.[151] Among communist trade unionists, particularly railworkers, Semard did now inspire the 'veritable cult' that Monmousseau had given voice to.[152] Nevertheless, the exclusion from this cult of Semard's role in party history did underline the hierarchical nature of the post-war cults and its binding character even retrospectively in the new thorézian narrative of party history. Marty would later cite Semard, along with Dimitrov, as one of those whose role had been obscured to Thorez's advantage.[153] Marty himself was once more not so grudging, not least because Semard epitomised the strongly proletarian party identity he sought to reaffirm. In tributes issued during the war and immediately afterwards, Marty thus recalled how Semard on becoming general secretary had been described as the 'consummate type of a worker-Communist', and how he was a pioneer at once of anti-fascist unity and of the 'workers' party of a new type' on which this unity was necessarily founded.[154] Unveiling a plaque where Lenin once had stayed, it was again with this class inflexion of the 'workers' party of a new type' that Marty cited Semard and not Thorez in his role as the party's general secretary.[155]

Marty for his own part was not in the business of being forgotten. Already in 1947, the reissuing of his *Black Sea Mutiny* had been scheduled for the following year.[156] Though the deadline came and went, Marty headed the Black Sea veterans' organisation and drove the campaign to mark the mutiny's 30th anniversary in April 1949. Peace was by this time the PCF's dominant preoccupation; the theme of a successful anti-war action could hardly have been more topical. Though characteristically Marty complained of 'abnormal resistance' to the campaign within the PCF, in July 1949 it received the authoritative endorsement of the Cominform journal *For A Lasting Peace, For a People's Democracy*. The Cominform was the co-ordinating body of communist and workers' parties established in 1947 and this in effect was the voice of Moscow. The PCF therefore extended the campaign to the end of the year, and *The Black Sea Mutiny* was at last reissued in a lavish edition, to supplement the shorter account by Marty already published for the anniversary.[157]

The result was like a covert battle of the books. At the very moment that leader and party were once more rendered indissoluble in the reissued

Son of the People, Marty's *Black Sea Mutiny* appeared as restoration of a formative moment of struggle—France's 'most important revolutionary movement' since the Commune, said the PCF's publishing director Joseph Ducroux—which Thorez could neither share in nor match from his own experience.[158] Dutiful party commentators linked the narratives as ones in which the personal found its meaning in history's larger movements, and the element of biography was unencumbered by the 'anecdotal bric-a-brac' of the conventional memoir.[159] Even so, the conception and appearance of the two volumes could hardly have been more different. Originating in the 1920s, Marty's was a survival of earlier practices in which multiple first-hand testimonies and contemporary documents and images combined in the collective representation of the heroic from which Marty himself, as both figurehead and narrator, derived his own biographical capital. More than anything, it also represented the merging of both personal and collective history with the event in a way not found in Thorez's narrative, and not required for the empty ceremonial of Thorez's birthday.[160]

Contrasting personal histories in this instance signified competing political perspectives. Although both books were promoted as weapons in the peace campaign, Marty's was a distinctly more militant conception in the spirit of the actions he had reconstructed through the activists who made them.[161] Marty also emphasised the immediate topicality of their example as new solidarities were called upon with the USSR and the people of Vietnam.[162] In both party commemoration and current campaigning, he thus presumed upon a sort of personal authority on issues of war resistance, always stressing that actions were the test of words, and citing Stalin to this effect from 'Foundations of Leninism'.[163]

The result was what Vanessa Codaccioni describes as a muffled confrontation with Thorez's more legalist approach as epitomised by the communists' mobilisation around the Stockholm peace petition.[164] Saluting him at the PCF's Gennevilliers congress in April 1950, Marty urged that the best birthday present Thorez could receive would be the intensification of efforts to get French troops back from Vietnam. As throughout the history of the cult phenomenon, the specification of some meaningful practical activity could imply a coded criticism of the mere offering of tribute. Marty also complained of citations in his speech having been missed by the stenographer; Stalin's test of actions may have been among them, and Marty certainly preserved an article for the party's education bulletin in which a paragraph expressing the same sentiments has been pencilled out.[165] It was

Thorez who had chaired the party history commission; and when instead of a party history there appeared an updated version of his *Son of the People*, it was this that henceforth provided the focal point of party education classes. Marty's own history course had to make way for it, and in the propositions he made regarding the new programme of study, Marty emphasised the pre-thorézian moment of the First World War in which the roots of French communism actually lay.[166]

It is hardly surprising that Marty should be seen as threatening an alternative conception of party history, both made and in the making. Within the PCF were many elements radicalised by the experiences of the 1930s–1940s and never properly reconciled to the dissolution of the resistance militias following Thorez's return from Moscow.[167] Why, one correspondent asked Thorez, were communists not demanding arms for Korea, as they had for Spain, or organising 'new international brigades' so that the 'American nazi tigers' also should not pass.[168] Thorez's party was one for which every unchecked militant action raised the spectre of adventurism: its guiding precept was, what we have we hold. Marty, on the other hand, had made himself synonymous with the idea of action. Reviews of his book singled this out as its decisive element; for the head of party publishing, he was the authentic marxist for whom 'action and thinking' were a unity, and who derived from this the 'highly personal qualities' he demonstrated as writer and as a political figure.[169] In the party's monthly journal there sit together one of Marty's Black Sea articles, with its moral that 'one does not defend peace with words alone', and an offering of Thorez's on the role of party functionaries, as if the PCF too were a machine for the production of leadership.[170]

Such juxtapositions would have mattered less had Marty's credit been confined to France itself. Communism, however, was a movement whose leaders were likeliest to be removed through some external initiative, as the PCF itself had served as instrument in the ousting of Earl Browder. As a form almost of quasi-factionalism from above, Marty in particular cut across his party's tapering cultic hierarchy by virtue of the kudos and connections he had built up internationally. The Spanish experience now counted for little within the PCF, and in Eastern Europe was a positive ground for suspicion. Even so, it was a basis for Marty's continuing standing with a 1930s' Comintern cohort now largely dispersed to its countries of origin. While in Italy Thorez's birthday in 1950 occasioned all the requisite formalities, it was Marty who immediately afterwards was 'madly cheered' at the PCI congress on being presented with the Garibaldi gold medal as an animator with Togliatti of the International Brigades.[171] The following year, his 65th birthday received extensive publicity in the GDR, including a substantial tribute by Franz Dahlem, erstwhile head of the International Brigades' political commission, that appeared in both national and regional party organs. Notwithstanding Marty's later claims to have discouraged celebrations of his birthday, he was not so unworldly as to let this mark of external esteem pass unnoticed in his own party.[172]

There were many threads in the Marty affair and these remain to be fully disentangled.[173] In his own account published in 1955, Marty alleged that its object was to stifle opposition to the PCF's opportunism and its relinquishment of any perspective of revolutionary transformation.[174] Of particular interest here was the emphasis he placed upon the cult of the individual. This may have demonstrated his alertness to the signals already coming from the post-Stalin USSR. Nevertheless, Marty had already almost a decade earlier raised with Ivan Stepanov the spirit of nepotism and 'monarchical absolutism' in which Thorez allegedly ran the party. Stepanov was a former member of the Marty secretariat with a long involvement in the PCF's relations with Moscow; in this sense, Marty was the rival mini-Stalin counting on an intervention from above like the one that had put paid to Browder. By nepotism, he particularly had in mind the elevation of Jeannette Vermeersch, whose 'paternalist' regime was allegedly undermining the communist women's movement and whose failure to perform any useful role in the war years Marty already at this point invoked.[175] Returning to these points in *The Marty Affair*, Marty extended the attack to the thorézian rewriting of party history, the 'counter-revolutionary' system of offering presents and the whole alien conception of the 'genius of a superman'.[176]

Though picking up on the incipient anti-Stalin reaction in the USSR, Marty did not so much as mention Stalin, or the cults of other Comintern leaders like Dimitrov. Whatever the inadequacies of such a treatment, it did nevertheless reveal Marty's familiarity with those traditions within the workers' movement that were inimical to the idea of leader-worship. Marty not only suggested that the word *chef* was itself of a fascistic character and justly equated with the German *Führer* and Italian *Duce*. Exceptionally, he also employed in a positive sense the notion of the *meneur* coming to the fore in movements of popular struggle. It was to these 'true *meneurs*', he wrote, that the success of the Black Sea mutiny was due, and not to any supposed *chef* like himself.[177] Despite Marty's obvious inconsistency, it was far more in this spirit than that of any individual cult that he had written

The Black Sea Mutiny. Whether as potential rival cult or as the antidote to such conceptions of the leader, Marty was manifestly ill-adapted to the echoes of the court system which he correctly detected in Thorez's party.

It is difficult to see that a cult like that of Thorez represented anything but the stifling of personality. If any party was one of Guevaras in every wood, it was the PCF at the moment of the liberation. The PCF was also the product of a political culture profoundly marked by the figure of the hero, and with Aragon to the fore the marking of this theme across the ages had been one of the key motifs of the resistance intellectuals. The 'French renaissance' which the liberation promised might have been a time of biographical profusion. Instead, the very reverse was true, and the biographically impoverished *Son of the People* stood almost alone as such a text.[178]

Marty's challenge was that he represented both personal political capital and a knowledge of how to deploy it, combined with the conviction that this was the necessary basis of political authority. The Marty–Tillon affair thus appears, amongst other things, as an archetypal case of the cauterisation of those thus endowed with their own personal resources, whether through the resistance, as in Tillon's case, or through an 'already significant activist life'.[179] For the period not only of Thorez's leadership, but of the entire party history which he was meant to incarnate, this also meant the backward projection of Thorez's singularity at the expense of any potentially distracting figure.

Like Peter the Great in Russia, Joan of Arc posed no such threat. Suzanne Masson was a real resistance hero, beheaded by the Nazis for refusing to work for the German army. A fortnight after Thorez's 50th birthday, a local communist ceremony on the anniversary of her death was severely sanctioned as a 'demonstration against the line of the party' because it coincided with the annual procession to the statue of Joan of Arc which by no means had the full approval of party members. Explanations were to be provided, the reporting of such events was to be tightened up, and a closer control of such activities was to be exercised through the participation of central committee members.[180] Though seemingly trivial in itself, the episode is suggestive of how the fully developed stalinist integration cult required the active management of a cultic hierarchy, and of every significant expression of the memory or political capital embodied in the individual.

The question is sometimes posed of why the PCF should have conformed more closely to these stalinist norms than other communist parties of the period. When all account is taken of deeper issues of culture and society, one may also wonder whether this is what one would necessarily have predicted of the fissiparous and disputatious PCF of the 1920s, or from the influx of a new generation of idealists during the war years. Doubtless in both these periods these were just the centrifugal pressures that could provide the rationale for the controlling mechanism of the integrating cult. At the same time, the cult's pervasive and highly ritualised character appears to have been here accentuated as nowhere else precisely because of Thorez's deficiency in personal capital and as a necessary compensation for it. To this extent, this really was the party that indelibly bore his imprint. Where monuments, as Marty intimated, were constructed to the living, perhaps it was because already in their lifetimes some such contrivance was needed to mark them out by. Paradoxically, it was just because Thorez's authority was so largely one of office that it did not act as a stimulus to the wider communist cult of the hero, but as a suffocating constraint upon it.

4.3 Office Boys and Lifelong Fighters

(i)

In the Comintern personal files on Thorez and Harry Pollitt, each has a cadre autobiography dating from within five months of each other in 1931–1932.[181] With the Comintern's systematisation of an international cadre policy, the provision of these autobiographies was being established at just this point as an instrument of selection, homogenisation and control. Though considerable variations existed according to period and party context, the prescriptive character of the exercise meant that narratives of self were adapted to the expectations of the institution and careers advanced or obstructed depending on how far these were realised in the individual.[182] Both the Thorez and Pollitt texts, for example, underline the crucial importance of a proletarian identity in the leadership cohort preferred by Stalin. Both autobiographies emphasise working-class origins and family background. Both men mention their lack of experience of foreign travel except as obtained through the Comintern, and some holiday excursions of Thorez to nearby Belgium. While Pollitt spoke only English, Thorez did have 'a little German'. Nevertheless, they described in strikingly similar terms a political education confined to such self-education as their day-to-day political responsibilities allowed. Even after joining the party, Thorez had 'read alone', and despite copious note-taking found a 'genuine study' of Marx and Lenin impossible to reconcile with his life as an activist. Pollitt also referred to a process of 'self-education through reading independently', and described how 'in all cases my chief weakness has been that my studies have had to be carried on in an unorganised and spasmodic fashion owing to my commitments in other directions'. Neither had published anything more substantial than a topical pamphlet. Later pretensions to a command of theory counted for nothing at this stage; if anything, they might have militated against their preferment.

Where the documents diverge is in respect of their authors' wider associations and activities. Thorez's account brings out his early working experience in the mines, and describes how three times between 1919 and 1923 he participated in miners' strikes. His time at the coalface was nevertheless cut short by military service after less than a year. While the subsequent combination of employer blacklisting and co-option into the apparatus was commonplace for Comintern-era cadres, its effects were in this instance compounded by its occurring at the very outset of Thorez's working life. Though he played some part in the miners' federation of the communist-aligned CGTU (Confédération générale du travail unitaire), the political bifurcation of the workers' movement meant that this was also undertaken as an extension of his party responsibilities.[183] In later tributes to Thorez, his coalfield origins are repeatedly invoked and provide a measure of what the one-time pitboy had achieved.[184] To this extent, this was a potent form of social or sociological capital, carried forward from Thorez's formative milieu and summed up in the well-founded claim of his *Son of the People* that his earliest memories were of the harshness of working-class life. Thorez's political capital, on the other hand, was confined to that acquired as a communist party worker, and the example he provided in his autobiography was that of the complete identification of the person with the party.[185]

Pollitt, apart from anything else, was ten years older. He was also the product of a minority socialist culture that predated the formation of either the CPGB or a national Labour Party and, particularly through the trade unions, continued to provide the milieu within which in Britain a communist politics had the best chance of flourishing. In personal terms this meant that Pollitt could also boast a record of wider activities that continued for several years even after he became a communist. Enrolled as a child in his Socialist Sunday School, he counted his activities as socialist propagandist from the age of 16 when he joined his local branch of the Independent Labour Party, later the Openshaw Socialist Society, and 'the largest and strongest ... in the North of England'. He placed much stress upon his socialist family environment, in particular the influence of his mother, 'a member from my earliest recollection of the revolutionary socialist movement in England, [who] when she worked in the factory was always accepted as the woman in the weaving shed who would lead deputations to the employers'. Pollitt himself assumed various roles within the Openshaw Socialist Society before succeeding an uncle as its secretary, and by this route became a CPGB foundation member.

He was also a time-served boilermaker, one of the elite of the metal-working trades, and until prevented by a change to his union's rulebook served for the most of the 1920s as a Boilermakers' delegate to the annual conferences of the Labour Party and Trades Union Congress. None but the most prominent officials spoke more often than Pollitt, and the German social democrat Egon Wertheimer described it as unfathomable to an outsider that he should be so warmly received by those politically opposed to him.[186] It was partly to retain these membership rights that Pollitt, according to his Comintern autobiography, continued working at his trade until 1928, and he listed a whole series of industrial actions in which he participated as an activist.

Whatever merely sat on a Comintern file could neither integrate nor enkindle. What therefore mattered in Pollitt's case was the congruence in most respects between his cadre biography and public persona. When he drafted this document in December 1931, a second Labour government had collapsed without any sign of the CPGB advancing in its place. Though like every other party it was bound for the moment by the Comintern line of 'independent leadership', the party's only real prospect of a more durable influence was through some orientation to the established labour movement and the active workers encompassed within it. This is where Pollitt's value lay, and it was not those possessing their own independent capital that threatened to undermine him, but those better practised or more amenable than he in reading the changing signals that came from Moscow.[187] It was on this account that in October 1939 Pollitt was displaced as CPGB general secretary after failing to adjust to the Comintern change of line on the war. Though this certainly demonstrated that the party was above any individual, the moral would have been still clearer had Pollitt not later been reinstated, and had a replacement been found for him in the meantime.

A sign of Pollitt's value was how precociously he had begun to be marked out as the CPGB's principal figurehead. Already in 1923, his then closest collaborator Dutt had had him depicted in a fictional serial in the party's weekly paper as part of an abortive bid to secure him the party leadership.[188] By 1925, it was Pollitt, followed by J.R. Campbell and then Gallacher, who topped the poll in the election for the party executive. In the political trial that year of 12 British communist leaders, these were the three who defended themselves, and whose speeches from the dock were issued as popular pamphlets. Whether in a British courtroom or at the Comintern, Pollitt knew how to strike the note of one whose natural environment was the boiler-shop. 'Members of the jury, nothing that Lenin ever wrote, or Trotsky ever said, or Marx ever found in the British Museum made a Communist', he told them. 'I saw the best woman in the world carry two children out, morning after morning, while I went out looking for work, that made me a Communist.'[189] As validated by his broad Lancashire accent, Pollitt would never pretend to embody the unity of theory and practice, but rather brought to it the authenticity of lived experience which was his principal political capital, and which frequently he set against the tyranny of hair-splitting and the party formula.

When, together with Dutt, Pollitt took the initiative in introducing the 'new line' of independent leadership, he was rewarded in August 1929 with the position of party secretary. Already in that year's general election, he had been the CPGB's standard-bearer against the Labour Party leader MacDonald, and the following year his candidacy in a Whitechapel by-election received extensive publicity and a first *Daily Worker* profile, 'A Lifelong Fighter in the Workers' Movement'.[190] From the setting out of party policy to the heading of campaigns like the Workers' Charter, Pollitt was already projected as de facto party leader, and reporters made space for the 'roar upon roar of thunderous applause' that would punctuate his flights of rhetoric.[191] Where the Soviets had led the way with Leniniana, an intimate of Pollitt's complained already in 1930 of the 'outburst of Pollittiana' which had taken hold of the British party:

> Pollitt Candidate for Whitechapel. Pollitt Principal and if one take the Daily [Worker] for it the only propagandist of our Party. Pollitt leading Charter Campaign. Pollitt overseeing the Daily Worker. Pollitt on the Youth Bureau and Pollitt General Secretary of the Party. This is not only bad for yourself but it is exceedingly bad for the Party.[192]

Pollittiana and its other national variants were not at this stage a recognised feature of communist politics, and Pollitt himself understood the force of these objections. Two years later, as 'class war' prosecutions proliferated, he warned that solidarity efforts should not just focus on 'Gallacher and Pollitt' at the expense of the 'little comrades down below'. Should a party leader be arrested, and a little comrade who was not a leader ('little is a bad word to use, but I can't think of another'), a grassroots mobilisation around the latter might indeed have a better political effect than the 'whole of the fancy speeches some of us might make at Bow Street'.[193]

But Pollitt did not maintain this position following Dimitrov's performance at the Leipzig trial and the wider Comintern turn to the figure of the leader. Immediately following Dimitrov's release, Pollitt and Tom Mann were faced with prosecution for sedition and the likelihood of lengthy prison sentences. There was no question now of missing the opportunity: a national campaign was launched and Pollitt prepared his own defence, promising to give them 'something to remember us for'. He even complained of those who in stinting their support seemed to relish the prospect of an enforced leadership change.[194] The charges however were dropped. Pollitt never again faced any similar threat, and with the turn to anti-fascist unity he attained a virtually unassailable position as its foremost British advocate and epitome. In the spring of 1937, Rose Cohen and her Ukrainian husband Petrovsky were among the countless victims of the terror. Both were Pollitt's intimate friends; Cohen was the woman he had wanted to marry.[195] Dutt later claimed that Pollitt made such vigorous representations over the issue that soundings were taken regarding his replacement as party leader.[196] Rumours of his censuring and possible ousting did certainly circulate in party circles, but also intimations of the resistance this would encounter because of Pollitt's personal popularity.[197]

To the extent that this popularity had a cultlike aspect, it combined the rituals and conventions of the radical platform with the mobilising power of the international movement whose principal British embodiment Pollitt was. Compared with the cultic system of the post-war years, the sense of a centred symbolic hierarchy was nevertheless far less distinct at an international level as well as nationally. It was not just that Pollitt, like Browder in the USA, was most likely to be located within an indigenous lineage of heroes. Even internationally, as he consolidated his leadership, his main source of political capital was not the USSR but Spain. Visiting the country five times in 1937–1938, Pollitt identified closely with the British volunteers and became inseparable from the conflict in the public mind. When in 1937 the CPGB's national congress gave full vent to the new cult ceremonial, Spain not Russia was the cause that was at its heart.

As delegates stood with clenched fists raised after Gallacher had introduced a group of International Brigaders, it was Pollitt who read out the names of those who had died in Spain, and it was Pollitt who returned to Spain in his concluding peroration and had many of the delegates reportedly weeping. Not only was Pollitt loved and honoured by his party, as the effusive preamble put it, but 'thousands of workers outside our Party see in Comrade Pollitt the type of man, the working-class man, who is the leader who is going to lead us all towards our final emancipation'.[198]

Borkenau's contention was that Stalin's use of secondary cults involved the wielding of a subordinate authority without its ever becoming so inflated as to threaten or diminish his own control.[199] Pollitt's was neither the prestige nor the independence of another Tito. Nevertheless, his initial defiance of the Comintern in 1939 was perhaps the most outspoken such outburst on the part of any general secretary of the Stalin generation. Curiously, it was the three individuals who defended themselves in 1925—Pollitt, Gallacher and Campbell—who now defended their party's anti-fascist stance against that other higher jurisdiction which was the Comintern. Just as in 1925, it was Pollitt who did so more particularly through the personal political capital which he deployed as a form of experiential intuition, or what, in a paraphrase of Lenin, he described as English common sense. 'I was in this movement practically before you were born', he reminded Dutt, who was now his principal immediate antagonist. Dutt in fact was barely five years his junior, but that was just the difference between Pollitt's formative experience of the First World War and the subsequent arrival of the Comintern:

> I was 24, had never heard of Bolshevism. Had never heard of the Basle resolution, but had a class instinct which was sound and I suppose I got as many physical beatings up for going round Lancashire endeavouring to get that war transferred into a civil war as any person in this country. Has got the same class instinct … now …[200]

An enduring component of the Pollitt myth was his returning forthwith to his work in the shipyards. In fact, this occurred some 18 months later, as a security against the possible internment of leading communists. Psychologically, Pollitt was nevertheless very differently situated from Thorez, who Robrieux notes had neither trade nor any other alternative prospects to his party career.[201] 'One thing I *do* know', Pollitt's mother wrote to him, 'I would not lose my dignity, by having an office boy's job,

& being dictated to, by someone not half as competent, because the tools are still vaselined'.[202]

Suitably modified, the letter was given pride of place in the autobiography which Pollitt now produced. While never threatening any significant controversy, this provided a vindication of Pollitt's 'apprenticeship to politics', as vividly symbolised by the frontispiece portrait of and preface devoted to his mother.[203] Assisted by the very fact of his demotion, Pollitt's independent standing was reinforced as never before. The *New Statesman* editor Kingsley Martin described him as a man whom socialists of all classes wanted to follow and who possessed a moral fervour 'utterly alien from the opportunism and Machiavellianism of current Marxism'.[204] The parallel is clear with Borkenau's implicit belief that Dolores Ibárruri was somehow of her party but apart from it.[205] Attacking the communists in 1940, a trade union delegate to the Labour Party excepted only Pollitt: 'one of the best fellows I have ever met in my life – but he is in the wrong party'.[206] When the communists in January 1941 attempted a wider political mobilisation around the People's Convention, the expelled Labour MP D.N. Pritt was supposedly the figurehead. Nevertheless, it was Pollitt who received the biggest ovation 'simply on announcement of his name … more people were trying to *see* him than … any other speaker'.[207]

Reinstated following the Nazi attack on the USSR, Pollitt was spared the experience of exile which Thorez shared with so many other communist leaders. By the same token, there was no British resistance movement that might have brought with it alternative claims to leadership. One result was the extraordinary continuity of the CPGB's inner leadership. Pollitt, now in his fifties, was essentially a figure of the public platform. From July 1941, he set about a gruelling schedule of meetings that still in 1944 amounted to over a hundred engagements across the country. A lifelong non-combatant, he urged on a public often unfamiliar with the rituals of the communist rally the urgency of the international effort required for fascism's defeat. When on May Day 1942 he spoke for an hour to an outdoor gathering of 17,000, there were this time no constant roars of approval:

> the excellence of his address may be judged by the fact that he was listened to in almost complete silence (though the applause when he had finished was immense) and by the fact that … I myself, who am by no means a disciple of Pollitt (and that is putting it mildly), did not at any time of his speech feel inclined to look at my watch, or indeed to take my attention off the speaker at all.[208]

'Martial you stand, with Promethean front / Able to daunt powerfullest dictators', wrote one enthralled admirer:

> And summer air charms not so still the night
> Nor lorn nightingale the woods, as your blunt
> Words rapt thousands, listening with applause ...[209]

Martin, also attending a London rally, likened Pollitt to that other figure looming larger than his party, Winston Churchill, and saw in both the kind of resolution and oratorical skill that he associated with an innate capacity for leadership.[210]

(ii)

A more obvious comparison in the present context might be with those other smaller communist parties whose effectiveness depended on some form of adaptation to a stronger mainstream labour movement retaining mass support and popular legitimacy. The Scandinavian parties were analogous cases, though these appear not to have produced any strongly marked cult figures. Though Belgium's labour movement was more centralised and less porous than Britain's, here too the Parti ouvrier belge (POB) was strongly entrenched and based on a powerful trade union movement. It was this similarity between the two countries as compared with France that the Belgian communist leader Xavier Relecom stressed as fraternal delegate to the CPGB congress in 1937.[211] Introduced by Pollitt as the leader of his party, the Parti communiste de Belgique (PCB), Relecom had assumed this role following the death the previous year of the better-known figure of Joseph Jacquemotte.

It was Jacquemotte, not Relecom, who was the nearest Belgian counterpart to Pollitt and Gallacher, exactly as in France it was the 'first proletarian general secretary' Semard and not Thorez. Born two years after Gallacher in 1883, Jacquemotte was a clerk by trade who had a continuous record of labour movement activity dating from before the First World War. As José Gotovitch has described, neither Relecom nor any other Belgian communist could rival him as a popular leader, and even party critics acknowledged that for a wider public 'the party is Jacquemotte'.[212] Moreover, where the PCB did resemble its French rather than its British counterpart was in the role played in the advancement of both Jacquemotte and Relecom by the Comintern's secret delegate to the party, the Hungarian Andor Berei. Drawing on Gotovitch's work, Jacquemotte's installation as party secretary in the spring of 1935 can be appreciated here as a calculating exercise in the politics of personality following the Comintern's turn to the figure of the leader the previous year.

If Jacquemotte prefigured Gallacher's role, it was through his election in 1925 as foremost of a tiny group of communist deputies which for three years from 1929 solely comprised himself. If he also bears comparison with Pollitt, it was through his deep immersion in trade union affairs, including 15 years as a full-time officer prior to his election as a deputy. Though the Belgian movement's sharper political divisions were reflected in Jacquemotte's expulsion from his union in 1927, he continued to exploit his parliamentary immunities to support striking workers like those in the mass strikes of 1932. Like Thorez's and Pollitt's, Jacquemotte's cadre autobiography described a political education of an unsystematic and 'autodidactic' character, principally carried out in spells in prison. He had no theoretical pretensions and, like Pollitt, by no means overestimated the benefits of a Lenin School training.[213]

Among the disparate Belgian groupings initially drawn towards the Third International, Jacquemotte had headed a left wing within the POB associated with the paper *L'Exploité*. He kept his distance when a first communist party was established by sections of the youth movement headed by War Van Overstraeten, and his political career henceforth was one of persistent conflict with successive tendencies usually younger than him and to his left. Jacquemotte, even so, was the one outstanding public figure of the party unified in 1921, and as such he was three years later installed as a member of the Comintern executive, ECCI. Pollitt, elected at the same congress, was initially a paper member and on his cadre autobiography the detail is added by hand almost as an afterthought. Jacquemotte, conversely, was by his own account able to attend all but one of the 13 ECCI plenums, and effectively combined the prerogatives of the international functionary with the wider public profile of his parliamentary mandate.

There were, in their different spheres, parallels with Barbusse in Jacquemotte's continuing conflicts with the young and zealous offset by the protection he enjoyed internationally on account of his basic political loyalty and wider public standing.[214] His value to the ascendant Stalin faction was demonstrated by the role he played in 1927 in the 'Pyrrhic victory' the Comintern secured over Van Overstraeten and the PCB's numerically preponderant pro-Trotsky elements.[215] As the leadership then passed to another impetuous cohort from the youth movement, relations once more deteriorated, and for a time in 1929–1930 Jacquemotte was excluded from the politburo. Despite his reinstatement, he remained in party terms a surprisingly detached figure, with a disinclination to collective work and disciplines. Also noted was a tendency to separate his political commitments from a private life that was rumoured to be less than spotless.[216] Gotovitch describes him as one of the PCB's few figures with a personal political identity, but one that was never really integrated into internal party life.[217] According to Berei, he symbolised communism and had authority with the masses—'but not within the party'.[218]

There was therefore a dual significance to Jacquemotte's installation as general secretary at the PCB's Charleroi conference in April 1935. On the one hand, it signalled the ousting of a leading group whose sectarianism towards the labour movement had been compounded by a laxity in respect of Trotskyism that went as far as agreement to a platform that included support for Trotsky's right to asylum. This by now was a heinous transgression, and in the manner of Souvarine's diptych Jacquemotte's elevation to the leadership was accompanied by the crushing self-criticism of his predecessor in a disturbing public ritual of integration by force of anathematisation.[219] On the other hand, his preferment was also the clearest possible signal of the PCB's turn towards unity with the broader labour movement. Rather than the latest phase in bolshevisation, it can be linked with the PCB's adaptation to the 'particularities of the structure of the Belgian workers' movement' as signalled at the same conference. Indeed, it was the direct corollary of the explicit prioritisation of experience within the reformist unions as a criterion in the renewal of the party's central committee.[220]

Jacquemotte himself was not so much the harbinger of new era, like Thorez, as the guarantor and embodiment of an older tradition of struggle. Symbolising this was his workman's cap, such as Thorez had lately spurned, but which for Jacquemotte was as purportedly 'legendary' an accoutrement as Stalin's pipe, and one that would be solemnly borne by children at his funeral.[221] A CPGB pamphlet addressed to trade unionists evoked those who missed the 'old days' when there were fewer officials, fewer committees, less respectability, and the taking to the streets of the hope of a better future with the red flag flying. 'You recognise now that hope and enthusiasm embodied in the Communist Party … You look on Harry Pollitt as your leader. You were as pleased as we were when Gallacher got into Parliament …'[222] Combining Pollitt's and Gallacher's roles, Jacquemotte offered this sort of legitimation of the PCB, and while he did not singlehandedly bring about the sudden upturn in its fortunes, he did symbolise the basis on which it took place. By the time of his death the following year, membership and parliamentary representation had trebled, and Jacquemotte's popularity was said to extend, not only to party sympathisers, but to the 'labouring masses in general'.[223]

He died suddenly in October 1936 and we cannot know how a living cult of Jacquemotte might have developed. What is clear is his party's eagerness to extract whatever advantage it could from his standing. Though Jacquemotte's funeral was conducted on a grand scale, it was the anniversary of his death the following year that occasioned the full cult treatment (Fig. 4.1). Already a subscription had been launched for a monument in bronze by the sculptor Dolf Ledel. There was also now produced a 64-page commemorative brochure in a print-run exceeding the PCB's membership. In default of any available published text, this began most unusually by reproducing the appropriate sections of Jacquemotte's cadre autobiography.[224]

Visually the emphasis was on Jacquemotte's obsequies, and on the human figure caught out on a stroll or fishing trip, inseparable, it seemed, from his legendary head-piece. There was no informality, however,

Fig. 4.1 Commemoration of Joseph Jacquemotte, Brussels, 10 October 1937 (Centre des Archives Communistes en Belgique)

regarding the campaign's political objects. A routine article upholding the PCB's latest positions on unity was now described as Jacquemotte's political testament. A mass demonstration in Brussels provided a carefully choreographed demonstration of the same theme. Workers were to attend in their working clothes, flowers but not wreaths were encouraged in a spirit of celebration, and banners and slogans were restricted to those made up beforehand according to a uniform design and political narrative.[225] Belatedly as he came to lead it, Jacquemotte was posthumously installed as the founding father of Belgian communism, and one who had only ever split the working-class movement so that he could afterwards reunite it on a better basis. When two years later Ledel's monument was unveiled, there was another popular mobilisation by the PCB, and the same deployment of plaudits from those beyond the party's ranks.[226]

Discontinuity of the PCB's leading personnel meant that the displacement of an enkindling figure by an integrating cult was in this instance demonstrated with particular starkness. Though Relecom appeared in the Jacquemotte commemorative brochure as if his designated successor, there was no real effort to promote him as such, and after an unfortunate accommodation with the Gestapo during the occupation Relecom was permanently excluded from any significant responsibility. With the Cold War turn to party cults, it was therefore the new party secretary Edgar Lalmand who was cast in the Thorez or Pollitt role. As Gotovitch has recounted, Lalmand was a former businessman bereft of either the personal history, social capital or political standing of a figure like Jacquemotte. With nothing to recommend him but his office, he was nevertheless treated with a veneration bordering on idolatry that was utterly incomprehensible beyond the shrunken ranks of the PCB itself. It was less than compelling even there, and already before the Khrushchev speech Lalmand was the first of the stalinist cult figures to be toppled from his pedestal at the end of 1954.[227]

Superficially, this contrasts markedly with the contemporaneous celebration of Pollitt for all that he had represented within his movement. Nevertheless, the same discontinuities were merely disguised in the CPGB's case by their being encapsulated within a single career as a result of the party's unusual stability of leadership. What Pollitt represented by the time of his 60th birthday was what he had been, not what he was, combined with the dignities of the office from which by now he seemed almost irremovable. Within months of his becoming general secretary in 1929, he had had the party intellectual Emile Burns drafted in to assist him so that he could focus on his wider campaigning role. Fourteen years later, Burns was said to have mooted the appointment of someone better fitted than Pollitt for the role of general secretary, with Pollitt himself as 'chairman and public representative of the Party' cultivating the influence he had among a wider public and political class.[228]

Though Pollitt had not the slightest intention of agreeing to this, the political leadership he provided not only followed the broader perspective that Moscow decided, but depended for its detailed exposition on devotees of a 1930s vintage very much resembling Thorez's acolytes in France. Whatever Pollitt's personal political capital, he added nothing to it in the post-war years in which his cult was formalised. 'To me Harry is linked with Spain, anti-appeasement and the Hunger Marches', wrote one of the younger party rebels of 1956. He had joined the party in 1934, just as Pollitt was coming into his own, and described how the 'affection for Harry' among this generation remained tremendous. But that did not take away from the fact that Pollitt by now was all 'washed up'.[229]

Increasingly Pollitt's speeches invoked his formative years, and when *Serving My Time* was reissued in 1950 he made no attempt to bring it up to date. At the same time, with the ebbing of the hope and enthusiasm once associated with his party, Pollitt obtained a compensatory satisfaction from his incorporation into a cult hierarchy that bound him into stalinism more closely than ever. After witnessing ovations to Gottwald in 1946, he wrote ingenuously of the 'nice feeling … to hear the gigantic concourse of workers cry out: "Long live Harry Pollitt."'[230] Three years later, he was again buoyed up by the bouquets presented him by young Czechoslovakian women comrades; and when Gottwald and Dimitrov entertained him in their palaces, he consoled himself that 'someone feels the old man is not so dusty'.[231] Pollitt's stance in 1939 remained a source of political capital; but what it also demonstrated in a Cold War environment was not so much his vindication against his party, but the 'grand and positive thing' of being brought into line by it.[232] Pollitt would not have orated from beneath his own gigantic portrait image, as Thorez did. He had no need to combine that image with a predecessor's, as Lalmand did with Jacquemotte. But this was because Pollitt in his own person now combined the attributes of office and collective memory that were the essence of the Cold War integration cult.

Notes

1. Isaac Deutscher, *The Prophet Unarmed. Trotsky: 1921–1929* (Oxford: Oxford University Press, 1970 edn), p. 458.

2. Trotsky, *Stalin. An appraisal of the man and his influence* (London: Hollis & Carter, 1947), p. xv.
3. Trotsky, *My Life. An attempt at autobiography* (Harmondsworth: Penguin, 1975 edn), p. 522.
4. Stephen Kotkin describes Trotsky's formulation as 'exactly backward', and it is true that Stalin as general secretary built up the machinery on which the *vozhd'* depended. Nevertheless, it was the party as already established in power that was the source of Stalin's authority, and Kotkin himself writes that he was handed 'exceptional power almost instantaneously'. See Stephen Kotkin, *Stalin: paradoxes of power 1897–1928* (London: Penguin, 2015 edn), pp. 424–5.
5. 'Interview with the first American labour delegation' (Sept. 1927) in Stalin, *Works*, vol. 10, pp. 124–5.
6. Stalin, *Works*, vol. 12, p. 146.
7. Stalin, *An interview with the German author Emil Ludwig* (Moscow: Co-operative Publishing House of Foreign Workers in the USSR, 1932).
8. Erik van Ree, *The Political Thought of Joseph Stalin. A study in twentieth-century revolutionary patriotism* (London: Routledge Curzon, 2002), ch. 12; Sarah Davies, 'Stalin and the making of the leader cult in the 1930s' in Balázs Apor et al. (eds), *The Leader Cult in Communist Dictatorships. Stalin and the Eastern bloc* (Basingstoke: Palgrave Macmilllan, 2004), pp. 29-46; Jan Plamper, *The Stalin Cult. A study in the alchemies of power* (New Haven, CT: Yale University Press, 2012), pp. 120–7.
9. Ivo Banac (ed.), *The Diary of Georgi Dimitrov 1933-1949* (New Haven, CT: Yale University Press, 2003), pp. 62–7, entry for 7 Nov. 1937.
10. Plamper, *Stalin Cult*, p. 37.
11. Maureen Perrie, *The Cult of Ivan the Terrible in Stalin's Russia* (Basingstoke: Palgrave Macmillan, 2001), p. 48; John Barber, *Soviet Historians in Crisis, 1928-1932* (Basingstoke: Macmillan, 1981), p. 26.
12. M.N. Pokrovsky, 'About a certain "experiment in autobiography"', *LM*, Sept. 1930, 569-73; George M. Enteen, *The Soviet-Scholar Bureaucrat. M.N. Pokrovskii and the Society of Marxist Historians* (University Park: Pennsylvania State University Press, 1978), pp. 175–6.

13. Dutt, '"Mirrors of the Kremlin, By a Comrade With a Duster"; or subjectivism in politics', *LM*, Jun. 1925, 379–80.
14. *Inprecorr*, 23 Apr. 1925, 486.
15. Browder, 'Trotsky admires Trotsky – His "life"', *DW* (L), 27 Jun. 1930.
16. V., 'Souvenirs d'un bolchévik', *CdB*, Apr. 1931, 235–6; see also Chap. 6.2 below.
17. Karl Radek, *Portraits and Pamphlets* (London: Wishart, 1935), pp. 1–34; also Jean-François Fayet, *Karl Radek (1885-1939). Biographie politique* (Bern: Peter Lang, 2004), pp. 643–4.
18. Emil Ludwig, *Leaders of Europe* (London: Ivor Nicholson & Watson, 1934), pp. 358–62.
19. George Orwell, *Animal Farm* (1945) (Harmondsworth: Penguin edn, 1951), p. 15.
20. Barbusse papers, Barbusse to Kurella, 6 Feb. 1934.
21. Barbusse to Kurella, 6 Feb. 1934.
22. Barbusse papers, Barbusse to Kurella, 6 Feb. and 7 Jun. 1934.
23. There are two extant versions of Stetsky's comments: a Russian version in RGASPI 558/11/699 and a French version in the Barbusse papers with a covering letter dated 15 Sept. 1934. Translations here are from the Russian version.
24. Barbusse papers, 'Petites anecdotes', notes of conversation, Moscow, n.d. but Oct.-Nov. 1934; Barbusse, *Staline*, pp. 47, 85–7.
25. Claude Pennetier and Bernard Pudal, 'Stalinism: workers' cult and cult of leaders', *TCC*, 1 (2009), 20–9.
26. Pokrovsky, 'About', 573.
27. See Chap. 6.3 below.
28. Sarah Davies, *Popular Opinion in Stalin's Russia. Terror, propaganda and dissent, 1934–1941* (Cambridge: Cambridge University Press, 1997), pp. 153–4.
29. Yves Cohen, *Le Siècle des chefs. Une histoire transnationale du commandement et de l'autorité* (Paris: Éditions Amsterdam, 2013), p. 795.
30. Rolland to Gorky, 17 Nov. 1934 in Jean Pérus (ed.), *Correspondance Romain Rolland Maxime Gorki* (Paris: Albin Michel, 1991), pp. 342–3.
31. 'Texte officiel de l'entretrien de Staline avec Romain Rolland', 28 Jun. 1935 in Bernard Duchatelet (ed.), *Voyage à Moscou. Juin-juillet*

1935 (Paris: Albin Michel, 1992), pp. 237–47; Beatrice Webb diaries (British Library of Political and Economic Science), entry for 16 Aug. 1939.

32. Gide, *Retour de l'URSS* (Paris: Gallimard, 1936) esp. pp. 69–78.
33. Lion Feuchtwanger, *Moscow 1937* (London: Gollancz, 1937), chs 2 and 6, also p. 169. Karl Schlögel, *Moscow, 1937* (Cambridge: Polity, 2012), p. 85 discusses the Soviet edition.
34. W.H. Chamberlin, *Russia's Iron Age* (London: Duckworth, 1935), p. 227; also Trotsky, *My Life*, p. 522.
35. Henri Barbusse, *Staline. Un monde nouveau vu à travers un homme* (1935) (Paris: Flammarion, 1936 edn), p. 60.
36. Dimitrov, 'Letter to the Austrian workers', *LM*, Jun. 1934, 364.
37. See notably Brigitte Studer, *The Transnational World of the Cominternians* (Basingstoke: Palgrave Macmillan, 2015).
38. Denis Peschanski (ed.), *Marcel Cachin. Carnets 1906-1947* (Paris: CNRS Éditions, 4 vols, 1993–8), vol. 2, pp. 570, 571-2, 611–2, entries for 19, 20 and 27 Jul. 1920; vol. 3, p. 291, entry for 27 Mar. 1925.
39. Peschanski (ed.), *Marcel Cachin. Carnets*, vol. 2, pp. 748–51, entries for 6–7 Jan. 1933.
40. Joseph Freeman, *An American Testament* (London: Gollancz, 1938), pp. 400–3, 529–30.
41. 'Pasionaria Tells of First Meeting People's Leader', *DW* (NY), 21 Dec. 1939.
42. Jordan, 'You'd never forget this!', *Russia Today*, May 1939, 12.
43. James G. Ryan, *Earl Browder. The failure of American communism* (Tuscaloose & London: University of Alabama Press, 1997), ch. 10.
44. For example, *Nos Rencontres avec Lénine* (Moscow: Éditions en Langues Étrangères, 1939).
45. Peschanski (ed.), *Marcel Cachin. Carnets*, vol. 4, p. 111, entries for 25 and 26 Jul. 1935.
46. Cachin, 'Long Live Stalin!' in *The World Hails Twentieth Anniversary of the Soviet Union* (Moscow: Foreign Languages Publishing House, 1938), pp. 137–40.
47. Cornford, 'Full moon at Tierz: before the storming of Huesca' in Pat Sloan (ed.), *John Cornford. A memoir* (London: Cape, 1938), p. 245; for the poem's specific evocation of Dimitrov's example, see Chap. 5.2 below.

48. Pat Sloan, 'Why they call him "our Stalin"', *DW* (L), 21 Dec. 1939.
49. Marcella and Maurizio Ferrara, *Palmiro Togliatti. Essai biographique* (Paris: Éditions Sociales, 1954), p. 87; Jorge Amado, *Le Chevalier de l'Espèrance* (Paris: Éditions Français Réunis, 1949), pp. 55–6; Frantisek Necasek, *Klement Gottwald. Communist Premier of Czechoslovakia* (London: CPGB, 1947), pp. 32–3; Aitken Ferguson, 'Under the shadow of Hitler's war plans', *DW* (L), 24 Apr. 1938; John McCarten, 'Party linesman', *New Yorker*, 1 Oct. 1938, 26; Ryan, *Earl Browder*, p. 293 n. 32.
50. Boris Souvarine, *Stalin. A critical survey of bolshevism* (London: Secker & Warburg, 1939), p. 412.
51. Kevin Morgan, *Harry Pollitt* (Manchester: Manchester University Press, 1993), pp. 119–20.
52. Henri Barbusse, *Connais-tu Thaelmann?* (Paris: Comité pour la Libération de Thaelmann et des Antifascistes Allemands emprisonnés, n.d. but 1934), pp. 5–7.
53. Philippe Robrieux, *Maurice Thorez. Vie secrète et vie publique* (Paris: Fayard, 1975), pp. 332–3. Jean Fréville, *Avec Maurice Thorez* (Paris: Éditions Sociales, 1950), pp. 16–17 preferred the comparison with Bossuet and a classical sobriety of discourse.
54. Barbusse, *Staline*, p. 16.
55. Barbusse papers, Barbusse to (Stefan) Pokhitonov, 1 Feb. 1933; *Henri Barbusse. Écrivain et révolutionnaire* (Paris: Éditions Sociales Internationales, 1935).
56. Koltsov, 'Zagadka – Stalin', *Pravda*, 21 Dec. 1929.
57. *DW* (L), 22 Dec. 1949.
58. 'Good Old Joe!', *Our Time*, Feb. 1942, 23–4.
59. Barbusse, *Staline*, p. 10.
60. Manuilsky, 'Lenin is as immortal as the people who gave him birth', *Sunday Worker* (NY), 21 Jan. 1940.
61. Orlando Figes and Boris Kolonitskii, *Interpreting the Russian Revolution. The language and symbols of 1917* (New Haven, CT: Yale University Press, 1999), p. 83.
62. Plamper, *Stalin Cult*, p. 25.
63. Greene, 'Lenin in October' (*Spectator*, 25 Nov. 1938) in idem, *The Pleasure-Dome. The collected film criticism 1935–40* (London: Secker & Warburg, 1972), pp. 206–7.
64. Plamper, *Stalin Cult*, p. 259 n. 34.

65. Barbusse, *Staline*, p. 87.
66. Souvarine, *Stalin*, p. 580.
67. William J. Chase, 'Stalin as producer: the Moscow show trials and the construction of mortal threats' in Sarah Davies and James Harris (eds), *Stalin: a new history* (Cambridge: Cambridge University Press, 2005), p. 247; Cohen, *Siècle*, pp. 786–7.
68. See however Andréas Mavroyiannis, 'La crise du PC cypriote Akel (1945-1952)', *Communisme*, 29–31 (1991), 162–9 for a less well-known example.
69. Charles Tillon, *Un procès de Moscou à Paris* (Paris: Seuil, 1971).
70. Cachin, preface to Marty, *La Révolte de la Mer Noire* (Paris: Éditions Sociales Internationales, 1939 edn), p. 10.
71. 'Les problèmes de la politique du Parti et l'activité fractionnelle des camarades André Marty et Charles Tillon', PCF politburo document, *CdC*, Oct. 1952, 953–6.
72. André Marty, *L'Affaire Marty* (Paris: Deux Rives, 1955), pp. 95–108.
73. See Claude Pennetier, 'Thorez-Marty: Paris-Moscou, Moscou-Paris' in Mikhail Narinsky and Jürgen Rojahn (eds), *Centre and Periphery. The history of the Comintern in the light of new documents* (Amsterdam: Institute of Social History, 1996), pp. 203–17.
74. Peschanski, entry on Tillon in José Gotovitch and Mikhaïl Narinsky (eds), *Komintern: l'histoire et les hommes. Dictionnaire biographique de l'Internationale communiste en France, Belgique, au Luxembourg, en Suisse et à Moscou (1919–1943)* (Paris: Éditions de l'Atelier, 2001), pp. 538–40.
75. Marie-Cécile Bouju, *Lire en communiste. Les Maisons d'édition du Parti communiste français 1920-1968* (Rennes: Presses Universitaires de Rennes, 2010), pp. 124–30.
76. Julian Jackson, *The Popular Front in France. Defending democracy, 1934–38* (Cambridge: Cambridge University Press, 1990 edn), p. 19.
77. See for example Paul-Franz Namur, *L'Histoire sainte et le martyre de Saint-Blum* (Paris, privately published, 1937).
78. Thorez papers 626 AP/231, collectively signed letter, n.d. but c. Apr. 1944.
79. Thorez papers 626 AP/271, Alfred and Charlotte Lebidon to Thorez, 4 May 1945 and 28 Apr. 1946.

80. *L'Humanité*, 23 Jan. 1936; 'Pour la victoire de la classe ouvrière', PCF central committee statement, *CdB*, 15 Jan. 1936.
81. 'Le Parti communiste vous parle …', *L'Humanité*, 17 Apr. 1936; Jackson, *Popular Front*, p. 49.
82. Simone Téry, 'Dimanche, Maurice Thorez le jeune chef de notre parti sera élu triomphalement', *L'Humanité*, 24 Apr. 1936.
83. 'Ecoutez la voix des dirigeants du Parti', *L'Humanité*, 21 Mar. 1936.
84. A. Rossi, *Physiologie du Parti communiste français* (Paris: Self, 1948), p. 34.
85. Annie Kriegel and Stéphane Courtois, *Eugen Fried. Le grand secret du PCF* (Paris: Seuil, 1997); for Stalin see Chap. 2 above.
86. Solomon, 'Un livre au service du Pain, de la Liberté et de la Paix', *CdB*, Nov.-Dec. 1937, 889–95; Bouju, *Lire*, pp. 135–6.
87. *La vie ardente de Paul Vaillant-Couturier. Quelques images de sa mémoire radieuse* (Paris: Éditions de L'Humanité, 1937).
88. *L'Humanité*, 24 Jan. 1936.
89. Jean-Richard Bloch, *L'Homme du Communisme* (Paris: Éditions Sociales, 1949), p. 34; Ernest Hemingway, *For Whom the Bell Tolls* (1940), ch. 42.
90. See the discussion in Rémi Skoutelsky, *L'Espoir guidait leurs pas. Les volontaires français dans les Brigades internationales 1936–1939*, (Paris: Bernard Grasset, 1998), pp. 251–3.
91. See Jean Vigreux and Serge Wolikow, 'General secretariat and general secretaries: the case of the French communist party' in Kevin Morgan et al. (eds), *Agents of the Revolution. New biographical approaches to the history of international communism in the age of Lenin and Stalin* (Bern: Peter Lang, 2005), p. 84.
92. Marty, *L'Affaire Marty*, p. 43.
93. See Marty papers (SSD) 281 J box 33, Marty to PCF secretariat, 26 Feb., 1 Apr. and 19 Apr. 1935; also Alexandre Courban, 'André Marty, responsable politique de L'*Humanité* dans les années trente' in Paul Boulland et al. (eds), *André Marty: l'homme, l'affaire, l'archive* (Paris: Codhos, 2005), pp. 63–8.
94. Téry, 'Dimanche'.
95. *L'Humanité*, 7 Nov. 1936.
96. Skoutelsky, *L'Espoir*, pp. 56–8; *La Voix du Peuple* (PCF Lyonnaise region) 14 Nov. 1936 in Marty papers (SSD) 281 J box 23.

97. See Chap. 3.4 above.
98. Marty papers (SSD) 281 J box 39, 'Directives générales pour l'histoire des B.I.' and 'Popularisation et histoire des Brigades Internationales' (21 Aug. 1939).
99. Marty papers (SSD) 281 J box 23, Rosa Michel, 'Un des meilleurs fils du peuple de France: *André Marty*', n.d. but 1939, place of publication (if any) not established.
100. Michel, 'Un des meilleurs fils'; 'Salut à André Marty', PCF central committee resolution, *CdB*, Aug. 1938, 374; 'Le Parti communiste français rend hommage à André Marty et aux volontaires de la liberté', *CdB*, Dec. 1938, 968.
101. 'Introduction générale' in Claude Pennetier et al. (eds), *Les Fusillés (1940–1944). Dictionnaire biographique des fusillés et exécutés par condamnation et comme otages ou guillotinés en France pendant l'Occupation* (Paris: Éditions de l'Atelier, 2015), pp. 18, 27.
102. Claudine Chomat, 'Le culte de souvenir. Février 1934', *Cahiers de l'Union des Femmes Françaises*, Feb. 1946, 4–6.
103. Aragon cited Pierre Juquin, *Aragon. Un destin français. 2: L'Atlantide (1939–1982)* (Paris: Éditions de la Martinière, 2013), 236.
104. *Des Français en qui la France peut avoir confiance* (Paris: Éditions du Parti communiste français, 1944 and 1945 edns).
105. Philippe Buton, *Les Lendemains qui déchantent. Le Parti communiste français à la Libération* (Paris: Presses de la Fondation Nationale des Sciences Politiques, 1993), pp. 176–9.
106. Rossi, *Physiologie*, pp. 424–30.
107. Robrieux, *Thorez*, p. 293.
108. Annette Wieviorka, *Maurice et Jeannette: biographie du couple Thorez* (Paris: Fayard, 2010), pp. 385–7.
109. On this see Stéphane Sirot, *Maurice Thorez* (Paris: Presses de Sciences Po, 2000), pp. 85–97.
110. Denis Peschanski, 'Introduction générale: du dirigeant à la figure emblématique' in idem (ed.), *Marcel Cachin. Carnets 1906-1947* (Paris: CNRS Editions, vol. 4, 1997), pp. 35–40.
111. Thorez papers 626 AP/273 Mme Duchesne, Rouen to Thorez, 13 May 1946.
112. Thorez papers 626 AP/231, works cell no 1506, Paris Xieme, 15 Oct. 1945, 626 AP/243, PCF Girard and Durupt cells to Thorez, received 28 Apr. 1947.

113. Thorez papers 626 AP/231, resolutions of St Jacques, Montlucon, 31 Jan. 1945 and Haubourdin (Nord), 16 Oct. 45.
114. My thanks to John Bulaitis for this observation.
115. Thorez papers 626 AP/231, Vergneau to Thorez, May 1946.
116. Duclos, 'Notre politique', *CdC*, May-Jun. 1946, 395.
117. Thorez papers 626 AP/273, Thorez to Roger Chalençon, Aug. 1945.
118. Peschanski, *Marcel Cachin*, vol. 4, p. 960, entry for 7 Jun. 1946.
119. Thorez papers, 626 AP/243.
120. See for example Thorez papers 626 AP/234 for resolutions occasioned by the threat to his parliamentary immunities in June 1949.
121. Thorez papers 626 AP/246, PCF Losserand-Chateau cell, Paris 14ème, to Thorez, 17 Oct. 1950.
122. For example, a note on a message from the PCF Puy-de-Dôme federation, 18 Oct. 1951 (Thorez papers 626 AP/251) records that there are over a thousand signatures.
123. Thorez papers 626 AP/249, message to Thorez from PCF Loire-et-Cher meeting at Blois, 8 Apr. 1951.
124. PCF secretariat, 6 Aug. 1951.
125. Thorez papers 626 AP/251, PCF Morbihan federal committee to Thorez, 1 Jul. 1951.
126. PCF secretariat, 14 Oct. 1947.
127. Jean Fréville, *La nuit finit à Tours. Naissance du parti communiste français* (Paris: Éditions Sociales, 1950), p. 156.
128. PCF secretariat, 23 Aug. 1950, letter of Auguste Lecoeur to party federations.
129. PCF central committee to Thorez on his fiftieth birthday, *CdC*, Jun. 1950, 40–2; Guy Besse, 'Maurice Thorez et son apport théorique au mouvement révolutionnaire français', *NC*, May 1950, 13–33; Marty papers (CHS) AM 21, 'Notes pour la lutte idéologique' (PCF central committee internal bulletin), special number 'Quelques éléments de trente ans de lutte du Parti communiste français' (23 Dec. 1950).
130. PCF secretariat, 31 Mar. 1947 for this explicit calculation.
131. André Parreaux, 'Maurice Thorez', *Pens*, Mar-Apr. 1950, 76–7; Fréville, *Avec Maurice Thorez*, p. 25.
132. Maurice Thorez, *Une politique de grandeur française* (Paris: Éditions Sociales, 1945).

133. Cachin, introduction to Paul Vaillant-Couturier, *Nous Ferons se lever le jour* (Paris: Éditions Hier et Aujourd'hui, 1947), pp. 1–5.
134. For Barbusse, see Chap. 5.2 below.
135. Fréville, *Avec Maurice Thorez*, p. 13.
136. Maurice Thorez, *Fils du peuple* (Paris: Éditions sociales, 1950 edn), pp. 138–9. Thorez's own directions for this section (Thorez papers 626 AP/211) refer not to Paul but to Vaillant-Couturier.
137. See Chap. 5.3 below.
138. Rémi Skoutelsky, 'Militants et militaires: les volontaires des Brigades internationales' in José Gotovitch and Anne Morelli (eds), *Militantisme et militants* (Brussels: EVO, 2000), pp. 51–2.
139. See PCF secretariat 2 Jan. 1945 for the earlier emphasis on this link.
140. Robrieux, *Maurice Thorez*, pp. 289–90.
141. Robrieux, *Maurice Thorez*, pp. 373, 387; Wieviorka, *Maurice et Jeannette*, p. 437.
142. Philippe Buton, 'Une génération évincée? Le recomposition des directions du Parti communiste français à la Libération', *Communisme*, 29–31 (1992), 54–5.
143. *Des Français en qui la France*, 1945 edn.
144. Marty papers (CHS) AM 29.
145. Marty papers (CHS) AM 42, 'L'affaire de L'Humanité', typescript dated 13 Mar. or May 1954; PCF secretariat, 20 Nov. 1944.
146. PCF secretariat minutes, 2 Aug. 1948; 'Georgi Dimitrov, le grand lutteur prolétarien antifasciste', *CdC*, Aug. 1949, 933–50.
147. PCF secretariat minutes, 19 Nov. 1948, 7 and 28 Feb. 1949.
148. Marty papers (CHS) AM 29 for various materials, also AM 17, Marty to PCF secretariat, 8 Jul. 1946 re ARAC and the resistance.
149. Monmousseau, 'Hommage à Pierre Semard', *CdC*, Mar. 1946, 59–63.
150. Genevée, 'Pierre Semard et la répression, essai d'interprétations' in Serge Wolikow (ed.), *Pierre Semard. Engagements, discipline et fidelité* (Paris: Cherche Midi, 2007), p. 233.
151. Wolikow, 'Le parcours d'un militant cheminot' and 'Un secrétaire générale oublié' in Wolikow, *Pierre Semard*, pp. 13–41 and 159–96.

152. Xavier Vigna, 'La mémoire de Pierre Semard chez les cheminots CGT' in Wolikow, *Pierre Semard*, p. 263.
153. Marty, *L'Affaire Marty*, pp. 95, 97.
154. 'The execution and victory of Pierre Semard' in André Marty, *Patriots of France* (London: Labour Monthly, n.d. but 1942), pp. 10–11; Marty, *Pierre Semard. Un de ceux grâce auxquels le France renaît* (Paris: Éditions du PCF, 1945).
155. Marty, 'Lénine et Staline, génies de la pensée et l'action', *CdC*, Oct. 1946, 932-3.
156. PCF secretariat minutes, 18 Nov. 1947.
157. Marty papers (CHS) AM 3 including Marty note for PCF secretariat, 10 Mar. 1949 and PCF secretariat circular, 5 Aug. 1949; also PCF secretariat minutes, 19 Jul. 1949.
158. Ducroux, 'André Marty: *Les Heures glorieuses de la Mer noire*', *CdC*, Mar. 1949, 378-9.
159. Jean Bruhat, 'Écrire et faire l'histoire en combattant. "Fils du peuple" et " La révolte de la Mer noire"', *CdC*, Jan. 1950, 96–108.
160. André Marty, *La révolte de la Mer noire* (Paris: Éditions Sociales, 1949 edn).
161. 'Deux ouvrages de lutte pour la paix: "Fils du Peuple" et "La Révolte de la Mer Noire"', *Apprendre*, Feb. 1950, 15–16; Guy Ducoloné, 'L'Union de la jeunesse française dans la lutte pour la paix', *CdC*, Jul. 1950, 45–53.
162. Marty papers (CHS) AM 3, Marty note for PCF secretariat, 10 Mar. 1949 and PCF secretariat circular 'Campagne du XXXème anniversaire de la révolte de la Mer Noire', 15 Mar. 1949.
163. Marty, 'La guerre d'Indochine et les traditions du mouvement ouvrier français', *CdC*, Mar. 1950, 20-34; Marty, 'Le Parti communiste français né et forgé dans la lutte contre la guerre', *CdC*, Dec. 1950, 25-45; Marty papers (CHS) AM 3, typescript article, 'Pourquoi et comment chaque membre de Parti doit étudier Les Heures Glorieuses de la Mer Noire'.
164. Vanessa Codaccioni, *Punir les opposants. PCF et procès politiques (1947–1962)* (Paris: CNRS Éditions, 2013), pp. 81–90.
165. Marty papers (CHS) AM 17, contribution at PCF 12th congress, 3 Apr. 1950 and covering letter 4 Apr. 1950; AM 3, typescript article, 'Pourquoi et comment'. The article appeared in *Apprendre*, Oct. 1949, 2-5.

166. PCF secretariat minutes, 14 Oct. 1947 and 23 Oct. 1950; Marty papers, 'L'affaire de L'Humanité'.
167. On this theme, see Codaccioni, *Punir*.
168. Thorez papers 626 AP/271, Maurice Agogué (?), Vierzou, to Thorez, 28 Sept. 1950.
169. Ducroux, 'André Marty'; also Pierre Daix, 'La morale nouvelle: à propos de la *Révolte de la Mer noire* d'André Marty', *NC*, Feb. 1950, 29–37.
170. Marty, 'La Révolte de la Mer noire' and Thorez, 'Le rôle du secrétaire fédéral', *CdC*, Apr. 1949, 419–35 and 436–42.
171. Raoul Calas, 'Le VIIe congrès du Parti communiste italien', *CdC*, Jun. 1950, 677–82.
172. Marty, *L'Affaire Marty*, p. 100; Marty papers (CHS) AM 29 for German materials including *Neues Deutschland* and *Junge Welt*, both 6 Nov. 1951.
173. For an overview, see Claude Pennetier, 'André Marty à l'épreuve des archives' in Boulland, *André Marty*.
174. Marty, *L'Affaire Marty*, pp. 258–61.
175. Marty to Stepanov, 7 Oct. 1946 cited Buton, *Lendemains*, pp. 260-1; for Vermeersch see Chap. 3.2 above.
176. Marty, *L'Affaire Marty*, pp. 95–108.
177. Marty, *L'Affaire Marty*, pp. 99, 100–1; Marty papers (CHS) AM 29, 'Comment a été écrite l'histoire de la Mer', 10 Nov. 1955.
178. See Chap. 6.2 below.
179. Pennetier and Pudal, 'Deux générations de militants communistes français (1931–1951) en proie à des procès d'épurations internes' in Gotovitch and Morelli, *Militantisme*, pp. 129–32.
180. PCF secretariat minutes, 16 May 1950.
181. RGASPI 495/108/1, Pollitt cadre autobiography, 6 Dec. 1931 and 495/220/82, Thorez cadre autobiography, 25 Apr. 1932.
182. Claude Pennetier and Bernard Pudal, 'Communist prosopography in France: research in progress based on French institutional communist autobiographies' in Morgan, *Agents of the Revolution*, pp. 21-36; Pirjo Kaihovaara, 'A good comrade, a good cadre: autobiographies and evaluation reports as a part of cadre policy in the Finnish Communist Party during the 1940s and 1950s' in Morgan, *Agents of the Revolution*, pp. 249–50.
183. Sirot, *Maurice Thorez*, pp. 166–72.

184. Thorez papers, 626 AP/250, CGT Fédération Nationale des Travailleurs du Sous-Sol et Similaires to Thorez, 28 Aug. 1950; 626 AP/243, PCF Cantonniers workplace cell resolution, 28 Apr. 1947.
185. See Chap. 6.2 below.
186. Egon Wertheimer, *Portrait of the Labour Party* (London: Putnams, 1929), pp. 29-30, 37–8.
187. See for example Kevin Morgan, *Harry Pollitt* (Manchester: Manchester University Press, 1993), pp. 148–51.
188. Morgan, *Harry Pollitt*, pp. 39–40.
189. Pollitt, *The Communist Party on Trial. Harry Pollitt's Defence* (London: CPGB, 1925), pp. 3, 31.
190. *DW* (L), 3 Dec. 1930.
191. *DW* (L), 22 Oct. and 3 Jan. 1931.
192. NA KV 2/1035, unnamed correspondent 'A' to Pollitt, c. Nov. 1930. Pollitt's name is misspelt and has been corrected here.
193. RGASPI 495/100/821/138, CPGB 12th congress, 1932, Pollitt reply to discussion.
194. RGASPI 495/100/951, Pollitt to Bob McIlhone, 7 Mar. 1934; Morgan, *Harry Pollitt*, p. 84.
195. See Kevin Morgan and Gidon Cohen, 'Rose Cohen (1894–1937), communist' in Keith Gildart, David Howell and Neville Kirk (eds), *Dictionary of Labour Biography. Volume XI* (Basingstoke: Palgrave Macmillan, 2003), pp. 31–9.
196. *Times Literary Supplement*, 5 May 1966, 387.
197. NA KV 2/1038, letter to J. Jones, Glamorgan chief constable, 22 Sept. 1937; report from Manchester, 23 Nov. 1937.
198. RGASPI 495/100/1025, CPGB 14th party congress, May 1937, contribution of Rose Smith; 495/14/17, 'Meeting of [Marty] Secretariat on English question', 29 Jun. 1937, contribution of Arnot.
199. See Chap. 3.4 above.
200. Pollitt at CPGB central committee, 2 Oct. 1939 in Francis King and George Matthews (eds), *About Turn. The British Communist Party and the outbreak of the Second World War* (London: Lawrence & Wishart, 1990), p. 199; Pollitt papers, CP/Ind/Poll, Pollitt's report, CPGB central committee, 24 Sept. 1939.
201. Robrieux, *Maurice Thorez*, pp. 247–8.

202. Pollitt papers CP/Ind/Poll, Mary Louisa Pollitt to Harry Pollitt, 11 Oct. 1939.
203. See Chap. 6.2 below.
204. Cited Morgan, *Harry Pollitt*, pp. 89–90.
205. See Chap. 3.4 above.
206. Labour Party 39th Annual Conference *Report*, 1940, 136, contribution of Frank Rowlands.
207. Mass-Observation report cited Morgan, *Harry Pollitt*, p. 119.
208. Mass-Observation archive, University of Sussex, TC 25/8/L, report on Montague Place demonstration, 1 May 1942.
209. Pollitt papers CP/Ind/Poll, Michael Marks, 'To Comrade Harry Pollitt', Jan. 1942.
210. *News Statesman and Nation*, 20 Sept. 1941, 274.
211. RGASPI 495/100/1026, CPGB 14th congress, May 1937, contribution of Relecom.
212. José Gotovitch, 'Construction and deconstruction of a cult: Edgar Lalmand and the Communist Party of Belgium', *TCC*, 1 (2009), 134–5; RGASPI 495/193/189, A. Legrand, evaluation of Jacquemotte, n.d. but early 1930s. The discussion here also draws on the entries by Gotovitch on all key figures in Gotovitch and Narinsky, *Komintern*.
213. RGASPI 495/193/189, Jacquemotte, cadre autobiography, 13 Oct. 1933; 495/93/250, 'Questions posées par la Cde Lebedeva', n.d., 1935?; for Pollitt see Gidon Cohen and Kevin Morgan, 'Stalin's sausage machine. British students at the International Lenin School 1926–37', *Twentieth Century British History*, 13 (2002), 327–55.
214. For Barbusse see Chap. 5.2 below.
215. RGASPI 495/193/189, De Boucke, 'La direction du PCB', 5 Jun. 1935; José Gotovitch, *Du communisme et des communistes en Belgique. Approches critiques* (Brussels: Éditions Aden, n.d.), p. 351.
216. De Boucke, 'La direction du PCB'; Legrand, evaluation of Jacquemotte; RGASPI 495/93/257, report of Berei, 31 Jul. 1936.
217. Gotovitch in Gotovitch and Narinsky, *Komintern*, p. 350.
218. Berei cited Gotovitch, 'Construction', 132–3.
219. Successive drafts of the self-criticism of Henri De Boeck dated 7 and 20 Mar. and 15 Apr. 1935 are in RGASPI 495/93/250; see also Gotovitch and Narinsky, *Komintern*, pp. 229–34.

220. RGASPI 495/93/246/55-9, 'Résolution sur la conférence nationale du PCB', 21 Mar. 1935.
221. *J. Jacquemotte. Sa vie, son oeuvre* (Brussels: Éditions Germinal, 1937), p. 56.
222. John Mahon, *Trade Unionism and Communism. A letter to a trade union branch secretary* (London: CPGB, 1936).
223. RGASPI 595/193/189, appraisal of Jacquemotte, Apr. 1936; Gotovitch, *Du Communisme*, pp. 48–9.
224. *J. Jacquemotte. Sa vie, son oeuvre.*
225. Cachin papers 290 J 50 for commemorative materials including the PCB's *Bulletin intérieur*, 15 and 23 Sept. 1937.
226. Etienne Neron, '20.000 travailleurs ont honoré la mémoire de Joseph Jacquemotte', *L'Humanité*, 14 Aug. 1939.
227. Gotovitch, 'Construction', 135–47.
228. NA KV 2/1040, note of 26 Aug. 1944.
229. John Saville to E.P. Thompson cited Morgan, *Harry Pollitt*, pp. 180–1.
230. Pollitt, *Impressions of Czechoslovakia* (London: CPGB, 1946), p. 38.
231. CPGB archives CP/Cent/EC/1/7, Pollitt and John Gollan, 'Report of the IXth Congress of the Communist Party of Czechoslovakia', May 1949; Morgan, *Harry Pollitt*, p. 179.
232. Pollitt papers CP/Ind/Poll/7/3, 'Points for September 11th speech', 1949.

CHAPTER 5

Cults of Circumstance

5.1 Comintern People

(i)

In March 1935, *The Communist International* ran a feature on the 'Comintern people' whom it described as the incarnation of its programme and the qualities that distinguished it from decaying social democracy. Three principal examples were given: two were in prison—the German Thälmann and the Hungarian Rákosi—and a third, Georgi Dimitrov, had been released the previous year following one of the most famous courtroom battles of the century (Fig. 5.1). Few articles convey so vividly how crucial to the emerging cult of the individual was the idea of being tested if necessary to the point of martyrdom. The German communist poet Erich Weinert provided an epigraph referring to 'the bloodstained five-sixths of the globe' where communism had suffered only different kinds of setback. Its vindication against social democracy therefore seemed, not a measure of achievement, but one of 'proletarian heroism on a mass scale' and the persecutions to which this gave rise. Where among the Hilferdings and Vanderverldes and 'Danish Royal Minister Stauning' were the names that inspired enthusiasm? The Comintern, conversely, had brought forth a 'phalanx of fearless proletarian revolutionaries who marched to the gallows singing the "Internationale"'. In Japan, in China, in Hungary—every one of the Comintern people in the article had been incarcerated, assassinated or tortured.[1]

K. Morgan, *International Communism and the Cult of the Individual*, DOI 10.1057/978-1-137-55667-7_5

Fig. 5.1 'Dimitrov lets in the light', cartoon by Buchan (James Boswell), *Daily Worker* (London), 21 October 1933 (Courtesy James Boswell Archive and Working Class Movement Library)

André Marty was one of this 'phalanx of heroes' and for some years one of the most celebrated of the Comintern's class-war prisoners.[2] When the following January he addressed the PCF congress, it was the same three names that he singled out, along with the Chinese Red Army, the heroes of Soviet science and exploration, and a nameless Asturias teenager shot down with slogans of the revolution on her lips. Repeatedly the passage was interrupted by the acclamations of the delegates. 'Yes, we are materialists', Marty assured them. 'But it's precisely because we represent humanity's future that our international gives rise to such examples of devotion and self-sacrifice while the great men of the bourgeoisie are sunk in mud and scandal ... .' Climaxing with Stalin as the best of these revolutionaries, Marty soaked, not entirely vicariously, in several minutes of applause.[3]

Along with the Comintern unperson Gramsci, Rákosi had had the longest experience of repressive state action and through his trials was known to many both in and beyond the communists' ranks. Nevertheless, it was Thälmann and Dimitrov who at this time provided the outstanding examples of international cult figures. As Marty addressed the PCF, it was their two giant portraits that flanked that of Marcel Cachin above the platform. It was Dimitrov, moreover, who had linked their two names in saluting Thälmann as the leader and paragon of the German workers to whom international efforts should turn following his own release.[4] As the campaigns segued into one another, the story could therefore be told as a consecutive tale of solidarity as projected through the figure of the leader. But it is also possible to approach the two cases comparatively; for despite their being so closely identified, Thälmann and Dimitrov exemplify the features we have identified respectively with the integrating and enkindling figure.

When he was arrested in 1933, Thälmann was already well-known internationally as 'undoubtedly the outstanding Communist leader in the Communist Parties in the capitalist countries'.[5] He was certainly the leader of the outstanding communist party, if that meant the largest of them and the one presented as a model to the others. Dimitrov, the head of the Comintern's West European Bureau, had by comparison been a man of the shadows. Through the platform of the Reichstag fire trial he nevertheless established an irreproducible kudos and moral capital that helped define the turn to anti-fascism which he, more than anybody, now articulated. Moreover, Dimitrov also brought into view a personal history by which his mastery of the occasion, so much in contrast with his communist co-defendants, was rendered explicable in terms of a character and experience that went beyond the collective party virtues which he exemplified. Where Dimitrov's coup de théâtre caught the Comintern unawares, the Thälmann campaign represented a concerted effort to mobilise an international public through projection of the individual as the 'living symbol' of a cause.[6] Considerable resources were devoted to the campaign; Barbusse gave it the slogan of winning Thälmann like a battle, and for communists internationally it was a crucial salient to be defended. Nevertheless, the role in this of Thälmann's personality was manifestly of a lesser order, in part, though only in part, because the Nazis denied him any platform from which to express it.

Dimitrov and his trial came first. Barbusse's pamphlet for the Thälmann campaign had the title 'Do you know Thälmann?' When Dimitrov in March 1933 was charged with involvement in the burning of the Reichstag, few outside of the Comintern apparatus and his native Bulgaria could have said that they knew him. Barbusse himself had encountered him through the West European Bureau, and already in June 1933 provided a biographical profile in his weekly *Monde*.[7] Nevertheless, even as the trial got underway, the communist press focused less on the 'three Bulgarians'—Dimitrov and his co-accused, Blagoy Popov and Vassil Tanev—than on their co-defendant Ernst Torgler, erstwhile head of the KPD's parliamentary group. 'Free Torgler And His Comrades', ran the headlines on the day the trial opened, and it was not until Dimitrov's electrifying appearance two days later that the focus shifted irrevocably to the Bulgarian.[8] Unlike the others, Dimitrov opted to defend himself when he was denied counsel of his own choosing. He did so with great dignity and cogency on the basis of his communist principles and a lifetime's record of commitment to his class. The Nazis had determined on the widest publicity as a sort of quasi-show trial, but without the later stalinist device of a prearranged script. The result in propaganda terms was a calamity; never more so than when Dimitrov in a famous encounter reduced the Nazi leader Göring to an object of ridicule. As the paper of the British communists put it, no class-conscious worker anywhere could not but at once feel inches taller.[9] Dimitrov himself was depicted in giant proportions; in *Monde*, and in the memorable photomontage of John Heartfield reproduced internationally, the image was that of a Brobdingnagian 'accused as accuser', towering over Göring or pointing accusingly at a cowering Nazi judge.[10] (Fig. 5.2)

Acquitted in December, two months later Dimitrov and his co-defendants were allowed to leave for the USSR, where their trial had also received extensive publicity. Dimitrov was in no doubt as to the political capital that he now represented for the Comintern.[11] Stalin was in any

Fig. 5.2 'The judge, the judged', montage by John Heartfield, *Arbeiter-Illustrierte-Zeitung*, 16 November 1933 (Collection of the Akron Art Museum, Gift of Roger R. Smith, © The Heartfield Community of Heirs/VG Bild-Kunst, Bonn and DACS, London 2016)

case turning to the outward projection of leadership figures, and at the first meeting between them told of how the masses had a herd psychology and would abandon their leaders only if better ones were found. Of the existing Comintern leaders, Manuilsky was an agitator, Kuusinen 'good, but an academic', Piatnitsky narrow, Knorin propagandist; none, Stalin might have added, had caught the popular imagination any more than had their social-democratic counterparts. Dimitrov, on the other hand, had 'looked the enemy in the face', exactly as the 'Comintern people' were to be described as doing.[12] Manuilsky summed up afterwards:

> In the Communist International we need a 'boss'. History has placed you at the forefront through the Leipz[ig] trial. You have enormous popularity among the masses. Your voice has colossal resonance. You must take over the leadership.[13]

Identified here with 'history', the spontaneity of the enkindling cult simply meant the generation of usable political capital independently of any deliberate preferment by the apparatus and attaching to an individual who commanded a wider political authority than had been formally vested in them. Alfred Kurella, the German communist now acting as Dimitrov's secretary, noted the relations of intimacy he had established with Stalin and anticipated his installation at the Comintern's head.[14] Although formally speaking Dimitrov became general secretary only at the seventh world congress, it was in 1934–1935, as the shift to the popular front was effected, that his political leverage was greatest. In the course of 1936 he would even creep in amongst the Four Giants, usually at Engels's expense, or as Stalin's counterpart in his own special sphere as the 'tested pilot' of the world's exploited and oppressed.[15] Though Dimitrov certainly enjoyed the prestige of his office, his political capital had not, even so, initially derived from this, but was the basis on which he achieved it.

Exploitation of this asset raised particular sensitivities precisely because of the interaction between the national and the international. The striking down so easily of the German workers' movement had been a crushing blow to European communists, and it is impossible otherwise to understand how Dimitrov's defiance could have so caught their imaginations. As Dimitrov himself put it, the denting of the myth of fascism's invincibility required 'the example of a living man' standing up to it.[16] On his first appearance in court, he had thus brought into play a personal history as worker, trade unionist and socialist that dated back more than 30 years.

'Like Socrates', a British admirer wrote, 'he could have claimed to have spent his whole life in preparing for his defence'.[17]

A key witness had been his sister Elena, who already at the London counter-trial had movingly evoked a family history of political commitment. This was silently corroborated at Leipzig by the attendance at the trial of Dimitrov's mother.[18] The Nazis had targeted bolshevism through its foreign agents. In deploying his biographical capital in its defence, Dimitrov did so both as a soldier of the international revolution, freely affirming his identification with the Comintern, and as a proud 'son of the Bulgarian working class'. The joke in Sofia was that there was one brave man in Germany, and he was a Bulgarian.[19] There was also a Brecht poem inscribed to Dimitrov that would have reminded them of the thousands who bravely resisted out of sight, and how Dimitrov on their collective behalf had seized upon Germany's one remaining public space.[20] It was in this spirit that at the seventh world congress he was presented by German communists with an album depicting the struggle within Germany for which he had furnished such an example.[21] The KPD had nevertheless suffered a devastating collapse, which Torgler's effacement during the trial, having accepted the services of a Nazi lawyer, had merely exacerbated. In due course, Torgler was to play the role in the Dimitrov myth of the counterfoil of traitor. But for the KPD in the meantime, the affirmation of some German symbol of defiance was an obvious political necessity.

The 'Thälmann committee' had originated on Dimitrov's acquittal as the International Committee for the Liberation of Dimitrov, Thälmann and All Imprisoned Anti-Fascists.[22] As Dimitrov was then released, Thälmann resumed centre stage and it was against Thälmann that the next big Nazi trial was initially anticipated. At the same time, the campaign offered the strongest projection yet of the Comintern's new cult of the party leader. According to the KPD chairman Wilhelm Pieck, while Dimitrov had 'fulfilled ... his duty as a representative of the working class', Thälmann's fate posed issues of a still higher order as Hitler now fixed upon the leader of the foremost body confronting him.[23] Barbusse's point was similar: 'He is not accused of some melodramatic and grotesque *attentat* ... They want his head because it's the head of the German Communist Party.'[24] The stark alternative 'Thälmann or Hitler?' was a key theme in Dimitrov's text and in others widely circulated.[25] In one, a parallel life of Thälmann was interwoven with extracts from *Mein Kampf* and contrasted with it in a Manichean commentary.[26] If it was Thälmann who symbolised the alternative for which the party stood, it also needed his flesh-and-blood leadership qualities in conditions of illegality. Pieck's text was not fine-tuned for a liberal public: 'You want to escape fascist servitude? You want to be free men? Then it is necessary that Ernst Thälmann take the place of Hitler.'[27]

For two years the campaign was one of the highest profile ever organised by the communists. Its centre was Paris, where both the KPD and Willi Münzenberg had transferred their main centre of operations, and where the French and international Thälmann committees operated from the same address. They had the same presiding luminaries, such as Barbusse, Rolland, André Gide and André Malraux, and crucial support from the PCF, including the secondment of the agitprop full-timer André Seigneur.[28] With the setting up in Germany of so-called people's tribunals, the campaign's focus turned to the threat of Thälmann's judicial murder, and 'international Thälmann days' were organised that included a Paris exhibition to which Ernst, Léger, Dali, Arp and Man Ray were among the artists donating works.[29] With the adoption of a platform of anti-fascist unity, the campaign was now conceived of as 'a vast popular front' and according to Gilbert Badia it contributed significantly to the realisation of such a movement in France itself.[30] Britain and especially the USA were also centres of activity, and in all three countries there were showings of a Thälmann film documentary.[31] During the peak of activity in 1934–1935, Dimitrov's name alone can have had a comparable resonance internationally.

There was a falling away after 1936 as Spain now made its greater call on solidarity. Even at the campaign's height Thälmann's imprint as an individual was much weaker than Dimitrov's, and this in a double sense because of his poverty in usable political capital. The first and more obvious issue was the failure to materialise of a Thälmann trial. If Leipzig provided Dimitrov's capital, Hitler seemed disinclined to risk a further such encounter, or to lose another communist like a battle.[32] At the same time, Barbusse's formulation of the issue in this way underscores how Thälmann's release on terms of clemency or collusion would have represented a political defeat for the thousands of other imprisoned anti-fascists whose defiance he was meant to symbolise.[33] Initially, Barbusse had envisaged a counter-trial in Washington, or else an 'international congress of thinkers, lawyers, idealists and technical workers'.[34] At the end of 1935 there was in fact a well-attended conference on national socialist law, and increasingly campaign materials focused on the legal expedients through which Thälmann was denied any possibility of an open trial.[35]

But if Thälmann lacked a public platform, nor could any use be made of more personal communications while his fate hung in the balance.

When the Italian–American anarchists Sacco and Vanzetti provided the solidarity cause célèbre of the 1920s, one important factor was that these were 'charismatic prisoners' who reaffirmed their ideals in moving and outspoken ways.[36] Dimitrov too had now published his *Letters from Prison*; but Thälmann's, like Gramsci's, could appear only posthumously and there was little in the meantime for supporters to feed upon. In the songs about these heroes on which Weinert collaborated with the Hungarian–French musicologist Paul Arma, it is notable that Thälmann was represented essentially as political symbol, and Dimitrov as the living revolutionary defying his persecutors from the dock.[37] While Dimitrov tended to be remembered on the anniversary of his trial, Thälmann was almost the first of the non-Soviet leaders to be marked out by the empty ceremonial of his birthday, albeit this was firmly in the longer tradition of demonstrating solidarity with political prisoners in this way.[38] Thälmann's 50th birthday was in any case both the high point of the campaign and its swansong. In Britain, 108 MPs supported a high-profile delegation for his release; in all communist papers, the coverage was extensive; in Paris, 2000 supporters gathered at the Mutualité—though the figure three months earlier for Romain Rolland had been three times that.[39] The occasion continued to be marked in smaller ways, and still in 1937 drew a thousand supporters to the Mutualité.[40] Nevertheless, in the illustrated brochure *From Dimitrov to Thaelmann*, the former stood out both visually and textually, and through its scrapbook-like format Thälmann as focal point was virtually supplanted by the campaigning activities around him.[41]

Initially Thälmann's cause was publicised through a profusion of biographical materials combining myth and outright invention in one of the earliest sustained exercises in such refashioning according to the stalinist mould.[42] Among the details of somewhat dubious veracity were Thälmann's tough and proletarian family background, his father's lifelong party commitment and the untameable spirit of insubordination which Thälmann himself had maintained throughout his spells of military service. Barbusse's in particular was a fantastical construction of the brother, guide, soldier and leader whose ardour and incorruptibility were associated with a yearning for education and spiritual enrichment which Thälmann himself had hardly even pretended to.[43]

What could not be conjured up was a 'living man'. Dimitrov's legitimising history had been vividly authenticated by his sister Elena, whose ability to move a wider public was such that she was for the time being denied re-entry into Britain.[44] That Prestes was 'conceived, nourished and raised' by the people was also symbolised for an international audience by the public appearances of his mother Leocádia Prestes, whom Amado described as one of modern America's great figures, and whose death in 1942 inspired Neruda's poem *Hard Elegy*.[45] Even Rákosi's sister sought to publicise his plight through the liberal press.[46] Thälmann's invented history could bring forth no such corroboration. His father, whose class and party credentials were largely invented, died in 1933; his wife Rosa, who would have a significant role in his posthumous cult, was constrained by conditions of access and correspondence. Even the willing Barbusse struggled to render Thälmann in terms of his readings, thoughts and associations. Under the very heading later used by Thorez, 'Son of the people', he offered instead the sort of 'personal social history' in which the complexity of individual commitment was all but stifled.[47]

The living man was elusive; and neither had Thälmann stood up to fascism. When Barbusse drafted his Thälmann pamphlet, he found on receiving his proofs that his text had been all but supplanted by one supplied by 'German friends' which he declined to put his name to.[48] If this is the text that then appeared with Pieck's endorsement, what principally distinguishes it is its forthrightness in condemning social democracy. Thälmann indeed is described as opposing this rather more strenuously than the fascism for which in any case the social democrats are held to bear sole responsibility.[49] Though this was the authentic Thälmann, it was singularly ill-adapted to his new symbolic role. Imprisoned as part of a train of events that brought about a drastic revision of Comintern strategy, Thälmann had been silenced without ever having the opportunity to trim his sails accordingly. Had he in any single utterance adequately forewarned of Hitler's dictatorship, campaigners might have made more of his own words and less of Barbusse's and Dimitrov's on his behalf. Only on the war threat was there a usable legacy, and Thälmann's expression of solidarity before a Paris audience in 1932 was for this reason repeatedly invoked. Even here, exemplars like Liebknecht were quotable at greater length, and Thälmann was reduced to a sort of anti-tribune figure whose voice hardly sounded in the campaign that was centred on him.[50] From the American Ruthenberg to Gabriel Péri and Vaillant-Couturier in France, communists would memorialise the absent or departed through the selective rendition of appropriate articles and speeches. In Thälmann's case they had nothing, and his principal call on solidarity was his victimhood.

Through a combination of personality and circumstance, it was therefore Dimitrov who had the opportunity to reach out to a wider radical public, and for the time being he seized it. Within four months of his release, a manuscript of 'hundreds of pages' was said to exist with excursions into matters 'historical, biographical, philosophical, political and anecdotal' and a 'whole series of entrancing episodes' from his childhood as well as the story of his trial and of his life as a revolutionary.[51] Publishers in Britain were keenly interested, and an interim biography was rushed out by the CI cadres department without, however, making any obvious concession to this wider interest.[52] In the 'Brown Book' of the Leipzig trial, appearing in French as *Dimitrov Against Goering* (Dimitrov contre Goering), a more vivid depiction did appear of the figure it described as 'the shining light of the trial to the world'.[53] In America there was talk of a film production, and a play by well-known playwright Elmer Rice, *Judgment Day*, which in Rice's words 'almost wrote itself' and also had a successful run in London.[54] A Dimitrov film scenario was produced by Kurella with the exiled theatre director Gustav von Wangenheim and the Dutch documentarist Joris Ivens, with initial guidance offered by Maxim Gorky.[55] There was also the volume of prison letters, collated by Kurella, that included a facsimile reproduction of Dimitrov's transcription into his prison notebook of the famous lines from *Hamlet*: 'This above all: to thine own self be true ... Thou canst not then be false to any man'.[56] This was the figure to whom a British publisher could write ingenuously of having no bias against the German government, but merely wishing to associate with 'a man who has so firmly had the courage of his convictions'.[57]

Assisted by Kurella, Dimitrov did not therefore underestimate the importance of the trial as a political platform. One British writer, Ralph Fox, described his as a courage and moral grandeur 'worthy to stand beside the greatest in our human history'.[58] Another, Harold Heslop, evoked the silence that fell among a fictional group of miners when Dimitrov's name was mentioned:

> It was a moment when the great heroism of one of the noblest creatures in the world stood amongst them ... Could it be possible that so great a miracle of heroism existed? Dimitroff lit up their world and sent that great, hopeful shudder thrilling through their spines, and stimulated anew their love of their own class, their pride in their own class. Dimitroff! Herculean in his simple bravery. They were with him, part of him, one with him. So they stood in silent tribute to a MAN ...[59]

Fox was of protestant antecedents and would not have spoken of miracles. In his *The Novel and the People*, he did nevertheless describe Dimitrov as the ideal hero of the new type of socialist novel and 'the symbol of man's spirit victorious against man's enemies'. Again it was a biographical narrative that Fox envisaged, as the Bulgarian working-printer 'grew mentally and morally' in the work of organising his fellow-workers.[60] On London's May Day procession, it was printworkers who provided the most eye-catching tableau with a life-size Dimitrov portrait bearing the slogan 'Long Live the Heroic Bulgarian Printer!'[61] In Fox's conception, a literary and political counterfoil was to be provided by the cowardice and treachery of Dimitrov's co-defendants.[62] In this he was only following Dimitrov's own lead, and in the course of their Moscow exile his comrades Popov and Tanev were both to face new charges as fantastical as those brought against them by the Nazis.[63]

(ii)

The distinction between the martyr and the victim was a basic one for communists, and more was required of Comintern people than mere fortitude in the face of affliction. In a negative sense, the persecutions of the enemy could indeed appear as charismatic stigmata inflicted by an external agency. Insofar as they provided a measure of pre-eminence, they were not infrequently manufactured, as with the alleged US attack on the aeroplane flying Thorez to Moscow in 1950, or the plots supposedly unearthed to murder Stalin.[64] It was not enough to die, however; one had to go to one's death singing the *Internationale*. The poet Aragon, who during the war used the pseudonym 'The martyrs' witness' (*Le témoin des martyrs*), emphasised this in his eulogy to Gabriel Péri, who not only died singing the *Marseillaise*, but did so in active refusal of the retractions that would have spared him.[65] That was why the deaths of partisan heroes were so often dramatised, and a concluding note of defiance recorded in their real or idealised final words or valediction.[66] Suicide, conversely, was regarded as inadmissible in a Bolshevik, as for example in the attempted suicide before the Leipzig trial of Tanev.[67] In the case of José Díaz, in exile and severely ill, the fact of his suicide was never admitted and the metaphor served instead of 'wounds received in the battle against Fascism' and the 'inhuman pounding' of his ceaseless toil.[68]

The fascination with death was thus a fascination with a manner of dying consistent with the manner of living which it thereby dignified.

Lenin, following his near assassination, was the first communist martyr, and when later he died so prematurely, Trotsky assembled his most cult-like effusions as Lenin wounded, ill and dead, like Stations of the Cross.[69] Nevertheless, there was nothing meek or passive about the figure he evoked. Clara Zetkin likened Lenin to the crucified Christ of Mathias Grünewald, a 'man of sorrows' exuding 'unspoken and unspeakable suffering ... the martyr, the tortured man, cruelly done to death ... burdened, pierced, oppressed with all the pain and all the suffering of the Russian working people'.[70] This note, however, was peculiarly Zetkin's own, and no published image of Lenin resembled the man of sorrows. Photographs that showed his debilitated condition were not released, and the first image taken as he convalesced in 1918 entered communist iconography with an arm now outstretched in challenge and exhortation.[71] From Eisenstein's *October* to the statues in a hundred city squares, Lenin's most characteristic pose conveyed not endurance but engagement and the church militant.

This was why the political trial loomed so large in the minds of communists. On the one hand were the trials in Moscow of those whom self-incrimination brought the ignominious deaths their treachery deserved. On the other hand were those whose bearing in capitalist courts provided both a model in itself and a confirmation of the guilt of those from whom proletarian justice had exacted compliance. Thälmann was at least spared the disavowal and vilification towards which Stalin's suspicions sometimes seemed to be leading him.[72] When Stefan Priacel compiled his manual of courtroom defiance *In the Name of the Law!* (Au nom de la loi!), he even made sure to include an unavailing journey 'In search of Thälmann'. Nevertheless, he had no means of demonstrating the eloquence, courage and self-possession displayed by other communist defendants such as Rákosi, Ana Pauker or the Finn Toivo Antikainen.[73] Barbusse in his *Stalin* evoked both the 'beauty' of Dimitrov's accusing voice and the symbol of the powerful Thälmann 'crucified on the Swastika'; but in fact, Hitler was as careful to spare Thälmann a martyr's death as he was to deny him a public platform.[74] Stories were relayed of a haggard but unbowed figure defiantly returning clenched fist salutes; the Thälmann committee urged that his silence sounded only the louder—but always as a 'flag' or as a 'symbol'.[75] On Thälmann's 50th birthday another Heartfield montage depicted him unconquerable in his cell, with a weeping angel beside him (Fig. 5.3). Russel Lemmons notes a debt to the *Melancolia I* of Durer, who as it happened had painted a Christ as the Man of Sorrows.[76] It was

Fig. 5.3 'When Hitler speaks of peace, remember this: Peace sits in jail with Ernst Thälmann. Freedom for Thälmann—peace for the world!', montage by John Heartfield, *Arbeiter-Illustrierte-Zeitung*, 12 April 1936 (International Center of Photography, purchase, with funds provided by the ICP Acquisitions Committee, 2005, © The Heartfield Community of Heirs/VG Bild-Kunst, Bonn and DACS, London 2016)

a very different image from the 'earthquake-Dimitrov' whom his French supporter Marcel Willard had likened to a crowd on the march.[77]

Being fought for like a battle encapsulated Thälmann's enforced passivity. In Britain again, Richard Goodman's poem 'For Ernst Thaelmann' had each stanza end by paraphrasing Barbusse, but otherwise made no actual reference to its dedicatee.[78] In John Cornford's 'Full moon at Tierz', written just before his death in Spain, the personalisation of the cause which brought him there had the force at once of example and instruction:

> Three years ago Dimitrov fought alone
> And we stood taller when he won.
> But now the Leipzig dragon's teeth
> Sprout strong and handsome against death
> And here an army fights where there was one.
> We studied well how to begin this fight,
> Our Maurice Thorez held the light.

From Germany, however, only a concentration camp is named, and even this was not where Thälmann was held:

> Now the same light falls over Germany
> And the impartial beauty of the stars
> Lights from the unfeeling sky
> Oranienburg and freedom's crooked scars.
> We can do nothing to ease that pain
> But prove the agony was not in vain.[79]

Cornford did not believe Dimitrov to be the only brave man in Germany, and he saluted the unbreakable spirit of the Germans he encountered in Spain.[80] But while they fought under Thälmann's name, for Cornford at least they evidently symbolised his cause better than he did theirs.

Speculating as to why Stalin failed to press for Thälmann's release, Lemmons ponders on his apprehensiveness of the 'all but untouchable' figure Thälmann had become.[81] In reality, few indeed were untouchable in the Russia of the late 1930s, and it is difficult to believe that Thälmann would have been among them. What the parallel with Dimitrov does confirm is that Stalin, as the decade progressed, was more concerned with the subjection and constraint of any other personality than his own than with its exploitation for some common political end. Dimitrov remained the

Comintern's secretary until its dissolution in 1943, and throughout the 1930s he served as symbol and reminder of its anti-fascism. Nevertheless, there were no major cult productions, and those already initiated were quietly buried. The biographical manuscript described in 1934 appears never to have been published. The von Wangenheim-Kurella film project did, following numerous vicissitudes and modifications, bear fruit in the production *Fighters* (Kämpfer), screened in Moscow in December 1936 and available in German and Russian-language versions. Even this, however, was consigned to an immediate obscurity from which it has never really emerged.[82]

In place of the self-assurance of Dimitrov's early diary entries, there begin to surface his anxieties as to the minutiae of protocol indicating his standing in Stalin's favour.[83] Kurella had been removed from political responsibilities because of alleged Trotskyist associations. His surviving the purges may conceivably demonstrate the value of Dimitrov's protection; if so, this was Kurella's good fortune, for in Moscow if not in Leipzig Dimitrov was caught up in a whirlwind which he neither resisted nor seriously mitigated. Thälmann's fate, meanwhile, was sealed by the Nazi–Soviet pact. Stalin did not take this opportunity to press for Thälmann's release, and the Comintern itself became caught up in his 'non-hostile' policy towards Thälmann's jailers by refraining from commemorating his 55th birthday.[84] Oblivious to such considerations, Hitler two months later launched his attack on the USSR.

Thälmann was shot in Buchenwald in August 1944; Dimitrov returned to Bulgaria as party leader in November 1945. As communist regimes were established in both their countries, each assumed his place among state-sponsored cults more profligate than those of the 1930s but also more politically circumscribed. That so much came to be invested in Thälmann's posthumous cult reflected the specificities of the German situation. In legitimising party, regime and even state, but not in any clear-cut way a protégé or successor, Thälmann's was not so much a buttress as a surrogate for the cult of the living leader emerging elsewhere in Eastern Europe. Quite apart from the sensitivities of denazification, the appearance of a quasi-state cult in eastern Germany might have sat uneasily with Stalin's professed commitment to the restoration of German unity. Thälmann, however, could symbolise the claim of a part of Germany, ideological as well as geographical, to represent the whole. He thus not only legitimised the communist GDR itself, but an anti-fascist legacy which in the rest of Germany had allegedly been usurped.

The reactivated Thälmann cult was therefore a quintessential product of the Cold War. Commemoration quickly followed Hitler's defeat, and the KPD veteran Willi Bredel had already prepared a biography whose origins lay deep in the period of the Thälmann committee.[85] It is nevertheless difficult to see that Thälmann's life was 'ideally suited' to a unity campaign or that he had ever 'fought valiantly for proletarian co-operation' against fascism.[86] Lemmons notes that Thälmann's name and image were largely absent from the launching of the Socialist Unity Party (SED) which in April 1946 brought together communists and amenable social democrats in Germany's Soviet sector.[87] In Alexander Abusch's widely circulated survey of German history, it is not the cult of Thälmann that one notices but his invisibility.[88] Though Bredel's biography appeared in 1948, this reputedly followed such extensive revisions by Otto Grotewohl, foremost of the SED's social democrats, that Bredel threatened to have his name removed from the title-page.[89] It was apparently also Grotewohl, not his communist co-chairman of the SED Wilhelm Pieck, who acted as principal German mouthpiece of a Stalin cult in whose lustre he could not directly share.[90]

Whatever the explanation, it was with the formation of separate German states that the Thälmann cult began to gather momentum, initially through the commemoration of the fifth anniversary of his death.[91] A Russian translation of Bredel's book was prepared, and justified as 'politically relevant and timely, in connection with ... the struggle of the German people for creating a single independent democratic state'.[92] Concerns were expressed to restore the emphasis on the Weimar years which had suffered from Grotewohl's excisions, and with the weak treatment in the published version of struggles against Trotskyists, social democrats and Anglo-American imperialists.[93] Concerns are also recorded regarding the delay to a Thälmann film, the sparseness of his portraits on demonstrations, the general underestimation of his legacy and the 'hidden resistance' to his popularisation which Rosa Thälmann linked with his 'divergences and mutual misunderstandings' with Pieck.[94] Whatever the role that Soviet pressure played, activity picked up rapidly and by the mid-1950s was bearing fruit in much public art and two expensive film productions, *Ernst Thälmann—Son of His Class* (Sohn seiner Klasse, 1954) and *Ernst Thälmann—Leader of His Class* (Führer seiner Klasse, 1955). It is hard to discern the same revival of interest further west. Even in Paris, centre of the pre-war campaign, Bredel's life was not translated, and for the time being at least commemoration continued to focus more on Luxemburg and Liebknecht. In contrast to the pre-war years, it was Rákosi and Prestes whose lives appeared in French translation, and the prison letters not of Thälmann but of Gramsci.

Dimitrov's case was more ambiguous. His dependence on Stalin was further impressed upon him by the 14-month delay before he was allowed to return from Moscow to Bulgaria. As premier from November 1946 he then frequently returned to Moscow for health or political reasons. Assuming his prerogatives as head of his party's 'Muscovites', his was now the mimetic small-state cult evidenced by his moving into the palace vacated by Bulgaria's departing monarch, and by the naming after him of the 1947 Dimitrov Constitution. Nor did imitation stop short of the elimination of party and non-party rivals through the use of political trials.[95] Both publicly and privately, Stalin took to cutting Dimitrov down to size, while Dimitrov appeared to rein in his own cult to emphasise its secondary character.[96] When he died in July 1949, he was nevertheless given the full Lenin treatment including embalmers, a mausoleum, a renamed city, an Order of Georgi Dimitrov, collected works, biography, monuments, oath-takings and songs.[97] Once the source of political capital for the Comintern, he was now described by his successors as the 'invaluable national capital' of his socialist fatherland.[98]

It was nevertheless as the hero of the Leipzig trial that Dimitrov remained embedded in the communists' collective memory. Willard's book *The Defence Accuses* was an archetypal representation of 'Comintern people' and a manual of how they should conduct themselves in the face of the enemy. Originally published in 1938, it drew on Willard's close involvement with Dimitrov to present him as the volume's central hero, but surrounded by an international cast of courtroom tribunes who figured either as his precursors or as his disciples.[99] Reissued in 1952 and 1955, according to priorities overseen by the PCF secretariat, the book's different editions vividly illustrate the vicissitudes of the politics of personality. By 1955, several of Willard's original examples have disappeared, whether on grounds of space, like the English Chartists, or of alleged political transgression, like Marty and Ana Pauker. Material dating from after 1938 shows a distinct reorientation towards France itself. There are also now included the latterly mandatory items on Stalin and on Thorez, despite neither having ever performed the accusing Dimitrov role or anything remotely like it.[100]

There could be no question now of the suggestion in 1938 of a sort of equivalence between Dimitrov and Stalin in their different spheres of activity. Originally styled 'the bolshevik Dimitrov', this itself was now amended to *stalinien*, and the characterisation no longer appeared of the 'tested pilot, rudder in hand' who had inspired the movement for unity internationally.[101] Despite all this, Dimitrov remained the core around which the book was organised, and it was he who in a country like France remained the central point of reference in the pantheon of communist heroes.[102] With the descent from a genuine communist heroism to the sequel of the show trial and the mausoleum, no figure better represents than Dimitrov the duality of communism's cult of the individual, and the process of stalinisation to which it was subjected.

5.2 Writers in Arms

(i)

If Dimitrov more than Thälmann was an enkindling figure, this in part was due to what he referred to as political capital. But it also required his ability to realise this capital through the written and spoken word, and the transformation even of the latter into printed text. It was not enough, therefore, that an enkindling figure be rendered visible; it was also indispensable that it be made articulate. It was because of this expressive power that the writer was a figure long ascribed a cultlike status by political radicals. On the other hand, it was the logic of the integrating cult that so crucial a matter as the command of text should also now be vested in the figure of the leader. It is this harnessing and appropriation of the writer's particular mystique that the following section traces.

In the beginning was not the image but the word. The word alone, in a double sense, was represented on one of the earliest and least compromised of the monuments to the hopes initially vested in the Russian revolution. The obelisk to commemorate Russia's ruling Romanovs had been erected near the Kremlin on the dynasty's tercentenary in 1913. When four years later the dynasty toppled, the obelisk did not follow, but was reinscribed to honour the forerunners of the Bolshevik ideal across the centuries. From Proudhon back to Thomas More and Campanella, the very names breathed the spirit of internationalism. From Owen and Bakunin to Jaurès and August Bebel, they also implied a generosity of outlook eschewing the narrowness of party or doctrinal orthodoxy. Strikingly, this was not so much a legacy of movements led and citadels stormed, but of the conjuring of possible futures through the alchemy of text. Thomas More was there, but not Thomas Münzer, and Saint-Simon and Fourier rather than Babeuf. It was text which John Reed saw pouring off expropriated printing presses in a 'frenzy of expression'; it was the ability to decipher text that was enshrined by Lenin himself as one of the core defining objects of the revolution. Where the cult of the ABC became combined with the lionisation of the individual, the writer as social demiurge might have seemed an obvious symbolic centre for this new and universal republic of letters.[103]

There was nevertheless an ambivalence inscribed upon the obelisk from the start. The train-loads of literature which stirred Reed's imagination did not only include works of social theory, philosophy and economics; there were also writings of the great Russian novelists like Tolstoy and Gogol. Lenin's 'plan for monumental propaganda', initiated within months of the revolution, was of similar compass; on the one hand it included 'social activists' as well as thinkers among the revolutionaries, but there were also categories for those whom the Commissar for Education Lunacharsky would style 'genuine heroes of culture'.[104]

Most of the heroes were writers. Though Chopin and Scriabin could demonstrate the cultural aspirations of the revolution, the writer was pre-eminent within the dissenting, critical tradition with which the Bolsheviks identified themselves. Moreover, where a political religions framework links the decline of traditional religion with the sacralisation of a ruling authority, a more familiar point of reference for European radicals was that which Paul Bénichou in a justly famous work described as the consecration of the writer.[105] For Victor Hugo, who both expressed and personified this notion, the writer's prescience and moral force were associated with the romantic quality of genius. That monuments to Byron and Heinrich Heine were among those erected under Lenin's plan suggests that this tradition still resonated with some strands in bolshevism. Indeed, both then and later, the claim was made that it was precisely in Russia that the writer had retained a sense of mission largely relinquished further west.[106] 'Bolshevik' or 'revolutionary' romanticism was a stock phrase summing up stalinism's heroic aspect.[107] Stalin's famous epithet the 'engineers of human souls' also played adroitly on its ambiguity. In one reading it might suggest a 'job category, and administrative slot', and the reduction of the writer to the status of technician.[108] On the other hand, it manifestly allowed the notion of educator and teacher of the people; and, as understood by the writer Romain Rolland, it signified an 'elite corps' of those whose special role and entitlement lay in seeing further and living more deeply than their fellows.[109]

The ambivalence of the obelisk was therefore that it implied both recognition and recasting of the writer's special role. It was not so much that this particular monument represented the 'great socialist thinkers and revolutionaries' rather than the cultural heroes who also figured in Lenin's scheme. Rather, it was the subsuming over time of the thinker in the revolutionary, and of the category of the writer in that of the party leader who also wrote. Bebel, Edouard Vaillant and even Jaurès were examples on the obelisk, and Lenin's cult itself owed something to the fascination with the writer of the nineteenth-century Russian intelligentsia.[110] Nevertheless, with the actualisation of the word, first in Lenin's party, and then in the revolution itself, the idea of its articulation as an independent activity became devalued and instrumentalised. The leninist mantra of the unity of theory and practice did not favour the self-standing political cult of the writer, and the requirement which Lenin already expressed for *partiinost'*, or party-mindedness, was easily generalised across a wide field of claimed party competence. Indeed, Lenin's own distrust of 'supermen of letters' was to be reflected after the revolution in his low regard for the party-minded but refractory literary charisma of the sometime futurist Vladimir Mayakovsky.[111] Ambivalence in Mayakovsky's case took the extreme form of disfavour and disillusionment culminating in his suicide in 1930, and his posthumous literary cult as founding laureate of the Soviet era.

To the extent that communism had been and remained a movement of diagnosis, indictment and anticipation, the texts in which it found expression nevertheless retained their talismanic quality. Historically, it traced its origins, not to the moment of its revolutionary breakthrough, but to the science of society by which it was guided and impelled. As the 1930s' turn to the individual then coincided with the reaching out to a broader public, the writer just as much as the martyr or political tribune commanded a respect and legitimacy which Stalin both valued and abused. Through Marx, through Maxim Gorky and Barbusse, it is therefore possible to trace the initial ascription to the writer or theoretician of qualities that were distinct from, but not obviously inferior to, those of the political leader. This, fleetingly, was the moment of the 'engineer of human souls'. It did not last, however, and following the deaths in the mid-1930s of Gorky and Barbusse no living writer was ever accorded a similar stature. Unlike the accomplishments of the composer, the mathematician or the visual artist, the potency and mystique of the written word were such as could not be allowed to detract from the integrating figure of the *vozhd'*. Not only was the writer's subordination perfectly explicit, but the unity of theory and practice, and therefore of the word and action, was realised at last in the genius of a new type whose palimpsest was society itself.

(ii)

In the beginning, of course, there was Marx; it was his profile that was borne aloft on the first May Day of the revolution, and whose features H.G. Wells complained two years later of seeing at every Russian street corner.[112] Marx was at the centre of Lenin's vision of monumental propaganda, and he would remain a key figure in both the iconography and the ideological edifice of Soviet power. In 1933, the 50th anniversary of his death occasioned one of the first such major commemorations in the spirit of the cult of the individual, and the depiction for the first time of the Four Giants image in Gustav Klutsis' poster 'Raise high the banner of Marx, Engels, Lenin and Stalin!' Though Marx's 60th anniversary fell in wartime and was little noticed, the 70th coincided with Stalin's death, resulting in a final iteration of his purported line of succession at the moment of its passing.

The appearance of continuity should not obscure the dilemmas to which even dead legends could give rise. In particular, Marx's abstraction from the obelisk's lineage of socialist thinkers to that of the retrospective founder of marxism–leninism required the reformulation of what Marx himself represented. When Lenin died, communists often spoke of two giants, Marx and Lenin, one of whom had executed in practice what the other had set out in theory. Mayakovsky in his famous Lenin eulogy wrote that Marx through his writings had put the workers 'on their feet' while looking ahead to the 'mighty man of practice' who would lead them 'on the field of battle and not of books!'[113] Though Mayakovsky's was not an orthodox text, its emphasis in this respect was consistent with the valedictory resolution of the Comintern which also described how Lenin had set about realising what Marx as his forbear had taught.[114] Karl Radek described how Marx after 1848 had even been reduced to the role of historical spectator; the British communist Strachey would later describe him as a Prometheus bound by the capitalism he had already grown far beyond.[115] As consequently Marx's genius exhausted itself in the study of capitalism's laws of development, it took Lenin, with 'both feet on the ground' of his teachings, to assume the role of practical leader of the revolution which Marx could only anticipate.[116] Though Dutt in Britain already referred to leninism as the 'union of understanding and action in the world sphere', it was still with the implication of the one preceding and making possible the other. 'What Marx saw, Lenin achieved. Marx taught the working class to think; Lenin taught them how to fight and win. Marx showed them how to understand history; Lenin how to make history.'[117] Lunacharsky had referred to Lenin's ability to 'raise opportunism to the level of genius'; Mayakovsky called him the organiser of victory.[118] It was this, not the quality of his writing, which as capital or charisma set Lenin apart from every other socialist pamphleteer.[119]

For those who had followed him longest, this was neither sufficient recognition of Lenin's achievement, nor the form in which it could be rendered permanent as the usable resource of leninism. Among the earliest proponents and potential beneficiaries of this notion were Zinoviev and Stalin. Already in 1918, the former had referred to Lenin as the revolution's Karl Marx and principal theoretician, having himself been forced into exile and the 'life of a scholar'.[120] Stalin two years later had outlined a simplified dialectic in which the active qualities of the revolutionaries and the theoretical faculties of the thinkers were combined in the higher synthesis which enabled Lenin to found and lead the party of the victorious revolution.[121] In his 'Foundations of Leninism' lecture following Lenin's death, he specifically discountenanced the view that leninism represented marxism translated 'into the realm of fact'.[122] His subsequent definition of leninism as 'the Marxism of the epoch of imperialism and of the proletarian revolution' was expressly intended as refutation of any notion that Lenin had merely had to apply Marx's teaching to the particular challenges confronting him.[123] Bukharin, in this period closely allied to Stalin, saluted Lenin as a 'genius theoretician' as well as 'genius practitioner', and noted that the former quality had suffered a relative neglect because of its scattered and frequently lapidary expression in topical writings and pronouncements. Leninism was not the application of marxism but the marxism of its times; and yet, this being an epoch 'of action', it was a marxism which was necessarily expressed in action and with the 'practical sense of every theoretical construction' that distinguished Lenin from the mere specialist in ideas.[124]

To register the synthesis of theoretician and practitioner called forth the characteristic cultic monument of the published works. Through a form of literary canonisation, the substantiality of literary accomplishment was thereby imparted to writings which frequently were routine, topical, fragmentary or simply trivial. As an exercise in bibliolatry, it lent itself to forms of study, exegesis and ritual citation whose organising principle was the author. When this was a figure of Marx's richness, depth and originality, validation lay in the precedent of those other thinkers, in other traditions, whom Marx had confronted with an alternative world-view and body of knowledge. But as progressively the communist movement aspired to the monolithic character encapsulated in the leader cult, the fetishisation of these texts by their removal from context or controversion disguised their frequently banal and formulaic character and distilled the axioms of the moment into the authoritative expression which the leader alone could give them.

Lenin belongs in this respect somewhere between the Second International and the Third. A product of marxism's so-called golden age, he ranks with those who justify close scrutiny simply as a thinker, let alone as a strategist.[125] Nevertheless, the biblification of his writings was also central to the process that brought critical thinking to a close. Bukharin, who would be among the victims, looked to the systematic rendering of 'everything new that Lenin gave us, scattered in endless quantities throughout his works', and allowing him to rise to 'his full gigantic height as a genius theoretician'.[126] Radek similarly wrote of how Lenin's preoccupation with practicalities had restricted his writing on matters of general principle, so that his followers had had to 'fight for the fragments of [his] ideas' while he captained the ship of revolution. 'But now everything is changed. Every member of the working class who is accustomed to think is now fully engrossed with the thought of how he can best learn from the work and life of Lenin, how he may find in Lenin's books the weapons for his struggle...'[127] Initiated in 1920, the collation of Lenin's works was charged to the Lenin Institute established in the months of his final illness, and which on completion of a first edition immediately set about production of a second.[128] The writings had a huge circulation, and in Vertov's tenth anniversary film *Three Songs of Lenin* (1934) the footage of them coming off the press combined the cults of word, machine and leader in a quintessential image of the time and place.

In respect of Marx there remained some ambiguity. Stalin himself was undecided as to how to demonstrate the communists' sole title to Marx's legacy without so extolling it that nothing remained but to follow in his footsteps.[129] In 'Foundations of Leninism' it was Russia that was given as the birthplace and Lenin as the founder of the 'theory and practice' of proletarian revolution. Marx, Engels and Germany, conversely, were accredited only with having founded the 'new doctrine' of scientific socialism.[130] In practice, direct responsibility for this legacy was not at this stage exercised by Stalin but by the Marx-Engels Institute, established under the directorship of David Riazanov in 1920. Devoted to the pursuit of *Marksovedenie*, or Marx-research, Riazanov underestimated neither social context nor the role of personality and through biographical and other materials depicted a Marx who was fully engaged as 'man, thinker and revolutionist'.[131] With the 50th anniversary of his death in 1933, the accent was on a communist Marx, not a desiccated social-democratic one, and the 'man of action' was stressed against the image of the literary recluse.[132] Klutsis showed the Four Giants looming over contemporaneous crowd scenes; the sequence over time was thus visualised, not as one from theory to practice, but from scenes of revolutionary struggle to the constructive achievements of the Stalin era. Ironically, Riazanov by this time had been arrested, the Marx-Engels Institute merged with the Lenin Institute and the project of a Marx and Engels collected works, initiated in 1924, put on hold.[133] Marx in this sense provided the first example of the writer's symbolic capital being subordinated to the ruler for whom the unity of theory and practice was in the end but a euphemism for personal power.

Klutsis has Marx and Engels gaze into a distance which may be the communist future, and which Lenin appears to have more immediately in view. Only Stalin, as if he were their future now made present, holds the viewer directly in his eye. There were of course cults of little Stalins, like those emerging in some secondary sphere of Soviet governance.[134] Nevertheless, should any figure emerge who might rival or diminish him, as conceivably with the Leningrad party secretary Kirov or the hero of the Soviet war effort Marshal Zhukov, this was soon put right in circumstances which in Kirov's case are still not fully clarified.[135] At least in death a posthumous Kirov cult could be allowed some fuller licence.[136] But in the aftermath of Kirov's murder in 1934, the only living contemporary enjoying a cultic status not manifestly derivative of Stalin's own was the writer Gorky.

Gorky was not alone in being depicted alongside the *vozhd'*: indeed the Stalin specialist Alexander Gerasimov established for a time a virtual subgenre of 'Stalin and ...' paintings, like the famous one with Voroshilov in the Kremlin in 1938.[137] There were nevertheless few public images conveying the same informality and sense of equality as that of Stalin and Gorky caught in seemingly intimate colloquy at Lenin's mausoleum in 1931. Three years later, the lifting of the figures from their original setting provided *Pravda*'s cover drawing for the opening of the Soviet Writers' Congress, at which Gorky's presence dominated and where the cultic epithets of the era were showered upon him. Golomstock in his *Totalitarian*

Art refers to it as 'something like an incarnation of [Stalin] himself in the field of literature'.[138] Gorky, however, was no empty vessel but his country's most famous living writer, and the publicity accorded the congress seemed to signal a new recognition of literature, and therefore of those who produced it, as a pre-eminent field of cultural activity.[139] While the giants of marxism–leninism provided a succession narrative stretching over time, Gorky alone could have been placed on the same level as Lenin and Stalin in giving his name to one of the 'airplane-giants' launched to such publicity in 1935. That the *Maxim Gorky* crashed turned out to be a fitting augury.[140]

In the words of his friend and admirer Romain Rolland, Gorky was virtually Europe's sole example of the 'great author who takes his genius, his fame, into the camp of revolution and addresses Western intellectuals from the other side of the barricade' (Fig. 5.4).[141] A Russian by origin, language and identity, he had been associated with the Bolsheviks since before the 1905 revolution, and despite initial misgivings had taken an active role under the Soviet regime before resuming his pre-war exile in 1921. While the writings on which his fame depended had by this time all been written, these had not lost their currency, and in 1926 the proto-socialist realist *Mother* (1906) inspired one of the finest of the early Soviet films, directed by Vsevolod Pudovkin. Add to this Gorky's well-documented intimacy with Lenin, and there was no other endorsement that could have offered both leader and regime such prestige at once in Russia itself and among the international public that Stalin had begun to cultivate. On his 60th birthday in 1928, Gorky arrived in Moscow for the first of countless ceremonial accolades. Returning henceforth annually, in 1931 he was said to have applied for party membership, and the following year he remained in Russia permanently.[142] That September he was rewarded with the truly cultic commemoration of the 40th anniversary of his literary debut. Renamings in his honour included his home town, Nizhny Novgorod, and Moscow's principal thoroughfare, Arts Theatre and new 'Park of Sport and Culture'. There were also Gorky bursaries, a Gorky day in schools, a lavish edition of his works, and a celebration at the Bolshoi with Stalin in attendance and an opening address by Stetsky. Barbusse, who also spoke, remarked upon the rarity in history's annals of any such apotheosis of a writer.[143]

Barbusse himself was one of Europe's foremost advocates of the writer's public function. He was also the one European writer of a stature comparable with Gorky's who from an early date had sought to harmonise this notion of the engaged intellectual with an active communist party

Fig. 5.4 Maxim Gorki by Fred Ellis, *International Literature*, 1933/1 (Courtesy Working Class Movement Library)

commitment. Rolland, who was closely connected with both, was also extravagantly fêted. On his 70th birthday in January 1936, he was saluted in Paris as an engineer of human souls, which certainly did not connote an administrative grading, and in Moscow as 'a spiritual *vozhd'* just as Stalin was a political one'.[144] Even so, Rolland was not a communist and his festooning with public honours must be placed somewhere between the softening up of the fellow traveller and the cult of literary greatness so evident in the following year's Pushkin centenary.[145] Barbusse, by contrast, was a longstanding PCF member who had several times met with Stalin, and had not done so primarily as a form of public display. When Barbusse died in 1935, Marty described him as his party's most popular figure second only to Cachin.[146]

Born five years later than Gorky in 1873, it was only in 1916 that Barbusse published the first-hand account of the trenches, *Under Fire* (Le Feu), that made his reputation both politically and as a writer.[147] His radicalisation followed swiftly, and with it a compelling sense of the writer's responsibility to bear witness to unpopular truths and link up across national boundaries. In 1919 he launched the Clarté movement as an International of the awakened intellect. Against the view that words changed nothing, his rationale was that nothing was beyond them, and that the writer's 'quasi-divine' gift lay in finding the words that would transform reality in this way.[148] Though such messianic overtones did not survive his joining the PCF in 1923, the idea of a transnational mobilisation of intellectuals remained Barbusse's abiding concern. In 1928 he launched his politico-cultural review *Monde* as a revival of the Clarté idea. He did so with the Bolsheviks' initial support and following the first of his meetings with Stalin. The timing, even so, was inauspicious; Barbusse's breadth of conception was anathema during the sectarian Third Period and his relations with his own party verged on open warfare. Even Gorky withdrew his association from *Monde*, while Fréville, one of numerous younger communist critics, deplored Barbusse's idealisation of the 'traditional, aristocratic individualism of the writer'.[149]

Barbusse in these controversies held to the conception linked here with rallying or *rassemblement* that a propagation or enkindling figure might personify. As he first developed the *Monde* initiative, it was this perspective of 'greatly expand[ing] the circle of our supporters' that distinguished it from the Comintern's plans for revolutionary writers.[150] The public he then reached through *Monde* he similarly characterised as a sort of personal following 'who one might ... lead towards more distinctly revolutionary conceptions, but who are not yet sufficiently ripe to accept the communist label'.[151] It was at the time of Gorky's apotheosis that the differences around Barbusse's activities were finally settled. Stalin at the Bolshoi publicly gave up his seat for him; privately, an understanding was reached as to the financial and other forms of support which would bring *Monde* into alignment with the Comintern; and for the next three years Barbusse's political capital was systematically exploited in the new political ferment that became the popular front.[152]

Notably this took place through the World Committee Against War and Fascism—the so-called Amsterdam-Pleyel movement—which was initiated in the spring of 1932 following a call issued by Barbusse and Rolland. Not all misgivings were dispelled, and Duclos within the PCF described the authority vested in Barbusse as a 'serious danger'.[153] Nevertheless, as the Comintern adopted positions so much more akin to *Monde*'s, Barbusse in turn became incorporated in the Comintern's machinery and relinquished the genuine spirit of heterodoxy which *Monde* had hitherto represented. When he died in Moscow in August 1935, Barbusse was accorded the dignities of a major public figure. For four days *Pravda* carried tributes, Molotov and Kaganovich paid the respects of Stalin's inner circle, and the funeral that followed in Paris provided a massive public affirmation of unity. It was as the fruits of Barbusse's labours that Cachin now described the Bastille Day demonstration of a few weeks earlier that had so spectacularly marked the arrival of the popular front.[154] Should the visitor to Paris seek out the enclave of communist luminaries buried in the Père-Lachaise cemetery, it is Barbusse's headstone that they will find was placed there first.

Long before the revolution Gorky had understood the dramatic effect of his own literary persona, with arms outstretched, wrote an American admirer, like 'a very Christ of the proletaire'.[155] It was the writer whom Gorky at that time envisaged as a sort of Nietzschean superman, and according to Mary Louise Roe he never fully resolved his ambivalence regarding the relationship between the individual and the collective.[156] Though Barbusse disclaimed any pretensions as an orator, he too acquired a compelling public persona whose authenticity as a former combatant was reinforced by his obvious physical frailty. When the worn, gaunt figure rose to speak, wrote Ralph Fox, 'a great burst of cheering ... enwrapped and shook him for a moment with the warmth of its love', as if Barbusse and the people before him were as one.[157]

For intellectuals in particular, Barbusse symbolised the defence of culture that was at the heart of their commitment to the popular front.

For Paul Langevin, scientist and anti-fascist, Barbusse was 'better than a leader', he was a guide.[158] For the writer Fox, he was 'more than either comrade or leader, he was one of those who knew how to express our thoughts and desires, our loves and hates, as no one else'. Fox quoted Shelley, that poets are trumpets calling to battle, and when he was killed in Spain, Fox himself was described as a modern-day Byron and a 'writer in arms'.[159] Others were to follow, and even Fréville, who in 1930 had dismissed the notion of clarions of the spirit, would by 1945 describe Barbusse as the model of the 'new type of writer' whose commitment had been proven in the resistance.[160]

Irene Masin-Delic refers to Gorky's as a personality cult fashioned to complement those of political leaders and bear the promise of a new socialist culture.[161] Barbara Walker writes that a Gorky cult was possible only on condition of a clientelistic relation to Stalin's as that of the 'master theatrical impresario'.[162] If privately Gorky admitted his antipathy to Barbusse, it is therefore hard not to see in this an element of competitive rivalry.[163] That Barbusse, unlike Gorky, accepted the commission of Stalin's biography, must have provided a further contributory factor. Having already mythologised Lenin, Gorky as biographer might have symbolised for Stalin both continuity and equivalence. Nevertheless, even as he adapted his Lenin text to new political orthodoxies, this did not extend to the writing into it of Stalin himself. Whatever the nature of his scruples, Gorky's failure to oblige Stalin in this matter coincided with his falling from political favour in just the period in which Barbusse took on the task in 1933–1934.[164]

That Barbusse performed such a role for Thälmann was an act of solidarity. That he did so for Stalin, and subject amongst other things to Stalin's personal reading of the manuscript, was like the gifting of his literary skills and reputation to the ruler who was also patron. In his *Pravda* tribute on Barbusse's death, Gorky did not even mention this culminating endeavour, and he failed to attend the author's Moscow commemoration on grounds, he said, of the inclement weather.[165] Paul Nizan, at one time the most aggressive of Barbusse's communist critics, had already used his review of *Stalin* in *Monde* itself to point out the deflating moral of 'the leaders who guide the masses and the writers who comment on their lives'.[166] Aragon, another of Barbusse's erstwhile assailants, now wound up a public celebration of his work by 'transform[ing] the evening into a stirring homage to Stalin, the beloved leader of the world revolution'.[167] Within the year, not only Barbusse but Gorky was to die in Moscow. Their passing in a time of looming terror has inevitably fed conjecture as to

Stalin's culpability, as it would when Dimitrov also died while visiting Moscow in 1949.[168] But if Gorky of the three is the likeliest victim, it is because he had in the end declined to gift his reputation to the political *vozhd'* in the way that Barbusse manifestly had done.

(iii)

However these figures died, it did not prevent their posthumous celebration. Gorky in particular inspired a flood of Soviet articles as well as a trilogy of films, and in the absence of an obvious successor he continued to function in the war years as the cynosure of Soviet literary culture.[169] Barbusse was also memorialised by his party, with the emphasis during Cold War peace campaigns shifting once more to the 'soldier of peace' motif.[170] But at the same time, as the party's history and collective identity were refashioned according to the integrating Thorez cult, Barbusse was among those called up from the Père-Lachaise to confirm it.

Even in the GDR, he popped up in the Thälmann cult films where his fragile frame and fervency of appreciation served to offset Thälmann's muscular command of the public platform.[171] Fréville meanwhile had devoted one of his Thorez 50th-birthday sketches to a slightly more than reconstructed encounter in April 1932 at Barbusse's home. This not only allowed Thorez's accreditation as inspiration behind both the Stalin biography and the Amsterdam-Pleyel movement. It also evoked the image of the ageing visionary tormented by anxiety and marvelling at Thorez the 'serene and smiling incarnation of the strength of the proletariat'. For days after he carried on talking about him as if driven prematurely senile. 'He spoke of my books with uncommon knowledge and wisdom. He admires my work, and nevertheless it's me, the intellectual, me, the writer, who has everything to learn from him! ... He is the brain of the class to whom the future belongs.'[172] Fréville himself had omitted to mention this interesting episode in his biographical profile of Barbusse five years earlier.[173] What the evolution of his narrative demonstrated was the clear and explicit subordination of the intellectual to the Cold War integration cult, even in respect of Barbusse's own recognised achievements and sphere of competence.

Barbusse by now could neither give nor withhold assent. In France, unlike the USSR, there was however another such figure of comparable standing from whom a more active compliance would be necessary. Born in 1897, Louis Aragon had joined the PCF in 1927, while still in transition between the surrealist revolution and the proletarian one. A writer of outstanding gifts, he was deeply impressed by Mayakovsky's example and initially expressed his communism with an onanistic verbal violence which Barbusse thought risible.[174] In due course Aragon nevertheless embraced the cultural politics of the popular front and according to his biographer and devotee Pierre Juquin was its archetype and incarnation.[175] While Thorez looked on from afar, Aragon during the war then achieved the threefold distinction of serving bravely with the French army, for which he received the croix du guerre; of playing an active role in intellectual networks of the resistance; and of publishing a volume of verse, *Le Crève-Coeur* ('What breaks the heart'), which in the dark days of 1940–1941 gave elliptical but unmistakable voice to the sense of a national spirit still unbroken. Aragon himself saw the analogy with *Under Fire*; others noted the influence of Hugo, whose *L'Année terrible* ('The terrible year') of 1870–1871 Aragon particularly admired. Philippe Forest, the latest of Aragon's biographers, describes him as principal emblem of the literary resistance, while even in Britain it was Aragon who was hailed as if the missing war poet.[176]

Immediately following the liberation, Aragon, together with his wife and fellow-writer Elsa Triolet, seemed an inescapable presence. To the young Pierre Daix, they carried themselves like royalty, while Claude Roy, who like Daix had come to the PCF through the resistance, gave vent to his hero-worship in a eulogistic portrait for Pierre Seghers's 'Poets of today' series.[177] If in some circles their celebrity prompted obloquy rather than acclaim, among communists there was no clearer vindication of the writer's role. In the spring of 1945, Aragon addressed communist intellectuals in London on the role that writers had played within the resistance. One of the audience later evoked the same feeling of hero-worship and the sense of 'enormous moral and poetic liberation' that Aragon inspired. 'He was still young enough to wear his daredevil debonair aura as a sort of pertly-tilted halo; and with his reputation as a poet-fighter he exercised an irresistible spell. Boyish, gasconading, gaily sincere he ... told his tale as clearly and forcibly as if he were addressing a maquis-group and priming them with the information necessary for an operation to be carried out within the hour.' Caught by Aragon's spell, several of the audience followed him onto the bus as the meeting finished.[178]

As controversy raged over Thorez's wartime record, Aragon was not alone in upholding the falsified version promulgated by his party. Where he led the way was in symbolically making over to Thorez his own political capital by presenting him with the military medal he had been awarded in

1940. Georges Friedmann had described the prevalent cultic practice in the USSR of publicly accrediting Stalin with disparate personal accomplishments achieved under his guidance.[179] While Thorez was still in Moscow, and to assist in his return, it was this which Aragon sought to symbolise through his medal. It was Thorez, he said, whose parting advice to do his duty had guided his every wartime action, and thus by extension the rallying of the intellectual resistance. 'Will you understand me if I say that of each of my acts, in the hour of danger as at the moment of writing, I always asked myself: "What would Maurice Thorez think of this?", and that I had only one idea, to be worthy of him so as to be worthy of France!'[180]

Roy would recall a party instructor warning that it was no use in the resistance asking what the party would do: 'In the place you're in, you are the Party. If you are cut off from comrades, you must think, decide and act as a communist.'[181] Aragon had had to do just this, notably in using the legal opportunities for publication from which *Le Crève-Coeur* resulted. Nevertheless, he would henceforth repeatedly reaffirm his debt to Thorez, as he did following the attacks upon Thorez as a deserter in 1946.[182] His boosting of Thorez may at the same time be linked with his scandalous defamation of Nizan, who having broken with the PCF over the Nazi–Soviet pact had been killed in action at Dunkirk, and whom Thorez had been the first to denounce as a police spy.[183] When subsequently Thorez was for a second time severed from his party, Aragon prepared a poem, 'He returns', of such excessively cultlike sentiment as to allow the suspicion of irony or deliberate parody.[184] It is certainly true that Thorez appeared to Aragon as his best security against the ouvriérisme to which he was otherwise so humiliatingly exposed. Even so, Thorez's party reciprocated his loyalty by drawing a veil over Aragon's role in the resistance, as if this itself were some unintended slur upon his leader.[185] Belatedly in 1950, Aragon was made a member of his party's central committee. Though this was certainly a mark of recognition, it was one that meant his incorporation in a formal hierarchy, rather in the fashion of a second-tier party secretary. When the previous year a Paris mass meeting had been convened to discuss Aragon's novel *The Communists* (Les Communistes), this again was a mark at once of distinction, subjection and public accountability that would have been unimaginable in the case of his general secretary. As Forest writes, Aragon was thus accorded a form of symbolic kingship, but on condition of his demonstrating to his party his overt submission to it.[186]

For the fuller apotheosis, not of the writer but of the leader, it required the vesting in that individual of the power of the word itself, and of the political acts and practices that were guided or inspired by it. It was Mao who would provide the best-known example of this through the quotation boards of the Cultural Revolution and the 'spiritual atom bomb' of the *Little Red Book*.[187] Already in this earlier period, both through his poetry and through the notion of Mao Zedong Thought, Mao exemplified this mastery of the text as act in a way the workers-turned-functionaries of the European parties had hardly yet pretended to. Claude Roy was drawn at first by Mao's poetry, as he had been by Aragon's, and when in 1950 he published a popular Mao biography he described him as encompassing the poet's and philosopher's qualities as well as those of soldier, statesman and revolutionary:

> This great and widely read Chinese ... has become the most sensitive and deepest *expression* of his people. He is the man capable of speaking a language, forming ideas, nurturing sentiments, in which all of his followers can *recognise* themselves. Militant benevolence and conquering reason speak with the voice of Mao, which registers today in the history of the immense awakening of his people. The words and the political and military writings of Mao Zedong have the clear sublimeness of the great text-actions bequeathed us by the history of men. Mao never speaks except to act ...[188]

Ho Chi Minh was another text-actor, whose sage-like image recalled the Confucianism of his upbringing.[189] So too, in an inversion betraying Amado's enthralment with the romantic synthesis of poet and hero, was Luis Carlos Prestes, whom Amado described as a poet whose verses were written 'with soldiers, sword, machine-guns, victuallers ... with his courage and with his dignity'.[190]

Standing above all these, the unity of theory and practice was realised in the figure of Stalin. Even as he presided over the cultural flowering of the popular front, Aragon caught this perfectly in a dithyrambic effusion on the 1936 Stalin constitution. In all the immense treasure-house of human culture, he asked, 'above the works of the imagination, above Shakespeare, Rimbaud, Goethe, Pushkin, should the first place not be taken by this radiant page written with the sufferings, labours and joys of 160 million people, with ... the wisdom of the Party and its leader, comrade Stalin, a philosopher according to Marx's wishes, who does not content himself with interpreting the world?'[191] Once more, it was the writer and the intellectual who had everything to learn from the party leader whose every text brought the new world closer.

It was thus that the leader's *Works* became such a characteristic product of Cold War communism. Stalin's had initially been projected in 1936, though the first volumes, largely comprising materials translated from the Georgian, did not appear until a decade later.[192] One opens a volume at random: 'Fraternal greetings to you, comrades! I wish you every success in your work. Long live our glorious Red Army!'[193] This does not conclude an item; it is the item, set on a page of its own. Here is another unabridged: 'Ardent greetings to *Pravda*, champion of Lenin's behests and standard-bearer of the proletariat's revolutionary struggle for communism!'[194] It was impossible, Molotov wrote on Stalin's 70th birthday, to overstate the importance of this page-by-page unfolding of genius 'in all its diversity and spiritual richness'.[195] Through the fetishistic collation of his published reports, interspersed with fragments, ephemera and outright banalities, Stalin thus assumed an equivalence or more with Lenin while displacing older projects on Luxemburg and even Marx in a stultifying monocracy of the word. A characteristic period image shows him reflective with pipe and a volume of Lenin, and behind him in sombre, uniform bindings the lineage of the Four Giants now distilled in print.[196] Within five years the print-run of Stalin's own works had reached 113 million; Deutscher in 1949 evoked the numbing effect on the written and spoken expression of an entire nation, as if it were gripped by a 'ventriloquial obsession'.[197] As translations then duly circulated internationally, not the least of their functions was to provide Stalin's followers with a continuing diet of aperçus and homilies in circumstances of his increasing disinclination to actual public utterance.

Thorez's *Works* were initiated on his 50th birthday. With the establishment of a full-blown cult, his every speech was hallowed as a political act by which great masses were animated and enlightened; as one commentary put it, Thorez's word transformed 'ideas into a material force'.[198] His pronouncement in 1949 that the 'people of France will not, will never wage war on the USSR' was endlessly invoked and supported by a mass campaign of endorsements. If in one aspect this recalled Barbusse, the hostility which Thorez encountered in the National Assembly also prompted analogies with the Leipzig trial.[199] Marcel Willard, Dimitrov's foremost French defender, even commended Thorez on the Barbussian premise that it was *clarté*—light—that warmongers could least of all abide.[200] The collection of such dicta in a published *Works* was in part an affirmation of the thorézian narrative of party history, and tellingly got underway in 1930 when Thorez was held to have taken charge of his party.[201] Equally, the *Works* were intended as the 'considerable doctrinal edifice' that marked out Thorez's pretensions as a theoretician.[202] Thorez's literary output did not even extend to his own autobiography. Nevertheless, he was saluted as a 'public writer' of his times, for if literature of its very nature was the work of circumstance, as Aragon maintained, Thorez's speeches and reports by the same token were entitled to consideration as 'genuine literary texts'.[203]

With volumes appearing every other month and sales initially exceeding 25,000, the *Works* were always envisaged as a central feature of party life and education. With Thorez's removal from active politics by his stroke they then became the central mechanism by which his leading presence continued to be exercised. A 'school year' was designated for individual study, with supporting commentaries, the registration of students and the launching of proceedings with 'a certain solemnity'.[204] Auguste Lecoeur, a key leadership figure in Thorez's absence, described the *Works* along with *Son of the People* and Thorez himself as 'the Trinity of our ideological leadership'. The formula of individual study therefore meant the unmediated encounter with the presence immanent in these writings. 'It is, each in their own home, to study marxism with Maurice Thorez beside them as their teacher.'[205]

In Jacques Duclos's papers, typed extracts from the *Works* are arranged by subject heading for facility of citation.[206] Perhaps Georges Cogniot had this in mind in describing the *Works* as an encyclopaedia of the working-class movement.[207] Equally, he might have intended an analogy with the great *Encyclopédie* of the Enlightenment. One cult commentary referred to Thorez as initiator of a 'new era in the way we write', a *'Son of the People'* style which marked him out as the 'man of the century' even as a literary stylist.[208] Usually the style recalled the classicism of a rising class; parallels were drawn with Montaigne and the *Discourse on Method* of Descartes, though his autobiography could also evoke recollections of George Sand.[209] Supporting citation confirmed the debt to Stalin's predilection for incantatory effects, with portentous ellipses reproduced here as in the original:

> Stalin, with Lenin, was the organiser and educator of the Bolshevik party ...
> Stalin, with Lenin, was the leader of the victorious insurrection of October 1917 ...
> Stalin, with Lenin, organised the revolutionary transformation of the economy ...
> Stalin, with Lenin, was the founder of the multinational Soviet state ....[210]

What Thorez's *Works* were held to demonstrate was the combination as never before of analytical power and intelligence with organisational skill, practical willpower, experience of mass movements and a knowledge of the people's soul.[211] The *Works* that justified such claims can therefore be seen as one of the most characteristic instruments of the integration cult.

Not all, however, chose to use it. André Marty described how Clemenceau had thought it improper to have a statue erected or square renamed in his honour while he was still alive.[212] A published *Works* was rather similar. Pollitt in Britain did inspire a feeble selection of 'speeches and articles' that was abandoned amidst general apathy with only two of its four volumes appearing. In Italy, however, the focus was on Gramsci's writings, and Togliatti's *Works* were initiated only after his death. Even Dimitrov's were announced as part of Bulgaria's posthumous commemoration programme. In France itself, the results of the first Thorez year of study were not 'fully crowned with success'; sales of the *Works* fell sharply, and volumes had to be withdrawn to keep pace with ever-changing taboos and anathemas. Remarkably, the project was maintained at a lower level until as late as 1965. In Thorez's case, like Stalin's, it was death which proved, not the occasion for such a project, but the opportunity to abandon it.[213]

5.3 The Red and the Grey

(i)

Commentary on the Soviet cult of Lenin tends to emphasise its relatively brief duration, at least as a primary integrating symbol for the new regime. Tumarkin in particular refers to its rapid diminution, and the three principal accounts of the subject all focus on the years preceding and immediately following Lenin's death.[214] If increasingly thereafter Lenin began to appear as Stalin's foil, he remained an indispensable source of posthumous legitimation; indeed, in a broader comparative perspective it is the longevity of his cult that stands out from all but a very few others.[215] It is probably true that Lenin's example resonated especially with the communists internationally who identified with further transformations still to be accomplished, and whose acquiescence in Stalin's paramountcy signified the subordination of these aspirations to the state which he headed. Nevertheless, for as long as the USSR itself claimed a revolutionary legitimacy rooted in a socialist teleology, Lenin bore a dual symbolic burden that could never simply be lifted onto another's shoulders.

Primarily, of course, he was the figure of October and a revolution personified as both process and outcome, whom a thousand statues caught as if alighting at the Finland station. At the same time, Lenin belonged within a longer socialist lineage, not exclusively Russian, that was personified in the Four Giants of Soviet iconography. The essential premise here was of a monolithic continuity, as Browder put it in 1939, now stretching for almost a century.[216] Stalin, of course, was not alone in the use of this foundation myth. From its earliest articulations it had served as the party's general validation as collective Lenin, and following his death the competing aspirants to its leadership had deployed whatever combination of affinity, association or appropriation was available to them in utilising Lenin as a source of political capital. As each sought to outbid the other, and none took the risk of being excluded, the authority vested in his memory was itself therefore sensibly increased.

No other party had or claimed a Lenin; no other party had a revolution whose guiding spirit a Lenin might have personified. Nevertheless, as the Comintern and its sections turned to other key individuals to substantiate their claims on history, the same basic elements of the legitimation and foundation cult may be recognised. In the earliest variants, these were political veterans who in adhering to the Comintern brought with them an anchorage in older traditions that offered a counter-teleology to social democracy. The most prominent cases, all born in the late 1850s, were the German Clara Zetkin, the Briton Tom Mann and the Japanese Sen Katayama. Though none could be imagined in the role of party chief, their value to the Comintern lay precisely in the possession of an independent political capital which nevertheless carried the risk of either neutralising or adulterating its collective disciplines. The veneration which they enjoyed, already in the 1920s, may consequently be counted a disbursement made to retain their disciplined attachment as well as one of the ways in which it was politically exploited. Cachin and the American Foster were younger figures. Though each also personified a longer political trajectory, when the turn to the individual took place in the early 1930s they were not yet beyond the performance of a primary leadership role, and in Foster's case the resulting tensions became fully exposed to public view. There was, finally, the foundation cult of the Italian Gramsci that could alone bear comparison with Lenin's in its obvious utility to his successor. In the following paragraphs, each of these cases will be considered in turn.

If Lenin's was the first of the Comintern's birthdays to be celebrated, Zetkin's followed shortly in revealing circumstances. No other western labour movement had been so violently rent in two as Germany's. Nor did any communist party bear so heavy a burden of expectation as the KPD, and when the quasi-insurrectionary 'March Action' of 1921 ended in fiasco it proved the principal matter of controversy at the third Comintern congress four months later. Zetkin, who along with Paul Levi resigned from the KPD's central committee over the issue, was the outstanding survivor of the Spartacist current within German social democracy and the one leading social democrat to have gone over to the KPD.[217] According to Cachin, when in 1920 she headed the KPD's first electoral lists she alone was 'popular and capable of carrying with her the masses'.[218] Provision at the third world congress was therefore made for the voicing of Zetkin's minority view; and through the too fortuitous contingency of her 65th birthday—for she was actually 64—Zetkin was then all but disarmed by the festooning of the congress hall in flowers and the leading of tributes by the fiercest of her adversaries, Fritz Heckert. 'Touched to tears, her backbone broken by loving embrace', wrote one observer, 'this pillar of the ... opposition sank into the open arms of the caucus ...'.[219] Not only was Levi now repudiated, but Zetkin's wider standing was used to maximum advantage in such very public settings as the 1922 show trial of Social Revolutionaries and the ill-fated conference of the three workers' Internationals.

By the time that Zetkin's 70th birthday fell in 1927, its celebration was a matter for public consumption, in Moscow, in Berlin and internationally. The years immediately following also saw the first birthday tributes to Mann, as in 1928 he turned 72, and to Katayama on his 70th birthday in 1929.[220] Though neither name resonated quite like Zetkin's, collectively these symbolised the claims of the Third International to carry forward all that was best in the Second. Zetkin herself had been the 'companion in arms of Engels', a pioneer of women's socialist activism and an internationalist 'by conception, action and sentiment' who had worked closely with Rosa Luxemburg.[221] Mann's profile, particularly in the English-speaking world, was that of the irrepressible industrial militant who had become synonymous with revolutionary syndicalism. Katayama was a pioneer of Japanese socialism whose embrace of Georgi Plekhanov at the 1904 congress of the International had symbolised workers' solidarity at the time of the Russo-Japanese war.[222] That theirs were complementary and mutually reinforcing roles was confirmed when Zetkin and Katayama addressed their own birthday greetings to Mann in 1928, and thus provided the opportunity to demonstrate 'how the reformists have rotted even from the meagre standards of the II International of twenty years ago'.[223] By virtue of their age, the trio combined an inalienable political capital with an adherence to current communist causes which by the late 1920s was almost the only semblance of breadth of which the Comintern was capable. With the launching of Barbusse's anti-war committee in 1932, theirs again were the endorsements—Gorky's, Cachin's and Jacquemotte's were others—allowing reputations to be exploited, each of which antedated the formation of the communist movement itself.[224]

In all these cases, including Barbusse, it was from the International that the initial impetus came for their vesting with a form of symbolic authority. In 1921 it had been the Comintern secretary Zinoviev who calculated on Zetkin's weakness for public approbation.[225] Critics thought her a pawn to be used on special occasions, or an icon provided for public genuflection.[226] Zetkin did also hold significant international positions as head of the International Red Aid and the CI's international women's secretariat. Nevertheless, her persistent differences with her own party leadership were tempered only by the Comintern's intermittent protection, and it was Thälmann who now took on the symbolic role of prospective presidential candidate.[227] The accolades Zetkin received in 1927 were such as advanced years alone could at this time license, and included the earliest and highest of the new Soviet system of honours, the Order of the Red Banner. Nevertheless, Zetkin herself by now was far warier of those who mingled public tribute and private slander, and who excluded her from any significant political influence.[228]

Both health and political commitments kept Zetkin increasingly in Moscow, where she found in Katayama a kindred spirit.[229] By this time she was sitting on ECCI in a personal capacity, just as Katayama by 1928 held his place in defiance of the Japanese party comrades who failed to understand the esteem in which he was held internationally.[230] Isolated within her own party, Zetkin wrote privately of her 'solitary confinement and solitary mood' and described the Comintern as a dead mechanism swallowing orders in Russian and spitting them out in some other language. Thälmann in particular she regarded as 'clueless' and theoretically uneducated, with a self-delusion bordering on megalomania.[231] None of this, however, was voiced in public. When Zetkin died in 1933, there was no jarring note in the Comintern eulogies, and her old antagonist Heckert delivered the funeral oration (Fig. 5.5). Only the Italian Tasca, expelled from his party for positions akin to Zetkin's, used the latitude of Barbusse's *Monde* to signal Zetkin's political misgivings and commend with obvious

Fig. 5.5 Clara Zetkin by Paula Illès-Kupka, *International Literature*, 1934/1 (Courtesy Working Class Movement Library)

irony the self-abnegation with which she had assented to a purely symbolic role.[232] Forcibly impressed on seeing her in Moscow, Aragon the following year concluded his novel *The Bells of Basle* with an evocation of Zetkin in her prime as a prototype of the new communist woman.[233]

The suggestion in 1928 that Mann's birthday deserved a full page of the CPGB's weekly paper had appeared to its editors as going 'off the handle' over the 'old boy'.[234] For several years already, Mann's importance as a public figure had been recognised in his close association with Pollitt as symbolic figurehead of the British section of the Red International of Labour Unions (RILU), the National Minority Movement. At RILU's insistence he had also been made a priority call on the subventions sent from Moscow. Nevertheless, it was only in the 1930s that initial reservations were fully overcome and Mann accorded the status of a living legend. Though he had earlier been linked with Zetkin and Katayama, the significance of Mann's deployment in this way was consequently rather different, as he now maintained his public activities into the popular front era, and did so while almost entirely based in Britain.

Mann's boosting must therefore be located within the Comintern's wider turn to the cult of the individual. Where Zetkin lent her lustre to the International first, the party second, and Thälmann not at all, Mann's public image was inextricably bound up with the emerging Pollitt cult that it complemented and authenticated. At the same time, Mann did not experience Zetkin's isolation, and he retained the platform presence by which his own store of political capital was continuously replenished. There were also significant differences of political formation. Zetkin's formal compliance with the Comintern's authority is ascribed by Tania Ünlüdag-Puschnerat to the cultures of party discipline into which she had long since been socialised as a social democrat.[235] Arguably that does too little justice to the oppositional trajectory that Zetkin had always followed. Nevertheless, there is certainly a contrast with the congenital rebel Mann, who had reached the age of 70 without any real notion of party discipline or even of a settled party attachment. Mann therefore epitomises in many ways the popular-front dilemma of the enkindling figure, who on the one hand promised such political advantages, but also threatened to elude the collective constraints of the party which wished to exploit them.

The final phase of Mann's long life in the public eye opened in the winter of 1932–1933 when at the age of 76 he once more found himself in prison. Such was the indignation that communists warned of Labour rivals seeking to jump on the Tom Mann bandwagon.[236] Mann himself on his release sought to capitalise on his renewed notoriety by launching a fortnightly paper, the *Militant Trade Unionist*, through highly personalised appeals to labour movement officers.[237] He and Pollitt were now a formidable double act: after one Edinburgh meeting Pollitt told of an audience some five times that attracted by the popular Labour Party leader Lansbury.[238] When in January 1934 the two men were charged with sedition, their names became still more closely yoked together as the personification of a tradition of struggle maintained across the generations. Pollitt in campaigning materials was certainly allowed a sort of precedence.[239] Nevertheless, with the CPGB's cultivation of its labour movement links, Mann was too valuable an asset to be employed only in an ancillary capacity. His 80th birthday in April 1936 was celebrated on a grand scale, and attracted the involvement of many prominent labour movement personalities. Falling fortuitously on the day before Thälmann's 50th birthday, it is perhaps not surprising that it should have overshadowed it in the British communist press. It does, however, seem odd that there was so little attempt to link the two.[240]

This was also the year that British communists discovered 'The march of English history'. Nobody living could have captured this impulse better than Mann. His Englishness was strongly emphasised in a *Labour Monthly* tribute that invoked Dimitrov's injunction to communists to 'acclimatise themselves' to their native soil.[241] Another article depicted him as a cavalier of sorts, but in the accents of his own particular culture and traditions of struggle:

> He can rouse and rally weak and dispirited forces and make from out of their scattered elements a united conquering force ... He has been, he still is, the dashing cavalry leader of the working-class ... snatching victories from under the guns of the enemy. He is possessed of just those qualities that make the great military captain ... the gift of appraising the agitational possibilities of a situation, of focussing discontents, and leading them on and on, from small beginnings, up to a mighty elemental force.[242]

The very definition of an enkindling figure, Mann did not require Moscow's prompting to acclimatise himself. For the earliest of his public birthdays, the contentious suggestion of a formal dinner was abandoned for a popular smoking concert which Mann himself wound up with a doubtless beery rendition of 'Ain't you coming out, my Juliet?'[243] This seems a long way from the immersion in German cultural and philosophical traditions to which Zetkin was held to owe the high regard even of political adversaries.[244] Mann on seeing Lenin would not have thought of the Man of Sorrows, and in his good-humoured readiness for a sort of martyrdom one would struggle to make out the 'saint's cult' with which Zetkin has been associated.[245] Born just a few months apart, what these two contrasting figures did nevertheless have in common was a frame of reference that went beyond the trammels of their party and predated it.

If Mann too was a symbol, he had his own ideas as to what he symbolised, and the opportunity to convey this through his continuing access to the public platform. Close as the two men were, this resulted in what Pollitt recalled as 'many bitter and heated scenes' between them.[246] The usual cause was Mann's refusal to deliver an article or speech on lines prepared for him. According to Pollitt, this made him a difficult act to follow: 'because of the character of his speeches, which are on his usual lines ... there is a double strain on me to try and get across our line before such huge audiences as we are now having'.[247] Pollitt himself was thus both the beneficiary of Mann's public kudos and the guarantor of an appropriate setting in which to exploit it. When challenged as to his communist convictions, Mann used to reply 'as Ruskin did 60 years ago, "Yes, indeed, I am a Communist, the reddest of the red!"'[248] When Pollitt in 1934 proposed that Mann be invited on a Soviet holiday, part of the reasoning was that he would thus acquire some 'new material for his speeches, and perhaps forget Robert Owen and Ruskin for a bit'.[249] Despite the legal costs, and the adamant objections of Mann himself, it was presumably on similar grounds that Pollitt alone was entrusted to handle his own defence at their anticipated trial for sedition.[250] Although Mann had already published a book of memoirs, it was thus also that the collation of a Mann biography was entrusted to Dona Torr, who had been working at the Marx-Engels-Lenin Institute and who had for the purpose abandoned a project on Eleanor Marx.[251] When Dutt in 1935 proposed Mann's addition to the central committee as 'our only ornament', Pollitt objected: '"no a thousand times no" ... big liability already, worse if actual part of leadership'.[252] Though two years later Dutt's view prevailed, Mann was by this time past making any but a token contribution to its activities.

(ii)

Cachin and Foster were different in that neither had yet reached the willingly ornamental stage. Until well into the 1930s, Cachin especially was the nearest to a symbolic centre that the PCF had. He was certainly the party's most popular figure, and when in 1934 *Le Petit Journal* polled its readers as to their preferred dictator, it was Cachin whom it offered as the communist candidate for such a role.[253] Cachin was not only editor-in-chief of *L'Humanité*, to which he contributed prolifically. Until 1932 he was also the PCF's most parliamentary representative, and from 1935 its first ever senator. His 65th birthday in September 1934 occasioned some of the first cultlike commemorations of an active party leader outside of the USSR, including a mass banquet, the exhibiting of gifts, a youth guard of honour, and the salutations as 'beloved leader' of the central committee. Thorez, who led the way, compared him with Thälmann and Dimitrov, not Zetkin and Katayama, and it was their three giant portraits that loomed over the 1936 Villeurbanne party congress.[254]

Cachin nevertheless laboured under several disadvantages. Originally a philosophy tutor, he had no experience of workplace struggle and was closer in this respect to the socialist politician of pre-Bolshevik formation. In the party, not so much of Thorez as of 'Maurice', even those addressing him on personal terms appear to have done so as Monsieur Cachin.[255] Political credentials were also compromised, for while Cachin embodied the marxist tradition associated in France with Jules Guesde, he had lurched with it into outright chauvinism after 1914. It was said that he had channelled subsidies to Mussolini before Italy entered the war, and it was well-established that he had promoted the Allied cause in Russia between the February and October revolutions.

When for the first time in 1930 his party formally saluted him on the confected anniversary of his entry into political life, these were represented as collective failings in which he had erred only in following his party. While this may have tempered individual culpability, it also reaffirmed the generational divide with a leadership cohort formed in 'the spirit of leninism' and an epoch of wars and revolutions.[256] When two years earlier Cachin had come in for criticism at the Comintern's sixth world congress, he kept his place on the party's leading bodies because of his wider influence and experience. Nevertheless, there was no question of him exercising any real political direction, still less of this being concentrated in his hands.[257] By 1931, Cachin was an almost invariable absentee from politburo meetings.[258] When even admirers referred to 'lovely old Clara Zetkin' or the revolution's 'revered grandmother', this could easily be mistaken for Zetkin's premature embalmment.[259] When Thorez, half

Cachin's age, saluted him as the PCF's 'old fighter', the tilting of the relationship between them may be said to have begun.[260]

Unlike Zetkin, Cachin accepted this with apparent complaisance. Victor Serge described him as likeable and intelligent but willing to swallow anything for the sake of popularity.[261] He remained a senior parliamentary figure, and as late as 1947 Thorez expressed to Stalin himself his displeasure at the prerogatives Cachin seemed to presume upon as president of the prestigious Commission for Foreign Affairs.[262] Within a party context, Cachin nevertheless deferred to Thorez even on the platform, where he functioned as something between a warm-up act and claqueur. Crucially, he played this role at Thorez's first Paris appearance following his wartime absence, and in the published account Thorez does not reciprocate his effusion even to the point of naming Cachin.[263] Though four years later, Cachin's 80th birthday was celebrated in considerable pomp, its coinciding with the reissue of Thorez's *Son of the People* allowed the further demonstration of the supporting role that Cachin had now assumed.[264] To younger correspondents by this time he was 'Papa' Cachin—'our good old papa' or 'Dearest Little Papa Cachin'.[265] Ostensibly out of concern for his health, it was also at this point laid down that requests for future speaking engagements be handled for him by the party secretariat.[266]

For Cachin, like Mann before him, there was little remaining but the emblematic status he had begun to acquire even before the war.[267] Where this most remained of value was in supplying the foundation narrative which the thorézian version of party history otherwise lacked. It was Cachin who at Tours in 1920 had made the crucial intervention at the socialist party congress which constituted itself a section of the Comintern. On the 25th anniversary in 1945, he was careless enough not to mention Thorez, who of course had played no role at Tours.[268] Five years later, with the Thorez cult now in full swing, the congress that signalled the break with social democracy was celebrated on a scale unthinkable in a period of unity.[269] Commemoration included a popular history by Fréville in which Cachin's pivotal role was recognised both in the text itself and the volume's dedication. For Fréville, of course, Tours could only be a first step towards 'Maurice Thorez's party', and in one plate Thorez is shown in a sort of father–son juxtaposition with a visibly ageing Cachin.[270] Cachin's own recollections now assisted such a narrative through the role he accorded Thorez's activity in the Pas-de-Calais and his entering thus obliquely through the 'great door of Tours' into the role of the PCF's man of destiny.[271] It was a *partiinost'* detail that may be likened to Cachin's attribution to the socialist leader Blum of the anachronistic allusion to Stalin supposedly made in the course of the same debates.[272]

Longevity for Cachin brought faltering health which contributed materially to his ceding position as the cult of party leader acquired a wider currency. The same was true of the American William Z. Foster, born in 1881. Though as much an embodiment as Mann of a militant syndicalist tradition, Foster was only five years older than Thälmann, and a near-contemporary of Jacquemotte and Gallacher. When he stood as the CPUSA's presidential candidate in 1932, he was supported by a league of prominent writers, among them Theodore Dreiser who saluted his 'Christ-like' devotion to his cause.[273] As Foster's health then deteriorated, it was Browder nevertheless who assumed the mantle of the all-American cult figure. When *Time* magazine featured Browder as its coveted cover image, it referred to Foster as 'pretty much the Elder Statesman' who had made way for him while 'out of commission'.[274] Foster was 57; Browder, a decade his junior, had at one time been his 'clerk' or 'chief lieutenant'.[275] The verdict of James P. Cannon, subsequently America's leading Trotskyist, was that Browder secured Stalin's preferment precisely because he lacked resources of his own and thus depended wholly on his favour.[276]

Few political cultures made as much of personality as America's. As early as 1927, the passing of the first American party secretary, Charles E. Ruthenberg, had brought forth an outpouring of sentiment and hyperbole, from 'Go to sleep Charlie' to 'Ruthenberg—the Leader' and 'Our Hero', and the transfer of his ashes to the Kremlin wall.[277] It was Foster, even so, who according to James Barrett was in this period 'by far America's most important communist—the party's perennial presidential candidate, the architect of its trade union work, a link to American radical traditions and to indigenous labour militants, and the person whom the public identified most closely with American communism'.[278] If the Zetkin–Katayama–Mann cohort had a counterpart here, it was not so much Foster as Ella Reeve or 'Mother' Bloor, whose comparable longevity of commitment was advertised as the proof of her party's home-grown pedigree.[279] To be identified in such a way was for Foster a demotion; and it was symptomatic of this that by 1938 the party's own daily organ could depict Foster along with Bloor flanking Browder's larger central profile.[280]

Foster did not languish in obscurity. For his 60th birthday in 1941, an audience of 18,000 looked on as Dreiser again called him a saint, a play was premiered based on his life and Paul Robeson sang *The Purest Kind of Guy*.[281] It was Foster, moreover, who in 1937 produced the first of his volumes of autobiography and gave it the title so suggestive of a culture of personalities, *From Bryan to Stalin*. Sometimes this is grouped with the similar productions of Thorez and Gallacher. It could, however, equally be compared with Mann, for Foster too, though far less willingly, was also becoming reduced to a party ornament. When Browder was imprisoned in 1941, he had his acolyte Robert Minor installed as acting secretary. Three years later, at a convention that opened on his birthday to the strains of *Happy Birthday to You*, Browder engineered the CPUSA's transformation into the Communist Political Association, replacing Foster's position as party chairman with a 14-strong collective vice-presidency.[282] Though Foster had waged what Browder regarded as 'constant guerrilla warfare' from the left, he did not even now bring this to a head, and dutifully chaired the commission that expelled his closest ally in the leadership.[283] As Cannon put it, Foster had his nose rubbed in the dirt, and if he accepted the role of 'honorary public figure' it was because his ambitions, like Cachin's, now seemed realisable to him only through his party.[284]

When in 1945 Moscow called time on Browder's liquidationism, using the PCF as its intermediary, it was Foster whose quietly registered dissent now recommended him for leadership of a reconstituted CPUSA. Exactly as in Belgium, the displacement of one cult figure by another signified more than just the filling of this role by interchangeable personalities.[285] Unlike Zetkin, Mann and Cachin, Foster's primary appeal was to the inner core of party members. He would always have had their vote as party leader, writes James G. Ryan, while Browder's forte lay in taking the party's message to Main Street America.[286] Like Thorez on a lesser scale, Browder was the figure of the popular-front breakthrough, and we can only speculate how his leadership might have developed in the so much less hospitable Cold War environment. Nowhere else as in America was a communist party so beleaguered short of outright suppression; nowhere else did it suffer so dramatic a contraction of support, and Starobin in his standard history describes it as a classic case of a party turning inward to survive.[287] It was at just this point, in 1949, that Foster for the first time received the full cult treatment.[288] One article on the CPUSA's 30th anniversary squeezed into a mere six pages some 35 references to its guiding 'Foster tradition'.[289] Not coincidentally, it was also at this point that anodyne dismissal of Browder's revisionism gave way to outright vituperation against the cast-out degenerate who poured out filth 'like pus from gangrene'.[290]

The Foster tradition that was thus rediscovered was one of theoretical even more than practical achievements. According to Edward

Johanningsmeier, 'Fosterism' had hitherto amounted to little more than 'an eclectic, empirical, opportunistic, and highly personal mode of activism'.[291] Doubtless Foster had smarted at Browder's condescension on this score; Foster now wrested from him the title of the hemisphere's foremost marxist–leninist through a series of leaden publications beginning with his *Outline History of the Americas* (1951).[292] Published as he reached his 70th birthday, this revealed one of the 'great scientific minds' of world communism, with '40 years of leadership on the theoretical front' stretching back to his syndicalist days. Dispelled were the 'left-handed compliments' as to his skills as a labour organiser, and Foster's excursion into 'Stalinist theory' was presented as itself a 'major political-ideological event', as if anticipating Stalin's own *Economic Problems of the USSR* the following year.[293] For a time further treatises appeared almost yearly, as Foster the theoretician inscribed his name on the obelisk of marxism–leninism.

This most singular of cults thus offers a distinctive variant on the enkindling–integration theme reflecting the peculiar predicament of Foster's party. In refashioning himself as a man of theory, Foster actively downplayed the authentic political capital he had acquired as an agitator and organiser, and sought instead the credentials of the 'great Marxist political leader and theoretician'. His popular-front memoirs had been quite warmly received beyond his party; his Cold War ventures into historical materialism were not much read even within it.[294] Foster reportedly did not care as long as his books were recognised internationally.[295] In this sense, his was a stronger version of the compensatory kudos which Pollitt also derived from acceptance within an international cult hierarchy in the context of relative party failure. Not the least of the American workers' achievements, claimed an acolyte, was to have 'produced a Foster ... People who have traveled throughout Asia and Europe ... have brought us stories how pictures of Foster and Dennis are carried by the people in all parades and how their photos are with those of other world leaders in all the workers clubs, union halls etc'.[296] Eugene Dennis, also held aloft, was the party's national secretary and a figure it depicted as a Eugene Debs redivivus.[297] A further distinctiveness of the Foster cult was therefore that he never assumed the position of party secretary, and through the 'Foster tradition' of collective leadership positively advertised his respect for the prerogatives of party institutions. Foster's in this sense remained a symbolic role, and the CPUSA remained a party of 'two outstanding leaders'.[298] But in a party which would itself become little more than a symbol, Foster's seniority, unlike that of Mann or Cachin, had at least been formally restored.

(iii)

The one truly great mind among the leaders of the communist parties, Antonio Gramsci was one of the founders of the PCI and by the mid-1920s its dominant personality and general secretary. Arrested in November 1926, he received a 20-year sentence and before his death in 1937 produced the famous prison writings that were published after the fall of fascism. Though these of course were unknown while he lived, the campaigns to which Gramsci's imprisonment gave rise still seem remarkably half-hearted compared with figures like Thälmann or even Rákosi. Ambivalence regarding the efficacy of public protest may have played a part, and the figure of the leader was not at first so central as it later became.[299] But there were also differences with the Comintern which in the early 1930s contributed to the 'order of silence' which it maintained in regard to Gramsci.[300]

Even as this relented, the turn to the leader signalled by the Thälmann campaign contrasted markedly with Gramsci's continuing neglect. In France, where there was a substantial Italian anti-fascist emigration, *L'Humanité* in 1934 had possibly 15 times as many references to Thälmann as to Gramsci.[301] Most prominent of the latter's supporters was Rolland, not even a communist, who pointedly dissociated himself from those for whom the plight of Gramsci and the Italians had been eclipsed by the Thälmann campaign. Gandhi's admirer as well as Lenin's, Rolland did not see in Gramsci the new proletarian hero but a figure who was physically frail and yet intellectually and spiritually indestructible, and whose very gaze and profile conveyed the rigour and the power of a mind steeped in the dialectic.[302]

Closely connected with émigré circles and the Italian solidarity movement, Rolland was able to draw for his tribute on materials lately circulating in these milieux. Already in March 1934 the PCI centre abroad approved measures for the intensification of the Gramsci campaign.[303] With the onset of the popular front, and the clearer recognition of Mussolini's role with the war in Abyssinia (1935–1936), Gramsci's case was now more widely taken up though hardly yet prioritised. It was not in fact until his death in 1937 that there appeared the first real harbinger of the post-war Gramsci cult. Rolland once more was to the fore in marking his passing; but crucially it was Togliatti who now came forward with a substantial published tribute, 'Antonio Gramsci, leader of the Italian working class'. In many respects this was an orthodox venture in the emerging genre of the stalinist party life. Gramsci, the 'son of the people', was thus accredited with a tough peasant upbringing and his studies at the university were not even mentioned.[304] Politically, what were judged his early weaknesses were freely admitted; and in the ECCI tribute that was published on his death their overcoming was attributed to the Bolshevik influence of Lenin and Stalin.[305] There was no invocation here of an older socialist lineage, and Gramsci was presented as the voice of a new political generation owing nothing to native precedents.[306]

Despite the conventional treatment, Togliatti's article has been seen, not merely as Gramsci's appropriation in the cause of stalinism, but as his preservation as a point of reference allowing Togliatti some room for manoeuvre in relation to the Kremlin.[307] As a motivation in 1937, this is necessarily conjectural. It is likely indeed that Togliatti was also concerned not to concede the party's founder to more heterodox readings like Rolland's, and he emphasised that Gramsci was above all else a 'man of the party' and 'did not have the status of the "intellectual", the "scholar", the "writer" in the sense that these posthumous eulogists would have one believe'.[308] Nevertheless, when Togliatti, like Thorez, returned to his country after the liberation, the notion that Gramsci's deployment helped him negotiate the conflicting pressures of the Cold War is one that the longer-term evolution of their parties would certainly lend credence to. The difference in this respect is particularly evident if one compares the uses made of Gramsci with the posthumous cults established in this period of Thälmann and Dimitrov.

Understandably, this is usually described in relation to Gramsci's theoretical legacy. As Gundle describes, between 1948 and 1951 there not only appeared a six-volume edition of the Prison Notebooks but the establishment in Rome of the Gramsci Foundation (Fondazione Gramsci).[309] Through Gramsci's writings, Togliatti was thus able to establish a national image and legitimacy for the PCI that was of particular significance for the appeal and credibility the party now exercised among Italian intellectuals.[310] Even so, it was only after 1956 that the more systematic exploration of Gramsci's legacy gathered momentum. In the Cold War context in which the enterprise began, Gramsci's image and biography were therefore also crucial. In party rooms and public gatherings, he appears to have been the only founder of a national communist party whose image was routinely displayed as prominently as the Giants of marxism–leninism. It was the youthful Gramsci whose image proliferated, and which authenticated the slogan '30 years of struggle' above the platform at the seventh

PCI congress in 1951. Nevertheless, Gramsci as a martyr for democracy was also brought vividly to life through the publication of a volume of prison letters even before the Prison Notebooks.

How often in this period were his profile and biography linked with Togliatti's–as they were each morning on the masthead of the PCI daily *l'Unità* which described them as its founders. In 1949, Togliatti's 'Leader of the Italian working class' article was reissued unchanged, along with two more recent anniversary addresses.[311] Also in 1949, Togliatti's brother-in-law Mario Montagnana completed his *Memoirs of a Turin Worker (*Ricordi Di Un Operaio Torinese) appearing in two volumes with the subtitles *Under the Guidance of Gramsci* (Sotto la Guida di Gramsci, 1947) and *Under the Guidance of Togliatti* (Sotto la Guida di Togliatti, 1949).[312] On cards or even coins, the two leaders also appeared together.[313] In 1953, following the first popular Gramsci biography two years earlier, a similar volume produced for Togliatti's 60th birthday accorded Gramsci a role of mentor, guide and collaborator that can only call to mind the legitimating role of Lenin.[314] In a tribute circulating internationally, invocation of the party 'founded by Lenin and Stalin' is directly echoed by that of its Italian counterpart 'founded and built' by Gramsci and Togliatti, and by a whole series of further conjoint references to the two leaders.[315]

The vicissitudes of their relationship did not of course figure in either biography. No texts could have been less a product of the apparatus than Gramsci's prison writings, and nor did Togliatti have to fabricate the collaboration of their earlier years, as Stalin had to with Lenin. Nevertheless, Togliatti's oversight of Gramsci's literary and biographical legacy, as exercised through the physical custodianship of his writings, did represent the assumption of a title to his political capital in its most literal sense. Even the decision to use the commercial publishers Einaudi might have signified both the ambition of reaching a wider audience and a certain independence of the controls of the party's own publishing houses.

Togliatti in fact was not only concerned with the PCI's wider legitimacy but with securing his own leadership against pressures both from above and from below. He had no obvious rival of Marty's pedigree, and Togliatti himself bore the credentials of the International through an exile experience which, in contrast with Thorez's, he positively advertised as a source of political capital.[316] The same is true of the assassination attempt with which his cult biography closes, and of the ensuing demonstrations which helped stoke up what Aldo Agosti describes as a 'naive and spontaneous' Togliatti cult.[317] Gundle nevertheless maintains that Togliatti's position was neither so dominant nor even so secure as Thorez's, and when Stalin in 1950–1951 sought to prise him away to the Prague-based Cominform, Togliatti in declining could not even count on his own colleagues' full support.[318] Himself an intellectual of the party's founding cohort, he cultivated figures like Giorgio Amendola, described by Silvio Pons as highly cultured and a genuine national communist.[319] Even so, the party leadership still predominantly comprised younger cadres from proletarian or popular milieux who met the sociological desiderata of the Stalin years.[320]

'There is nothing proletarian about him', observed a British interlocutor, whom Togliatti reminded of a prelate of the Catholic church, and Togliatti apparently did not have the easy rapport with the party base of a Thorez or a Pollitt.[321] Gramsci was the founding figure that he needed, and the value to him is obvious of the model of leadership, legitimising personal link and narrative of party history which Gramsci represented. Through the fortuitous and tragic circumstances of his imprisonment, Gramsci to the end had been insulated from stalinism and its control mechanisms. It was thus that the PCI alone of Europe's communist parties could deploy a legitimising cult that was not only a product of its stalinist times but pointed the way beyond them.

Notes

1. 'Comintern people', *CI*, 4 Mar. 1935, 291–3.
2. See for example André Marty, *Dans les Prisons de la République* (Paris: Librairie de L'Humanité, 1924); Marcel Cordier, *Andre Marty* (Moscow: Central Committee of MOPR SU, 1931). Marty by 1931 had spent seven-and-a-half years in prison.
3. *L'Humanité*, 25 Jan. 1936.
4. 'Dimitroff nous écrit', *Monde*, 31 Mar. 1934.
5. 'Thaelmann's fight for German workers', *DW* (L), 12 Mar. 1932.
6. Romain Rolland cited Stefan Priacel, *Au nom de la loi!... Les grands procès politiques de notre temps* (Paris: Éditions Sociales Internationales, 1936), p. 13.
7. Barbusse, 'L'incendie du Reichstag', *Monde*, 17 Jun. 1933.
8. *DW* (L), 28 Aug. 1933; RGASPI 539/3/38, 'Appeal for the German section of the International Labour Defence', n.d. but 1933.
9. 'Heroes in the dock', *DW* (L), 29 Sept. 1933.

10. Boris Yefimoff, 'L'accusé accusateur', *Monde*, 7 Oct, 1933; Heartfield reproduced in e.g. *Pravda*, 13 Dec. 1933; *DW* (L), 23 Dec. 1933.
11. See Chap. 3.4 above.
12. Ivo Banac (ed.), *The Diary of Georgi Dimitrov 1933–1949* (New Haven, CT: Yale University Press, 2003), pp. 12–15, entry for 7 Apr. 1934; Bernhard H. Bayerlein gives the translation *Hausherr* or head of household for 'Chasjain' (boss); see Bayerlein (ed.), *Georgi Dimitroff: Tagebücher 1933–1943* (Berlin: Aufbau-Verlag, 2000), p. 103.
13. Banac, *Diary of Georgi Dimitrov*, p. 16, entry for 25 Apr. 1934.
14. Barbusse papers, Kurella to Barbusse, 24 May 1934.
15. Harry Pollitt, 'Join the party that builds unity', *DW* (L), 1 May 1936; PCF fraternal greetings to Swiss communist party fifth congress, *CdB*, 15 Jun. 1936, 750–1; Marty papers (SSD) 281 J box 23, PCF Aisne-Marne region 50th birthday greetings to Marty in *L'Exploité*, 14 Nov. 36.
16. 'Dimitrov to writers. A speech before the Soviet Writers' Association', *Left Review*, Jun. 1935, 343.
17. Ralph Fox, *The Novel and the People* (1937) (London: Cobbett Press, 1944 edn), p. 121.
18. 'Helène Dimitrova est à Paris', *L'Humanité*, 20 July 1933; 'A complete alibi for Dimitrov', *DW* (L), 19 Sept. 1933; 'Dimitrova Receives Great Welcome', *DW* (L), 18 Nov. 1933.
19. Marietta Stankova, *Georgi Dimitrov. A biography* (London: Tauris, 2010), p. 107.
20. Bertolt Brecht, trans. Alexander Benzion, 'Adresse au camarade Dimitrov qui lutte à Leipzig devant le tribunal fasciste', *Commune*, Dec. 1933, 410–11.
21. Dimitrov, concluding address to CI seventh world congress in idem, *The United Front. The struggle against fascism and war* (London: Lawrence & Wishart, 1938), p. 133.
22. Russel Lemmons, *Hitler's Rival. Ernst Thälmann in Myth and Memory* (Lexington, KY: University of Kentucky Press, 2013), pp. 78–9.
23. Pieck, preface to *Thaelmann* (Paris: Éditions La Défense, 1934), pp. 3–7.
24. Barbusse, *Connais-tu Thaelmann?* (Paris: Comité pour la Libération de Thaelmann et des Antifascistes Allemands emprisonnés, 1934), pp. 17–18.

25. Georgi Dimitrov, *Thaelmann* (London: British Anti-War Movement, n.d. but 1934), pp. 4–5.
26. Anna Seghers et al., *Ernst Thaelmann. What he stands for* (London: Workers' Bookshop, 1934), pp. 3–21.
27. Pieck, preface, pp. 1, 3.
28. 'Le comité Thaelmann' in Gilbert Badia, 'Le comité Thaelmann' in Badia et al, *Les bannis de Hitler. Accueil et lutte des exilés allemands en France 1933–1939* (Paris: Études et Documentation Internationales, 1984), pp. 202–7.
29. *Monde*, 20 Jul. 1934.
30. Andres, 'La lutte pour Thaelmann, Bataille pour la paix et la défense de l'URSS', *CdB*, 1 May 1935, 530; Badia, 'Le comité Thaelmann' , pp. 203, 259.
31. See below Chap. 6.1.
32. Norry LaPorte informs me that a properly documented explanation of the Nazis' abandonment of the trial has yet to be produced.
33. Thus a message from Heinrich Mann discussing such possibilities (Barbusse papers, Mann to Barbusse, 7 Jul. 1934) was reduced on publication to a one-sentence truncation (*Monde*, 20 Jul. 1934).
34. Barbusse papers, Barbusse to Dimitrov, n.d.
35. *Information About the Trial of Thaelmann* (Paris: Comité International pour la Libération de Thaelmann et de tous les Antifascistes Emprisonnés, 1935).
36. Moshik Temkin, *The Sacco-Vanzetti Trial. America on trial* (New Haven, CT: Yale University Press, 2009), pp. 302–3 n. 91.
37. Lemmons, *Hitler's Rival*, pp. 101–2; Weinert and Arma, 'Le chant de Dimitroff', *Commune*, Jan. 1934, 667.
38. See for example Marie-Cécile Bouju, *Lire en communiste. Les Maisons d'édition du Parti communiste français 1920–1968* (Rennes: Presses Universitaires de Rennes, 2010), p. 184; Banac, *Diary*, p. 284; PCF secretariat minutes, 12 Feb. 1945.
39. Lemmons, *Hitler's Rival*, pp. 82–6; *DW* (L), 29. Apr. 1936; 'Le meeting de la Mutualité', *L'Humanité*, 17 Apr. 1936; Cachin, 'Romain Rolland', *L'Humanité*, 30 Jan. 1936.
40. Badia, 'Le comité Thaelmann', pp. 230–3.
41. *De Dimitrov à Thaelmann. Échec au fascisme* (Paris: Bureau d'Éditions, n.d. but 1936).
42. *Thaelmann* (Paris: Éditions La Défense, 1934), pp. 11–22; Seghers, *Ernst Thaelmann*, pp. 3–13; Barbusse, *Connais-tu*

Thaelmann?, pp. 6–9; Dimitrov, *Thaelmann*, pp. 5–8. For details of Thälmann's early years, see Norman LaPorte, 'Ernst Thälmann: the making of a German communist, 1886–1921', *Moving the Social*, 51 (2014), 127–58.

43. Barbusse, *Connais-tu Thaelmann?*, pp. 5, 9–11.
44. NA KV 2/1664, Home Office file 638472/8 cited MI5 5 Jan. 1934.
45. See Chap. 3.3 above; also Jorge Amado, *Le Chevalier de l'Espèrance* (Paris: Éditions Français Réunis, 1949), pp. 33, 64–72, 364–7.
46. *DW* (L), 3 Mar. 1936.
47. *Thaelmann*, pp. 10–11; also Claude Pennetier and Bernard Pudal, 'Les autobiographies des "fils du peuple". De l'autobiographie édifiante à l'autobiographie auto-analytique' in idem (eds), *Autobiographies, autocritiques, aveux dans le monde communiste* (Paris: Belin, 2002), pp. 225–6.
48. Barbusse papers, copy letter to Barbusse, 2 Feb. 1934, Barbusse to 'cher camarade', 28 Mar. 1934.
49. Pieck, preface, pp. 4–5.
50. *Crime Contre Thaelmann. Crime Contre Nous Tous* (Paris: Comité pour la Libération de Thaelmann et de Tous les Antifascistes Emprisonnés, 1935); Émile Belfort, 'L'acte d'accusations contre Thaelmann', *CdB*, 15 Apr. 1936, 444–66.
51. A. Kypers, 'Ce que sera le livre de Dimitroff', *Monde*, 8 Jun. 1934.
52. Stella D. Blagoyeva, *Dimitrov. A biography* (London: Martin Lawrence, 1934).
53. *The Reichstag Fire Trial. The Second Brown Book of the Hitler Terror* (London: Bodley Head, 1934), pp. 136–58.
54. Banac, *Diary of Georgi Dimitrov*, p. 6, entry for 5 Feb. 1934; Frank Durham, *Elmer Rice* (New York: Twayne Publishers, 1970), pp. 95–100.
55. Günter Agde, *Kämpfer. Biographie eines Films und seiner Macher* (Berlin: Das Neue Berlin, 2001).
56. Alfred Kurella (ed.), *Dimitroff's Letters from Prison* (London: Gollancz, 1935), ill. at 60.
57. NA, KV 2 1664, Lovat Dickinson to Dimitrov, 7 Mar. 1934; see also Gollancz to Dimitrov, 6 Apr. 1934 for the interest of a rival publisher of more decidedly left-wing sympathies.

58. Fox, *Novel*, p. 121.
59. Harold Heslop, *Last Cage Down* (1935) (London: Lawrence & Wishart, 1984 edn), pp. 61–2.
60. Fox, *Novel*, pp. 122–4.
61. 'All set for great rally to Hyde Park on May Day', *DW* (L), 29. Apr. 1936.
62. Fox, *Novel*, p. 127; also Marcel Willard, *La défense accuse ... De Babeuf à Dimitrov* (Paris: Éditions Sociales Internationales, 1938), pp. 137–8, 163–9.
63. Stankova, *Georgi Dimitrov*, pp. 125, 129, 140.
64. For the former see Philippe Robrieux, *Maurice Thorez. Vie secrète et vie publique* (Paris: Fayard, 1975), pp. 396–7.
65. Aragon, 'Ballade de celui qui chanta dans les supplices' in *Un Grand français: Gabriel Péri. Une vie de combat pour la paix et la sécurité de la France* (Paris: Éditions Sociales, 1947), pp. 15–17.
66. See for example Serge Wolikow, 'Le parcours d'un militant cheminot' in idem (ed.), *Pierre Semard. Engagements, discipline et fidelité* (Paris: Cherche Midi, 2007), pp. 13–41; Chang-tai Hung, *Mao's New World. Political culture in the early People's Republic* (Ithaca, NY: Cornell University Press, 2011), pp. 220–1; Peter J. Conradi, *A Very English Hero. The making of Frank Thompson* (London: Bloomsbury, 2013 edn), pp. 339–41.
67. Stankova, *Georgi Dimitrov*, p. 129; also Karl Schlögel, *Moscow, 1937* (Cambridge: Polity, 2012), ch. 10.
68. Marty papers (SSD), 281 J box 40 (M16A), Milton Wolff and Irving Fajans for the Veterans of the Abraham Lincoln Brigade, message of tribute to Díaz, 31 Mar. 1942.
69. L.D. Trotsky, *O Lenine. Materialy dlya Biografa* (Moscow: Gosudarstvennoe Izdatel'stvo, 1924).
70. Zetkin, *Reminiscences of Lenin* (New York: International Publishers, 1934), p. 20.
71. David King, *Red Star Over Russia. A visual history of the Soviet Union from 1917 to the death of Stalin* (London: Tate Publishing, 2010 edn), pp. 212–13; Victoria E. Bonnell, *Iconography of Power. Soviet political posters under Lenin and Stalin* (Berkeley, CA: University of California Press, 1993), p. 144.
72. Banac, *Diary of Georgi Dimitrov*, p. 197, entry for 15 Oct. 1941.
73. Priacel, *Au nom de la loi!*

74. Henri Barbusse, *Staline. Un monde nouveau vu à travers un homme* (1935) (Paris: Flammarion, 1936 edn), p. 73.
75. '"I saw Thaelmann." Refugee's story', *DW* (L), 15 Feb. 1936; Harry Pollitt, 'Three years in a Nazi jail—they can't break him', *DW* (L), 3 Mar. 1936; 'Depuis trois ans Ernst Thaelmann est incarcéré' and 'Thaelmann est un symbole' (*Trud* interview with Pierre Cot), *L'Humanité*, 4 Mar. 1936.
76. Lemmons, *Hitler's Rival*, pp. 98–9.
77. Marcel Willard, 'Figure de Dimitrov', *Commune*, Nov. 1933, 167.
78. Richard Goodman, 'For Ernst Thaelmann', *Left Review*, Jan. 1935, 122–3.
79. Cornford, 'Full moon at Tierz: before the storming of Huesca' in Pat Sloan (ed.), *John Cornford. A memoir* (London: Cape, 1938), pp. 245–6.
80. Cornford, 'Diary letter from Aragon' in Sloan, *John Cornford*, pp. 209–11.
81. Lemmons, *Hitler's Rival*, pp. 71–3.
82. Agde, *Kämpfer*, p. 190.
83. See Stankova, *Georgi Dimitrov*, pp. 145, 153.
84. Banac, *Diary of Georgi Dimitrov*, pp. 152–3, entry for 29 Mar. 1941.
85. Lemmons, *Hitler's Rival*, pp. 120–1, 125, 281–4.
86. Lemmons, *Hitler's Rival*, p. 123.
87. Lemmons, *Hitler's Rival*, pp. 127–8.
88. Abusch, *Der Irrweg einer Nation. Ein Beitrag zum Verständnis deutscher Geschichte* (Berlin: Aufbau-Verlag, 1949 edn).
89. RGASPI 17/137/330, Yur. Korol'kov to Kabin, 1 Jul. 1950.
90. Jan C. Behrends, 'Exporting the leader: the Stalin cult in Poland and East Germany (1944/5–1956)' in Balázs Apor et al (eds), *The Leader Cult in Communist Dictatorships. Stalin and the Eastern bloc* (Basingstoke: Palgrave Macmillan, 2004), p. 170.
91. Lemmons, *Hitler's Rival*, pp. 130–3, 136–7.
92. RGASPI 17/137/174, L. Grachev to M.A. Suslov, 29 Aug. 1950.
93. RGASPI 17/137/174, B. Ponomarev (CPSU Foreign Political Commission, deputy chairman) to M.A. Suslov, 31 Aug. 1950; note of Suslov, 1 Sept. 1950.
94. Yur. Korol'kov to Kabin, 1 Jul. 1950.

95. On this period see Stankova, *Georgi Dimitrov*, ch. 5.
96. Stankova, *Georgi Dimitrov*, pp. 214–16.
97. *Dimitrov's Union of People's Youth* (Sofia: CC of the Dimitrov Union of People's Youth, 1949).
98. Todor Zhivkov, 'Invaluable national capital' in *Memories of Georgi Dimitrov* (Sofia: Sofia Press, 1972), pp. 13–17.
99. Willard, *La défense accuse* (1938 edn), p. x and passim.
100. Marcel Willard, *La défense accuse* (Paris: Éditions Sociales, 1955 edn), pp. 72–3, 92–3 and passim; also PCF secretariat minutes, 27 Feb. and 13 Mar. 1951.
101. Willard, *La défense accuse* (1938 edn), pp. ix-x, 205, 340; (1955 edn), pp. 159, 348.
102. Vanessa Codaccioni, *Punir les opposants. PCF et procès politiques* (*1947–1962*) (Paris: CNRS Éditions, 2013), p.194.
103. John Reed, *Ten Days That Shook the World* (London: Martin Lawrence, 1932 edn), pp. 11–12; René Fülöp-Miller, *The Mind and Face of Bolshevism. An examination of cultural life in Soviet Russia* (London: Putnams, 1927), ch. 11. On Moscow as the 'lettered city', see *Katerina Clark, Moscow, the Fourth Rome. Stalinism, cosmopolitanism, and the evolution of Soviet culture, 1931–1941* (Cambridge, MA: Harvard University Press, 2011), ch. 2.
104. Christine Lodder, 'Lenin's plan for monumental propaganda' in Matthew Cullerne Bown and Brandon Taylor (eds), *Art of the Soviets. Painting, sculpture and architecture in a one-party state, 1917–1992* (Manchester: Manchester University Press, 1993), pp. 20–1; see also Chap. 6.3 below.
105. Paul Bénichou, *Le Sacre de l'écrivain 1750–1830. Essai sur l'avènement d'un pouvoir spirituel laïque dans la France moderne* (Paris: José Corti, 1973).
106. *Literaturnaia Gazeta*, Jun. 1944 cited George Reavey, *Soviet Literature Today* (London: Lindsay Drummond, 1946), pp. 26–7.
107. Schlögel, *Moscow, 1937*, p. 310.
108. Jeffrey Brooks, *Thank You, Comrade Stalin! Soviet public culture from revolution to Cold War* (Princeton, NJ: Princeton University Press, 2000), p. 111 citing David Joravsky.
109. Romain Rolland, 'Du rôle de l'écrivain dans la société d'aujourd'hui', *Commune*, May 1935, 934.
110. Nina Tumarkin, *Lenin Lives! The Lenin Cult in Soviet Russia* (Cambridge, MA: Harvard University Press, 1983), pp. 7, 62.

111. See A. Kemp-Welch, *Stalin and the Literary Intelligentsia, 1928–39* (Basingstoke: Macmillan, 1991), pp. 14–16.
112. Wells, *Russia in the Shadows* (London: Hodder & Stoughton, 1920), pp. 69–70.
113. Mayakovsky, 'Vladimir Ilyich Lenin. *Dedicated to the Russian Communist Party*' (1924) in Herbert Marshall (trans. and ed.), *Mayakovsky* (London: Denis Dobson, 1965), pp. 270–1.
114. *Inprecorr*, 28 Jan. 1924, 35–6.
115. Karl Radek, 'Lenin's life and work', *Inprecorr*, 6 Mar. 1924, 141–8; Strachey, 'Prometheus Bound', *DW* (L), 25 May 1936.
116. Radek, 'Lenin's life and work'.
117. Dutt, 'Leninism', *LM*, Mar. 1924, 135.
118. Anatoly Lunacharsky, *Revolutionary Silhouettes* (London: Allen Lane, 1967), pp. 45, 47, 49.
119. Mayakovsky, 'Vladimir Ilyich Lenin', p. 313.
120. G. Zinovieff, *Nicolai Lenin. His life and work* (London: CPGB, 1920), pp. 14–15, 28–9, 43.
121. Joseph Stalin, 'Lenin as the organiser and leader of the Russian Communist Party' (*Pravda*, 23 April 1920) in *Stalin on Lenin* (Moscow: Foreign Languages Publishing House, 1939), pp. 9–17.
122. Joseph Stalin (trans. Eden and Cedar Paul), 'Foundations of Leninism' (Apr. 1924) in *Leninism* (London: Allen & Unwin, 1928), pp. 94–6.
123. Stalin, 'Problems of Leninism' (Jan. 1926) in idem, *Leninism*, pp. 13–14; 'Foundations of Leninism', 85–6.
124. Bukharin, *Lenin as a Marxist* (London: CPGB, 1925).
125. See notably Neil Harding, *Lenin's Political Thought. Theory and practice in the democratic and socialist revolutions* (London: Macmillan, 1983 edn); also Leszek Kolakowski, *Main Currents of Marxism. Its rise, growth and dissolution. Volume II: the golden age* (Oxford: Oxford University Press, 1978).
126. Bukharin, *Lenin*, p. 6.
127. Radek, 'Lenin's life and work'.
128. Olga Velikanova, *Making of an Idol. On uses of Lenin* (Göttingen: Muster-Schmidt Verlag, 1996), ch. 6; Bouju, *Lire en communiste*, p. 33.
129. See Chap. 6.3 below.
130. Stalin, 'Foundations of Leninism', p. 86.

131. Colum Leckey, 'David Riazanov and Russian Marxism', *Russian History/Histoire Russe*, 22 (1995), 134, 146; also Riazanov (ed.), *Karl Marx. Man, thinker, and revolutionist* (London: Martin Lawrence, 1927); Riazanov, *Karl Marx and Friedrich Engels* (London: Martin Lawrence, 1927).
132. 'Comment les cellules doivent organiser la campagne de Karl Marx', *L'Humanité*, 8 Mar. 1933; V. Masson, 'Marx, homme d'action', *L'Humanité*, 25 Feb. 1933; T.A. Jackson, *DW* (L), 10 Mar. 1933.
133. Leckey, 'David Riazanov'; Bouju, *Lire*, pp. 32–3.
134. Ronald Grigor Suny, 'Stalin and his Stalinism: power and authority in the Soviet Union, 1930–53' in Ian Kershaw and Moshe Lewin (eds), *Stalinism and Nazism. Dictatorships in comparison* (Cambridge: Cambridge University Press, 1997), pp. 34–5.
135. For the latest overview of the Kirov debate, see Matthew E. Lenoe, *The Kirov Murder and Soviet History* (New Haven, CT: Yale University Press, 2010); for Zhukov, see Geoffrey Roberts, *Stalin's General. The life of Georgy Zhukov* (London: Icon Books, 2012).
136. Lenoe, *The Kirov Murder*, ch. 12.
137. Matthew Cullerne Bown, 'Alexsandr Gerasimov' in Bown and Taylor, *Art of the Soviets*, p. 131.
138. Igor Golomstock, *Totalitarian Art in the Soviet Union, the Third Reich, Fascist Italy and the People's Republic of China* (London: Collins Harvill, 1990), p. 87.
139. For *Pravda*'s coverage including the cover drawing see Brooks, *Thank You, Comrade Stalin!*, pp. 106–8.
140. Clark, *Moscow*, p. 149.
141. Cited 'A real call to arms', *DW* (L), 12 Jul. 1933.
142. *DW* (L), 27 Apr. 1931.
143. Barbusse, 'À Moscou, devant la nouvelle pièce de Gorki', *Monde*, 5 Nov. 1932; Kemp-Welch, *Stalin*, pp. 124–5.
144. Aragon, 'Une entrevue avec Romain Rolland, l'ingénieur des âmes', *CdB*, 15 Mar. 1936; Michael David-Fox, *Showcasing the Great Experiment. Cultural diplomacy and western visitors to the the Soviet Union, 1921–1941* (New York: Oxford University Press, 2012), 243–4.
145. Schlögel, *Moscow, 1937*, ch. 9.

146. Marty, 'Henri Barbusse, héraut du front unique des travailleurs contre la guerre impérialiste et le fascisme', *CdB*, Oct. 1935, 1176.
147. The best biography is Philippe Baudorre, *Barbusse. Le pourfendeur de la Grande Guerre* (Paris: Flammarion, 1995).
148. Barbusse, *La Lueur dans l'Abîme. Ce que veut le groupe Clarté* (Paris: Éditions Clarté, 1920), pp. 124, 129–31; Barbusse, *Le couteau entre les dents. 'Aux intellectuels'* (Paris: Éditions Clarté, 1921), pp. 5–6.
149. Baudorre, *Barbusse*, p. 330; Fréville, 'Réponse à un manifeste', *L'Humanité*, 15 Dec. 1931.
150. Barbusse papers, Barbusse to comrades Pepper and Kurella (Comintern), 19 Aug. 1926.
151. Barbusse papers, 'Rapports de *Monde* avec les communistes', typescript notes, c. 1932.
152. Denis Peschanski (ed.), *Marcel Cachin. Carnets 1906–1947* (Paris: CNRS Éditions, 4 vols, 1993–8), vol. 3, p. 757, entry for 10 Jan 1933.
153. Baudorre, *Barbusse*, p. 363.
154. Cachin, 'En avant dans la voie tracée par le grand disparu', *CdB*, Oct. 1935, 1190–1.
155. Leonard D. Abbott, 'An impression of Maxim Gorki', *Mother Earth*, Mar. 1908, 32–4.
156. Mary Louise Roe, 'Gorky and Nietzsche: the quest for a Russian superman' in Bernice Glatzer Rosenthal (ed.), *Nietzsche in Russia* (Princeton, NJ: Princeton University Press, 1986), pp. 270–3.
157. Fox, 'Henri Barbusse: in memoriam' in John Lehmann et al (eds), *Ralph Fox. A writer in arms* (London: Lawrence & Wishart, 1937), p. 240.
158. Jacques Duclos and Jean Fréville, *Henri Barbusse* (Paris: Éditions Sociales, 1946), p. 24.
159. Ralph Fox, 'Henri Barbusse', *Left Review*, Oct. 1935, 3–6; Pollitt in Lehmann, *Ralph Fox*, p. 6.
160. Duclos and Fréville, *Henri Barbusse*, pp. 42–4.
161. Irene Masin-Delic, 'Purges and patronage: Gor'kii's promotion of socialist culture' in Klaus Heller and Jan Plamper (eds), *Personality Cults in Stalinism—Personenkulte im Stalinismus* (Göttingen: V&R Unipress, 2004), pp. 443–67.

162. Barbara Walker, 'Kruzhok culture: the making of patronage in the early Soviet literary world', *Contemporary European History*, 11 (2002), 123.
163. Gorky to Rolland, 27 Nov. 1932 in Jean Pérus, intr., *Correspondance Romain Rolland Maxime Gorki* (Paris: Albin Michel, 1991), p. 285.
164. David-Fox, *Showcasing*, pp. 144–5; Kemp-Welch, *Stalin*, pp. 227–8; David Brandenberger, 'Stalin as symbol: a case study of the personality cult and its construction' in Davies and Harris, *Stalin: a new history*, pp. 256, 258.
165. *Pravda*, 1 Sept. 1935; Gorky to Rolland, 1 Sept. 1935 in Pérus, *Correspondance Romain Rolland Maxime Gorki*, p. 358.
166. Nizan, 'Staline humaniste', *Monde*, 13 Jun. 1935.
167. 'Pour Barbusse! Pour Staline!', *L'Humanité*, 1 Jun. 1935.
168. Arkady Vaksberg, *The Murder of Maxim Gorky. A secret execution* (New York: Enigma Books, 2007), pp. 350–2 and passim; Stankova, *Georgi Dimitrov*, pp. 227–31.
169. Sheila Fitzpatrick cited Kemp-Welch, *Stalin*, p. 317 n. 107; Vladimir Yermilov, *Gorky—Staunch Fighter Against Fascism* (Moscow: Mezhdunarodnaya Kniga, 1941).
170. See Kevin Morgan, '"Soldado de la Paz". Henri Barbusse y la paradoja del comunismo antimilitarista' in Francisco Morente and Javier Rodrigo (eds), *Tierras de nadie. La Primera Guerra Mundial y sus consecuencias* (Granada: Comares, 2014).
171. *Ernst Thälmann—Führer seiner Klasse* (1955).
172. Jean Fréville, 'Une visite à Henri Barbusse (5 avril 1932)' in his *Avec Maurice Thorez* (Paris: Éditions Sociales, 1950), pp. 33–46.
173. Duclos and Jean Fréville, *Henri Barbusse*.
174. 'Rapports de *Monde* avec les communistes'.
175. Pierre Juquin, *Aragon. Un destin français. 1: Le temps des rêves (1897–1939)* (Paris: Éditions de la Martinière, 2012), p. 725.
176. Philippe Forest, *Aragon* (Paris: Gallimard, 2015), ch. 37; John Bennett, *Aragon, Londres et France Libre* (Paris: L'Harmattan, 1998).
177. Pierre Daix cited Pierre Juquin, *Aragon. Un destin français. 2: L'Atlantide (1939–1982)* (Paris: Éditions de la Martinière, 2013), p. 229; Claude Roy, *Aragon* (Paris: Pierre Seghers, 1945).
178. Jack Lindsay, *Meetings With Poets* (London: Frederick Muller, 1968), pp. 167–8.

179. Georges Friedmann, *De la Sainte Russie à l'URSS* (Paris: Gallimard, 1938), p. 214.
180. *Ce qu'a écrit de Maurice Thorez un grand poète de la Résistance: Louis Aragon* (Paris: Imprimerie Centrale du Croissant, n.d.).
181. Claude Roy, *Les chercheurs de dieux. Croyance et politique* (Paris: Gallimard, 1981), p. 172 citing Réné Blech.
182. See Chap. 4.2 above.
183. Pierre Daix, *Aragon: une vie à changer* (Paris: Seuil, 1975), p. 351; Annie Cohen-Solal, *Paul Nizan, communiste impossible* (Paris: Bernard Grasset, 1980), pp. 243–69.
184. For the poem and Aragon's contemporary commentary, see Aragon, *L'Oeuvre poétique* (Paris: Messidor, 1990 edn), vol. 5, pp. 35–46.
185. Juquin, *Aragon. 2: L'Atlantide*, p. 259.
186. Forest, *Aragon*, chs 43, 46.
187. Daniel Leese, *Mao Cult. Rhetoric and ritual in China's Cultural Revolution* (Cambridge: Cambridge University Press, 2011), chs 5–6; Alexander C. Cook, 'Introduction. The spiritual atom bomb and its global fallout' in Cook (ed.), *Mao's Little Red Book. A global history* (Cambridge: Cambridge University Press, 2014), pp. 1–22.
188. Claude Roy, *Premières Clefs pour la Chine. Une vie de Mao Tse Toung* (Paris: Éditeurs Français Réunis, 1950), pp. 12–13.
189. Pierre Brocheux, *Hô Chi Minh* (Paris: Presses de Science Po, 2000), p. 32.
190. Amado, *Chevalier*, p. 151; see Chap. 3 n. 85 above.
191. *Commune*, Aug. 1936 cited Juquin, *Aragon. Un destin français. 1*, p. 681.
192. Aldred J. Rieber, 'Stalin, man of the borderlands', *American Historical Review*, 106 (2001), 1652 and n. 5.
193. Stalin, *Works*, vol. 10, p. 257.
194. Stalin, *Works*, vol. 9, p. 235.
195. V.M. Molotov, 'Stalin and stalinist leadership' in *'Pravda' Articles on the Occasion of the 70th Birthday of Joseph Vissarionovich Stalin December 21, 1949* (London: Soviet News, 1950), p. 21.
196. Viktor Ivanov, 'Great Stalin—Beacon of Communism' reproduced in Bonnell, fig. 6.10.
197. Deutscher, *Stalin*, pp. 366–7.

198. 'Union pour le combat de la grande espérance', *CdC*, May 1949, 531.
199. Thorez papers 626AP/233, Berthe Leblanc to Thorez, 25 Feb. 1949.
200. Thorez papers 626AP/233, Willard to Thorez, c. Feb. 1949.
201. On which aspect see Fernand Dupuy, 'Les oeuvres de Maurice Thorez, pages d'histoire, de doctrine et d'action du Parti Communiste Français', *CdC*, Jul. 1950, 71–4.
202. Dupuy, 'Oeuvres'.
203. Maurice Mouillaud, 'Maurice Thorez: écrivain publique du XXe siècle', *NC*, May 1950, 37; also Forest, *Aragon*, pp. 591–6.
204. 'Pour l'essor de l'étude individuelle', *CdC*, Nov. 1951, 1326–9.
205. August Lecoeur, 'Le précieux apport des "Oeuvres" de Maurice Thorez pour l'étude individuelle de masse', *CdC*, Dec. 1951, 1410–27.
206. Duclos papers 293 J 7.
207. Georges Cogniot, 'Un guide indispensable', *Pens.*, Mar-Apr. 1952, 52–8.
208. André Parreaux, 'Maurice Thorez', *Pens*, Mar-April 1950, 73.
209. Garaudy, 'Doctrine et vie dans "Fils du Peuple" de Maurice Thorez', *NC*, Dec. 1949, 69–71; Victor Leduc, 'Un livre de sagesse', *NC*, Oct. 1949, 106–12; Thorez papers 626 AP/211, Sadoul to Thorez, 30 Sept. 1949.
210. Mouillaud, 'Maurice Thorez', 45.
211. Luce Langevin, 'Oeuvres de Maurice Thorez', *Pens*, Sept.-Oct. 1950, 86–93
212. André Marty, *L'Affaire Marty* (Paris: Deux Rives, 1955), p. 99.
213. Bouju, *Lire*, pp. 225–6, 287; also Fernand Dupuy, 'À propos de l'étude individuelle. Des enseignements de l'année écoulée à la préparation de l'année nouvelle', *CdC*, Sept. 1952, 917–21.
214. Namely Tumarkin, *Lenin Lives!*; Velikanova, *Making*; Ennker, *Anfänge des Leninkults in der Sowjetunion* (Cologne: Bohlau Verlag, 1997).
215. Notably Kemalism in Turkey, for which see the suggestion of a conscious adaptation of the Lenin-Stalin relationship in M. Şükrü Hanioğlu, *Atatürk. An intellectual biography* (Princeton, NJ: Princeton University Press, 2011), pp. 192–7.
216. Browder, 'Joseph Stalin's 60th Birthday', *DW* (NY), 21 Dec. 1939.

217. See Jean-François Fayet, 'Paul Levi and the turning point of 1921: Bolshevik emissaries and international discipline in the time of Lenin' in Norman LaPorte et al. (eds), *Bolshevism, Stalinism and the Comintern: perspectives on Stalinization* (Basingstoke: Palgrave Macmillan, 2008), pp. 105–23.
218. Peschanski, *Marcel Cachin. Carnets*, vol. 2, p. 407, entry for 2 Jun. 1920, conversation with Georg Ledebour.
219. Peter Petroff, unpublished autobiography (International Institute of Social History), ch. 27, pp. 18–19; 'Une cérémonie en l'honneur de Clara Zetkin', *L'Humanité*, 13 Jul. 1921.
220. Tania Ünlüdag-Puschnerat, 'A German communist: Clara Zetkin (1857–1933)' in Kevin Morgan et al. (eds), *Agents of the Revolution. New biographical approaches to the history of international communism in the age of Lenin and Stalin* (Berne: Peter Lang, 2005), p. 94; Hyman Kublin, *Asian Revolutionary. The life of Sen Katayama* (Princeton, NJ: Princeton University Press, 1964), p. 333.
221. 'Clara Zetkin notre guide ...', *L'Humanité*, 7 Jul. 1927; Charles Rappoport, 'Clara Zetkin' and August Thalheimer, 'Son rôle dans le mouvement ouvrier en Allemagne', *L'Humanité*, 10 Jul. 1927; greetings of CPSU central committee on Zetkin's birthday, *Communist International*, 1 Aug. 1932, 455.
222. Cachin, 'Sen Katayama est mort', *L'Humanité*, 6 Nov. 1933 and 'Le congrès international d'Amsterdam', *L'Humanité*, 18 Mar 1934.
223. RGASPI 495/100/491, R. Page Arnot to Walter Holmes (*Sunday Worker*), 28 Apr. 1928.
224. Signatories listed in *Monde*, 10 Sept. 1932.
225. Angelica Balabanoff, *My Life as a Rebel* (1938) (Bloomington, IN: Indiana University Press edn, 1973), pp. 288–90.
226. Gilbert Badia, *Clara Zetkin, féministe sans frontières* (Paris: Éditions Ouvrières, 1993), p. 243; Petroff, unpublished autobiography.
227. Badia, *Clara Zetkin*, p. 272; Ünlüdag-Puschnerat, 'German communist', p. 96.
228. Zetkin to Wilhelm Pieck cited Badia, *Clara Zetkin*, p. 307.
229. Peschanski, *Marcel Cachin. Carnets*, vol. 3, p. 385, entry for 17 Jul. 1928.

230. Badia, *Clara Zetkin*, p. 245; Kublin, *Asian Revolutionary*, pp. 316–17 and 319 n. 2; Peschanski, *Marcel Cachin. Carnets*, vol. 3, p. 509, entry for 1 Sept. 1928.
231. Ünlüdag-Puschnerat, 'German communist', p. 96; Horst Helas, 'Clara Zetkin's "filthy letter"', *Revolutionary History*, n.s., 1 (2015), 128–34.
232. A.R., 'Clara Zetkin. Une militante, une femme de coeur …', *Monde*, 31 Jun. (sic) 1933.
233. Aragon, *Les Cloches de Bâle* (Paris: Denoël et Steele, 1934), pp. 424–5, 440–1.
234. This paragraph draws on Kevin Morgan, *Labour Legends and Russian Gold: Bolshevism and the British left part 1* (London: Lawrence & Wishart, 2006), pp. 219–23 and Antony Howe, '"Our only ornament".Tom Mann and British communist "hagiography"', *TCC*, 1 (2009), 91–109.
235. Ünlüdag-Puschnerat, 'A German communist', pp. 103–7.
236. 'Exploiting Tom Mann' and 'Labour leader exploits Tom Mann case', *DW* (L), 9 and 17 Jan. 1933.
237. Mann, 'To my friends and comrades holding office in the trade unions', *DW* (L), 15 Feb. 1933.
238. RGASPI 495/100/911, Pollitt to Rust, 14 Mar. 1933.
239. See *Free Our Fighters* (London: Labour Defence Publications, 1934), pp. 4–6.
240. See *DW* (L), 15–17 Apr. 1936. Howe, '"Our only ornament"', 97 suggests that the occasions were sometimes linked in other years.
241. Allen Hutt, 'Tom Mann', *LM*, Apr. 1936, 221–2.
242. Tom Quelch, 'A great revolutionary fighter', *LM*, Jun. 1936, 379–80.
243. RGASPI 495/100/497, CPGB political bureau, 2 and 30 Mar. 1928; *Workers' Life*, 23 Mar. and 13 Apr. 1928; *Sunday Worker*, 13 May 1928.
244. Thalheimer, 'Son rôle'.
245. Ünlüdag-Puschnerat, 'A German communist', p. 94.
246. Pollitt, 'Memories of Tom Mann' in CPGB archives, Tom Mann papers.
247. Pollitt to Rust 14 Mar. 1933.
248. Mann, 'Why I am a communist', *DW* (L), 15 Apr. 1932.

249. RGASPI 495/100/951, Pollitt to Bob McIlhone, 18 and 27 Jul. 1934.
250. Pollitt, 'Memories'; RGASPI 495/100/951, Pollitt to Bob McIlhone, 9 and 28 Jun. 1934.
251. Howe, '"Our only ornament"', 100.
252. Kevin Morgan, *Harry Pollitt* (Manchester: Manchester University Press, 1993), p. 13.
253. Jean Garrigues, *Les hommes providentiels. Histoire d'une fascination française* (Paris: Seuil, 2012), p. 87.
254. Thorez, 'Marcel Cachin "bon serviteur du prolétariat" artisan de l'unité ouvrière', *L'Humanité*, 18 Sept. 1934.
255. Dominique Desanti, *Les Staliniens (1944–1956). Une expérience politique* (Paris: Fayard, 1975), p. 41; André Wurmser, *Fidèlement vôtre. Soixante ans de vie politique et littéraire* (Paris: Grasset, 1979), pp. 173–4.
256. 'Quarante années de militantisme! Quarante années consacrées au service du prolétariat!', PCF politburo statement, *L'Humanité*, 18 Nov. 1930.
257. Serge Wolikow, 'Préface' to 'Année 1928' in Peschanski, *Marcel Cachin. Carnets*, vol. 3, pp. 337–52.
258. Girault, 'Préface' to 'Année 1931' in Peschanski, *Marcel Cachin. Carnets* vol. 3, p. 519.
259. Rappoport, 'Clara Zetkin'; Riazanov, *Karl Marx and Friedrich Engels*, p. 214.
260. Thorez, 'Marcel Cachin', *L'Humanité*, 18 Nov. 1930.
261. Victor Serge, *Memoirs of a Revolutionary 1901–1941* (Oxford: Oxford University Press, 1967 edn), p. 167.
262. Denis Peschanski, 'Introduction générale: du dirigeant à la figure emblématique' in Peschanski, *Marcel Cachin. Carnets*, vol. 4, p. 44.
263. *L'accueil enthousiaste de Paris au grand patriote Maurice Thorez de retour en France* (Paris: Editions du PCF, n.d., 1944?).
264. Compare for example the treatment in the PCF education bulletin *Apprendre*, Sept. 1949.
265. Thorez papers 626 AP/231, Huguette Batteux to Thorez, n.d but Jan. 1945; Cachin papers 290 J 6/11, Paulette Alché (?) to Cachin 19 Sept. 1949.
266. PCF secretariat minutes, 19 Jul. 1949.
267. Peschanski, 'Introduction générale', pp. 42–6.

268. Cachin, 'Il y a 25 ans naissait à Tours le PCF', *CdC*, Dec. 1945, 50–8.
269. See Chap. 4.2 above.
270. Jean Fréville, *La nuit finit à Tours. Naissance du parti communiste français* (Paris: Éditions Sociales, 1950), pp. 15–16, 114–15, 155–6, also ill. at 144.
271. Cachin, 'Souvenirs du Congrès du Tours', *Pens.*, Nov-Dec 1950, 10.
272. Cachin papers 290 J 36, typescript speech, 'URSS—Lénine-Staline', 1947.
273. James R. Barrett, *William Z. Foster and the Tragedy of American Radicalism* (Urbana, IL: University of Illinois Press, 1999), p. 182.
274. 'Rain check on communists', *Time*, 30 May 1938, 9–11.
275. James R. Barrett, 'Revolution and personal crisis: communist politics and personal narrative in the life of William Z. Foster' in Morgan, *Agents of the Revolution*, p. 121; Joseph R. Starobin, *American Communism in Crisis, 1943–1957* (Cambridge, MA: Harvard University Press, 1972), p. 51.
276. Cannon, *The First Ten Years of American Communism. Report of a participant* (New York: Pathfinder Press edn, 1973), pp. 114–15.
277. Contributions of A.G. Magil, Meilech Epstein and Max Karp in *DW* (NY), 9, 10 and 12 Mar. 1927.
278. Barrett, 'Revolution and personal crisis', p. 115.
279. Charlotte Todes and Sasha Small (eds), *Mother Bloor's 75th Birthday Souvenir Book* (New York: Mother Bloor Celebration Committee, 1937).
280. *DW* (NY), 1 Jun. 1938.
281. Barrett, *William Z. Foster*, p. 212.
282. James G. Ryan, *Earl Browder. The failure of American communism* (Tuscaloose: University of Alabama Press, 1997), pp. 234–5.
283. Barrett, *William Z. Foster*, pp. 204, 209, 220.
284. Cannon, *First Ten Years*, p. 124.
285. For the Belgian case, see Chap 4.3 above.
286. Ryan, *Earl Browder*, pp. 146–7; Edward P. Johanningsmeier, *The Forging of American Communism. The life of William Z. Foster* (Princeton, NJ: Princeton University Press, 1994), p. 249.
287. Starobin, *American Communism in Crisis.*

288. Elizabeth Gurley Flynn, *Labor's Own. William Z. Foster: a communist's fifty years of working-class leadership and struggle* (New York: New Century Publishers, 1949).
289. Alexander Bittelman, 'Our party's thirtieth anniversary', *Political Affairs*, Sept. 1949, 7–13.
290. John Gates, *On Guard Against Browderism, Titoism, Trotskyism* (New York: New Century Publishers, 1951), pp. 5–6, 10; Starobin, *American Communism*, p. 198.
291. Johanningsmeier, *Forging*, p. 310.
292. For Browder's pretensions, see Barrett, *William Z. Foster*, p. 223; Browder Library publicity material, *DW* (NY), 3 Jan. 1940.
293. Bob Thompson in *William Z. Foster. 70th birthday celebration* (New York: Communist Party Educational Department, 1951), pp. 4–13.
294. Barrett, *William Z. Foster*, p. 202; Johanningsmeier, *Forging*, p. 331.
295. John Gates cited Starobin, *American Communism*, p. 264 n. 15.
296. Gus Hall in *William Z. Foster. 70th birthday celebration*, pp. 28–9.
297. Elizabeth Gurley Flynn, *Debs and Dennis. Fighters for Peace* (New York: New Century Publishers, 1950).
298. Bittelman, 'Our party's thirtieth anniversary', 12–13.
299. Paulo Spriano, *Antonio Gramsci and the Party: the prison years* (London: Lawrence & Wishart, 1979), pp. 52–3, 119–21.
300. Giuseppe Fori, *Antonio Gramsci. Life of a Revolutionary* (London: New Left Books, 1970), pp. 252–3, 269–70; Aldo Agosti, *Palmiro Togliatti. A biography* (London: Tauris, 2008), pp. 110–11; Spriano, *Antonio Gramsci*, pp. 54–5, 72–3.
301. Calculated from the on-line version at http://gallica.bnf.fr/ark:/12148/cb327877302/date.langFR.
302. Romain Rolland, *Antonio Gramsci. Ceux qui meurent dans les prisons de Mussolini* (Paris: no publisher, n.d. but 1934), pp. 3–4.
303. Cited Spriano, *Antonio Gramsci*, p. 102.
304. 'Il capo della classe operaia italiana' (1937) in Togliatti, *Gramsci* (Milan: Sera, 1949), pp. 16, 20–1; Fori, *Antonio Gramsci*, p. 1.
305. Togliatti, 'Il capo', pp. 51–5; 'Le Comité exécutif de l'Internationale communiste rend hommage à la mémoire d'Antonio Gramsci', *L'Humanité*, 30 Apr. 1937.
306. Togliatti, 'Il capo', pp. 25–6.

307. Stephen Gundle, 'The legacy of the prison notebooks: Gramsci, the PCI and Italian culture in the post-war period' in Christopher Duggan and Christopher Wagstaff (eds), *Italy in the Cold War. Politics, culture and society 1948–58* (Oxford: Berg, 1995), p. 135.
308. Togliatti, 'Il capo', p. 18.
309. Gundle, 'Legacy', p. 145; Gundle, *Between Hollywood and Moscow. The Italian communists and the challenge of mass culture, 1943–1991* (Durham, NC: Duke University Press, 2000), pp. 51–2.
310. My thanks to Silvio Pons for this observation.
311. Togliatti, *Gramsci*.
312. Bruno Groppo, 'Entre autobiographie et histoire. Les récits autobiographiques de communistes italiens publiés après 1945' in Pennetier and Pudal, *Autobiographies*, p. 251.
313. Marzia Marsili, 'De Gasperi and Togliatti: political leadership and personality cults in post-war Italy', *Modern Italy*, 3 (1998), 253.
314. Lucio Lombardo Radice and Giuseppe Carboni, *Vita di Antonio Gramsci* (Rome: Edizione di Cultura Sociale, 1951); Marcella and Maurizio Ferrara, *Palmiro Togliatti. Essai biographique* (Paris: Éditions Sociales, 1954), pp. 33–6, 86–7.
315. Pietro Secchia, 'Palmiro Togliatti—leader of Italian communists and working people', *For A Lasting Peace, For a People's Democracy*, 27 Mar. 1953.
316. Ferrara and Ferrara, *Palmiro Togliatti*, chs 14–15, 21–5.
317. Agosti, *Palmiro Togliatti*, p. 200.
318. Gundle, *Between Hollywood and Moscow*, p. 15; Agosti, *Palmiro Togliatti*, pp. 209–12.
319. Silvio Pons, *The Global Revolution. A history of international communism 1917–1991* (Oxford: Oxford University Press, 2014), p. 197.
320. Groppo, 'Entre autobiographie et histoire', pp. 255, 257.
321. Article by Richard Crossman, *New Statesman*, 27 Jun. 1953, cutting in NA KV 2/1816.

CHAPTER 6

Cult Representations

6.1 Remembering Stalin's Pipe

(i)

Admitted into Stalin's inner precincts, Emil Ludwig was surprised to see him with a packet of cigarettes. 'Where is your legendary pipe, Mr Stalin? ... millions of people abroad, who know nothing of certain of your words and deeds, nevertheless know about your legendary pipe.' Ludwig was right: in graphic images, portrait shots and carefully regulated public appearances, Stalin seemed inseparable from his legendary accoutrement. The more studiedly iconic his pose, the likelier the pipe was to be seen, not merely dangled but actively attended to or drawn upon. Already the previous year, Stalin's first western interviewer, Eugene Lyons, had nevertheless experienced the same mild sense of deflation on being offered one of his cigarettes. Stalin's dry response to Ludwig was that he had left his pipe at home.[1]

Like the cap which Lenin apparently started wearing only after returning to Russia in 1917, Stalin's pipe suggests that he was far from inattentive to the impression these details made.[2] What the encounter with Ludwig also highlights is how different media supported different strategies for the representation of key individuals and different conceptions of the public to which they were addressed. The Stalin of Ludwig's anticipation was a highly visual figure whose silhouette was more familiar than either his

K. Morgan, *International Communism and the Cult of the Individual*, DOI 10.1057/978-1-137-55667-7_6

written or his spoken word. His cult indeed is described by Jan Plamper as an 'overwhelmingly visual phenomenon'; like Mao's symbolic politics of the 1950s, it was tailored to a population in which mass literacy campaigns had, according to this view, yet to displace the centrality of the image as a tool of political communication.[3] Even within a Soviet context, other historians urge the primacy of the text.[4] The key point here, however, is that an unfledged Soviet reading public was not the only one which at this stage concerned Stalin. The very granting of an audience to Ludwig suggests that he did not underestimate the power of words as a means of impressing himself upon an activist and wider public beyond the reach of his dictatorship. It was Ludwig after all, not a painter or photographer, who was internationally recognised as the period's most successful political portraitist. If Stalin's deeds as well as appearance were to be known to those millions abroad, this was the instrument by which it might be achieved.

The representation of such figures was therefore influenced both by the skills and expectations of different audiences and by the forms of mass communication that were available with which to reach them. The projection of personality across state and linguistic boundaries was one obvious challenge. So, crucially, were the different constraints and opportunities of ruling and non-ruling communist parties. In some respects, there was even an increasing disparity over the period of the cults' development, as technologies of mass communication developed faster than the ability of oppositional communist parties to make use of them. Not every communist party monopolised the means of symbolic production, and those that did not were subject in every case to some combination of legal and material constraint in the construction of a cult community.

Even Stalin's cult had the same voluntary, partisan and sectional character in that wider world that initially comprised everywhere but the USSR itself. One may wonder whether messages of greeting really were smuggled out of capitalist prisons on the occasion of Stalin's 50th birthday. One can be sure that there were communists for whom no other means of greeting him existed. If it is true that labour movements failed to harness the cinema and radio as they had done other cultural forms, this as much as anything was a matter of material resources.[5] One result was that the communist parties' attempted exploitation of these new media tended to mean a greater dependence on the surrogate state patronage of the Soviets, either for financial and technical support, or more directly for materials like radio broadcasts and film productions. While this could only accentuate a sense of hierarchy and dependence, the uneven access to new technologies did also mean the persistence and continuing validation of an older labour movement culture in which the printed word was paramount and could now be supplemented by the more accessible innovation of the typewriter. Entangled modernities were conflicted modernities, and if communists and others persisted in well-established practices, from the cyclostyled leaflet and chalked pavement to the agitational meeting, these were neither modern nor premodern, but a reflection of unequal resources and relationships of power.

In his diary in 1941 Dimitrov wrote that already in the USA the cinema was the primary means of influence, the radio next, and the press only third.[6] He would not have made such an observation of the USSR, and it is *Pravda* which has been described as the normative and informational centre of Soviet political culture.[7] Nevertheless, the terms in which Dimitrov put the issue were common to every modern state with variations only of tempo and emphasis. It was Lenin who was so often quoted describing the cinema as most important of the arts, and it was Boris Shumyatsky, head of the Soviet film organisation Soyuzkino, whose ambition it was to create a Soviet Hollywood.[8] By 1938 there were also twenty million Soviet radio sets, a more than tenfold increase in the previous decade, and within a month of his diary entry Dimitrov would hear the normally diffident Stalin deliver the most effective and symbolically resonant of his radio broadcasts as the German army stood at the gates of Moscow.[9] Even *Pravda*'s daunting appearance had been broken up by the increasing intrusion of cultlike visuals, and until his perishing in the purges the montage work of Gustav Klutsis also circulated in poster editions of as many as a quarter of a million.[10]

Despite the advances in literacy, the Stalin depicted by *Pravda* on his 60th birthday was thus a more visual one than a decade earlier. At the same time, the Stalin depicted on the screen was one now equipped with the faculty of speech, albeit in a language that only his compatriots could comprehend. If in both cases the image and the word were thus brought more closely together, a complicating factor in the Soviet context was the establishment in the early 1930s of single approved bodies of writers, artists and composers, and similarly of Soyuzkino as the overarching body for the cinema. Inevitably this influenced how rival claims for preferment were advanced within a closed environment of state and party patronage. It is that Plamper refers to in the Soviet context as the 'battle for the place of master medium' in the representation of Stalin's cult.[11] Nevertheless, beyond this Soviet context it was not so much patronage, except as sometimes deriving from some ruling state or party, but the diverse forms of legal restriction and material constraint that most decided the preference for one medium over another.

Whatever the medium, the Bolsheviks in the early years were well aware of the international dimension of their activity. In no other field of culture had they achieved such prestige as through the films in which directors like Eisenstein and Pudovkin demonstrated their mastery of the visual esperanto of the silent era. Acclaimed by cineasts, these also provided the capital of the workers' film societies, like those which Bert Hogenkamp describes in Britain.[12] While Eisenstein could call on thousands for his crowd scenes, home-grown productions were restricted to the 'lower-than-low budget' agitational films that Hogenkamp mentions, or the *Workers' Newsreels* made by the Workers' Film and Photo League in the USA. Even in France, the popular-front initiative Ciné-Liberté focused on popular newsreels and documentaries and its only major production was Jean Renoir's film of the French revolution *La Marseillaise*. Intended as a challenge to commercial cinema, *Ciné-Liberté* consequently functioned in practice as a large-scale film club and distribution agency, which Pascal Ory characterises as a ghetto, albeit a spacious one.[13] In the words of the American radical film-maker Leo Hurwitz, documentary dominated because 'revolutionary dramatic films', like those produced in the USSR, were neither economically nor technically feasible.[14]

Documentary, in any case, was the obvious and appropriate vehicle for the projection of key individuals. Lenin in his lifetime had refused to sanction a hagiographical film treatment proposed by the then head of Soviet film production.[15] But if it is true that he also had initial reservations about himself being filmed, he certainly overcame them. The documentarist Dziga Vertov, whose fifth 'Cine-Pravda' newsreel in 1922 included a first 'Cine-portrait' of one of the lesser Bolshevik leaders, generated enough Lenin footage to be able on his death to produce a 'Leninist Cine-Pravda' or 'film poem'.[16] It was Vertov again who in late 1931 was commissioned to produce the first feature-length cult film for the tenth anniversary of Lenin's death. This was a production of the Moscow studio Mezhrabpom-Film, one of the most successful enterprises of the Workers' International Relief (Internationale Arbeiterhilfe), whose concern with international themes and audiences was actually accentuated in the early 1930s.[17] With its strongly internationalist message, *Three Songs of Lenin* thus seemed to have been made 'with half an eye on international distribution'.[18] Preliminary screenings in Moscow and at the Venice Film festival were widely publicised, and privately Vertov commented mordantly on the contrast between the film's reception at home and abroad.[19] An American reviewer described as 'virtually counter-revolutionary' the mystic, devotional way the film promoted Lenin worship. But Léon Moussinac, France's leading communist film critic, also recorded how viewers were moved to tears by the second 'song' depicting Lenin's death and funeral.[20]

Perhaps its example helped stimulate the further productions that signalled the turn to the cult of the individual. Already on his arrival in Moscow, Dimitrov had noted that a film was being made about him in America.[21] With the shift of campaigning focus to Thälmann, it could be that this was actually displaced by the four-reel sound documentary *Ernst Thaelmann—Fighter Against Fascism*, which included footage from the Leipzig trial as well as opening and closing remarks by Browder.[22] There was also a shorter silent British version and a French film, *Life and struggle of Ernst Thaelmann* (Vie et lutte d'Ernst Thaelmann), of uncertain relationship if any to the English-language one.[23] Other productions of this type included a Ciné-Liberté tribute to Vaillant-Couturier, *The Life of a Man* (La vie d'un homme, 1938) and Vertov's similarly valedictory *In Memory of Sergo Ordzhonikidzhe* (1937). The difference between French and Soviet conditions for such productions was that the former had to circumvent the almost total absence of film material depicting Vaillant-Couturier.[24]

Between the commissioning of *Three Songs of Lenin* and its completion, the Stalin cult had re-emerged to rival Lenin's own. Between completion of the film and public viewing, there consequently followed a delay of some months which is usually attributed to the need to accommodate the new cult figure without whom Lenin himself could not now be presented. The problem with documentary in this respect, as Jeremy Hicks observes, was its reliance on actual recordings: like the 13th Cine-Pravda, perhaps, produced on the revolution's fifth anniversary and featuring Trotsky more even than Lenin, and Stalin not at all.[25] Stalin did reluctantly begin to feature in newsreels, and Shumyatsky singled out his appearance at the inauguration of the Moscow metro as a cinematic highlight.[26] The first to envisage a genuine Stalin cult film nevertheless appears to have been Barbusse on completion of his Stalin biography. Also commissioned by Mezhrabpom-Film, Barbusse's scenario was sent to Stalin's secretary with the assurance that it was quite differently conceived from Vertov's documentary and heralded 'a new form of film' for the depiction of Stalin's genius.[27]

Its vaunted novelty lay in combining a fictionalised family saga with a Stalin who was evoked but not actually depicted as the architect and symbol of his people's better destinies. In the literature of the period, Stalin was also most often presented either obliquely or through some similar mediating device.[28] In the case of film or theatre, taboos regarding the portrayal of the living ruler may also have lingered from the censorship regime of the tsarist era.[29] Even the posthumous depiction of Lenin by an actor, notably in Eisenstein's *October* (public release, 1928), provoked enormous controversy. There was for the time being no repetition and Barbusse's scenario was explicitly conceived with this constraint in mind. Stalin is thus variously glimpsed in silhouette, or in semi-darkness, or through a priest's denunciation or a character reading from his *Marxism and the National Question*. The scenario concludes with an indistinct figure with his hand raised in greeting on Lenin's mausoleum. 'He is too far away to be made out, but we can guess that it is Stalin. Everything is coloured red, giving a background of fire and dawn.' A continuity as yet with Vertov's Lenin, projected as leader of the world's oppressed, was that Stalin's dawn was not Russia's alone but that of the 'masses of different nationalities joining with the first people to go down the path of the salvation of humanity'.[30]

Barbusse's collaborator Alfred Kurella was by this time in Moscow working on a similar treatment for Mezhrabpom-Film of the Leipzig trial. Kurella attributed the 'curious "coincidence"' of their having hit upon the same hybrid form of the 'artistic-documentary' to their facing the same basic challenge of presenting the living revolutionary hero without lapsing into the 'bad taste' of simulation.[31] The Dimitrov project did at least enjoy a brief exposure on completion of the film now called *Fighters* (Kämpfer) in 1936.[32] There is little sign, however, that Shumyatsky was ever much taken with Barbusse's proposal. With Barbusse's death in August 1935, he did not even mention the project in the tribute he wrote for *Pravda*, and the following summer Mezhrabpom-Film itself was closed down.[33]

It is *Lenin in October* which must therefore be regarded as the first Stalin cult film. When the ban on an acted Lenin was lifted with the competition for the scenario, no specific mention was made of Stalin.[34] Despite the initial uncertainty that this caused, Stalin's ostensible role in the revolution was by now so inseparable from Lenin's that it is difficult to see how the latter could have been represented without him. In just this way, the same year, 1937, also marked Stalin's debut as a stage character in Nikolai Pogodin's Lenin play *The Man With a Gun*, and his depiction in that other imagined world of the novel in Alexei Tolstoy's *Bread*.[35] Jay Leyda in his history of Soviet cinema notes that the flood-gates now were open. A trio of Gorky biopics were soon to follow, and an intended series of Bolshevik film biographies that began in 1940 with the infant Soviet republic's first president, Yakov Sverdlov.[36]

Where Stalin alone burst through conventional taste barriers was in providing the role of principal hero while still alive.[37] It is hardly surprising that stage performers in this role were reduced to panic-stricken incoherence by the presence in the audience of Stalin himself.[38] Though Stalin roles at first were relatively modest, already in *Lenin in 1918* (1939) he was moving centre stage, and in the post-war cult films of Mikhail Chiaureli he assumed the lead role now requiring no legitimising co-star.[39] Other dictators would have scorned the reliance on actors. Hitler was apotheosised through Leni Riefenstahl's pseudo-documentary *Triumph of the Will* (1935); and Mussolini exclusively through newsreel images.[40] Stalin, on the other hand, was by 1937 retreating from even this mediated form of public view.[41] This was not the invention of tradition but the invention of the leader. On Stalin's 70th birthday, the Moscow veteran Marty evoked Stalin's qualities of leadership by recalling an 'old Soviet film' depicting him during the civil war.[42] That the figure Marty conjured up was a professional stand-in, enacting scenes increasingly of pure invention, was a peculiarity of Stalin's cult, and a measure of its deficiency in the personal history and public presence on which ostensibly it was founded.

Among the communists too, Stalin alone of his contemporaries seems to have required or allowed impersonation. Major productions initiated in his final years were the highly romanticised German dramatisations of the life of Thälmann. These, of course, were allowable as a posthumous depiction, albeit with legitimising cameos for current GDR leaders that recalled Stalin's in *Lenin in October*.[43] In Hungary, proposals for a film treatment of Rákosi's life were not taken forward; like other ruling leaders, Rákosi starred in newsreels and documentaries, but the main production for his 60th birthday focused on the commemoration of the anniversary itself.[44] Where western parties had some limited capacity for such productions, the practice rather than the object of the cult also offered most in the way of visual spectacle. This was true for example of Carlo Lizzani's *Togliatti Has Returned* (1948) which celebrated its hero's recovery from attempted assassination through the popular demonstrations and expressions of solidarity to which it gave rise.[45] Similar images of a countrywide mobilisation were also a feature of the PCF film *The Man We Love the Most* (1949), which evoked the occasion of Stalin's 70th birthday, rather as Barbusse might have, through the tributes and the offerings that it prompted.

Despite the efforts that were put into them, productions even in France and Italy were often banned from public viewing or restricted to use by party sections and workplace groups. The gathering in closed halls for such observances could perform an integrating function. But it was nevertheless impossible on these terms to compete with the commercial cinema for a wider audience, or replicate the easier hand-to-hand interaction that the distribution of political literature allowed. Even the Soviet cult films were confined, on the one hand, to a captive home market, and on the other to an audience politically predisposed to appreciate them. Despite the legal obstacles that these had also faced, Richard Taylor notes that the classics of the Soviet silent era spoke to aspirations and stereotypes that were by no means exclusive to the communists themselves.[46] The same could not be said of productions reflecting the turn to national bolshevism. The communist film critic Georges Sadoul maintained that the shift to sound coincided with the transition from a cinema of the masses to one of heroes, and thus, quite self-consciously in Shumyatsky's case, to a form of cinematic populism.[47] Nevertheless, these heroes not only spoke a national language; they did so in productions that were, to paraphrase the socialist realist formula, national in content as well as form. The Soviet cinema of the 1920s had revealed a quality of universality in the specificities of the Russian revolution, and Stalin himself had spoken of films reaching a public that books in Russian could never reach.[48] *The Fall of Berlin*, on the other hand, rendered the international drama of the anti-fascist war as a national epic centred on the Kremlin, in which the voices of the once united nations are heard only for the purpose of rendering Stalin homage. In this, they faithfully reflected the transnational but politically circumscribed character of the Cold War cult community.

(ii)

The strengths and limitations of radio were like a mirror image of those of the early cinema. Launched in 1930, the British *Daily Worker* would sometimes show the stark metallic functionalism of Vladimir Shukov's Moscow radio tower as a symbol of modernity bound up with internationalism. Klutsis in his images for *The Language of Lenin* (1925) had also shown the radio in constructivist depictions as a central tool of communication.[49] Overstepping physical and legal obstacles, Shukov's transmitter not only carried foreign-language broadcasts, as many as five a week in German, but Soviet materials like the wireless oratorio and collective Lenin poem which in 1931 formed part of its offerings for the Lenin anniversary.[50] 'Hear Lenin's Own Voice!', ran an advertisement for *Three Songs of Lenin*, as if this were now a relic which all could touch.[51] It was Stalin's rule, however, which coincided with the age of wireless, and Shukov's transmitter had been erected in the very year that Stalin became general secretary. There was, even so, no prospect of Stalin projecting himself into one's living space as bourgeois politicians like Baldwin and Tardieu did, and with that immediacy and even intimacy of address that was radio's contribution to the personalisation of political leadership. Even among his compatriots, Stalin's leaden delivery and heavy accent did not always inspire.[52] It was the language barrier, however, which was finally insurmountable, and Stalin despite his best efforts had never attained a fluency in any but his native languages of Russian and Georgian.[53]

There were in theory no such issues with the national-level figures that emerged with the communists' growing political presence. Thorez's first opportunity to broadcast nationally came during the popular front elections of 1936. When his party organised 'collective listenings', just as in the USSR, this also recalled the collective readings of an earlier, not yet fully literate age of activism.[54] Pollitt's opportunity did not come until 1945, also in the form of an election broadcast. Browder, on the other hand, used the opportunities offered by American commercial radio to establish a profile as a radio as much as a platform speaker, reaching audiences plausibly described as 'far beyond the numerical strength of his party'.[55] Most effective and widely noticed of the popular-front broadcasts were Ibárruri's during the Spanish war, in one of which, in September 1936, she used the famous words 'No pasarán!' (They shall not pass) which came to symbolise resistance to fascism internationally.

The wider conflict which followed proved the heyday of the political radio broadcast. Churchill and Roosevelt are obvious examples; Stalin too recognised the need for tangible proofs of continuing leadership, and de Gaulle in broadcasting from London demonstrated the particular utility of radio in laying claim to leadership from a position in exile. Few of de Gaulle's compatriots had any idea what he looked like, and he was probably the first such figure in history to establish a genuine aura of authority as a disembodied voice.[56] This was also the opportunity for the communist leaders exiled in Moscow, for whom the Comintern by the time of its dissolution in 1943 was functioning as much as anything as a broadcasting operation.

Togliatti, Rákosi and Ibárruri all performed this role; conspicuously failing to was Thorez, whose incognito deprived him of even this more distant record of public activity. Togliatti's biographer Aldo Agosti points out that few Italians would have had receivers powerful enough to pick up his thrice-weekly broadcasts. Nevertheless, these did provide the material for a post-war compilation documenting the continuous leadership that he had sought to exercise.[57] Thorez, by contrast, had to be pressurised into giving a weekly broadcast even in 1944; and though a pamphlet of sorts was thus belatedly made possible, it did nothing to settle the issue of Thorez's silent war.[58] Ironically, as afterwards in France he sought to avail himself of such opportunities, for example on the reissuing in 1949 of his *Son of the People*, the denial of his right to do so prompted a vigorous campaign of protest on the part of his supporters.[59]

Next to the typewriter, the camera was the most accessible of the new tools of communication to oppositional movements as well as ruling parties.[60] According to Margarita Tupitsyn, photography was also at the height of its prestige within the USSR at the time that Stalin cult's was initially launched.[61] In 1930 the photo-journal *The USSR in Construction* began publication in the four main Comintern languages, and until its demise in 1941 it supplied a widely circulated visual account of Soviet achievements. The major figures of Soviet constructivism were involved, among them the Latvian Klutsis, who in 1930 produced the first of the montage images of Stalin which henceforth dominated in his work. Klutsis's famous 'Four Giants' image of 1933 would circulate in more than 20 different languages, and his commemorative album for Stalin's 55th birthday the following year was issued in leather, cloth and dauntingly steel-bound versions.[62] In comparison with the use of film, photojournalism was also practised more extensively by western communist parties. Münzenberg again was a pioneer with the *Arbeiter Illustrierte Zeitung* (Workers' Illustrated Newspaper), which was launched as such in 1924 and became notable for the montage work of Heartfield. In France, it was to be the illustrated weekly *Regards*, rather than any biographical text, that most conveyed the distinctively familial and domesticated character of Thorez's post-war cult.[63] In the British *Daily Worker*, neither Stalin's words nor those about him enjoyed the prominence of his image. Even George Orwell thought he had a likeable face; and from the giant facsimile surmounting the Czechoslovakian party congress, to the youthful companion of Lenin and the filmstrip-type depiction of 'The architect of socialism', it is primarily through Stalin's image that his cult was discernible in the *Worker* as it built towards its pre-war apogee.[64]

Photography's advantage as a medium was that it circulated beyond the reach of Stalin's political apparatus while remaining dependent on his control of the supply of images. A key component in the development of a modern politics of personality, the photograph had long since moved beyond the formal portrait shot to the exposure either of the seemingly unrehearsed or less public setting, or of the active performance of leadership whether at the desk or on the platform. Thorez's depictions in *Regards* were of just this character, and Joseph Jacquemotte after his death was shown in seemingly unstudied poses of unusual informality.[65] That this engendered concerns with the medium's control as well as exploitation was not peculiar to communism. In 1899 America's *Penny Pictorial Magazine* had introduced a 'Taken unawares' feature, and the British politician Gladstone, on being surprised by excursionists at his home, had reached quickly for an axe to assume his favoured pose of Carlylean woodchopper.[66] 'The Dictatorship of the Photographer', a voice called out as Trotsky was asked to re-enact a speaking gesture at the first Comintern congress.[67] Still at this stage it was possible to photograph Lenin crouching with his notes by a congress podium, and the Frenchman André Morizet thought it the one published image that caught something of his personal dynamism.[68]

Stalin had no intention of being caught unawares, or crouching down, or (unless he so decided) smoking a cigarette. He was shorter than he liked to appear and self-conscious about his pock-marked face; he was also getting older. He was, moreover, de facto co-author of every image that not only required his presence but, like Mao's later on, was approved for reproduction according to a painstaking visual censorship.[69] Both Ludwig and Lyons could practise a verbal lese-majesty in their unauthorised Stalin biographies.[70] A flurry of such volumes marked Stalin's emergence as Soviet leader, and he could do nothing to prevent the most sensationalist textual images of his rule. Notably this was true of the 'career of a fanatic' delineated by the former Georgian Socialist Revolutionary writing as Essad-Bey.[71] Nevertheless, the visual matter that accompanied these texts was in every case approved and supplied by official agencies. Few observers wrote with better insight than the American W.H. Chamberlin in his *Russia's Iron Age* (1935). Whether designedly or of necessity, Chamberlin's text even gave the effect of subverting the official images interwoven with it, as in his 'Ordeal of the peasantry' chapter, with its incongruous supporting visual

'Tractors at work on a collective farm'. While text therefore eluded Stalin's control, the fact that so many were beguiled by *The USSR in Construction* was due not least to the lack of any visual counter-narrative.

On two occasions, and seemingly only two, Stalin admitted a western photographer into his Kremlin sanctum. The first occasion, shortly following on the Ludwig interview, saw him entertain the then Berlin-based American photographer James Abbe in April 1932. Well-practised in celebrity portraits and photo-journalism, Abbe took counsel from Stalin's favourite western correspondent Walter Duranty and by his own account secured his unprecedented entry by arguing that an outsider's sighting alone could convincingly dispel the rumours of Stalin's ill-health that had lately circulated in the West. Abbe like Ludwig had his own obvious interest in penetrating where others could not, and the previous year had similarly secured exclusive admission into Hitler's presence and the not-yet ruling Nazis' Brown House headquarters. As Bodo von Dewitz observes, Abbe's published shots of Stalin were both his finest hour and most compromised one, and showed how successfully Stalin had exploited his hunger for a scoop to bring before a wider public the image of the smiling father figure posing with such serenity and affability amongst his unassuming surroundings.[72]

It was with a similar assurance of control that Stalin in 1941 entertained the well-known *Life* photographer Margaret Bourke-White. Despite the wartime easing of Soviet-western relations, Stalin did not much open up to western journalists and literati, and the British correspondent Alexander Werth referred with a tinge of jealous resentment to the single off-the-record interview he granted the American Ralph Ingersoll. Werth was not much more impressed with 'Mrs Bourke-White ... as usual, bothering us with her camera and flashlights'. Her credentials, like Abbe's, included earlier commissions in the USSR, notably three professional visits in the early 1930s. Presumably on this last occasion too her negatives had to be submitted for approval, and it is therefore revealing that for a western audience, as if recalling Cromwell's 'warts and all', Stalin apparently did not object to the clear sight of his pock-marks, which in any approved Soviet depiction were indiscernible.[73] It does not appear that controls were otherwise relaxed. Finding Stalin standing stiff and straight in a long bare room, Bourke-White told of how she 'wanted badly to get him sitting down, or talking, but I don't know what you can do with a dictator when he thinks he wants to stand in the middle of the rug'. It was Bourke-White, therefore, who dropped to her knees to provide the obligatory low camera angle that made for a striking portrait image for circulation in the West. Once more, it was only in Bourke-White's written commentary that another Stalin was depicted, not unsympathetically, with great strength of countenance, but 'like a man who has been stout and got thinner lately ... [with] a kind of grey and tired look ... of almost physical fatigue'.[74] This itself, however, was again far from unhelpful in signalling the leader sharing in his people's trials as they bore the brunt of the German war offensive.

The limitations of the photograph were in a double sense those of its static character. It was claimed in Lenin's case, as it was of Gladstone, that no fixed image could capture his dynamic quality and mobility of expression. If film alone could do him justice, as Vaillant-Couturier maintained, this might help explain the appeal of *Three Songs of Lenin* and the outrage provoked by Lenin's impersonation by an actor.[75] Stalin impressed Bourke-White, not by nimbleness or vitality, but by granite-like solidity and strength, which seemingly might have lent itself to the photographer's or the sculptor's art.[76] But if photography was losing its privileged status, it was because of its failure to represent movement in a second and less superficial sense: that of the defining precept of socialist realism which recognised the active, transformative quality of reality, not as an end, but as a process of becoming.

It was at the Soviet Writers' Congress of August 1934 that the new guiding line was for the first time comprehensively expounded.[77] Scattered among the proceedings are numerous references to the photograph as the symbol becoming cliche that connoted a 'dry' or lifeless naturalism.[78] Rosalind Sartorti has suggested that in *Pravda* photomontage had by this time become established as a method appropriate to Stalin alone among living leaders, and one which through juxtaposition and the manipulation of proportion depicted the idealised reality that was beyond the grasp of the discrete photographic shot.[79] In the form of pseudo-documentary falsification, surreptitious montage would of course remain a crucial part of stalinism's visual armoury.[80] So too would the use of giant photographic enlargements creating the same effect of disproportionality at congresses and mass rallies. While the ubiquity of the leader's features was achievable only where communism ruled, such set-piece effects were widely employed by some western parties like the PCF. At the same time, the non-illusionist montage of the Klutsis type fell from favour. Already in 1934, Barbusse had sought for his Stalin biography an image that sounds rather like Klutsis's Four Giants poster. Nevertheless, neither this nor anything similar was included in the dossier of images that was sent him, and it was Barbusse himself who through his highly coloured prose achieved a visual quality somewhat lacking in the studied portrait shots which interspersed his text.[81]

Rather than montage, it was the painted image that Sartorti suggests began to supplant the photograph as a mark of Stalin's distinction. Particularly in a context like a daily newspaper, it counteracted the 'democratic' medium of photography with the exclusive and quasi-monarchical anointment of power by the painter.[82] There was also a history to be falsified, through a genre of historical painting that predated and prefigured Stalin's similar depiction on the screen. At its most basic this could simply mean the intrusion of a pipe, which in the French volume *Stalin in Images* appears in painted scenes predating the First World War.[83] Deutscher also referred to the 'oddly handsome daredevil Stalin' who appeared in 1935 in *The History of the Civil War in the USSR*. Nevertheless, the crucial point was that, even in this far-from-scrupulous collation, a greater licence was allowed in Stalin's 'strikingly false' visual record of activity than in the accompanying written text.[84] While photography lent itself to the purging or the massaging of the image, it could not supply the missing or unrecorded scenes in Stalin's life, and to this extent the camera proved a reluctant instrument of hagiography. While the painting of Stalin's portrait was like the patent of nobility of the Soviet art elite, it was in the representation of stalinist apocrypha that the traditional art forms of an age of faith retained a documentary function they were otherwise thought to have lost.[85] It is telling that in the quintessential cult compilation *Stalin on Lenin* the historical scenes are all drawn or painted, and the portrait images all photographs.[86]

Control of artistic production could not extend in the same way beyond the territorial limits of the cult. Hostile visual caricatures were as insusceptible to such controls as hostile biographies. Even positive depictions were fraught with difficulty and mostly avoided. In Britain, the only significant art works devoted to Stalin appear to have been two monumental heads by the Hungarian émigré sculptor, Peter Peri. Rituals of gift-giving could extend to items of personal significance for the giver, who made them over to the recipient as if of some part of themselves. This did not, however, imply the right to represent Stalin himself as he figured in their imaginations.

This distinction is particularly clear in France. Post-war Paris was a centre of the art world as well as Stalin's cult, and Wieviorka suggests that painting even supplanted writing as the foremost of the PCF's cultural activities.[87] Such a claim would be unthinkable had it not been for the recruitment to communism of the best-known painter of the age, Pablo Picasso.[88] One of those who rallied to the *parti des fusillés*, Picasso remained a PCF member until his death and lent its campaigns not only his name and material support, but such instantly recognisable images as the famous dove of peace.[89] No case better illustrates the tension between the harnessing and subjection of the individual's cultural or political capital. The retention and advertisement of Picasso's allegiance coincided with the Cold War cultural reaction known as Zhdanovism and the anathematisation by Soviet bodies of the so-called formalism which served as the artistic analogue of Trotskyism. Picasso was an obvious target, and morbid, repulsive and pathological were among the epithets used of him. His emblems might appear at peace rallies, but where communism ruled his major works were forbidden and condemned.[90]

Even in these difficult circumstances, the PCF was not so oblivious to its wider credibility as to alienate in this way its most illustrious recruit. Picasso in return had avoided provoking unnecessary controversy, particularly in depicting communist personalities. Images like those of the victimised anti-war activist Henri Martin and the executed Greek resistance leader Nikos Beloyannis adopted a naturalistic style which one journal identified with 'a marked turn towards realism'.[91] In fact, the drawings Picasso made of Thorez in May 1945 already respected these conventions, and one was later used as frontispiece of a luxury edition of *Son of the People* published in 1950. Where Togliatti's pictorial biography would comprise a photographic record of documents, personalities and events, the intermittency of Thorez's documentation was circumvented by using the work of leading communist artists. Though one image portrayed Thorez as a youthful farm-hand, and another the Courrières mining disaster with which *Son of the People* begins, Picasso's was the only real portrait as such (Fig. 6.1). Rather as Sartorti suggests, he was thereby dignified with the attentions of an acknowledged artistic prodigy from which no lesser portrayal was allowed to detract.

Thorez was drawn by Picasso in at least three distinct manners, as if offering him alternatives. Picasso similarly provided a choice of images for the festivities to mark the PCF's 30th anniversary.[92] But if greatness was to figure greatness, and Picasso turn his hand to Stalin, there could clearly be no provision for the scrutiny that would have been accorded a Soviet artist. Asked for a drawing to mark Stalin's 70th birthday, Picasso had on this occasion sidestepped the dilemma with a wine glass raised and the motto, 'Stalin, to your health' (Fig. 6.2). Perhaps this was offhand or even

Fig. 6.1 Maurice Thorez by Pablo Picasso, pen-and-ink drawing, 23 May 1945, as reproduced in Maurice Thorez, *Fils du peuple*, Éditions sociales, 1950 (Courtesy Tate Images, © Succession Picasso/DACS, London 2016)

Fig. 6.2 'Stalin, to your health' by Pablo Picasso, pen-and-ink drawing, November 1949 (Courtesy Tate Images, © Succession Picasso/DACS, London 2016)

CE QUE NOUS DEVONS A STALINE

par ARAGON, Frédéric JOLIOT-CURIE, PICASSO
Henri BASSIS, Pierre COURTADE, Pierre DAIX, Georges SADOUL

LES LETTRES françaises ARTS Spectacles

Prix : 35 fr. Directeur : ARAGON Prix : 35 fr.

STALINE *le marxisme et la science*

par F. JOLIOT-CURIE

STALINE *et la* FRANCE

par ARAGON

Poème pour le Vél' d'Hiv'

par Henri BASSIS

Fig. 6.3 Stalin by Pablo Picasso, drawing, 8 March 1953, as reproduced in *Les Lettres françaises*, 12–19 March 1953 (Courtesy Tate Images, © Succession Picasso/DACS, London 2016)

impertinent, as Wieviorka suggests; but perhaps it was also simply politic.[93] The wishing of Stalin's health was certainly part of the PCF's repertoire of cult cliches, though not usually, it is true, with the familiar 'tu' form. On the other hand, Picasso again produced multiple versions of the drawing, one of which has 'STALIN' not merely underlined but heading the page as if emitting light, like the rays of the sun.[94] Whatever rumblings there may have been, the conceit was not so controversial as to prevent it being used both in Aragon's cultural review, *Les Lettres françaises*, and in the film *The Man We Love the Most*, which Éluard narrated. Nor did it deter Aragon from again approaching Picasso in this connection at the time of Stalin's death.

Why Picasso responded with the drawing he did is still not fully clear (Fig. 6.3).[95] *Les Lettres françaises* was a weekly paper; there was no time for detailed directions or proper oversight, and he was simply requested to 'send us whatever you want text or drawing'.[96] But he did not this time send alternatives, or take the easier option offered of a written message. The image he provided of a younger Stalin was free, as Aragon would note, of the 'distortions' thought synonymous with formalism.[97] Nevertheless, the commonest complaint was of not being able to recognise Stalin in the drawing, and the young Annie Kriegel, then a committed communist, called it a daub.[98] Picasso was well-practised in such commissions; he did not on this occasion seek to avoid controversy, and in contrast with his other communist portrait sketches offered a type as much as a likeness. Wieviorka expresses doubts as to Picasso's feelings towards the commission, and it is hard not to see in the image both a comment on the pomposity of official Soviet art, and at least a semi-ironical response to the criticisms to which his own work had been subjected.

Whatever Picasso's intentions, it proved a cause célèbre. Critical responses were published by order of the party secretariat, and Picasso's socialist realist bête noire André Fougeron weighed in urging that a photograph would have been better, or 'the honest work of a Soviet Artist'.[99] Stalin, nevertheless, was not the only sacrosanct figure in this affair. When shortly afterwards Thorez returned to France, he immediately signalled his continuing approval of Picasso's work. Even among the criticisms, care was usually taken not to impugn Picasso's greatness as an artist, and Fougeron's aspersions gave rise to indignation. When the following year *L'Humanité Dimanche* published Picasso's drawings of the imputed atomic spies Julius and Ethel Rosenberg, there was neither scandal nor possible pretext for one in the somewhat anodyne images themselves. When a decade later a volume of Cachin's portrait sketches appeared,

Picasso now supplied the cover drawing with that freedom of line conspicuously absent from his Stalin.

Nobody by this time was under any illusion that this was not an act of tribute by Picasso but one of patronage. Alain Badiou has lately defended the communist personality cults with a reminder of our readiness to accept the notion of creative genius in the arts.[100] It is true that no field of activity shows a greater predilection for the cult of the individual than that of art. For communists themselves, conversely, it was in Lenin and the field of politics that a cult of genius was first recovered that was now restored to the field of culture. As Kriegel the fervent stalinist put it at the time, 'the genius of Stalin was tamed by the genius of Picasso'.[101] Having bought into the culture of artistic celebrity, the PCF even in the Cold War was unable fully to control it. Picasso's genius came up against Stalin's, and with a sketch dashed off in an afternoon proved beyond its sanction.

What Picasso brought to the encounter was the mystique of his genius rather than its material expression. How telling it is that Aragon, knowing fully Picasso's rapidity of execution, should have offered him the option of a text as well as an image. Perhaps the crucial distinction is not that between one medium and another but that between the narrative and pictorial. Svetlana Alpers and Michael Baxandall suggest that even the visual arts are conventionally evaluated according to 'the performance of a typical language task such as telling a story'.[102] The mobilising of support for a political cause is certainly a language task, and the compelling and often empowering nature of a communist commitment was very much that of narratives to be enacted and counter-narratives to be resisted. The image, by contrast, was an emblem of identification and belonging: in other words, of the integrating cult. One may have interviewed a hundred communists, as the present author has, and struggle to recall the political commitment that arose from an image rather than a text. The power of the image thus presupposed some familiarity with the narrative scheme that unlocked its political meaning. 'Will not the caption', wrote Walter Benjamin, 'become the most important part of the photograph?'[103] Or, as one of Vertov's critics put it, though the sight of Mussolini might arouse one's interest, that of a 'straightforward plump and bald-headed man' entirely failed to do so.[104]

What quantities of metal, Giovanni Germanetto wrote, had been moulded into badges in Lenin's effigy.[105] Already with the fate of the revolution still in the balance, an Italian medallion was said to bear Lenin's image and the inscription *ex oriente lux*.[106] Both the image and the inscription were like a cipher connoting the revolution as incarnated in its leader, and it was thus alone that Lenin's physically unremarkable profile acquired its symbolic resonance. A published *Works* could also serve as emblem, and Mao's Little Red Book has been described precisely as a badge book.[107] Songs about communist leaders could serve a similar function, from the Thälmann and Dimitrov songs that rallied activists in the 1930s, to the lifting up of voices in celebration of Rákosi, Thorez or even Browder.[108] Music that was strong enough, like Prokofiev's *Toast* to Stalin, could survive the circumstances of its creation.[109] Nevertheless, even the Briton Ewan MacColl, whose musical gifts certainly did reach a very wide audience, can have had no illusions of appealing to that audience when in 1952 he set the doggerel of his *Ballad of Stalin* to 'jaunty banjo licks'.[110]

It was nevertheless the image as a password unlocking a common identity and history that served as an integrating device that, in Soviet public places, was literally inescapable. Within this Soviet context, arguments have been advanced for the primacy in stalinist culture both of visual media and of a narrative that was paradigmatically a biographical narrative.[111] For the communist parties of the West, on the other hand, there was not only the narrative task of delineating on a human scale an epochal process of social transformation. There was also a labour movement culture to which the written and spoken word were central, and print, along with the photograph, was the most accessible medium in conditions of legality. Communists in France might uphold the idea of Thorez's ubiquity; but they could do so only by putting it in a song. They did not control the principal public spaces except when temporarily occupying them by mass demonstrations. They were also excluded from the dominant forms of mass communication, and the ones they principally used were not so very far removed from the age of Gladstone or even Garibaldi. Biography for all these reasons provided the more obvious vehicle for the personalisation of political leadership. But it was precisely its delineation of a personal history that proved so difficult to reconcile with the cult of the individual that was always in some degree a cult of party.

6.2 The Impossible Cult Biography

(i)

When Werth arrived in Moscow in July 1941, he commented on how little westerners knew of Stalin and how 'practically all the well-known books' about him were hostile.[112] Previously based in Paris, Werth's contention that Stalin had been severely handicapped by a deficit in effective propaganda seems difficult to credit. Nevertheless, the dearth of published material detailing Stalin's personal record of activity was by this time established as a truism. Barbusse in 1935 had referred to Stalin as 'the most visible man in the world, and yet one of the least familiar'.[113] Though Barbusse's was at this point the only authorised attempt to put this right, within months of its appearing the Russian translation was withdrawn and it was not until the end of the decade that any similar account of Soviet provenance finally appeared. Even so, the defining stalinist text of the cult years was not a biography but the *History of the CPSU (B)*, or famous *Short Course*. Originally published in 1938, this circulated internationally in huge editions; in France at least its appearance was thought sufficiently a watershed to justify its birthday being marked just like a leader's.[114] Nevertheless, biography was not the history's organising principle, and biographical materials were even edited out at Stalin's behest. His premise was that party education was not best served by a history constructed around particular individuals.[115]

This is the more surprising given biography's centrality to the stalinist culture of the 1930s. This was an age, writes Katerina Clark, when it seemed that 'virtually everyone who put pen to paper was writing a heroic biography'.[116] Communism was a narrative of becoming, and a work upon society which was simultaneously a work upon the self. Framed as both a challenge to history and its enactment, it was also an affirmation of what the Webbs in their *Soviet Communism* described as a vocation of leadership, authenticated by the exemplary lives which validated this calling in a spirit of service to the collectivity.[117] It was biography, not the motionless statue or portrait bust, that Clark describes as the cornerstone of stalinist culture, and Jochen Hellbeck as the tangible expression of the new man (or woman) in the making.[118]

That Stalin at the system's apex should require the legitimation of biography was therefore intrinsic to the claims he made upon it. Tucker maintained that nothing mattered more than this to his pretensions as Lenin's successor.[119] Whether as *chef* or *grand meneur*, there was in fact hardly a leader of modern times whose credentials had not been expounded biographically. In the case of Mussolini, whose cult loomed largest as Stalin's first took shape, the number of such productions had increased 'exponentially' during the first years of his rule.[120] In Moscow, by contrast, there were 103 Stalin busts to be counted in the renamed Gorky Street, but no biography to be had from any of its bookstalls.[121]

In biography, more than any other mode of expression, the paradoxical quality of the cult of the individual is thus encapsulated. David Brandenberger clearly demonstrates that biography was central to the cult phenomenon.[122] Nevertheless, it was as a challenge and ambition that in Stalin's case, precisely because of the discrepancy between his actual personal history and that which his cult required, could never be fully accomplished. Stalinism as a result was never an age of biographical flourishing. On the contrary, this was a time of biographical devastation in which those lives and persons were decimated that cast a shadow over the consummate personal history that was irretrievably beyond Stalin's reach.[123]

It was for this reason that his life was most convincingly represented by his detractors. Werth mentioned Souvarine and Trotsky. By the time of Stalin's death, they would be joined by another dissenting communist, Isaac Deutscher. Though Stalin therefore failed to secure biographical legitimation with a wider international public, he was for a time seriously exercised by such an ambition. Moreover, while his approved biographies did in time epitomise the monolithic qualities of the integrating cult, there remained elsewhere a manifest tension between these disciplines and that deployment of an individual's political capital that was of such proven effectiveness in popularising some wider cause or movement.

It was hardly surprising, wrote a Jesuit historian, that the reading of hagiographic texts should prove such monotonous work, or so many resemblances become apparent between the actions they described.[124] The fundamental challenge of the cult biography was similar. This too required the delineation of an individual life history as the distillation of some higher ideal, which in this case was the collective ideal of the party. To the extent that this object was given priority, three characteristic features of the modern biography were consequently minimised if not excluded. The first was that of any personal detail tending to the differentiation of the individual from the collective. The second was the development of the individual through experience in the manner of the Bildungsroman. The third was the interplay between life and times in which the public life found its meaning and distinction. These were the principal constraints within which individual texts were produced, and it is worth expanding briefly upon them before proceeding to examples.

One advantage of the parallel storylines in the film treatments of Stalin and Dimitrov was that they channelled all domestic interest into the fictional lesser characters. Indeed, while Dimitrov's family had initially figured prominently in publicity around the Leipzig trial, his mother was edited out of any significant role in *Fighters*, while the tragic death in Moscow of his estranged wife would never have made it into the storyline.[125] Communist biographies were not alone in not allowing a private sphere to intrude upon the public engagements which they held up for display. What was more distinctive was the leninist party model to which all public roles and undertakings were formally subordinated, so that even activist and secondary political commitments had to be assimilated into a party-centred narrative.

With the casting of the narrative over time, this also posed the second challenge, of the protagonist's development from a lower to a higher level of consciousness. This was in fact a feature of much western communist autobiography, in which joining the party or meeting with Lenin could provide a moment of catharsis and a radical rupture between past and present. Stalin, on the other hand, would have reminded the Jesuit of the saints who were born with their aureole already in place. In a telling adaptation of an older trope, Malte Rolf refers to him as the 'unmoved mover' among the continuously moving, and this quality of motionlessness was represented biographically over time as well as spatially in the Kremlin.[126] The same was also true of the traitors who filled the other half of the diptych. Notoriously in the show trials, old Bolsheviks were unmasked who had not so much fallen away as concealed an inner rottenness from the start. It was this which Trotsky in his own case referred to as a state cult, and the same pattern was subsequently repeated in the East European trials.[127] In France in similar fashion, Marty, following his expulsion from the PCF, was retrospectively divested even of the role he had played in the Black Sea mutiny.[128]

Not even a Jesuit might fully have grasped the difficulty of linking life and times for a movement of constantly changing lines and anathemas. What this bewildering volatility meant in practice was that an appearance of unwavering rectitude was achievable only at a level sufficiently general as to remain unaffected by compromising exposures or turns of events. Notoriously this was the case during the Soviet terror, when seemingly almost any past or present party contact risked possible unmasking as an enemy of the people.[129] Even in the more settled world of the western parties, reconciling past and present phases of policy and personnel was a matter of fine judgement that was always liable to be undone by events. Willi Bredel, for example, discovered this with his life of Thälmann, and Aragon when he was asked to remove sundry characters from his novel *Les Communistes*.[130] As a general rule, the more intermittent one's relations with Moscow, the greater the feasibility of a biography avoiding excessive levels of abstraction and approximating to the genre's wider conventions. Combined with a liberal publishing environment, and its reflection in a long-established tradition of labour autobiography, this was attested in the profusion and relative insularity of such works emanating from the small British communist party.[131] No British communist, on the other hand, had either the temerity or the authority to attempt a life of Stalin.[132]

That such a life was needed was at first a reflection of the evident appetite for Bolshevik biography both within and beyond the USSR. Until 1935, when Stalin liquidated it, the Society of Old Bolsheviks was an authoritative source of such materials, and some of these were widely translated. The *Memoirs of a Bolshevik* of Osip Piatnitsky, one of the Comintern's best-known leaders, was originally published in 1925, and progressively translated into German, Czechoslovakian, Japanese, Spanish and English. The French edition, with a preface by Marty, appeared in a collection of 'Revolutionary memoirs' that also included Marty's own account of the Black Sea mutiny, Giovanni Germanetto's *Memoirs of a Barber* and the autobiography of the Moscow-domiciled former Wobbly, Big Bill Haywood.[133] There was also, as we have seen, a spate of Lenin biographies.[134] Whether commercially or politically motivated, a common feature of these was that Stalin's name barely registered. Crucially, there was also the exiled Trotsky, whose own autobiography treated Stalin as a rival almost too negligible to expend effort upon.[135]

Stalin as yet had only the biographical sketch prepared in 1927 by his secretary Ivan Tovstukha.[136] Two years later this featured in *Pravda*'s 50th birthday materials, and when a selection of these appeared in English they were actually packaged as *The Life of Stalin*. Even the friendliest reviewer could nevertheless note the absence of 'the "personal"', and of that 'softer side' to Stalin which might have won over a wider public.[137] Münzenberg, with his instinctive grasp of the need for an effective counter-propaganda, wrote to Tovstukha of the urgent need for a corrective to accounts like Essad-Bey's.[138] But even in the USSR, the promised popular biography failed to appear.[139]

It was no accident that Stalin should have chosen Ludwig for his first high-profile colloquy of the 1930s. Ludwig was the most popular biographer of the day, scathingly characterised by Trotsky as the epoch's 'court portrait painter', and a public sounding board for Mussolini in just this period.[140] He had also published a sketch of Lenin that must have given assurance by its description of Lenin and Trotsky as 'antipodal' characters.

It also described how Lenin had reshaped Russia through 'the pure but relentless will of the leader', and in defiance of the marxist theories he formally upheld.[141] Whatever Stalin's motivations, within a week of the meeting with Ludwig, Tovstukha was writing to Gorky with materials that might have been used for a biography or memoir, like the one which Gorky too had devoted to the regime's founding *vozhd'*.[142]

Gorky was not to be drawn, and still in 1933 Tovstukha was using a co-authored editorial in the CPSU history journal *Proletarskaya Revolyutsiya* to deplore the absence of 'dynamically written' lives of the revolution's major leaders.[143] While the issue of some such Soviet production remained unresolved when Tovstukha died in 1935, Barbusse offered the prospect of just such a livelier treatment of Stalin's biography. His international standing and connections were crucial to the enterprise, and it was by no means just a French public that Stalin had mind. In particular, following his acceptance of the commission in Moscow in July–August 1933 Barbusse embarked directly upon a first American speaking tour. A contract was signed with Macmillan, and Barbusse, who had an obvious interest in talking it up, reported on the eager anticipation with which the American edition was awaited.[144]

The impossible challenge facing him was to meet the expectations of such readers while observing the official conventions which were becoming established for Stalin's depiction. Events in 1931–1932 had dealt a double blow to any prospect of a credible portrayal. Publicly, Stalin's brutal intervention in *Proletarskaya Revolyutsiya* in October 1931 was the signal for a *partiinost'* conception of Bolshevik history in which Lenin in particular was to be represented as a figure incapable of error.[145] The clear implication, Tucker noted, was that Stalin too should be regarded as a figure in whom no past or present fault was even conceivable.[146] The following year, the suicide of Stalin's second wife Nadezhda Alliluyeva extinguished what little possibility there ever was of breaching his external wall of privacy. The popular memoir of Lenin by his widow Krupskaya had offered various glimpses of their life together and of a community of exiles that included other companionate pairings like the 'Zinovievs' and 'Bukharins'. Stalin had had no part in this milieu, nor any other personal ties that were now admissible. A model of the revolutionary biography was demanded in which 'the "personal"' intruded only in the earliest stages, and only in such ways as actively confirmed the qualities of the later public figure.

That Tovstukha in these circumstances should lament the absence of the 'living portrait' exposed the incoherence of a cult of the individual that was also its denial. Among the plethora of Lenin biographies in the West, some did represent the attempt of communists to meet the manifest demand for such a portrayal. In Britain, this was conspicuously the case with Ralph Fox's effort drawing on materials he had collected working at the Marx-Engels(-Lenin) Institute (IMEL). Perhaps the influence lingered of the Institute's ousted director David Riazanov, who had urged acceptance of Marx's human limitations against the 'elevated and solemn tones' of hagiographers.[147] Fox had certainly had to defend himself against charges of 'theoretical and political deviation' in an article on Marx's life for the *Daily Worker*.[148] He was in any case a sometime novelist writing for a commercial publisher under the laxer controls of one of Moscow's remoter satellites. If the Lenin he depicted seemed a providential figure, this was through the overcoming of defects rather than their absence. The hero was a difficult child, lacked application and self-control, was unruly as a student, and afterwards prone to moments of deflation requiring temporary respite from the life of a professional revolutionary. Crucially, in his judgements of his fellows, Lenin's impulsive humanity was 'constantly leading him into mistakes', as in his initial estimation of Trotsky—whose positive qualities, even so, Fox himself did not entirely deny.[149]

Fox had still been working at the IMEL when Stalin wrote to *Proletarskaya Revolyutsiya*. Indeed, it was he who then took up the cudgels against rotten liberalism within the CPGB.[150] But it seems that he had no more grasped its implications for the writing of such a life than had Pollitt as general secretary in approving his manuscript. Fox now conceded that one of the most serious charges that could be made against a communist writer was that of attributing 'mistakes' to the Giants, as he had been ill-advised enough to do even in the case of Stalin. Dutt, in adjudicating upon the episode, absolved Fox of the charge of Trotskyism. He did, on the other hand, deplore his framing of a purely personal narrative, like a conventional bourgeois biography, and the effacement of the party's 'collective outlook and movement' by the 'psychological isolating and subjectivising' of the volume's hero.[151]

It was Dutt himself who provided the necessary antidote in a thoroughly disembodied *Lenin* for another commercial publisher. Throughout his career, it insisted, Lenin had acted never as an individual, 'but always as the conscious and responsible representative of a movement greater than any individual' which both predated and survived him.[152] If Fox's by intent was a living biography, Dutt's was one of those pseudo-biographies 'more like party histories' which Tovstukha deplored.[153] Nevertheless, no approved Lenin biography ever was or could be written that was not more like a party history. Fox's *Lenin* was ignored by the communist press and he turned for his next biographical subject to Genghis Khan. When he died in 1937, Sidney Webb remarked upon the unaccountable omission of any mention of *Lenin* in Fox's obituaries.[154]

Barbusse in preparing his *Stalin* was not merely dependent on sources provided him on Stalin's behalf. In writing his Thälmann pamphlet, and doubtless in agreeing this new commission, he had also indicated his amenability to correction either factually or 'for political reasons'.[155] Like Gorky's, his writing had the further advantage that it was not constrained by an over-scrupulous literalism; and in the method which Barbusse described as 'integral realism' it was frequently impossible to distinguish between the observed, the documented and the invented.[156] Already demonstrated in the novelisation of his wartime experiences, it was a mark of Barbusse's heterodoxy as a communist that he had since applied this method to the life of Jesus, and even recounted it in the first person.[157] Barbusse did therefore have his own ideas as to how best to reach the wider potential readership that was his principal recommendation as Stalin's biographer. It should not be 'a purely technical book, but a living book'—exactly as Tovstukha urged. Barbusse had earlier amended the suggested title of his Thälmann pamphlet to 'Do you know Thälmann?' In just the same terms, he now aimed at providing a complete Stalin portrait so that the reader would also 'get to know him well'. But what above all he needed for this were the unpublished materials through which alone such an object was achievable.[158]

To Barbusse's obvious frustration, documentation of Stalin's 'actual life' failed to materialise.[159] Conscious of publishers' deadlines, he did what he could with recycled materials like those circulating on Stalin's 50th birthday and returned to Moscow in the autumn of 1934 to meet once more with Stalin and obtain from Béla Kun some desultory 'little anecdotes' for use in his concluding section.[160] He also received the detailed comments of the head of Kultprop, Alexei Stetsky. It is symptomatic of the contradictory impulse which both denied biography and sought its legitimation that Stetsky criticised Barbusse's draft for doing Stalin insufficient justice 'as a man'. What Stetsky meant by this was Stalin's style of work and language and his 'many-sided links with the masses' who surrounded him with their love.[161] It was the image of the 'man at the helm' with which the published narrative opened and concluded, and which depicted Stalin precisely as the object of mass love and veneration. But it was anything but a living portrait.

The book's most famous claim was that Stalin was the 'Lenin of today'. It was just such a claim that resisted demonstration through the medium of biography. If anything, it required the evisceration of Lenin's own biography so as to render him, as it were, in Stalin's own dimensions. Ironically, it is a second Barbusse biographical project that best illustrates the flattening process this required. Completed by Kurella only after Barbusse's death, its object was a volume of Lenin family letters of the sort that Stalin's biography so conspicuously lacked. The introductory sections are evidently Kurella's work, and the rationale they offer is not that of Lenin's softer side, but of the consummate revolutionary who had no sides and could at no time desist from embodying the revolution. Though incidentally they revealed 'the aspect of the "man" of this superman', primarily the letters demonstrated the 'interpenetration, the complete unity, of person and cause'. Lenin was thus presented as creator of a new human type, the professional revolutionary, prefiguring the 'true superman' of the future which Nietzsche had only been able to caricature. As detailed through his years of exile and the comradeship he shared with Krupskaya, a life of Lenin was therefore still presented that was not only very different from Stalin's but also untouched by it.[162] In Barbusse's life of Stalin, the relationship with Lenin was pivotal; from the perspective now of Lenin himself, there was no corroboration, and Stalin's role was rendered in its true proportions by being overlooked entirely.[163]

One can understand why a romantic Lenin cult might seem to pose a danger for the 'sober reality' of the Stalin regime.[164] By the time Krupskaya died in 1939, her *Memories of Lenin* had ceased to circulate in the USSR, and there was certainly no desire for volumes of family letters.[165] Whatever Barbusse's original ambitions, his *Stalin* was for long sections a bloodless institutional history merely structured as biography and losing sight of Stalin even as a name. Objecting to Barbusse's statement that Stalin after 1912 had no private life, Stetsky insisted that hadn't had one 'since 1898'—the year of his joining the party as a teenager. Erring on the side of caution, Barbusse's published text states that Stalin had never had a private life, and allows no domestic detail to impinge upon the relationships that did matter: those with Lenin, with the party and with the masses.[166] Despite his several meetings with Stalin, Barbusse had not even got as close to him as biographical subject as he had to Jesus. It was just because of this that his film scenario needed a parallel narrative to carry a story line of human scale and interest. Exactly such an approach was subsequently used in *Lenin in October*, with its fictional foil Comrade Vasily, and in *The*

Fall of Berlin the lives and loves of ordinary Russians interconnect with the larger human drama, still devoid of any personal aspect, that has Stalin at its centre.

Such was the publishing climate under Stalin that the Russian translation of Barbusse's book proved a popular success.[167] Though it continued to provide a quotable source of eulogy, the book was nevertheless withdrawn from libraries as collaborators like Kun and Stetsky, who contributed a foreword, fell victim to the terror. At last on Stalin's 60th birthday there appeared two Soviet-produced biographies. Compared with the anonymous short volume emanating from the IMEL, the treatment by the party historian Emelyan Yaroslavsky was almost vivacious, and did at least provide a semblance of biographical and pseudo-biographical detail for Stalin's early years. Nevertheless, the demands of official biography were again attested in the absence of any single blemish, beginning with Stalin's childhood popularity, and the depiction of his telepathic convergence with Lenin through long years of minimal or non-existent contact. The text is thinly populated, especially by the living, and even in respect of Stalin pseudo-biography gives way in later chapters to a *Short Course* type of history rendered through the leader's public pronouncements.[168] In 1946, there did appear a book of memoirs by Stalin's sister-in-law, written with the approval and oversight of key figures in the apparatus. Like Barbusse's *Stalin*, this enjoyed considerable success; but the following year it was severely censured in *Pravda* for its 'impermissible familiarity', and its author was later imprisoned.[169]

By the time of Stalin's 70th birthday, a second edition of the IMEL volume had been produced, more popular in character and circulating in huge numbers in the USSR.[170] There was no consideration by this time of a western readership, nor do the western parties themselves appear to have commemorated Stalin through biography.[171] In France, there was one curious volume, *The Man of Communism* (L'Homme communiste), which the writer Jean-Richard Bloch left unpublished on his death, having spent the war years in Moscow. Approving the public taboo regarding Stalin's personal circumstances, Bloch disowned psychological biography and eschewed either social or political biography. The result was a collation of journalistic impressions and anecdotes that rather confirmed Stalin's enjoyment of arbitrary power by commending the spirit in which he exercised it.[172] Even such well-meaning indiscretions meant that only a censored version of the volume was to be found in the restricted access section of Moscow's Lenin Library.[173] The empty shell of stalinist biography was at last encapsulated for the PCF by two minimally captioned volumes on Lenin and Stalin 'in images'. Comprising both photographs and the compensatory school of historical painting, these may or may not attest the survival in the West of traditions of image-worship. But what they did surely demonstrate was the vulgarisation to the point of collapse of the falsified biographical narrative at the heart of Stalin's cult.[174]

(ii)

While Stalin's biography continued to prove elusive, there appeared in France the quintessential cult production *Son of the People* that arguably defined its party's political identity as no such text did. Not only was Thorez's pseudo-autobiography distributed on an almost Soviet scale, but its successive editions also illustrate quite clearly the changing imperatives of the enkindling figure and the integration cult. The first edition, appearing at the height of Thorez's pre-war popularity in September 1937, was supported by a large-scale promotional campaign targeting readers beyond the communists' own ranks. The text itself, written by Fréville, began with the vivid evocation of Thorez's proletarian origins that would prove so central a component of his legend. 'Read this book, especially if you are not a communist', one reviewer exhorted, and the volume did sell some 130,000 copies, equivalent to around a third of the PCF's membership. Nevertheless, though this compared most favourably with other communist titles, Marie-Cécile Bouju's verdict is that the ambition of reaching a wider readership was not achieved.[175]

The volume's most striking feature was Thorez's abandonment of the autobiographical voice as he attained simultaneously to manhood and party membership. Scantly endowed with biographical capital, Thorez in *Son of the People* resolved the issue through a party history that once again was merely projected in its leader's name. Bloch, at this point still to formalise his commitment to the PCF, wrote to him to applaud just this blend of collective assertion and individual self-effacement, and the respite that it provided from the self-absorption of the confessional autobiography. From the moment that Thorez joined the party, Bloch wrote approvingly, his 'destiny and biography' were so closely bound up with it that 'in reality, in telling your own story, you give us seventeen years of the history of communism in France'.[176] Preliminary notes for the project had urged the continuous 'I' of a narrative as 'seen by' Maurice as well as through him.[177] As has often been pointed out, Thorez's 'I' in reality was not 'a lived "I"', and his eye was not a seeing one; everything was renounced, Stéphane Sirot notes, 'that might set him apart or single him out', and the first-person Thorez intruded only to announce some passage from a speech or article.[178]

Other biographies were conceived with the same basic object of popularising communism through the individual. It is hard to see that they used a common template to achieve this. Published the same year as *Son of the People*, Foster's *From Bryan to Stalin* was possibly its nearest counterpart as an exercise in anti-individualism. By virtue of Foster's greater age it also conveyed an even stronger sense of the communist teleology that was summed up by the volume's title. Though Foster's 'I' was also elusive, he did then attempt a volume of ostensibly more personal reminiscences, though without ever really surfacing from the collectivities he described. Foster's if nothing else was an authentic American social history, and even mainstream reviewers were generally well-disposed. Elizabeth Gurley Flynn, a prominent communist, praised him as one who lived, moved and had his being as a worker, and had 'no personal life nor ambition outside of theirs'.[179] Flynn would prove prolific in cultlike tracts, and on returning to Foster after Browder's eclipse would celebrate this identification of the individual with the collective as the antidote to notions of charisma. 'William Z. Foster has blazed the trail, forged the path, pointed out the goal and led the way', she wrote in 1949, evidently with the aid of *Roget's Thesaurus.* But all his life as a communist he had nevertheless 'fought all notions of inspirational and personal leadership attempting to substitute for it a collective leadership, which is based upon the sound theoretical foundations of Marxism-Leninism'.[180]

The Brazilian Amado located his life of Prestes within an epic tradition centred on the hero who was etched on every page, with the world about him as a backdrop. There was an echo of Barbusse in the dialectical notion of the people's son who becomes its father, and having been nurtured by the people now marches at its head and serves to constitute it precisely as a people. 'The Poet and the Hero', Amado pronounced with a characteristic flourish, 'make peoples, give them personality, dignity and life'. What was missing, whether as leitmotiv or unspoken constraint, was a party-centred teleology, or even, for the most part, any very clearly articulated role for the party. It was through the story's lustrous centrepiece of the Prestes Column that its hero took his place in a longer historical lineage which was conspicuously not a Bolshevik one.[181] Even following his embrace of communism, Prestes remains a sharply delineated individual of almost magical capacities deriving from that 'inner strength which makes leaders, saints and heroes'. The crucial years he spent in the USSR are evoked, somewhat perfunctorily, in the prophetic register of the Marx who announced that destiny 'was not written in the heavens', and of the Lenin and Stalin who came after him—just as it was Prestes whose third coming, following his exile and his martyrdom, Brazilians awaited as for the resolution of their own destiny.[182] Though Amado was a fervent communist and future recipient of the Stalin Peace Prize, there is no stock figure here that links his text with those of Foster and Thorez.

It is true that assumptions as to the unblemished party life had to some degree been codified in the biographical questionnaires which had become a central feature of Comintern cadres policy.[183] How these assumptions were reflected in narratives for public consumption had not, however, been formalised, and scope therefore existed for the refashioning and even subverting of established procedures. Harry Pollitt and Picasso are names not often juxtaposed. Both of them, nevertheless, knew enough of prevailing political conventions to know when they were disregarding them. Pollitt's autobiography *Serving My Time* was produced in the unusual circumstances of his temporary removal from the CPGB's general secretaryship during the Nazi–Soviet pact.[184] Cachin at this point was also urged by colleagues to work upon the memoirs that he had evidently already embarked upon.[185] Zetkin in later years had become habituated to such requests; Foster similarly had written his memoirs when sidelined by ill-health.[186] Pollitt's, however, seems to be the only case of an exemplary leader's life being produced in circumstances of its author's political demotion.

The CPGB, compared to the PCF, was a small party whose publications nevertheless reached far beyond the membership of the party itself. In the difficult circumstances of the pact, Pollitt's deployment as the party's most plausible public asset was of obvious political utility, but it also required some licence for Pollitt to express these qualities. Though the English translation of *Son of the People* had borne his endorsement, Pollitt disregarded the precedent that it offered. Instead, he used the opportunity for a more personalised and idiomatic narrative to express subliminally the disaffection with the Comintern's direction so evident in his contributions to the inner-party debate over the war.[187]

Stylistically, there was less trace here of socialist realism than of the popular literary models of Pollitt's youth. These included the use of bathos, self-mockery, the intrusion of incongruous detail and a sense of the ridiculous. Bathos in particular was inimical to teleology. In Pollitt's account the expected progression from lower to higher was in many respects inverted, as he depicted his own 'glorious salad days' with nostalgic fervour and confounded the 'clever people' who had fallen under the spell of phrase-mongering and who scoffed at such sentimentalism. There was also in these chapters a specificity of time, place and occupational and associational culture that conjured up a life and personality very clearly distinguishable from the collective. Significantly, the account ended with Pollitt's assumption of the party leadership in 1929. While this could therefore be presented as the culmination of his ambitions, it also meant that the book as a whole was like an extension of the apprenticeship narrative that Thorez had disposed of in his opening chapter. If Pollitt therefore disarranged the clear-cut 'before' and 'after' of the putative stalinist master-narrative, he also blurred another set of boundaries by evoking his easy social intercourse with a cast of chance acquaintances going far beyond the party or even labour movement. Notably these included an employer, a prison governor, an undercover policeman and a Conservative Party worker. The impression conveyed, of a residual fondness for Britain's liberal polity, could hardly have been so accentuated had it not been for the war against fascism, which formally speaking Pollitt now repudiated, and the brutal stalinist realpolitik with which he was now once more publicly reconciled.

There is no evaluation of the book in Pollitt's Comintern personal file. There is, however, in the files of the Marty secretariat a report on a contemporaneous article of Pollitt's which is described as like the 'call of a – shall we say – *British revolutionary movement* (which ignores the Soviet Union)'. To emphasise its disapproval 'British' is underlined three times, and Pollitt himself can hardly have intended otherwise.[188] He knew perfectly well how such texts were scrutinised; he also knew when he was 'talking bolshevik', and when he was failing to do so: just as Picasso knew quite well what sort of face he was drawing. In a Soviet context, reference is often made to the use of aesopian themes and language to give some vent to what was otherwise inexpressible. Communists beyond the reach of Stalin's censorship were also disciplined enough not to speak out what could not be spoken. Pollitt in *Serving My Time*, for example, would not have referred to the disappearance of internationalism in Soviet pronouncements as he had done within the confines of the CPGB's central committee. Nevertheless, he did not thereby forego the more serpentine forms of expression which, in London or in Paris, were so much more difficult to control than in Moscow. There was thus an inherent tension in the exploitation of a personal prestige that had meaning only because it was not reducible to the sanction of the apparatus. What Pollitt had in common with Picasso was that both were at once indispensable to their parties and at the same time irrevocably committed to them.

Stalin's rationale for the post-war revision of his IMEL biography was the enlightenment of those unable to tackle his or Lenin's political writings.[189] The object here was not so much the wider readership that Barbusse might have promised, but the integration of a well-defined cult community through a common text accessible to all. When the updated *Son of the People* was reissued in September 1949, this too was intended, not as the 'simple narrative of the life of a man', but as a veritable history manual in the 'agreeable form of autobiography'.[190] Alongside the *Short Course* history of the CPSU, it was envisaged as the 'bedside reading, guide and friend' of thousands.[191] Nevertheless, the wider promotion of the first edition now gave way to the saturation coverage of the PCF itself, and its closer integration through the diffusion, citation and collective study of this quintessential cult artefact. Sales on this occasion quickly exceeded a third of a million.[192] A further estimate impressed by both the scale and staggering precision of 148,270 copies 'signed and dedicated'.[193] Whatever the figure's accuracy, the encounters with readers which these copies represented, and those despatched unsolicited to key party workers, were crucial to the binding function which the book was meant to serve. Numerous letters in Thorez's papers express a sense of honour, indebtedness or reward at being thus distinguished, and pledge the recipients to still further efforts for a party so closely held together by reciprocal ties of loyalty.

The limitations of the text as a biography were most of all demonstrated in what *Le Monde*'s reviewer referred to as *le black-out total* regarding the war years.[194] The original text of 1937 was left relatively unscathed, mainly because specificity had already been avoided in the original edition. Newly inserted passages were devoted to Vaillant-Couturier and Rolland, both now deceased and therefore threatening neither political embarrassment nor immediate rivalry. Rolland, who had died without ever having joined the PCF, was now described as if he had, to his family's understandable dismay.[195] In the evocation of the resistance, it was again the martyr-figures like Péri and Semard who figured most, and the absence of a reproducible personal history required at this point a broadening out of the narrative to encompass that history which could not be documented through Thorez himself. Even so, the position that Thorez now occupied as a central integrating figure was not only reflected within his text, but meant the de facto proscription of any other narrative of this type. For as Pennetier and Pudal have demonstrated, even in the wake of destalinisation no similar account ever emanated from the PCF in Thorez's lifetime—unless it was the third edition of *Son of the People*.[196]

Cachin's published life was one obvious casualty. Though Cachin lived until 1958, performing a symbolic role precisely on account of what his life represented, the idea of giving this some literary form was apparently abandoned. There is an obvious contrast here with the Briton Gallacher, whose further instalments of biography were promoted to younger communists at once as textbook, history primer and model for emulation.[197] When Cachin, by contrast, received from a Paris schoolboy a similar encomium to such personal histories, it was Thorez's life which he singled out, along with Marty on Dimitrov and the socialist realist classic *How the Steel Was Tempered*.[198] Cachin's voluminous journals do not seem to indicate a diminished capacity for such an enterprise, but French readers had as yet to dispense with the veterans' and founders' lives so familiar in Britain and the USA.

Still more conspicuous by their absence were the personal histories by which the PCF might have exploited the abundant political capital of the resistance. In 1947, there did appear the party's one other published autobiography of the period, a document produced by Gabriel Péri during his final imprisonment by the Nazis in 1941.[199] Péri's really was the stuff of legend: Aragon in 'The passion of Gabriel Péri', the text now adapted as the volume's introduction, likened him to a Mediterranean prince and modern Ulysses, even physically resembling a Greek statue.[200] Péri's own account described an intellectual's trajectory through the party that was wholly distinct from Thorez's and so little centred on it that it failed to mention him. It was actually Cachin whom Péri invoked in the parting evocation of the 'tomorrows that sing' that became one of the most widely cited documents of the communist resistance. Even *Son of the People* cited it, though not of course its allusion to Cachin. Aragon also commented on how Péri in his text constantly spoke as 'I', but was nevertheless the exemplary communist and 'profound incarnation of the Party in a man'. It was an image of the resistance hero that could not help but cast a shadow over Thorez.[201]

Péri's text could not have been published any time much after 1947. His was one of the names to have featured in the 'Memorial-example' series devoted to the resistance by the communist publishers Éditeurs Français Réunis. In 1949, the series was nevertheless abandoned with only four of its 77 titles having appeared, and Jean Chaintron, whose responsibility it had been, was subsequently charged with the Stalin and Thorez birthday celebrations. It was not in fact until the year following Thorez's death that another series was launched featuring resistance testimonies.[202] Produced adventitiously and issued only posthumously, Péri's was in fact the only competing autobiographical narrative to appear under communist auspices in the three decades of Thorez's party leadership. The thorézian cult of the individual had thus come to represent, not the harnessing of the PCF's biographical capital, but its control, curtailment and even obliteration in favour of the bureaucratic scale of values whose real personification the cult of the leader provided.[203]

Biography, more typically than autobiography, was in this sense one of the characteristic monuments of the Cold War cult system. Examples from eastern Europe included those of Pieck, Gheorghiu-Dej, Bierut and Rákosi as well as Tito, and Balázs Apor describes how the construction of an 'impersonal persona' was common to nearly all of them.[204] But if by this time it was in the nature of the cult phenomenon that major biographical productions were focused on the party leader, a continuity with the 1930s across the communist world was the relative profusion of a school of historical biography. For given the centrality to marxism of a narrative of social transformation spanning the centuries, there could be no cult of the individual in the present without the cult of the individual in history.

6.3 The Cult of the Individual in History

(i)

Whatever Stalin's motives in agreeing the interview with Ludwig, it was the chance for him to clarify his understanding of the claims on history that he now appeared to be assuming for himself. Ludwig's métier was the advertisement of the moving force of personality, and his *Genius and Character* had been dedicated to Thomas Carlyle, the nineteenth-century writer almost synonymous with this conception of the heroic. As Ludwig now reminded Stalin, it was with the outright denial of any such belief that marxism was associated in the public mind. As first Lenin, then Stalin, was lifted high above the masses, it is not therefore surprising that this was sometimes discussed as if an anomaly requiring explanation, and the exorcising of the spectre of Carlyle himself.[205] Stalin, however, held that it was not marxism but only its vulgarisation that discountenanced the role of the outstanding personality. Historical greatness, according to this conception, lay in the individual's ability to understand and act upon conditions which were not fundamentally of their own making. The genuine hero, in other words, was not the maker of history, but its finest product.[206]

The obvious authority for such a position was the 'father' of Russian marxism Georgi Plekhanov, a figure at this time held politically and intellectually in public scorn. Nevertheless, by the time these principles were reaffirmed in the *Short Course* history in 1938, Plekhanov's influence was once more openly acknowledged, and his *Role of the Individual in History* (1898) was reissued and translated.[207] Essentially, this offered a personalisation of the base-superstructure metaphor in which leading individuals influenced the course of events, but 'in the last analysis'—Engels's famous formula—these were still determined by social forces and relations of production.[208] As the *Short Course* put it, any refusal of this logic spelt ignominious failure, and the only heroes that mattered were those who met the challenge of their time and correctly expressed the needs of its foremost class.[209]

Elaborating on this theme, Fréville would describe how every epoch had found its realisation in a particular social type, from the crusader and conquistador of such dubious repute to the modern entrepreneur like Ferdinand de Lesseps.[210] The 'communist man' was thus the pre-eminent social type of the twentieth century in whom the incarnation of the collective in the individual was in two respects raised to a higher level than previously conceivable. In Stalin's much cited words, such figures were first of all rooted in the masses, who in this mediated way were thus confirmed as 'the genuine makers of history'. At the same time, these figures demonstrated that mastery of the science of society which marxism–leninism represented, and through which alone the agency of the masses could be effectively realised. 'The strength of an outstanding individual', a new gloss on Plekhanov summarised, 'lies in his contact with a class, with the masses, with the people … in his ability to organise the masses, in his ability to foresee the course of historical progress'.[211] Fréville's authority for his 'new social type, the communist' was Lenin's *What Is To Be Done?*, and the casting of the individual in this role was like a projection and corollary of the leading role of party with which it was, for the most part, inextricably conflated.[212]

As Stalin was arbiter of what both masses and marxism truly stood for, there was of course an obvious circularity to these arguments. There was also a parallel with right-wing dictators like Hitler, whom supporters like

Carl Schmitt also described as incarnating some larger collective, albeit one conceived of in national and racial terms.[213] It is not surprising that those subjected to these cults did sometimes see similarities in the practices of veneration to which these claims of symbiosis gave rise.[214] Criticism of the fascist cults could therefore pose some awkward questions regarding that of Stalin himself, as clearly they were intended to in the Webbs' *Soviet Communism*.[215] Jean-Richard Bloch would even express his concern at the 'treacherous ambiguity' of Elmer Rice's play about the Leipzig trial because it did not clarify sufficiently the political character of the tyrant at its centre.[216] Communists, even so, refused the premise of totalitarian theorists of a 'deep parallelism' between Bolshevik and Nazi conceptions of leadership, and with it too the ideal of the 'superman-leader' that was supposed to unite them with their enemies.[217]

That communists turned more or less simultaneously to anti-fascism and to the leader cult was thus not only paradoxical in itself but helps explain the tentativeness of the cult's adoption internationally. Adulation of Stalin in such compromising forms was clearly not driven by this anti-fascist agenda, and the warmest of sympathisers saw in it something ill-adapted to western sensibilities and requiring explanation or extenuation.[218] Feuchtwanger, describing it openly as a 'cult' of Stalin-worship, did so with that note of revulsion that allowed Stalin, as we have seen, to convey to a western audience his own supposed lack of responsibility for such practices.[219] Western communists might themselves attribute the appearance of adulation in the USSR to differences of culture or linguistic idiom.[220] They did not therefore admit of the 'frenzied' and 'absolute' obedience which in Italy was a matter for self-congratulation.[221] Indeed, obedience, as opposed to discipline, was almost never invoked except in a pejorative sense; for whereas obedience implied the individual's subjection to another's will, discipline was the common bond through which the individual and collective were reconciled.[222] 'Our opposition to the totalitarian state or to the "Fuehrer princip"', wrote the British scientist J.D. Bernal, 'is not only that it is a diminution of human capacity merely to obey orders, but ... because a population that merely obeys orders puts demands on those that have to give the orders which no actual or conceivable human being could adequately fulfil'. Few were less stinting in their praise for Stalin than Bernal. Bernal, however, also evoked Lenin's precept that every cook must learn to rule the state, and even in extolling Stalin described his achievement as one in which not his orders but his thought and example were embodied.[223]

Gorky at the 1934 writers' congress had thus distinguished sharply between the communist conception of leadership and the 'leaderism' (*vozhdizm*) which under capitalism produced such 'festering sores' as Hitler and the social democrat Ebert.[224] The same distinction was developed in Pierre Merin's disquisition on the 'two categories of leader' as a contribution to the Thälmann campaign. Merin was the pseudonym of the Yugoslavian communist Oto Bihalji-Merin, who had been active in KPD cultural organs and subsequently helped initiate the short-lived Institute for the Study of Fascism in Paris.[225] Citing as usual Stalin's interview with Ludwig, he described how the idea of the leader was at once discredited by fascism and vindicated by the example of the resistance it engendered. Charisma, in this instance, was a dividing line, for Merin insisted that there was nothing of the charismatic summons attaching to the proletarian leaders chosen by virtue of their class sense and as the 'most visible expression of the collectivity of the class'.[226] Merin's examples were of the oppositional 'Comintern people' type, including Gramsci, Rákosi, Tim Buck and even the New Zealander Griffin. Nevertheless, a similar rationale could also be used in relation to Stalin's rule in the USSR, as it was for example by Merin's British contemporary John Strachey.[227] Reviewing *Son of the People*, Paul Nizan observed as usual that its real hero was Thorez's party, and contrasted this with the Belgian neo-socialist Hendrik de Man, whose *Masses and Leaders* (Masses et Chefs) did certainly betray a susceptibility to *vozhdizm*.[228] Fifteen years later, Waldeck Rochet made similar points regarding the 'barbaric' idea of the leader cult he now associated with de Gaulle.[229]

It is difficult in these statements to see the stalinism that 'privileged the individual rather than the collective as the defining basic entity of human behavior'.[230] Communism is certainly identified with the flourishing of the individual, but through the overcoming of that opposition between individual and collective that capitalism was held to have taken to new extremes. This at least was true of Bernal. Just as he invoked the paradoxical freedom of necessity, he also wrote of how socialism offered greater scope for individuality than any previous society while at the same time requiring the strenuous employment of the individual's gifts for the public good, and in a spirit that was free of independence on the one hand and of self-abasement on the other.[231]

Gorky was frequently the authority for such views, and few contributed more to the new conception of the hero than he did through projects like *The Lives of Remarkable People*.[232] It was certainly to Gorky more than anyone that was due the Nietzschean accent so evident in the heroic discourse of the Stalin years. Writing in 1908, Gorky had identified the power of the individual with times of social stress in which this became the 'focal point of thousands of wills which have selected it for their instrument'. Illuminated by the desires of people, class or party, it did not matter who the individual was: 'what matters is that all these heroes appear ... as carriers of collective energy or mouthpieces of mass desires'.[233] The text was anthologised in the Stalin years, and Bernal was among those who cited it, mistakenly believing it a product of Gorky's Soviet commitments.[234] Its echoes did certainly remain in Gorky's address to the 1934 Writers' Congress and the claim that the 'socialist individuality' of the USSR's new heroes was conceivable only in conditions of collective labour. At the same congress, not only Gorky but Radek and Bukharin distinguished this individuality from the 'effete, impotent and impoverished individualism' of the old order and rejected any attempt to confuse the enrichment of personality with 'that which one divides one man from another'.[235]

The ideal expressed in these contributions was expressly anti-individualistic, as Bukharin put it, and yet not only consistent with the flourishing of the individual but alone consistent with it. Freedom was the recognition of necessity, and individuality the recognition of wider social forces, thus empowering the individual to the point of potential greatness. Whether in the frictionless relations of the new society, or in the struggle to attain them, communism was itself an ideal that ennobled those who worked to achieve it. According to Radek, the USSR was already producing 'millions of new individualities', and hundreds of thousands deserving the attentions of a Michelangelo.[236] Browder in extolling Stalin drew the contrast with a capitalist society that elevated the individual over the masses but was incapable of producing any great individual except through the struggle for its overthrow.[237] Vaillant-Couturier in France evoked the particular plight of the cultural worker, trapped in a termites' nest that stifled the human spirit and recognised only the 'shameful driving force' of material gain. Denouncing the values of a commercial society, Vaillant-Couturier rejected the association of communism with egalitarianism, but at the same time extolled an extended conception of the heroic in the figures of the 'hero-scholar, hero-mechanic, hero-engineer, hero-peasant, hero-poet, heroine-mother'. Reprinted after the war, the passage bore the sub-heading: 'For the convocation of the States General of the French intellect'.[238]

Published as a cultural manifesto for the popular front, Vaillant-Couturier's address evoked this convocation of the mind and spirit not only in the present but as inheritance from the past. Communists, he insisted, did not polemicise against history, but recognised the creative spirit wherever it was to be found, not only in the revolutionary Robespierre but in Napoleon.[239] There is an extensive literature on this development in Stalin's Russia, with the accent more on Napoleon's counterparts than on Robespierre's.[240] Indeed, Napoleon himself figured through the biography of the rehabilitated academician Eugene Tarlé, and the turn to the history of great men was colloquially ascribed to Stalin having discovered that his son did not know who Cromwell was.[241] The result in any case was a concerted campaign against the once dominant 'Pokrovsky school' of historiography, which certainly had polemicised against figures like Peter the Great. When Peter's biographer B.F. Kafengauz assailed the now defenceless Pokrovsky, it was the interview with Ludwig which as usual he cited to validate the importance that was now attached to such figures.[242]

The Bolsheviks apart, there were no communists in the party sense before 1917. In every case, laying claim to such figures therefore represented an act of appropriation or at least of active contestation. In representing the issues of contemporary politics as two distinct and opposing world-views, Merin had simply set one figure, Thälmann, against another, Hitler. However, when the following year he wrote on the English socialist forbear Thomas More, it was with the rather different object of retrieving the humanist vision of More's *Utopia* from the clutches of the Catholic church which had lately canonised him.[243] It was in this spirit that the Bolsheviks had earlier inscribed More's name upon their Moscow obelisk, along with diverse rebel spirits across the ages.[244] Their inclusion of Jean Jaurès, wrote a critic, was like a second assassination—just the expression the communists would use to characterise Jaurès' incorporation into the bourgeois republic's Valhalla of the Panthéon.[245] These were the contested legacies that may be regarded as appropriation cults.

In respect of a figure like Peter the Great, Nicholas Riasanovsky referred to the Bolsheviks' 'bipolar' attitude in celebrating their historically progressive character while locating them within oppressive and now superseded systems of class rule.[246] Though not usually in such extreme forms, there was always a degree of ambivalence regarding figures caught within the limitations of their own times while anticipating those to come. Coinciding with the cult of the present-day hero, the retrieval of such figures was by the late 1930s one of the characteristic features of communist politics. Following his return from the USSR, Friedmann in 1937 launched the 'Socialism and culture' series for the principal PCF publishers. Bouju describes it as an elitist version of the earlier 'Revolutionary episodes and lives' series, but it was also more wide-ranging both politically and chronologically.[247] Already Vaillant-Couturier, along with Aragon, had taken the lead in marking Victor Hugo's half-centenary, just as communists across the Channel laid claim to figures like Bunyan and Dickens.[248] The naming of the International Brigades was an obvious case in point; for whereas the Red Army units of the Russian civil war had been known by their numbers, the units of the Spanish volunteers provided a veritable roll-call of cultural and political heroes including Garibaldi, Lincoln, Adam Mickiewicz, Louise Michel and George Washington.

The giants of tsarism meant nothing to communists beyond the USSR. None but a French communist could have thought of commemorating Joan of Arc. There was therefore a twofold distinction between the appropriation of conservative national heroes and the recovery of those, including the luminaries of the ascendant bourgeoisie, who were identified with the challenge to established political and intellectual orthodoxies. Not only were these rebels of their time credibly presented as the forerunners of a modern radical politics. Despite the strong claims made upon distinct national histories, there was also a more than residual sense of an international inheritance going beyond particular projects of state-building. Already in Lenin's 'plan for monumental propaganda', there was at first a division between exclusively Russian cultural figures and the international cast of 'revolutionaries and social activists'.[249] On the other hand, the 'Socialism and culture' series had titles on Cervantes, Darwin and Heine as well as socialism's various forerunners in France. Even the Russified internationalism of the Cold War allowed space for the commemoration of figures like Leonardo and Victor Hugo on the initiative of the stalinist World Peace Committee. Though in France, there was a strongly national slant to the PCF's claim to Hugo, it was actually the Chinese writer and culture minister Mao Dun who had proposed Hugo's commemorations internationally.[250]

(ii)

The Pushkin centenary in 1937 was the first such commemoration on a grand scale, and within the 'national bolshevism' of the USSR it may perhaps be said to have prevailed over Marx.[251] Nevertheless, at both a national and an international level it was the claim to a contested socialist inheritance which mattered most to communism's political identity. Marx's was the earliest but also the pre-eminent appropriation cult, and as the founder of the Giants' immortal lineage he was, moreover, the one such figure who was not trapped within the limitations of his own times.

The claim to Marx was the claim to represent the authentic traditions of the workers' International which social democracy had betrayed in 1914. That was why Marx's statues were the first to proliferate after the revolution. That was also why Riazanov and the Marx-Engels Institute had the resources to acquire the research holdings which were then the focus of the enormous enterprise of dissemination that Riazanov himself had earlier pursued within the ranks of German social democracy.[252] Despite a falling off of activity following Riazanov's arrest in 1931, the 50th anniversary of Marx's death in 1933 saw a massive commemoration conducted in a spirit of fratricidal warfare. 'Marx belongs to us', was the principal slogan; as applied to different cases, as we shall discover, it would become the defining formula of the appropriation cult. 'Although the Parties of the Second International have distorted and openly betrayed Marxism for years, still they refuse to relinquish Marx, and exploit the reverence of the working masses for [his] name', ran one contribution which typified the tenor of the campaign. It would, as a result, have a wholly communist character, and be informed throughout by 'relentless exposure of the Second International, and of every description of pseudo-Marxism'.[253]

The role of Marx's collaborator Engels was initially more ambiguous. Outliving Marx by more than a decade, Engels remained a strong supporter of the Second International until his death in 1895. His seeming qualification of key tenets of historical materialism in his final years was seized upon by revisionists like Bernstein, and could consequently bring Engels himself under suspicion of degeneration.[254] The alternatives in respect of these contested figures were appropriation, repudiation or effacement. In Engels' case, there was never any chance that the communists would by some form of relinquishment have left marxism's co-founder to be exploited by their opponents. Not only did Engels have an international stature setting him apart from national founding figures like Plekhanov or Jules Guesde. He also provided the crucial chronological link between the death of Marx and Lenin's emergence in the mid-1890s. Fox in his Lenin biography even speculated hopefully on Lenin's having visited Engels in his London home. It was therefore the reformists who were accused of doctoring Engels' final writings and seeking to set off one great revolutionary against the other. It was Manuilsky who on the 40th anniversary of Engels' death gave authoritative expression to the crucial point about continuity. As delegates gathered in Moscow for the Comintern's seventh world congress, he thus saluted Engels as one of the 'two great geniuses' who prefigured Lenin and Stalin and thus confirmed the principle of uninterrupted succession by which the necessary and symbiotic relationship between movement and leader was continuously maintained.[255]

The challenge of this narrative was simultaneously to affirm immortality and delimit it with temporality lest it appear that Marx's successors had nothing left to do but follow in his footsteps. Stalin was clearly exercised by this dilemma, and Riazanov's purging in 1931 has been attributed in part to his implicit depreciation of Lenin's theoretical achievements through preoccupation with Marx's.[256] Three years later Stalin took issue with the editors of *Bol'shevik* for equating the views of Engels and Lenin in just such a way as detracted from the latter's originality. On the one hand, Stalin held that the papering over Engels's mistakes meant marxism's mummification and the obscuring of Lenin's role in developing it further. On the other hand, Engels remained the Bolsheviks' teacher, and Stalin was also dissatisfied when what followed was a heavy-handed attempt to cut him down to size.[257] The validation of greatness and even genius had therefore to be accommodated within a narrative of progression now culminating in Stalin himself.

More delicate still was the issue of those of Lenin's contemporaries who in some way or other had become separated from him. Plekhanov was one, and for just that reason there was nothing remotely resembling a Plekhanov cult. Far more significant, as the third outstanding figure in the German revolutionary tradition, was Rosa Luxemburg.[258] Holding the social democrats responsible for Luxemburg's death through the unleashing of the murderous Freikorps, the communists through their annual Luxemburg-Liebknecht campaign reaffirmed a strident anti-reformism and the binary political world-view characteristic of German communism.[259] Though in one sense Luxemburg was thus the KPD's founding figure, to whom increasingly social democrats renounced all claim, she was also the first of the dissident communists who shortly before her death had expressed with great lucidity her concerns regarding bolshevism's basic ethos and cult of organisation.[260] Beginning with the KPD expellee Paul Levi, who in 1922 published the most compelling of these assessments of the Russian revolution, Luxemburg thus provided a crucial reference point for critics of the apparatus and one of equal stature to Lenin himself. Critically, this therefore posed the issue of whether Luxemburg's legacy should be accommodated within the bolshevising Comintern or repudiated by it.

It was Lenin who set the pattern in saluting Luxemburg as an eagle whose memory communists cherished in spite of her mistakes. As well as the January '3 Ls' campaign, this was reflected in the project of Luxemburg's collected works agreed at the Comintern's third world congress. Amongst other things, this served to conciliate Levi's sometime ally Clara Zetkin while exacting from her the now obligatory disavowal of Luxemburg's shortcomings.[261] As the KPD during the 1920s swung between left and right, a precarious balance was maintained between the honouring of Luxemburg the revolutionary and the repudiation of her errors in the form of 'Luxemburgism'. The object of the *Works* was thus, on the one hand, to counter the claims to Luxemburg of heterodox elements like Levi, while at the same helping to prise social-democratic workers from the grip of reformism.[262]

The project of the *Works* was nevertheless one of the casualties of Stalin's tightening ideological orthodoxy. When in his 1931 letter to *Proletarskaya Revolyutsiya* he inveighed against suggestions of a flaw in Leninism, the pretext if not the cause was the willingness of some in certain crucial aspects to vindicate Luxemburg against Lenin. Momentarily, Luxemburgism appeared, if not exactly equivalent to Trotskyism, at least as the masked form which Trotskyism now assumed.[263] As one British communist observed, the disciplinary intent was all the more blatant in a country like Britain in which so few communists could even read the writings in which alleged transgressions were supposed to be found.[264] Like Engels, Luxemburg was nevertheless too valuable an asset, or one too potent in the hands of rivals, to be finally relinquished. It was Thälmann who thus restored a sort of equilibrium with the claim that Luxemburg and those around her, even despite their errors, 'belong to us'. The formula entered into wider usage, and would later provide the GDR with one of its legitimising myths. Luxemburg and Liebknecht, as the '3 Ls' campaign restated in 1933, 'belong entirely to the Comintern, which reveals their mistakes, but regards and will regard them as its own and will not surrender them to anyone'.[265]

The Clydeside socialist John Maclean offers a variation on the Luxemburg theme within a purely national context. Though of no comparable stature internationally, Maclean according to Gallacher was Britain's foremost revolutionary and yet until his death in 1923 had been adamant in his condemnation of the CPGB and its Moscow connections.[266] Where Levi in Germany had access to crucial Luxemburg manuscripts, and Paul Frölich passed from editor of her works to Luxemburgian dissenter, Maclean's political legacy was entrusted by his widow to the MP Jimmy Maxton, whose Independent Labour Party occupied a somewhat analogous position on the British left. For as long as Maxton's planned biography showed no sign of materialising, the CPGB did nothing to supply the deficiency and Maclean sank into 'near-oblivion'.[267] In 1936, however, following Gallacher's tendentious portrayal of Maclean's final years in *Revolt on the Clyde*, the Maxton commission was taken on by the poet Hugh MacDiarmid. MacDiarmid was a fervent nationalist as well as a communist; and where Luxemburgism had been a matter of democracy, 'spontaneity' and the role of the party, what Maclean most signified for MacDiarmid was the 'Scottish workers' republicanism' he set against the CPGB's false internationalism.[268] The party, he wrote, had 'the wind up – and with cause' about his biography, and the claims he made to Maclean were central to MacDiarmid's expulsion from the CPGB as protractedly carried through in 1936–1938.[269]

As MacDiarmid following his expulsion continued to promote Maclean's 'Red Scotland' line, the CPGB in effect sought to separate Maclean from Macleanism.[270] An eagle in spite of mistakes was just how Maclean appeared in *Revolt on the Clyde*, and eight years later this prompted one of the earliest substantial British communist biographies, by Tom Bell. Despite his 'limited national outlook' and refusal of the necessary collective agency of the party, Maclean was there laid claim to as one of communism's 'great family'—precisely as one who belongs to us.[271] Though neither Levi nor Frölich were ever reconciled to stalinism, MacDiarmid's own predilection for a communist politics of personality was afterwards turned to party advantage, not only through his Maclean commemorations, but through the reprinting of his *Hymns to Lenin* and the cult poem he now inscribed to Gallacher himself.[272]

In France, the PCF had swung between denouncing the influence of a figure like Jaurès and seizing him back from those who traduced his memory—as in the counter-demonstration on the transfer of Jaurès's ashes to the Panthéon in 1924.[273] With the turn to the popular front, it was nevertheless Jaurès's bust which adorned the platform at the PCF's 1936 Villeurbanne congress, and which henceforth remained more or less continuously on its pedestal.[274] Flanking Jaurès at Villeurbanne was France's pioneering marxist Guesde, who had sometimes been presented as himself beyond political redemption.[275] Nevertheless, the handling of Luxemburg once more set the pattern, for Guesde even with his failings could not simply be ceded to the socialists. 'He belongs to the revolutionary proletariat and to its vanguard, the communist party.'[276] Following the war, the names and anniversaries of Jaurès and Guesde were linked in a spirit of retrospective solidarity that could either be shared fraternally with other claimants on the left or else provide the measure of their betrayals.[277] One distinctive strand in France was the commemoration of the insurrectionary socialist Auguste Blanqui and its linking with the anniversary of the Paris Commune. Characteristically, it was Marty who was associated with this initiative, and 'neo-Blanquism' was to figure among the charges later brought against him.[278]

An important element in the cult of the party veteran was the sense of upholding a direct line of succession from such figures. Pieck was esteemed in Germany as the last of the Spartacists. Mann would invoke his association with Labour pioneer KeirHardie.[279] Cachin was linked with Guesde, and to a much lesser extent Jaurès, as symbol at once of continuity and advance.[280] It was only over time that the narrative came to culminate in the present-day party leader. When Vaillant-Couturier saluted the French revolution's 'Friend of the people' Jean-Paul Marat, it was the party itself, not its leader, which he described as continuing this role in modern times.[281] When Gallacher countered those who held that Spain most needed a Lenin, it was again 'Lenin's party', not Stalin or any other individual, that he presented as the continuator of Lenin's legacy.[282] The 1936 'March of English History' was performed as a poster parade of great personalities, including Mann, but whose principal legatee once again was the collective Lenin of the party. Pollitt's profile had not yet been borne among them. 'It was of great interest to me', he had written the previous year, 'to learn that my photograph was being carried in a procession alongside that of Comrade Katayama, but it is my devout wish that this happy combination does not indicate that I am shortly to join Katayama as I prefer to walk about on two legs, and not in the form of In Memoriam placards'.[283]

Even in Britain, where these instincts seem generally to have prevailed, the elevation of the leader's image in this literal sense is occasionally documented in old photographs. Though Stalin or Dimitrov were more likely to be depicted in this way, when the CPGB in 1939 staged the historical pageant *Heirs to the Charter* the climax was now provided by Pollitt himself appearing on stage as the living personification of history's onward march.[284] Browder in the USA had called ambiguously 'for a Lincoln, for a new party, for a new programme', as if once more the party itself were that collective Lincoln. Nevertheless, it was Browder now who personified it, and whose image began to be juxtaposed with Lincoln's own.[285] Lincoln was also among the litany of New World heroes cited in Neruda's poem *Hard Elegy*, and Prestes, who was the poem's centrepiece, was described by Amado as the Bolívar of the new American independence.[286] By 1951, a Paris exhibition and published brochure linked the annual commemoration of the Commune with Thorez's 51st birthday. It was as if these were analogous events, and Thorez now the 'living connection' between this genuine epic of the proletariat and his own work as party secretary. The link between the cult of the centralised party and the cult of its leader was never perhaps more clearly attested. What the Communards were held to have lacked, despite their heroism, was a party uniting revolutionary will and understanding. This was the party that Thorez had forged; 'here is what Maurice Thorez has given to the French people'.[287]

What was here called the 'merging' of party and leader was by this time a familiar idea. If the balance tilted in Stalin's final years, it was in this notion of the leader, not only as the party's instrument or embodiment, but as its benefactor, creator and animating force. In 1945, the PCF reprinted from *Bol'shevik* a further exposition of the Plekhanov theme in the light of Stalin's contribution to the defeat of fascism. Carlyle was there among the usual reference points, and it was argued now that he had not so much exaggerated the role of the hero as underestimated that of the masses in the making of the hero. Stalin's genius was thus once more located within a wider heroic discourse, and with the achievement of a hitherto unattainable measure of individual greatness precisely because of the growth in the historical role of the masses. At the same time, the faculty of 'scientific prevision' with which marxism empowered the individual was now still further accentuated. History's final destination could never be in doubt. Nevertheless, the experience of entire generations depended on this personal factor; in particular, it had not been predetermined that the Russian revolution should have found those leaders who were indispensable as the condition of its success.[288] Trotsky had said precisely this of Lenin, and in this sense the entire epoch of socialist construction was conditional upon the agency of the individual.[289] But what at one stage might have appeared as the exercising of leadership at some decisive historical turning point had in Stalin's time become installed as a system of personal power whose only limitation is that it was a system.

The paradox, if such it was, was not unique to stalinism. Fréville once described how something deep within Thorez responded to the 'tranquil majesty' of the seventeenth-century theologian Bossuet. Though the analogy Fréville intended was with Bossuet's limpid prose, it is intriguing that he should have come across Thorez reciting France's most illustrious expositor of the divine basis of royal authority.[290] Historians both of communism and of absolutism have from time to time noted the parallels between these periods, and by the time of Stalin's 70th birthday the tributes of his retainers did certainly resonate with the echoes of earlier conceptions. 'Paternal concern' for the people, who were sometimes 'his' people, was thus matched by Stalin's role as inspirer and creator of their achievements, through the 'Stalin policy of industrialisation', the 'Stalin Five-Year Plans', his 'stalinist' foreign policy or even stalinist military science. Socialism's distinctiveness as a social system, according to the arch-sycophant Beria, was that it required consciously bringing into being, and it was on this account that Stalin ranked among the greatest geniuses of mankind.[291] Nevertheless, historians of absolutism also remind us of the monarch's dependence upon the conception of sovereignty from which royal authority derived, and of the conundrum of 'King-State' which was also the 'State-King' and a form of symbiosis as constraint.[292] There are certainly resemblances here with the communist party leader who might claim to have 'forged' the party they surmounted, but who still counted for nothing without it.

There is one further possible parallel in the scope of the cult community. It was in the nature of the enkindling-type cults that these were themselves susceptible to appropriation by political rivals. This was certainly the case with Lenin, whose 'canonisation' by non-communists Dutt deplored.[293] Dimitrov earned the attention of bourgeois publishers; there were for a period suggestions even of Stalin as a sort of appropriation figure, initially surfacing in the 1930s and revived on a wider scale during the popular period of the Soviet war effort. In Europe at least, that feeling had been dissipated among all except the communists' closest associates by the time of Stalin's death. Instead, one is reminded of the 800 pamphlets in Dutch libraries attacking the Sun King whom Bossuet had glorified.[294] Stalin's, unlike that of Louis Quatorze, was a truly international cult. But it was just as much the focus of a bounded cult community, only one defined by party and ideology rather than state alone.

In the valedictory panegyric cited at the beginning of this book, Palme Dutt recorded how Stalin's death was mourned almost universally, 'with the exception of a tiny handful of evil maniacs'.[295] No delusion could have better conveyed the occult nature of the claims on which the Cold War integration cult depended. Less than three years were to pass, and with the Khrushchev speech that denounced him the ranks of evil maniacs would extend to Stalin's successors. The result was a crisis for the communist parties considered in this book, and one from which in many ways they would never recover.

Notes

1. Joseph Stalin, *An interview with the German author Emil Ludwig* (Moscow: Co-operative Publishing House of Foreign Workers in the USSR, 1932); Eugene Lyons, *Assignment in Utopia* (London: Harrap, 1938), p. 384.
2. Olga Velikanova, *Making of an Idol. On uses of Lenin* (Göttingen: Muster-Schmidt Verlag, 1996), pp. 39–40, 150.
3. Jan Plamper, *The Stalin Cult. A study in the alchemies of power* (New Haven, CT: Yale University Press, 2012), p. xv; Chang-tai Hung, *Mao's New World. Political culture in the early People's Republic* (Ithaca, NY & London: Cornell University Press, 2011), pp. 5–6, 13.
4. Katerina Clark, *Moscow, the Fourth Rome. Stalinism, cosmopolitanism, and the evolution of Soviet culture, 1931–1941* (Cambridge, MA: Harvard University Press, 2011), ch. 2; Jochen Hellbeck, *Revolution On My Mind. Writing a diary under Stalin* (Cambridge, MA: Harvard University Press, 2009 edn), pp. 19–20.
5. Dieter Langewiesche cited Bert Hogenkamp, *Deadly Parallels. Film and the left in Britain 1929–1939* (London: Lawrence & Wishart, 1986), p. 65.
6. Ivo Banac (ed.), *The Diary of Georgi Dimitrov 1933–1949* (New Haven, CT: Yale University Press, 2003), p. 196, entry for 9 Oct. 1941.
7. Jeffrey Brooks, *Thank You, Comrade Stalin! Soviet public culture from revolution to Cold War* (Princeton, NJ: Princeton University Press, 2000), p. xviii.
8. Richard Taylor, 'Ideology as mass entertainment: Boris Shumyatsky and Soviet cinema in the 1930s' in Richard Taylor and Ian Christie (eds), *Inside the Film Factory: new approaches to Russian and Soviet cinema* (London: Routledge, 1991), pp. 193–216.
9. Karl Schlögel, *Moscow, 1937* (Cambridge: Polity, 2012), ch. 14.
10. Victoria E. Bonnell, *Iconography of Power. Soviet political posters under Lenin and Stalin* (Berkeley, CA: University of California Press, 1993), p. 158.
11. Jan Plamper, 'Georgian Koba or Soviet "Father of Peoples"? The Stalin cult and ethnicity' in Balázs Apor et al. (eds), *The Leader Cult in Communist Dictatorships. Stalin and the Eastern bloc* (Basingstoke: Palgrave Macmillan, 2004), pp. 125–6.
12. Hogenkamp, *Deadly Parallels*, p. 59.

13. Pascal Ory, 'De "Ciné-Liberté" à "La Marseillaise", hopes and limitations of a liberated cinema (1936–1938)' in Ginette Vincendeau and Keith Reader (eds), *La Vie est à nous* (London: BFI, 1986), pp. 5–36.
14. Leo T. Hurwitz, 'The revolutionary film – next step' (May 1934) in Lewis Jacobs (ed.), *The Documentary Tradition. From Nanook to Woodstock* (New York: Hopkinson & Blake, 1971), pp. 91–3.
15. Rashit Yangorov, '*Onwards and Upwards!*: the origins of the Lenin cult in Soviet cinema' in Richard Taylor and Derek Spring (eds), *Stalinism and Soviet Cinema* (London: Routledge, 1993), pp. 23–7.
16. Graham Roberts, *Forward Soviet! History and non-fiction film in the USSR* (London: Tauris, 1999), pp. 17–18, 21, 37–9; Jeremy Hicks, *Dziga Vertov. Defining documentary film* (London: Tauris, 2007), pp. 11–12.
17. Jamie Miller, 'Soviet politics and the Mezhrabpom studio in the Soviet Union during the 1920s and 1930s', *Historical Journal of Film, Radio and Television*, 32 (2012), 521–35.
18. Hicks, *Dziga Vertov*, p. 126.
19. Herbert Marshall, *Masters of the Soviet Cinema. Crippled creative biographies* (London: Routledge& Kegan Paul, 1983), p. 91.
20. *New York Herald Tribune* cited Hicks, *Dziga Vertov*, p. 127; Moussinac, 'Trois chansons de Lénine', *Monde*, 24 Aug. 1934.
21. Banac, *Diary of Georgi Dimitrov*, p. 6, entry for 5 Feb. 1934
22. Russell Campbell, *Cinema Strikes Back. Radical Filmmaking in the United States, 1930–1942* (Ann Arbor, MI: UMI University Press, 1982), pp. 84–5.
23. Gilbert Badia, 'Le comité Thaelmann' in Badia et al, *Les bannis de Hitler. Accueil et lutte des exil és allemands en France 1933–1939* (Paris: Études et Documentation Internationales, 1984), pp. 230–3; see also Chap. 5.1 above.
24. Ory, 'De "Ciné-Liberté"', pp. 14–15; Hicks, *Dziga Vertov*, p. 117.
25. Hicks, *Dziga Vertov*, p. 102; Roberts, *Forward Soviet!*, pp. 23–5.
26. Shumyatsky, 'Fifteen years of Soviet cinema' in A. Arossev (ed.), *Soviet Cinema* (Moscow: VOKS, 1935), pp. 28–9.
27. RGASPI 558/11/700, Mezhrabpom-Film to Poskrebyshev, 21 Apr. 1935.
28. Rolf Hellebust, 'Reflections on an absence: novelistic portraits of Stalin before 1953' in Nina Kolesnikoff and Walter Smyrniw (eds), *Socialist Realism Revisited. Selected papers from the McMaster conference* (Hamilton, Ontario: McMaster University, 1994), pp. 111–20.

29. Richard S. Wortman, *Scenarios of Power: myth and ceremony in Russian monarchy. Volume two: from Alexander II to the abdication of Nicholas II* (Princeton, NJ: Princeton University Press, 2000), pp. 486–7.
30. RGASPI 558/11/700, Barbusse draft screenplay, 1935.
31. Barbusse papers, Kurella to Barbusse, 8 Mar. 1935.
32. See Chap. 5.1 above.
33. Shumyatsky, 'Barbusse and cinema', *Pravda*, 2 Sept. 1935.
34. Judith Devlin, '"Recreating history on film". Stalin and the Russian revolution in feature film, 1937–1939', *Media History*, 13 (2007), 153.
35. Laurence Senelick and Sergei Ostrovsky (eds), *The Soviet Theater. A documentary history* (New Haven, CT: Yale University Press, 2014), pp. 493–4; Hellebust, 'Reflections'.
36. Jay Leyda, *Kino. A history of the Russian and the Soviet film* (London: Allen and Unwin, 1960), pp. 352, 362.
37. As memorably noted by André Bazin, 'The myth of Stalin in the Soviet cinema' (1950) in idem, *Bazin at Work. Major essays and reviews from the forties and fifties* (New York: Routledge, 1997), pp. 23–40.
38. Senelick and Ostrovsky, *Soviet Theater*, pp. 381–2.
39. See Chap. 2 above.
40. James Hay, *Popular Film Culture in Fascist Italy. The passing of the Rex* (Bloomington, IN: Indiana University Press, 1987), pp. 222–33; Stephen Gundle, *Mussolini's Dream Factory. Film stardom in fascist Italy* (New York: Bergahn, 2013), pp. 35–7; David Welch, *Propaganda and the German Cinema 1933–1945* (Oxford: Oxford University Press, 1983), pp. 146–7. The one comparable case I am aware of is *Battle of Sutjeska* (1973), the Yugoslav cult film starring Richard Burton as Tito.
41. Devlin, '"Recreating history"', pp. 150, 152.
42. Marty, 'Comment ils ont conquis le bonheur', *CdC*, Dec. 1949, 1466–7.
43. For these films, see Russel Lemmons, *Hitler's Rival. Ernst Thälmann in Myth and Memory* (Lexington, KY: University of Kentucky Press, 2013), ch. 4.
44. Balázs Apor, *The 'Invisible Shining': the cult of Mátyás Rákosi in stalinist Hungary, 1945–1956* (Budapest: Central European University Press, forthcoming 2017), ch. 4.
45. Accessed at http://cinemadipropaganda.it/search/record/567 July 2013.

46. Richard Taylor, *Film Propaganda. Soviet Russia and Nazi Germany* (London: I.B. Tauris, 1998 edn), pp. 61–2.
47. Georges Sadoul cited Antoine de Baecque, 'Georges Sadoul, *les Lettres françaises* et le cinéma stalinien en France' in Natacha Laurent (ed.), *Le Cinéma 'stalinien': questions d'histoire* (Toulouse: Presses Universitaires du Mirail, 2003), pp. 222–4.
48. G. Alexandrov (1939) cited Leyda, *Kino*.
49. Alexander Shklyaruk and Sergei Larkov, *Gustav Klutsis – Valentina Kulagina: posters, book graphic arts, magazine graphic arts, news photomontage 1922–1937* (Moscow: Contact-Cultura, 2010), pp. 86–7.
50. 'Over the air', *DW* (L), 22 Jan. 1931; sample details of broadcasts taken from 'Les émissions soviétiques', *L'Humanité*, 27 May 1932.
51. Hicks, *Dziga Vertov*, p. 127. Vertov combined a sound recording with surviving silent footage to create a 'scene which literally amazes the spectators' (Timofei Rokotov, 'Recent Soviet historical films', *International Literature*, Apr. 38, 102).
52. Schlögel, *Moscow, 1937*, p. 225.
53. Miklós Kun, *Stalin. An unknown portrait* (Budapest: Central European University Press, 2003), ch. 8.
54. 'Le Parti communiste vous parle ...', *L'Humanité*, 17 Apr. 1936.
55. Elizabeth Gurley Flynn, *The Man From Kansas* (New York: Citizens' Committee to Free Earl Browder, 1941), p. 17.
56. Garrigues, *Les hommes providentiels*, pp. 157–8 citing Georges Cattaui and Maurice Herr.
57. Aldo Agosti, *Palmiro Togliatti. A biography* (London: Tauris, 2008), pp. 139–44; Palmiro Togliatti (as Mario Correnti), *Discorsi agli Italiani* (Rome: Societa Editrice Unita, 1945).
58. See Banac, *Diary of Georgi Dimitrov*, pp. 317 and 322, entries for 5 and 16 May 1944; Maurice Thorez, *Un Grand français vous parle. Allocutions prononcées au micro de Radio-Moscou (Mai-Octobre 1944)* (Paris: Éditions du PCF, 1944).
59. As documented in Thorez papers 626 AP/211.
60. In Britain at least, 'communist party activists, real activists, always used to reckon they had a typewriter of their own and access to a duplicator, so they could get a leaflet out at a minute's notice' (author's interview with Edmund Frow, 10 Sept. 1987).
61. Margarita Tupitsyn, *The Soviet Photograph 1924–1937* (New Haven, CT: Yale University Press, 1996), p. 126
62. Bonnell, *Iconography*, p. 158; Shklyaruk and Larkov, *Gustav Klutsis – Valentina Kulagina*, pp. 42–3.
63. See notably the 50th birthday issue, 28 Apr. 1950.

64. Orwell, review of Eugene Lyons, *Assignment in Utopia* (Jun. 1938) in Sonia Orwell and Ian Angus, *The Collected Essays, Journalism and Letters of George Orwell. Volume 1: an age like this 1920–1940* (Harmondsworth: Penguin edn, 1970), pp. 370–1; *DW* (L), 24 Apr., 8 May and 16 Jun. 1936. For the infrequency of textual references in this period, see Chap. 2 above.
65. See above Chap. 4.3.
66. Mary Warner Marien, *Photography: a cultural history* (London: Laurence King, 2014 edn), p. 165; Ruth Clayton Windscheffel, *Reading Gladstone* (Basingstoke: Palgrave Macmillan, 2008), pp. 215–19.
67. Arthur Ransome cited Robert Service, *Trotsky. A biography* (London: Pan edn, 2010), p. 250.
68. André Morizet, *Chez Lénine et Trotski. Moscou 1921* (Paris: Renaissance du Livre, 1922), p. 68.
69. Plamper, *Stalin Cult*, pp. 33–4 and 249 n. 10; Benno Enkker, 'The Stalin cult, Bolshevik rule and Kremlin interaction in the 1930s' in Apor, *Leader Cult*, p. 84; Daniel Leese, *Mao Cult. Rhetoric and ritual in China's Cultural Revolution* (Cambridge: Cambridge University Press, 2011), p. 39.
70. Emil Ludwig, *Stalin* (New York: Putnams, 1942); Eugene Lyons, *Czar of all the Russias* (London: Harrap, 1940).
71. Essad-Bey, *Stalin. The Career of a Fanatic* (London: Bodley Head), 1932; see also Kun, *Stalin*, 69–70.
72. Bodo don Vewitz and Brooks Johnson (eds), The 'Wonderful' Years of Photographer James Abbe (Göttingen: Museum Ludwig, 2004), pp. 40–2, 216–25, 324–8.
73. Plamper, *Stalin Cult*, pp. 138–9; also Alexander Werth, *Moscow '41* (London: Hamish Hamilton, 1942), pp. 81, 88, 101, 160–1, 163; Jonathan Silverman, *For the World to See. The life of Margaret Bourke-White* (London: Secker & Warburg, 1983), p. 37.
74. Margaret Bourke-White, 'Introduction' to idem with Erskine Caldwell, *Russia at War* (London: Hutchinsons, n.d. but 1941 or 1942), p. 14.
75. Morizet, *Chez Lénine*, p. 68, also citing Vaillant-Couturier; Pankhurst papers (International Institute of Social History), file 119, memoirs of Comintern second congress, 1920; also Joseph S. Meisel, 'Gladstone's visage: problem and performance' in Roland Quinault, Rogert Swift and Ruth Clayton Windscheffel (eds), *William Gladstone: new studies and perspectives* (Farnham: Ashgate, 2012), pp. 73–98.

76. Bourke-White, 'Introduction', p. 14.
77. For helpful insights on these themes see Jean-Pierre A. Bernard, *Le Parti communiste français et la question littéraire* (Grenoble: Presses Universitaires de Grenoble, 1972).
78. Contributions of Radek, Bukharin and Stetsky in *Problems of Soviet Literature. Reports and speeches at the First Soviet Writers' Congress* (Moscow: Co-operative Publishing Society of Foreign Workers in the USSR, 1935), pp. 181, 253, 264, 270.
79. Rosalinde Sartorti, *Pressfotografie und Industrialisierung in der Sowjetunion: die Pravda, 1925–1933* (Wiesbaden: Osteuropa Institut, 1981), pp. 257–8.
80. See David King, *The Commissar Vanishes. The falsification of photograph and art in Stalin's Russia* (Edinburgh: Canongate, 1997).
81. Barbusse papers, Barbusse to Alfred Kurella, 6 Feb. 1934 and 'Photos de Staline mises à la disposition des Editeurs pour l'illustration de *Staline*'. For the Four Giants image, see Chap. 5.2 above.
82. Sartorti, *Pressfotografie*, pp. 258–60.
83. *Staline par l'image* (Paris: Éditions Sociales, 1950), pp. 28, 39, 61.
84. Isaac Deutscher, *Stalin. A political biography* (Oxford: Oxford University Press, 1949), p. 167.
85. On stalinist portraiture, see Plamper, *Stalin Cult*, ch. 5.
86. *Stalin on Lenin* (Moscow: Foreign Languages Publishing House, 1939).
87. Annette Wieviorka, *Maurice et Jeanette: biographie du couple Thorez* (Paris: Fayard, 2010), ch. 16.
88. For which see Gertje R. Utley, *Picasso: the communist years* (New Haven, CT: Yale University Press, 2000), ch. 3.
89. For which see Lynda Morris and Christoph Grunenberg (eds), *Picasso: peace and freedom* (London: Tate Publishing, 2010), pp. 110–51; Utley, *Picasso*, ch. 7.
90. Igor Golomstock, *Totalitarian Art in the Soviet Union, the Third Reich, Fascist Italy and the People's Republic of China* (London: Collins Harvill, 1990), pp. 145–6; Piotr Bernatowicz and Vojtěch Lahoda, 'Picasso and Central Europe after 1945' in Morris and Grunenberg, *Picasso*, pp. 44–51.
91. Bernatowicz and Lahoda, 'Picasso and Central Europe', p. 49.
92. Utley, *Picasso*, pp. 120–1.

93. Wieviorka, *Maurice et Jeanette*, p. 490; Utley, *Picasso*, p. 182. See also Wieviorka, 'Picasso and Stalin' in Morris and Grunenberg, *Picasso*, pp. 26–33.
94. See the reproductions in Utley, *Picasso*, p. 182 and Morris and Grunenberg, *Picasso*, p. 28.
95. Much depends on the vivid testimony of Pierre Daix (for which see his 'Encounters with Picasso' in Morris and Grunenberg, *Picasso*, pp. 18–25) dating from after Picasso's death.
96. Telegram cited Utley, *Picasso*, p. 182.
97. Aragon, 'À haute voix', *Les Lettres françaises*, 9. Apr. 1953 in Aragon, *L'Oeuvre poétique* (Paris: Messidor, 1990 edn), vol. 5, p. 49.
98. See Aragon, *L'Oeuvre poétique*, vol. 5, p. 928; Annie Besse (Kriegel) cited Wieviorka, 'Picasso and Stalin', p. 30.
99. Aragon, *L'Oeuvre poétique*, vol. 5, p. 929.
100. Alain Badiou, 'The Cultural Revolution: the last revolution?' in idem, The Communist Hypothesis (London: Verso, 2015 edn), pp. 112–18.
101. Besse cited Wieviorka, 'Picasso and Stalin', p. 30
102. Svetlana Alpers and Michael Baxandall, Tiepolo and the Pictorial Intelligence (New Haven, CT: Yale University Press, 1994), p. 2.
103. Benjamin, 'A small history of photography' (1931) in idem, One Way Street and Other Writings (London: Verso, 1985 edn), p. 256.
104. Viktor Shklovsky cited Taylor, Film Propaganda, pp. 75–6.
105. Giovanni Germanetto, Memoirs of a Barber (New York: International Publishers, n.d.), p. 235.
106. M.A. Landau-Aldanov, *Lenin* (New York: Dutton, 1922 edn), pp. 18–19.
107. Quinn Slobodian, 'Badge books and brand books. The Mao bible in East and West Germany' in Alexander C. Cook (ed.), *Mao's Little Red Book. A global history* (Cambridge: Cambridge University Press, 2014), pp. 206–24; see also Leese, *Mao Cult*, ch. 5.
108. For the former see Anna Langenbruch, 'Medium Kampflied: Kulturtransfer im Pariser Exil am Beispiel der Kampflieder von Paul Arma', *Lied und populäre Kultur / Song and Popular Culture*, 57 (2012), 143–60.
109. Vladimir Orlov, 'Prokoviev and the myth of the father of the nations: the cantata *Zdravitsa*', *Journal of Musicology*, 30, 4 (2013), 577–620.

110. Ben Harker, *Class Act. The cultural and political life of Ewan MacColl* (London: Pluto, 2007), pp. 104–5.
111. See respectively Plamper, *Stalin Cult* and Clark, *Moscow*, p. 13.
112. Werth, *Moscow '41*, pp. 47–8.
113. Barbusse, *Staline. Un monde nouveau vu à travers un homme* (1935), (Paris: Flammarion, 1936 edn), p. 4.
114. PCF secretariat minutes, 25 Oct. 1948.
115. Sarah Davies, 'Stalin and the making of the leader cult in the 1930s', *Leader Cult*, pp. 36–7.
116. Clark, *The Soviet Novel. History as ritual* (Chicago: University of Chicago Press, 1981), pp. 121–2.
117. Kevin Morgan, *The Webbs and Soviet Communism: Bolshevism and the British left part 2* (London: Lawrence & Wishart, 2006), ch. 10.
118. Clark, *Moscow*, pp. 14, 104; Hellbeck, *Revolution*, pp. 29–30.
119. Tucker, 'Rise', 352–3.
120. Simonetta Falasca-Zamponi, 'The "culture" of personality: Mussolini and the cinematic imagination' in Heller and Plamper, *Personality Cults in Stalinism*, p. 96.
121. Eugene Lyons cited Tucker, 'Rise', 362.
122. David Brandenberger, 'Stalin as symbol: a case study of the personality cult and its construction' in Davies and Harris, *Stalin: a new history*, p. 251.
123. On this see Moshe Lewin, 'Ego and politics in Stalin's autocracy' in *Jahrbuch für Historische Kommunismus-Forschung* (2003), 29–50.
124. H. Delehaye, *The Legends of the Saints. An introduction to hagiography* (London: Longmans, Green & Co, 1907), pp. 24–5.
125. Günter Agde, *Kämpfer. Biographie eines Films und seiner Macher* (Berlin: Das Neue Berlin, 2001), p. 190. Dimitrov's wife Ljubica Ivosević had committed suicide in Moscow in May 1933.
126. Malte Rolf, 'Working towards the centre: leader cults and spatial politics in pre-war stalinism' in Apor, *Leader Cult*, p. 141; also Delehaye, *Legends*, p.69.
127. Leon Trotsky, *My Life. An attempt at an autobiography* (Harmondsworth: Penguin, 1975 edn), p. 376.
128. See Chap. 4.2 above.
129. For the effects more generally on Soviet history-writing, see David Brandenberger, *Propaganda State in Crisis. Soviet ideology,*

indoctrination, and terror under Stalin, 1927–1941 (New Haven, CT: Yale University Press, 2011), ch. 7; Brandenberger, *National Bolshevism. Stalinist mass culture and the formation of modern Russian national identity 1931–1956* (Cambridge, MA: Harvard University Press, 2002), pp. 38–41.

130. For Bredel, see Chap. 5.1 above; for Aragon, Marie-Cécile Bouju, *Lire en communiste. Les Maisons d'édition du Parti communiste français 1920–1968* (Rennes: Presses Universitaires de Rennes, 2010), pp. 224–5.
131. See Kevin Morgan, 'Ainsi pour Gallacher? Quelques regards sur la construction de la vie communiste modèle en Grande-Bretagne', *Communisme*, 87 (2006).
132. Unless one counts Ivor Montagu's popular pamphlet *Stalin. A biographical sketch* (London: CPGB, 1942).
133. Titles advertised *Monde*, 23 Jan. 1932.
134. See Chap. 2 above.
135. See Chap. 4.1 above.
136. For Stalin's Soviet biographies see Brandenberger, 'Stalin as symbol'.
137. 'Stalin – at the focus of struggle', *Russia Today*, Jan. 1931, 8.
138. Kun, *Stalin*, p. 70.
139. David Brandenberger, *Propaganda State in Crisis. Soviet ideology, indoctrination, and terror under Stalin, 1927–1941* (New Haven, CT: Yale University Press, 2011), p. 53.
140. Trotsky, *Stalin. An appraisal of the man and his influence* (London: Hollis & Carter, 1947), p. 8. Ludwig had first encountered Mussolini in 1929 though his *Talks with Mussolini* was based on interviews in early 1932.
141. Ludwig, 'Lenin' in *Genius and Character* (1924; London: Cape, 1927), pp. 137–56.
142. Tovah Yedlin, *Maxim Gorky. A political biography* (Westport, CT: Praeger, 1999), pp. 195–6.
143. Cited Brandenberger, *Propaganda State*, p. 57; also Erik van Ree, *The Political Thought of Joseph Stalin. A study in twentieth-century revolutionary patriotism* (London: Routledge Curzon, 2002), p. 308 n. 21 and 33.
144. Barbusse papers, Barbusse to Kurella, 6 Feb. 1934.
145. John Barber, *Soviet Historians in Crisis, 1928–1932* (London: Macmillan, 1981), ch. 10.

146. Robert C. Tucker, 'The rise of Stalin's personality cult', *American Historical Review*, 84 (1979), 356.
147. D. Riazanov, *Karl Marx and Friedrich Engels* (London: Martin Lawrence, 1927), p. 214.
148. NA KV 2/1377, Fox to William Rust 8 Apr. 1930.
149. Ralph Fox, *Lenin. A biography* (London: Gollancz, 1933), pp. 12–13, 34, 97–8, 108, 110–11, 207–8, 224.
150. Fox, 'Comrade Stalin's letter and the CPGB', *CR*, Apr. 1932, 199–207.
151. Dutt papers CP/Ind/Dutt/16/4, 'On Ralph Fox's work "Biography of Lenin"', Sept. 1933; Fox, 'Reply to criticism on my book "Lenin"'; Dutt to Pollitt, 4 Oct. 1933; NA KV 2/1377, Pollitt to Dutt, 9 Oct. 1933.
152. Dutt, *Lenin* (London: Hamish Hamilton, 1933), p. 87.
153. Brandenberger, *Propaganda State*, p. 57.
154. Webb, 'Ralph Fox' in John Lehmann, T.A. Jackson and C. Day Lewis (eds), *Ralph Fox. A writer in arms* (London: Lawrence & Wishart, 1937), p. 7.
155. Barbusse papers, copy letters to Barbusse [from Thälmann committee?], 2 and 20 Feb. 1934; Barbusse to unidentified correspondent, 25 Feb. and 28 Mar. 1934.
156. Barbusse, *Zola* (London: Dent, 1932), pp. 265–70.
157. Barbusse, *Jésus* (Paris: Flammarion, 1927).
158. Barbusse papers, Barbusse to Kurella, 6 Feb. 1934; also RGASPI 495/60/246, excerpt from letter 28 Jan. 1934, unidentified author and addressee with handwritten annotation 'to Comrade Bela Kun. E[lena] S[tassova]'.
159. Barbusse papers, Barbusse to Kurella, 11 Apr., 24 May and 7 Jun. 1934.
160. Barbusse papers, 'Petites anecdotes', n.d. but Sept.–Nov. 1934.
161. There are two extant versions of Stetsky's comments: a Russian version in RGASPI 558/11/699 and a French version in the Barbusse papers with a covering letter dated 15 Sept. 1934. Translations here are from the Russian version.
162. Henri Barbusse (ed., with Alfred Kurella), *Lettres de Lénine à sa famille* (Paris: Rieder, 1936), pp. 7–8, 15–16, 23–4, 34–5.
163. See the biographical summaries in Barbusse, *Lettres*, pp. 91–3, 116–19, 272–80, 303–7, 398–402.

164. *Sotsialisticheskiivestnik*, 25 Jan. 1934 cited Sarah Davies, *Popular Opinion in Stalin's Russia. Terror, propaganda and dissent, 1934–1941* (Cambridge: Cambridge University Press, 1997), pp. 178–9.
165. Robert H. McNeal, 'Krupskaya: the feminine subcult' in Bernard W. Eissenstat (ed.), *Lenin and Leninism. State, law, and society* (Lexington, KY: Lexington Books, 1971), pp. 222–4; Velikanova, *Making*, ch. 9.
166. Barbusse, *Staline*, pp. 17, 86.
167. Michael David-Fox, *Showcasing the Great Experiment. Cultural diplomacy and western visitors to the Soviet Union, 1921–1941* (New York: Oxford University Press, 2012), p. 234; Kun, *Stalin*, p. 20 n. 53; Brandenberger, *National Bolshevism*, p. 82.
168. E. Yaroslavsky, *Landmarks in the Life of Stalin* (London: Lawrence & Wishart, 1942); *Joseph Stalin. A short biography* (London: Lawrence & Wishart, 1940).
169. Kun, *Stalin*, ch. 26; Deutscher, *Stalin*, p. 571.
170. Brandenberger, 'Stalin as symbol', pp. 263–4, 266.
171. A French translation of the IMEL volume appeared in 1950. There appears to have been no English translation of the second edition.
172. Jean-Richard Bloch, *L'Homme du communisme* (Paris: Éditions Sociales, 1949), pp. 14–15, 38–41.
173. Sergueï Feodossiev, 'Sur les archives et les textes de Jean-Richard Bloch en URSS' in Annie Angremy and Michel Trebitsch (eds), *Jean-Richard Bloch ou l'écriture et l'action* (Paris: Bibliothèque nationale de France, 2002), pp. 316–17.
174. *Lénine par l'image*, pref. François Billoux (Paris: Éditions Sociales, 1950); *Staline par l'image*, pref. Raymond Guyot (Paris: Éditions Sociales, 1950).
175. Thorez papers 626 AP212, André Ribaud, '"Fils du peuple"', *Paix et Liberté*, Dec. 1937 (cutting); Bouju, *Lire en communiste*, p. 126.
176. Thorez papers 626 AP212, Bloch to Thorez, 19 Dec. 1937.
177. Thorez papers 626 AP212, 'Conseils de *Vaillant* pour le livre *Fils du Peuple*', comment attributed to Léon Moussinac; for the fuller citation see Wieviorka, *Maurice et Jeannette*, p. 237.
178. Claude Pennetier and Bernard Pudal, 'Stalinism: workers' cult and cult of leaders', *TCC*, 1 (2009), 26–8, here citing Marie-Françoise Chantrault-Duchet; Sirot, *Maurice Thorez* (Paris: Presses de Sciences

Po, 2000), p. 28; also Claude Pennetier and Bernard Pudal, 'Les autobiographies des "fils du peuple". De l'autobiographie édifiante à l'autobiographie auto-analytique' in Claude Pennetier and Bernard Pudal (eds), *Autobiographies, autocritiques: aveux dans le monde communiste* (Paris: Belin, 2002), pp. 223–7.

179. James R. Barrett, *William Z. Foster and the Tragedy of American Radicalism* (Urbana, IL: University of Illinois Press, 1999), pp. 202–3, citing Elizabeth Gurley Flynn; Edward P. Johanningsmeier, *The Forging of American Communism. The life of William Z. Foster* (Princeton, NJ: Princeton University Press, 1994), pp. 269–71.
180. Flynn, *Labor's Own. William Z. Foster: a communist's fifty years of working-class leadership and struggle* (New York: New Century Publishers, 1949), pp. 42–3, 46.
181. See Chap. 3.3 above.
182. Amado, *Le Chevalier de l'Espèrance* (Paris: Éditions Français Réunis, 1949), pp. 30–1, 87–8, 230–1, 244–6, 351, 367; see Chap. 3 n. 85 above.
183. On these themes see Gina Hermann, *Written in Red: the communist memoir in Spain*, 2010 (Urbana, IL: University of Illinois Press, 2010), pp. 1–25.
184. See Chap. 4.3 above.
185. Denis Peschanski, 'Introduction générale: du dirigeant à la figure emblématique' in Peschanski (ed.), *Marcel Cachin. Carnets 1906–1947* (Paris: CNRS Editions, 4 vols, 1993–8), vol. 4, p. 34.
186. Henri Barbusse, *One Looks at Russia* (London: Dent, 1931), p. 170; Flynn, *Labor's Own*, pp. 37–8.
187. The discussion that follows draws on Kevin Morgan, 'Harry Pollitt, Maurice Thorez and the writing of exemplary communist lives' in Julie Gottlieb and Richard Toye (eds), *Making Reputations: power, persuasion and the individual in British politics* (London: Tauris, 2005), pp. 56–69.
188. RGASPI 495/74/49, Rosa Michel, report on CPGB, 9 May 1940.
189. Cited Brandenberger, 'Stalin as symbol', p. 265.
190. Victor Joannès, '"Fils du peuple" et la lutte pour les principes du léninisme', *CdC*, Oct. 1949, 1203.
191. 'La campagne de diffusion de "Fils du peuple"', *Apprendre*, Sept. 1949, 19–20.

192. On the second edition, see Jean-Marie Goulemot, *Pour l'amour de Staline. La face oubliée du communisme français* (Paris: CNRS, 2009 edn), pp. 119–30; Wieviorka, *Maurice et Jeannette*, pp. 423–32.
193. Thorez papers 626 AP211, 'Signatures et dédicaces de "Fils du peuple"', 1950.
194. André Fontaine, *Le Monde*, 20 Oct. 1949, cutting in Thorez papers 626 AP211.
195. Thorez papers 626 AP/211, Marie Rolland to Thorez, 5 Dec. 1949.
196. See the bibliographical annexe in Pennetier and Pudal, 'Les autobiographies', pp. 240–6.
197. Gallacher papers CP/Ind/Gall/2/3, Andrew Rothstein to Maurice Cornforth (Lawrence & Wishart), 1 May 1951. For the appeal of such works to younger communists, see for example the letters to Gallacher from Julian Kay, Peter Berman and John Downes (all 1953) in CP/Ind/Gall/1/8.
198. Cachin papers 290 J 6/171 Pierre Coureille (?) to Cachin, Sept. 1949.
199. Gabriel Péri (intr. Aragon), *Les Lendemains qui chantent* (Paris: Éditions Sociales, 1947).
200. Aragon in Péri, *Lendemains*, pp. 8–9.
201. Aragon in Péri, *Lendemains*, pp. 11–12; also *Un grand français: Gabriel Péri. Une vie de combat pour la paix et la sécurité de la France* (Paris: Éditions Sociales, 1947).
202. Alexander Courban, *Gabriel Péri: un homme politique, un député, un journaliste* (Paris: La Dispute, 2011), pp. 180–1; Bouju, *Lire en communiste*, p. 293; Jean Chaintron, *Le vent soufflait devant ma porte* (Paris: Seuil, 1993), pp. 300–5.
203. See Bouju, *Lire en communiste*, p. 230.
204. Apor, *'Invisible Shining'*, ch. 2.
205. Albert Rhys Williams, *Lenin: the man and his work* (New York, Scott & Seltzer, 1919), pp. 117–21; Trotsky, 'Lenin wounded' in idem, *Lenin* (London: Harrap, 1925), p. 231; 'Stalin' in *The Life of Stalin: a symposium* (London: Modern Books, 1930), pp. 12–14.
206. Stalin, *Interview.*
207. See for example 'Le rôle de la personnalité dans l'histoire', *CdB*, Mar. 1939, 374–87, originally published, *Pravda*, 27 Nov. 1938.

208. G.V. Plekhanov, *The Role of the Individual in History* (London: Lawrence & Wishart, 1940), pp. 49, 55.
209. *History of the Communist Party of the Soviet Union (Bolsheviks): Short Course* (Moscow: Foreign Languages Publishing House, 1939), p. 14.
210. Fréville, 'L'homme communiste: Gabriel Péri', *NC*, Dec. 1949, 63.
211. Plekhanov, *Role*, unattributed preface, pp. 7–8; also 'Le rôle de la personnalité', 375–80.
212. Fréville, 'L'homme communiste', 63.
213. Cited Yves Cohen, *Le Siècle des chefs. Une histoire transnationale du commandement et de l'autorité* (Paris: Éditions Amsterdam, 2013), pp. 146–7.
214. Ian Kershaw, *The 'Hitler Myth'. Image and reality in the Third Reich* (Oxford: Oxford University Press, 1989 edn), p. 151; Davies, *Popular Opinion*, pp. 171–3.
215. Morgan, *Webbs*, pp. 229–33.
216. Bloch papers 394 J2, Bloch to Andrée Ducret, 21 May 1945.
217. F. Borkenau, *The Totalitarian Enemy* (London: Faber & Faber, 1940), p. 209.
218. As well as the Webbs, see for example Georges Friedmann, *De la Sainte Russie à l'URSS* (Paris: Gallimard, 1938).
219. See Chap. 4.1 above; Lion Feuchtwanger, *Moscow 1937* (London: Gollancz, 1937), pp. 12, 85–8. Michael David-Fox (*Showcasing*, p. 272) describes how a reference to the Stalin 'cult' was removed from Feuchtwanger's draft at the behest of his Soviet minder. Nevertheless, the published version still includes unambiguous references to '[den] geschmaklosen und maßlosenKult, der mit seiner Person getrieben wird' (the tasteless and immoderate cult made of his person); see Feuchtwanger, *Moskau 1937. Ein Reisebericht für meine Freunde* (Amsterdam: Querido Verlag, 1937) pp. 76, 83.
220. Pat Sloan, *Soviet Democracy* (London: Gollancz, 1937), pp. 206–9.
221. Giorgio Pini, *The Official Life of Benito Mussolini* (London: Hutchinson, 1939), p. 117.
222. There is a rare positive allusion to obedience in Amado, *Chevalier*, p. 77.
223. Bernal, 'Stalin as scientist', *MQ*, summer 1953, 133; also 'The freedom of necessity' (1945), 'Belief and action' (1945) and 'Science and the humanities' (1947) all in Bernal, *The Freedom of*

Necessity (London: Routledge & Kegan Paul, 1949), pp. 62, 79–80, 160–1.
224. Gorky, 'Soviet literature' in *Problems of Soviet Literature*, p. 62.
225. Jean-Michel Palmier, *Weimar in Exile. The antifascist emigration in Europe and America* (London: Verso, 2006), pp. 205–6, 328–30.
226. Anna Seghers et al., *Ernst Thaelmann. What he stands for* (London: Workers' Bookshop, 1934), pp. 13–21; also the shorter version, 'Chefs de classe. Le rôle du personnage dans l'histoire', *Monde*, 22 Jun. 1934.
227. John Strachey, *The Theory and Practice of Socialism* (London: Gollancz, 1936), pp. 162–3.
228. Nizan in *Ce Soir*, 18 Nov. 1937, cutting in Thorez papers 626 AP/212.
229. Waldeck Rochet, 'Le rôle des personnalités dans l'histoire', *CdC*, Apr. 1952, 389–90.
230. Jochen Hellbeck, *Revolution*, p. 28.
231. Bernal, 'Freedom and necessity', p. 62.
232. Clark, *The Soviet Novel*, pp. 118, 121–2.
233. Gorky, 'The destruction of personality' in *Literature and Life. A selection from the writings of Maxim Gorki* (London: Hutchinson, 1946), p. 117.
234. Bernal, 'Leonardo da Vinci', *LM*, Apr. 1952, 170–6.
235. *Problems of Soviet Literature*, pp. 62, 65, 176–7, 254–5.
236. *Problems of Soviet Literature*, p. 159.
237. Browder, 'Joseph Stalin's 60th Birthday', *DW* (NY), 21 Dec. 1939.
238. Paul Vaillant-Couturier, *Au Service de l'Esprit* (Paris: Éditions Sociales Internationales, n.d. but 1936), pp. 13–15; Vaillant-Couturier, *Nous Ferons se lever le jour* (Paris: Éditions Hier et Aujourd'hui, 1947), pp. 241–2.
239. Vaillant-Couturier, *Au Service*, p. 14.
240. For example Brandenberger, *National Bolshevism*; Maureen Perrie, *The Cult of Ivan the Terrible in Stalin's Russia* (Basingstoke: Palgrave, 2001); Nicholas V. Riasanovsky, *The Image of Peter the Great in Russian History and Thought* (New York: Oxford University Press, 1985), pt. 4.
241. Friedmann, *De la Sainte Russie*,p. 215.
242. Riasanovsky, *Image*, pp. 258–9. For Pokrovsky, see Chap. 4.1 above.

243. Merin, 'Saint Thomas More. Humanisme bourgeois et humanisme prolétarien', *Monde*, 6 Jun. 1935.
244. See Chap. 5.2 above.
245. Landau-Aldanov, *Lenin*, ch. 11; Vincent Duclert, *Jaurès 1859–1914. La politique et la légende* (Paris: Autrement, 2012), pp. 106–8.
246. For this theme, see Riasanovsky, *Image*.
247. Bouju, *Lire en communiste*, p. 104.
248. Madeleine Rebérioux, '1935 – fascisme et antifascisme' in Pierre Georgel et al. (eds), *La gloire de Victor Hugo* (Paris: Éditions de la Réunion des musées nationaux, 1985), pp. 233–5; Jack Lindsay, *John Bunyan. Maker of myths* (London: Methuen, 1937); T.A. Jackson, *Dickens. Portrait of a radical* (London: Lawrence & Wishart, 1937).
249. See Chap. 5.2 above; also Christine Lodder, 'Lenin's Plan for Monumental Propaganda' in Matthew Cullerne Bown and Brandon Taylor (eds), *Art of the Soviets. Painting, sculpture and architecture in a one-party state, 1917–1992* (Manchester: Manchester University Press, 1993), pp. 20–1.
250. Aragon, 'Le Parti communiste français et Victor Hugo', *Pens.*, May-Aug 1952, 37–51; Georges Cogniot, 'Le cent-cinquantième anniversaire de Victor Hugo', *CdC*, Feb. 1952, 161–79; also Madeleine Rebérioux, '1952: Les communistes et Hugo' in Georgel, *Gloire*, pp. 235–41.
251. Brandenberger, *National Bolshevism*, ch. 5.
252. For Riazanov, see Chap. 5.2 above.
253. 'Fiftieth anniversary of the death of Karl Marx', *DW* (L), 31 Jan. 1933; D.Z. Manuilsky, *Marxism: the doctrine of the proletarian dictatorship* (London: Modern Books, 1933).
254. See for example Max Beer, 'The testament of Engels', *LM*, May 1922, 366–71.
255. D.Z. Manuilsky, *Engels in the Struggle for Revolutionary Marxism* (London: Modern Books, 1935); also Dutt, 'Notes', *LM*, Mar. 1933, 142–3; Fox, *Lenin*, p. 50.
256. Colum Leckey, 'David Riazanov and Russian Marxism', *Russian History/Histoire Russe*, 22 (1995), 151.
257. Stalin to members of CPSU politburo, Vladimir Adoratsky and others, 19 July and 5 Aug. 1934 and Stalin to V.G. Knorin, after 16 Aug. 1934 in R.W. Davies et al. (eds), *The Stalin-Kaganovich*

Correspondence 1931–36 (New Haven, CT: Yale University Press, 2003), pp. 225–6, 251–2, 375–82.

258. Except as indicated, the account that follows draws on J.P. Nettl, *Rosa Luxemburg* (Oxford: Oxford University Press, 2 vols, 1966), ch. 18 and Eric D. Weitz, '"Rosa Luxemburg belongs to us!"' German communism and the Luxemburg legacy', *Central European History*, 27 (1994), 27–64.
259. Eric D. Weitz, *Creating German Communism 1890–1990: from popular protest to socialist state* (Princeton, NJ: Princeton University Press, 1997), p. 185.
260. Nettl, *Rosa Luxemburg*, p. 818 for the SPD view.
261. See Chap. 5.3 above for Zetkin and the third world congress.
262. Paul Frölich, 'Rosa Luxemburg: "Against reformism"', *Inprecorr*, 26 Nov. 1925, 1267–8.
263. See Kaganovich's 'For a Bolshevist Study of the History of the Party' (speech at Institute of Red Professors, 1 Dec. 1931) published in instalments in *Inprecorr* in December 1931 with extracts prominently featured in national organs like *Rote Fahne*, 8 Jan. 1932 and *DW* (L), 6 Jan. 1932.
264. T.A. Jackson, 'Rosa Luxemburg and her mistakes', *DW* (L), 12 Feb. 1932. Jackson followed with a retraction and self-criticism three months later ('Lenin and Rosa Luxemburg', *DW* (L), 4 May 1932).
265. 'For Marxist-Leninist theory', *CI*, 15 Feb. 1933, 95–6.
266. 'Did Maxton Write The Lenin "Biography"?', *DW* (L), 18 Jun. 1932 (article by a 'special correspondent' either written by Gallacher or deriving from him). The most helpful of Maclean's several biographies is B.J. Ripley and John McHugh, *John Maclean* (Manchester: Manchester University Press, 1989).
267. David Howell, *A Lost Left. Three studies in socialism and nationalism* (Manchester: Manchester University Press, 1986), p. 157.
268. See his articles in *Scots Socialist*, Nov-Dec, 1940, 2–7; Jan.–Feb. 1941, 2 and Apr.-May 1941, 4
269. C.M. Grieve (Hugh MacDiarmid) to Catherine Carswell, 5 Oct. 1936 in Alan Bold (ed.), *The Letters of Hugh MacDiarmid* (London: Hamish Hamilton, 1984), pp. 428–9; MacDiarmid papers 7361/7, CPGB Scottish district committee to MacDiarmid, 30 Oct. 1936.
270. 'The Red Scotland Thesis. Forwards to the John Maclean Line' in *Voice of Scotland*, Jun.-Aug. 1938, 7–14.

271. Tom Bell, *John Maclean. A fighter for freedom* (Glasgow: Communist Party Scottish Committee, 1944), pp. xiii, 152–3; also MacDiarmid, 'John Maclean, Scotland, and the Communist Party', *Scots Socialist*, Nov-Dec, 1940, 2.
272. Grieve (MacDiarmid) to Sean O'Casey, 20 Dec. 1949 in Bold, *Letters*, p. 637; MacDiarmid papers 7361/20, Scotland-USSR Society to Victor Holthum, literature section, 7 Jun. 1949. For Gallacher, see Chap. 3.3 above.
273. J. Klément, *Jaurès réformiste* (Paris: Bureau d'Éditions, 1931); Duclert, *Jaurès*, pp. 106–8.
274. *L'Humanité*, 23 Jan. 1936. For the congress see Chap. 4.2 above.
275. For example J. Rocher, 'À propos du livre de A. Ferrat: "Histoire du Parti communiste français"', *CdB*, Aug. 1932, 1037–40.
276. A. Fer, 'Le Parti communiste français et le guesdisme', *CdB*, 1934, 908–18.
277. See for example PCF secretariat minutes, 23 and 31 Jul. 1945, 27 Jul. 1946; also the article by Raoul Calors, with supporting texts, *CdC*, Jun.-Jul. 1945,50–76.
278. Roger Garaudy, 'Le néo-blanquisme de contrabande et les positions antiléninistes d'André Marty', *CdC*, Jan. 1953,38–50; also PCF secretariat minutes, 21 Mar. and 13 Nov. 1950, 13 Mar. 1951.
279. 'Tom Mann's appeal to members of the ILP', *DW* (L), 8 Apr. 1933.
280. *Des Français en qui la France peut avoir confiance* (Paris: Éditions du Parti communiste français, 1944 and 1945 edns); 'La vie et les combats de Marcel Cachin', *Apprendre*, Sept. 1949, 22–31.
281. Vaillant-Couturier, 'Marat, l'ami du peuple', *CdB*,25 Jul. 1936,834–6.
282. RGASPI 495/100/1025, CPGB 14th congress, May 1937, contribution of Gallacher.
283. RGASPI 495/100/1006, Pollitt to 'Dick', 2 May 1935.
284. Mick Wallis, 'Heirs to the pageant. Mass spectacle and the Popular Front' in Andy Croft (ed.), *A Weapon in the Struggle. The cultural history of the Communist Party in Britain* (London: Pluto, 1998), pp. 51, 63.
285. Browder, *Lincoln and the Communists* (New York: Workers' Library, 1936), pp. 11–12; Edward P. Johanningsmeier, *The*

Forging of American Communism. The life of William Z. Foster (Princeton, NJ: Princeton University Press, 1994), p. 278.

286. Amado, *Chevalier*, pp. 132, 363; see also Chap. 3.3 above.
287. Victor Leduc, 'De la Commune à Maurice Thorez' in *Vive la Commune! Edité pour le 51e anniversaire de MT et le 80e anniversaire du Commune de Paris* (Paris: Éditions Sociales, 1951), pp. 3–6.
288. C. Gak, 'Du rôle de l'individu et de celui des masses populaires dans l'histoire', *CdC*, Dec. 1945, 81–96.
289. Trotsky, 'Lenin ill' (1923) in idem, *Lenin*, p. 238.
290. Jean Fréville, *Avec Maurice Thorez* (Paris: Éditions Sociales, 1950), pp. 16–17.
291. V.M. Molotov, 'Stalin and stalinist leadership' and L.P. Beria, 'The great inspirer and organiser of the victories of communism' in *'Pravda' Articles on the Occasion of the 70th Birthday of Joseph Vissarionovich Stalin December 21, 1949* (London: Soviet News, 1950), pp. 11–26 and 27–42.
292. Joël Cornette, 'Figures politiques du Grand Siècle: Roi-État ou État-Roi?' in idem (ed.), *La Monarchie entre Renaissance et Révolution* (Paris: Seuil, 2000), pp. 137–276.
293. Dutt, 'Marxism is communism', *DW* (L), 11 Mar. 1933.
294. Cornette, 'Figures politiques', p. 217.
295. Dutt, 'Stalin and the future', *LM*, Apr. 1953, 145–6.

CHAPTER 7

Cult Reflections: No Saviour from on High

Communism's cult of the individual does not end with the Khrushchev speech. More than ever this was now a movement of global reach, and it was in Asia in particular that leader cults came to be practised on a scale surpassing even Stalin's. In China's Cultural Revolution of the late 1960s, this reached such a pitch of 'cult anarchy' as to undermine the integrative role of Mao's cult and require its drastic curtailment in the interests of the party's own authority.[1] In North Korea, the cult of Kim Il-sung is said to have matched or exceeded even Mao's, and the landmark of the leader's birthday was still further institutionalised in such forms as the 8 February Film Studio and the 8 February House of Culture. While the Ceauşescu regime in Romania developed the familial aspect already prefigured in the Thorez cult, Kim's authority was actually inherited on his death by his son Kim Jong-il. With the collapse in 1989 of Europe's communist regimes, and the public execution of the Ceauşescus in the presence of film crews, North Korea was left to keep alive the traditions of the communist state cult. It did so as the only communist country, as one American party veteran put it, to have a communist monarchy.[2]

In focusing on communism 'under Lenin and Stalin' the present account has therefore observed a chronological limitation that broadly corresponds with the centring of the communist world on Moscow, and in a secondary sense on Europe as its principal field of activity reaching out from Moscow. In this respect, it sits quite comfortably with constructions of the modern personality cult developing in these countries from the later

K. Morgan, *International Communism and the Cult of the Individual*, DOI 10.1057/978-1-137-55667-7_7

nineteenth century, or with the 'century of leaders' which Yves Cohen dates more precisely from the mid-1890s to the watershed moment of 1968.[3] Whether delineating this wider fixation on the leader, or the specifically communist variations upon it, a chronologically and geographically partial account is thus alone conceivable unless at very least the second great communist cult of Mao is treated less perfunctorily than it is here. Within its limitations, the present study does nevertheless seek to register how the plural conception of a 'century of communisms' was also reflected in the different temporalities and functionalities according to which these communist notions of the leader were constructed. The cult of the individual, in other words, was not restricted to any one particular phase or variant of these communisms, as tendentious commentary of the Khrushchev type sought to suggest. Not the cult alone but the cults of the individual must therefore be historicised as communism itself is, according to its changing political imperatives and the disparate conditions in which these were or could be made effective.

Discussion centred on the Stalin cult offers a carefully calibrated periodisation which nevertheless has a certain linearity. Compressed into a sentence, it postulates a cult of the actual or mummified Lenin which is held to prefigure that of Stalin, which itself attained its pre-war apogee in the period of the Moscow trials and was then both further inflated and generalised across the dictator's expanded dominions in the years immediately preceding his death. This basic periodisation is also valid for the internationalisation of the cult phenomenon. Here a first phase can be traced from 1933–1934, broadly coinciding with the popular front, and a second one from around 1947, reflecting the culture of high stalinism and the polarising logic of the Cold War. The glorification of the leader was perhaps the most visible expression of Stalin's ascendancy over world communism, and it may seem plausible to regard these as phases of the same ongoing stalinisation narrative differing only in degree and on the surface. This, however, is only part of the story. Using the heuristic devices of the integrating and enkindling cults, these interconnected studies have attempted both the differentiated analysis of these communisms (plural) that the use of a comparative method requires, but also the recognition of what held them together as the transnational phenomenon of communism (singular).

It was at the high point of international cult-building during the Cold War phase that the esoteric character of these cultic practices was most pronounced. This was not only true of the highly ritualised forms which they took but could mean the vesting of cultic properties in individuals who excelled, if at all, only in their capacity to alienate and affront a wider public. Politically noxious though Stalin's cult in particular must seem, there was nevertheless some basic congruence between the binding practices of a formalised cultic hierarchy and the turning in upon themselves of the European communist parties. The communist movement in effect had become its own cult community: there was no inherent tension between the national and international, and in the short term at least the cults performed the integrating role of holding the movement still more closely together. The experiences in this period of the western fortress parties are thus relatively easily assimilated into a literature hitherto focusing mainly on communist state systems and Stalin's territorial empire. In France, where these connections have most of all been explored, it is on the period of the Cold War that the most detailed accounts have focused.[4] If one can speak of the stalinisation of international communism, this if any was the period in which it was essentially accomplished.[5]

If these were the features of the integrating cult, they were already clearly evident before the war, both within the USSR and in the presence which Stalin exercised for a population of 'Cominternians' directly exposed to Soviet practices. Nevertheless, communism was not in this period a movement seeking to insulate itself from the world beyond. On the contrary, it was precisely in these years that those wider connections were established which, in the worst cases during the Cold War, were to be invoked as the evidence of contamination or even treachery. In this earlier phase, the promotion of a communist cult of the individual coincided with the opening out of communist politics, often with some considerable degree of success, and with the establishment of a political identity founded crucially on resistance to the cult regimes and movements of the political right. It is therefore not surprising that from Stalin downwards there was some appreciation of the need to adjust the communists' public face to the wider constituencies it sought to mobilise, align with or recruit.

If Stalin's cult, as Cohen writes, was functional and situational, then other situations required a different type of figure, or the attempt to connect with this wider public of Stalin himself.[6] This is the figure characterised here as an enkindling one, and if Stalin ever achieved this role internationally, it was not yet in the 1930s, but rather in the 1940s as the vaunted architect and symbol of the Soviet war effort. Though Soviet practices had been taken up across the international communist movement, these did not so much focus on Stalin himself as on that wider cultivation of the hero within which the Soviet cult of the *vozhd'* must be located. The plausible intuition that it was Stalin's authority which attracted westerners to communism is in fact less strongly supported by contemporary sources than one might imagine.[7] Even well-wishers sought rather to account for the cult phenomenon, or warn against its consequences, than necessarily to celebrate it. 'Is this adulation of one citizen among many thousands … consistent with their relative merits, or in harmony with the spirit of equalitarian comradeship?', the Webbs asked in their *Soviet Communism*. Was it detrimental to veracity and conducive to the evils suggested by the 'contemporary experience of leadership' in Italy and Germany? 'Will it always be necessary to create such a "head of the community", rather than to give impersonal prominence to the highest council of administrators?'[8]

J. Arch Getty, as we noted at the outset, has recently cited Shils in postulating just such a universal human tendency to anthropomorphise political power.[9] Whatever implications this may have for Getty's insistence on a sort of Russian exceptionalism, it does seem consistent with the claim that a cult like Lenin's tells us more about the character of the new Soviet state than it does about communism in general.[10] Even so, what slips from view in this national and teleological reading is how Lenin also anthropomorphised revolution, and how his biography was read as a life-course in accomplishing that revolution. In politics, as in the world of mythology, very different qualities could be represented through the individual, and so therefore were forms of social and political conflict personified in this way. If Lenin did indeed become a symbol of the Soviet state, his only real peer in the shape of Trotsky was taken to symbolise some demoniacal force that threatened it. Moreover, through the figure of the enemy of the people, systemic failings that went far beyond the possible agency of any individual or group of individuals were represented as human transgression and fallibility.

This itself is a theme that would certainly merit more consideration in discussions of the Stalin cult. Nevertheless, the primary focus of the present study has been on how the cult phenomenon was generalised across a movement pursuing different objects in different political environments, and how the vesting in the individual of some supra-personal quality could equally represent either the contestation or defiance of some central authority or the veneration of the figure of the ruler. The construction of different cult figures was not itself unique to communism: a regime like Hitler's thus also promoted a cult of remembrance in which the casting over time of the martyr-figure and the pioneer represented one of the foundations on which the Nazis' subsequent assumption of power was supposed to have been founded.[11] Communism's distinctiveness, as an international movement and thus one simultaneously of revolutions achieved and still to come, was that its intersecting narratives of protest, power and sacrifice were all caught within the turn to the individual that it promoted from the early 1930s.

The enkindling cult as postulated here is a concept borrowed from Eduard Bernstein via Eleanor Marx that evoked a period when socialism was not yet a party but a movement only just beginning to stir. It is easy to see how this could be discounted in the present context. Already for Bernstein, looking back as a fin de siècle social democrat, a figure like Lassalle had been able to assume such a role in temporary default of organisation and as a way of establishing its foundations. In a longer perspective still, the subsequent communist cults can appear as an epitome of an age of organisation, deriving from a manufactured institutional charisma and apotheosising, if not the principle of hierarchy, then the sanctity of the apparatus. If internationally speaking the Stalin cult was most actively promulgated in the years that followed the Comintern's dissolution, no doubt this was a means of reasserting international disciplines in the absence of the institutional charisma that had earlier been vested in the Comintern itself.

Readings of the dominant Soviet cults tend to fall between the commonalities over time and national specificity of the *longue durée* of Russian history, and the commonalities over space and period specificity of the modern leadership figure or personality cult. As noted at the outset of this book, the positing of an age of dictators and would-be dictators is sometimes sharply distinguished from a world we have lost, of the authentic democratic hero. Particularly in accounts emanating from the left, there is also proposed a second chronological watershed and fundamental discontinuity between the leader-fixated age of command-and-comply and the new social movements emerging since the 1960s. In Claus Offe's influential treatment, this appears as a paradigm shift in which the rejection of hierarchy, bureaucracy and vertical differentiation was at the heart of the revivified conception of democracy that marked the new politics from the old.[12] Cohen's verdict is that the 'century of leaders' not only had an unambiguous starting point, but an end-point that is identified with still greater precision with the moment of '68 and the emergence of the 'crowd without a master'.[13]

In practice, recognition of the specificity of particular national histories does not preclude a sense of how these interconnected with each other. The banal contention of the present study is simply that oppositional histories and counter-narratives may also be viewed in a longer historical perspective which was also in part a transnational one and which in its communist phase was established as a defining element of ideology and organisation. In other words, the wider appeals of communism, which seemed so compelling to a generation of European radicals, must be located within both the immediate imperatives of a bolshevised mass politics and the longer lineages of radical protest to which communism for the time being staked its claim. Or at least this is how it appeared to communists themselves. If in one aspect the 1930s–1940s appears as the apogee of the fixation on the leader, in another this was E.P. Thompson's 'decade of heroes' with its Guevara in every wood.[14] When Thompson used these words in the 1970s, it was in precisely the sense already familiar to any reader of his *Making of the English Working Class*, with its agent-centred narrative of an earlier phase of radical activism. At the same time, in evoking the Guevaras of anti-fascism he might have been assimilating his own communist experiences to more recent times, or else intimating the persistence of the figure of the *grand meneur*, whose features a later generation not only bore on its Che Guevara lapel badges but on the new cultural artefacts of the celebrity poster and tee-shirt.

The forms were certainly different, and did not meet with Thompson's approval.[15] Nevertheless: when the demonstrators of '68 signalled their support for struggling Vietnam, it was in the person of that survivor of the age of birthday cults, Ho Chi Minh, and according to the time-honoured ritual of rhythmically chanting his name. If Ho in his very different way was like a Pasionaria figure, symbolising resistance to external aggression, the young black American Angela Davis was reminiscent of a Thälmann or Dimitrov. The latest in the communists' long line of political prisoners, Davis became the focus of an international campaign that linked official communism with the counter-culture, and with the love–hate relationship with America that was common to both. John and Yoko, Herbie Hancock and the Rolling Stones all paid tribute in their different ways, as the awarders of the Lenin Peace Prize did in theirs. Above all there was Mao, whose cult was not confined to China, but flourished as nowhere else in the West in the same Left Bank milieux that 20 years earlier had made so much of Stalin.[16] Even now the echo survives in the resounding reaffirmation by Alain Badiou of the functional and political necessity of a revolutionary cult of personality.[17] The moment of '68 was, inter alia, one of a leninist revivalism that was branded with the very names of Mao and Trotsky, and in the former case continued to idealise the revolutionary state and leader as if each were the incarnation of the other. Thompson referred to 'old and discredited arguments under a new label', but not even the system of labelling was all that new.[18]

There was, however, no system or hierarchy to link these figures with a single dominant party of the left. Moreover, by the time that Mao died in 1976, the wider veneration of a leading state and personality was at last falling into desuetude. Within the Soviet bloc, or its individual component parts, pastiche cults persisted of such obvious products of the machine as Stalin's next-but-one successor Leonid Brezhnev. In a feeble echo of Barbusse's *Stalin*, Soviet détente strategy included the seeking out of accommodating western publishers for Brezhnev biographies that offered no concessions to western readers.[19] Doubtless it lingered on among some older communists, but the integrating cult as an international phenomenon was now something manifestly belonging to the past. Where there had been a simple replication or transfer of Stalin's authority, it might seem reasonable to speak, as Agnes Heller has, of the 'borrowed charisma' of the mini-Stalins of post-war Eastern Europe.[20] As communist leaders further afield also took on a mini-Stalin aspect, the cult system centred on the Kremlin may certainly be regarded as the symbol of their parties' continuing and even intensified subjection to its overriding authority.[21] The integrating cult had thus been a function of the monolith; its high point was Stalin's 70th birthday, and as subsequently the monolith was undermined by sclerosis and internal fragmentation, the symbol at its centre gave way at once to the reassertion of the parties' collective authority, the restoration of the founding cult of Lenin and the vesting of authority in the individual primarily at the national level. In this sense it was Brezhnev, in this respect resembling Nicholas II more than he did Lenin or even Stalin, whose cult was exercised only within the physical limits of a closed society.

Where the echoes of the cult phenomenon remain is in the greater durability of the enkindling figure. The initial phase of researching this project in Paris libraries was completed in the final weeks of 2013. It was then that news broke of Nelson Mandela's death, and the themes from yellowing pamphlets were brought into the here-and-now with the most extraordinary immediacy. Within a purely national context, Mandela may be thought of as a benign example of the transformation of the enkindling resistance hero into a symbol of national integration and the new post-apartheid state. The struggle against apartheid, however, had not been a purely national one, and Mandela's was a name that reverberated internationally as only a very few like Lenin's ever had. For a moment that December, it appeared as if every Paris bookshop felt obliged to display Mandela's autobiography. Every reputable newspaper seemed to have its special supplement or *hors-série* prepared, and at every metro station posters sprouted up for the Mandela biopic that good taste and opportunism now permitted. Mandela's, however, was also an appropriation cult, and it was the communist daily *L'Humanité* which rightly claimed to have been earliest and most steadfast in his support. In the stories which *L'Humanité* once more recounted of Mandela's life, the classic themes of the political trial, unbroken dignity and clarity of vision were again rehearsed; and to the recollections of a 'Mandela generation' of solidarity activists was added the renewed internationalist note of the attendance of the Palestinian people's representative at the commemorative rally held outside the PCF's Paris headquarters. Surmounting the scenes was the giant image of the leader whom speakers apostrophised as the familiar *tu*, or referred to as Madiba, just as they might once have referred to Ilyich or Pasionaria.[22]

With Mandela's times the transition is made from the hero to the celebrity, or in Mandela's case the celebrification of the hero. Though represented in this instance through a non-communist figurehead, the rally in the Place du Colonel-Fabien might also be seen as a swansong to the communist politics of personality, or one at least umbilically connected to the communist tradition. Nevertheless, the anthropomorphising, not of power, but of its contestation, is a phenomenon that not only predates the Bolshevik experience but survives it; and what Bernstein described as the 'craving to personify' has not yet been dissipated by the further relentless development of mass communications. In every project of the radical left, whatever its different notions of how the world might be changed, there is always and inherently the prescriptiveness of what the syndicalist Émile Pouget called 'the minority who carry the future within themselves', and whose claims to prefigure that future have so often been embodied in the exemplary individual.[23] In every such project that has a wider resonance, there is also some capacity to symbolise the cause it represents through the centring on some space, event, text, or sometimes a person.

The Zapatistas movement of indigenous Mexicans is often invoked as a prototype or epitome of a movement refusing traditional forms of authority and confounding hierarchy with the network.[24] Even so, there can be few social movements in history that became so identified with an individual, here in the person of Subcomandante Marcos.[25] As with Prestes, there was very much the consciousness of a longer lineage. Indeed, the movement took its very name from the revolutionary peasants' leader Emiliano Zapata, whose image appeared on placards and public murals with the slogan *Zapata lives, the struggle continues!* Marcos, however, was not an indigenous peasant but a former lecturer, and through mastery of fable and epigram he exercised what in some respects appears once more as the charisma of the word. Ostensibly, this was the cult of impersonality taken to its extreme, as the Subcomandante appeared only in a ski-mask, and with a pipe protruding incongruously in what might have been an ironic commentary on an early age of ostentatious modesty. The mystique, of course, was all the greater. 'We are all Marcos!', declaimed Zapatistas also wearing ski-masks; but in a movement which maintained its ethos of collective leadership and horizontalism, there were also complaints of *protagonismo*—excessive focus on the leader—and of 'Marcotrafficking'. That might perhaps recall Mayakovsky's warning against trafficking in Lenin; but one might also go much further back, to the Chartist leader Feargus O'Connor, famous as the 'Lion of Freedom', whose fustian dress symbolised the 'unity of leader and led', but whom a democratic movement also accused of cultivating 'Lionism'.[26] The tension, perhaps, may never be resolved; for without Marcos's consummate command of communications, one may certainly wonder whether *Zapatismo* would ever have exercised the profound influence internationally that it subsequently did.

Travelling practices are like travelling theory; relocated from one time and place to another, a practice like a theory is not simply reproduced or replicated, but may become something altogether different.[27] In his study *Power in Movement*, Sidney Tarrow defined the social movement as one galvanised by 'culturally resonant, action-oriented symbols' which mobilises large numbers of people by means of 'meetings, processions, demonstrations, petitions, slogans, symbols, committees, publicly proclaimed strategies, and related means', and which has its greatest effect in the presence of binding elections or visible opportunities for more radical forms of action.[28] On a scale without historical parallel, communism in one aspect was the attempt to institutionalise and co-ordinate these forms of activity not only nationally but internationally, and by virtue of its internationalism to circumvent the denial of elections or other 'visible political opportunities' by particular regimes. Through the 'cycles of contention' that one may identify with the upheavals of 1917–1921 and with the anti-fascist mobilisations of the 1930s–1940s, communism and its ancillaries emerged as, for the time being, arguably the primary vehicle for such activities and for the cultures of solidarity that developed around the defence of the right to practise them. Travelling theory may also have its bearing on the variations that emerged as it did so. The turn to the individual that marked the second of these cycles was certainly a corollary and reinforcement of the centralising principle that was now embodied in the figure of the general secretary. But at the same time, this was also a form of action-oriented symbol long familiar in radical politics, by which a Thälmann or Dimitrov could be won or lost 'like a battle', and using just the repertoires of social-movement action which communists now laid claim to as their own.

Communism's distinctiveness did not necessarily lie in the entanglement of these symbols with a highly bureaucratised form of party authority, for this to some extent had already been anticipated by the parties of the Second International. What fundamentally set the communist experience apart was the harnessing of a radical symbolic politics to a process of state-building and international realpolitik of the utmost cynicism and brutality, and thus to the manufactured adulation of the leader as the instrument of public conformism and the securing of the cult community against both internal and external contagion. The ambivalence of Thompson's decade of heroes gave way to what Thompson himself called 'the era of Stalin's birthday and the Doctors' Plot', with a fitting recognition of how inextricable the practices of cult and coercion had now become. Even now, Thompson identified his rediscovered ideal of socialist humanism with those very individuals, William Morris and the communist Mann, whom he had also claimed for the party of Stalin's birthday.[29] But what was not to be repeated was the vesting of such authority in the domineering political structures whose instrument and beneficiary the leader was. 'No saviour from on high delivers', the communists still sang in their anthem the *Internationale*; 'our own right hand the chains must shiver'. With all the historical complexities necessarily registered here, the cult of the individual under communism shows how well-founded that basic impulse was.

Notes

1. Daniel Leese, *Mao Cult. Rhetoric and ritual in China's Cultural Revolution* (Cambridge: Cambridge University Press, 2011), ch. 7.
2. Anders Stephanson, 'Interview with Gil Green' in Michael E. Brown et al. (eds), *New Studies in the Politics and Culture of US Communism* (New York: Monthly Review, 1993), p. 322; also

Jane Portal, *Art Under Control in North Korea* (London: Reaktion, 2005), ch. 4.

3. Yves Cohen, *Le Siècle des chefs. Une histoire transnationale du commandement et de l'autorité (1890–1940)* (Paris: Éditions Amsterdam, 2013), pp. 815–21.
4. For example Jean-Marie Goulemot, *Pour l'amour de Staline. La face oubliée du communisme français* (Paris: CNRS, 2009 edn); see also Chap. 1 above.
5. See Norman LaPorte, Kevin Morgan and Matthew Worley (eds), *Bolshevism, Stalinism and the Comintern: perspectives on Stalinization* (Basingstoke: Palgrave Macmillan, 2008); the point is developed in the editors' introduction, pp. 1–21.
6. Cohen, *Siècle*, p. 795.
7. Cohen, *Siècle*, p. 794.
8. Sidney and Beatrice Webb, *Soviet Communism: a new civilisation* (1935) (London: Gollancz, 1937 edn), pp. 995–6.
9. J. Arch Getty, *Practicing Stalinism. Bolsheviks, boyars and the persistence of tradition* (New Haven, CT: Yale University Press, 2013), p. 77.
10. See Chap. 1 above.
11. Daniel Siemens, *The Making of a Nazi Hero. The murder and myth of Horst Wessel* (London: Tauris, 2013).
12. Claus Offe, 'New social movements: challenging the boundaries of institutional politics', *Social Research*, 52 (1985), 817–68.
13. Cohen, *Siècle*, pp. 815–21.
14. See above, Chap. 2; also Cohen, *Siècle*, p. 815.
15. Thompson, 'An open letter to Leszek Kolakowski' in idem, *The Poverty of Theory and other essays* (London: Merlin, 1978), pp. 99–100.
16. See Julian Bourg, 'Principally contradiction. The flourishing of French Maoism' in Alexander C. Cook (ed.), *Mao's Little Red Book. A global history* (Cambridge: Cambridge University Press, 2014), pp. 225–44.
17. Alain Badiou, *The Communist Hypothesis* (London: Verso, 2015 edn), pp. 112–18 and 186–8.
18. Thompson, 'Open letter', p. 99.
19. These included Hachette, Simon & Schuster and Robert Maxwell's Pergamon Press.
20. Agnes Heller, 'Legitimation deficit and legitimation crisis in East European societies' in Vladimir Tismaneanu (ed.), *Stalinism*

Revisited. The establishment of communist regimes in East-Central Europe (Budapest: Central European University Press, 2009), p. 144.
21. François Furet, *Le Passé d'une illusion. Essai sur l'idée communiste au xxe siècle* (Paris: Robert Laffont, 1995), p. 450.
22. See for example Pierre Laurent, 'Le symbole de la lutte pour l'emancipation humaine nous a quittés' and 'L'hommage du peuple parisien au père de la nation arc-en-ciel', *L'Humanité*, 11 Dec. 2013.
23. For discussion of this point see my 'Heralds of the future? Emma Goldman, Friedrich Nietzsche and the anarchist as superman', *Anarchist Studies*, 17, 2 (2009), 55–80.
24. For example John Holloway, *Change the World Without Taking Power* (London: Pluto, 2010 edn), pp. 20–1 and 204–15.
25. The discussion that follows draws on Jeff Conant, *A Poetics of Resistance. The revolutionary public relations of the Zapatista insurgency* (Oakland, CA: AK Press, 2010).
26. Paul Pickering, *Feargus O'Connor. A political life* (London: Merlin, 2008).
27. Edward Said, 'Traveling theory' in idem, *The World, the Text and the Critic* (Cambridge, MA: Harvard University Press, 1983), pp. 226–47.
28. Sidney Tarrow, *Power in Movement: Social movements and contentious politics* (Cambridge: Cambridge University Press, 1998 edn), p. 2.
29. John Saville and E.P. Thompson, 'Editorial', *New Reasoner*, 1 (1957), 2; also Thompson, 'Socialist humanism. An epistle to the philistines', ibid., 119–29.

Select Bibliography

This select bibliography lists archival sources and the principal scholarly texts relating to communism and the cult of the individual consulted specifically for this study. Full references will be found in the endnotes, and these include extensive contemporary printed sources which are not separately listed here.

Principal Archival Sources

Archives Départmentales de la Seine-Saint-Denis

Parti communiste français archives including PCF secretariat and central committee; Fonds Jean-Richard Bloch; Fonds Marcel Cachin; Fonds André Marty

Archives Nationales, Paris

Fonds Maurice Thorez

Centre d'Histoire Sociale du XXe siècle, Paris

Fonds André Marty

National Archives, London

Security Service personal files (KV 2)

K. Morgan, *International Communism and the Cult of the Individual*, DOI 10.1057/978-1-137-55667-7

Parti communiste français, Paris

Fonds Henri Barbusse

People's History Museum, Manchester

Communist Party of Great Britain archives including CPGB central committee, R. Palme Dutt papers, William Gallacher papers, Tom Mann papers, Harry Pollitt papers

Russian State Archive of Socio-Political History (RGASPI), Moscow

Comintern archives including Comintern personal files, Marty secretariat, CPGB and Parti communiste belge opisi

Scholarly Books and Articles

Günter Agde, *Kämpfer. Biographie eines Films und seiner Macher* (Berlin: Das Neue Berlin, 2001).

Aldo Agosti, *Palmiro Togliatti. A biography* (London: I.B. Tauris, 2008).

Gleb J. Albert, '"Esteemed Comintern!" The Communist International and world-revolutionary charisma in early Soviet society', *TCC*, 8 (2015), 10–39.

Balázs Apor, *The 'Invisible Shining': the cult of Mátyás Rákosi in stalinist Hungary, 1945–1956* (Budapest: Central European University Press, forthcoming 2017).

Balázs Apor, 'Leader in the making: the role of biographies in constructing the cult of Mátyás Rákosi' in Apor et al., *Leader Cult*, pp. 63–82.

Balázs Apor, 'National traditions and the leader cult in communist Hungary in the early cold war years', 1 (2009), 50–71.

Balázs Apor et al. (eds), *The Leader Cult in Communist Dictatorships. Stalin and the Eastern bloc* (Basingstoke: Palgrave Macmillan, 2004).

Gilbert Badia, *Clara Zetkin, féministe sans frontières* (Paris: Éditions Ouvrières, 1993).

Gilbert Badia, 'Le comité Thaelmann' in Badia et al., *Les bannis de Hitler. Accueil et lutte des exilés allemands en France 1933–1939* (Paris: Études et Documentation Internationales, 1984), pp. 199–260.

James R. Barrett, 'Revolution and personal crisis: communist politics and personal narrative in the life of William Z. Foster' in Morganet al., *Agents of the Revolution*, pp. 111–32.

James R. Barrett, *William Z. Foster and the Tragedy of American Radicalism* (Urbana & Chicago, ILL: University of Illinois Press, 1999).

Philippe Baudorre, *Barbusse. Le pourfendeur de la Grande Guerre* (Paris: Flammarion, 1995).

Jan C. Behrends, 'Drei Gesichter der Führerkults. Eine vergleichende Skizze zu Bolschewismus, Faschismus und Nationalsozialismus' in Ennker and Hein-Kircher, *Der Führer im Europa des 20. Jahrhunderts*, pp. 325–46.

Jan C. Behrends, 'Exporting the leader: the Stalin cult in Poland and East Germany (1944/5-1956)' in Apor, *Leader Cult*, pp. 161–78.

Jean-Pierre A. Bernard, 'La liturgie funèbre des communistes (1924–1983)', *Vingtième Siècle. Revue d'histoire*, 9 (1986), 37–52.

Jean-Pierre A. Bernard, *Le Parti communiste français et la question littéraire* (Grenoble: Presses Universitaires de Grenoble, 1972).

Andrew G. Bonnell, 'The Lassalle cult in German social democracy', *Australian Journal of Politics and History*, 35 (1989), 50–60.

Victoria E. Bonnell, *Iconography of Power. Soviet political posters under Lenin and Stalin* (Berkeley, CA: University of California Press, 1993).

Marie-Cécile Bouju, *Lire en communiste. Les Maisons d'édition du Parti communiste français 1920–1968* (Rennes: Presses universitaires de Rennes, 2010).

David Brandenberger, *National Bolshevism. Stalinist mass culture and the formation of modern Russian national identity 1931–1956* (Cambridge, Mass.: Harvard University Press, 2002).

David Brandenberger, *Propaganda State in Crisis. Soviet ideology, indoctrination, and terror under Stalin, 1927–1941* (New Haven, CT: Yale University Press, 2011).

D.L. Brandenberger and A.M. Dubrovsky, '"The people need a tsar". The emergence of national bolshevism as stalinist ideology, 1931-1941', *Europe-Asia Studies*, 50 (1998), 873–82.

David Brandenberger, 'Stalin as symbol: a case study of the personality cult and its construction' in Davies and Harris, *Stalin: a new history*, pp. 249–70.

Pierre Brocheux, *Hô Chi Minh* (Paris: Presses de Science Po, 2000).

Jeffrey Brooks, *Thank You, Comrade Stalin! Soviet public culture from revolution to Cold War* (Princeton, NJ: Princeton University Press, 2000).

Peter Burke, *The Fabrication of Louis XIV* (Cambridge, MA: Yale University Press, 1992).

Luciano Cavalli, 'Considerations on charisma and the cult of charismatic leadership', *Modern Italy*, 3 (1998), 159–71.

William J. Chase, 'Stalin as producer: the Moscow show trials and the construction of mortal threats' in Davies and Harris, *Stalin: a new history*, pp. 226–48.

Ian Christie, 'Canons and careers: the director in Soviet cinema' in Richard Taylor and Derek Spring (eds), *Stalinism and Soviet Cinema* (London: Routledge, 1993).

Katerina Clark, *Moscow, the Fourth Rome. Stalinism, cosmopolitanism, and the evolution of Soviet culture, 1931–1941* (Cambridge, MA: Harvard University Press, 2011).

Katerina Clark, *The Soviet Novel. History as ritual* (Chicago, ILL: University of Chicago Press, 1981).

Vanessa Codaccioni, *Punir les opposants. PCF et procès politiques (1947-1962)* (Paris: CNRS Éditions, 2013).

Yves Cohen, 'The cult of number one in an age of leaders', *Kritika: Explorations in Russian and Eurasian History*, 8 (2007), 597–634.

Yves Cohen, *Le Siècle des chefs. Une histoire transnationale du commandement et de l'autorité (1890–1940)* (Paris: Éditions Amsterdam, 2013).

Alexander C. Cook (ed.), *Mao's Little Red Book. A global history* (Cambridge: Cambridge University Press, 2014).

Alexander Courban, *Gabriel Péri: un homme politique, un député, un journaliste* (Paris: La Dispute, 2011).

Sarah Davies, 'The "cult" of the *Vozhd'*: representations in letters from 1934-41', *Russian History*, 24 (1997), 131–47.

Sarah Davies, *Popular Opinion in Stalin's Russia. Terror, propaganda and dissent, 1934–1941* (Cambridge: Cambridge University Press, 1997).

Sarah Davies, 'Stalin and the making of the leader cult in the 1930s' in Apor et al., *Leader Cult*, pp. 29–46.

Sarah Davies and James Harris (eds), *Stalin: a new history* (Cambridge: Cambridge University Press, 2005).

Isaac Deutscher, *The Prophet Unarmed. Trotsky: 1929–1940* (Oxford: Oxford University Press, 1970 edn).

Isaac Deutscher, *The Prophet Outcast. Trotsky: 1921–1929* (Oxford: Oxford University Press, 1970 edn).

Isaac Deutscher, *Stalin. A political biography* (Oxford: Oxford University Press, 1949).

Judith Devlin, '"Recreating history on film". Stalin and the Russian revolution in feature film, 1937–1939', *Media History*, 13 (2007), 149–68.

Benno Ennker, *Die Anfänge des Leninkults in der Sowjetunion* (Cologne: Bohlau Verlag, 1997).

Benno Ennker, 'The origins and intentions of the Lenin cult' in Ian D. Thatcher (ed.), *Regime and Society in Twentieth-Century Russia. Selected papers from the Fifth World Congress of Central and East European Studies, Warsaw, 1995* (Basingstoke: Macmillan, 1995).

Benno Enkker, 'The Stalin cult, Bolshevik rule and Kremlin interaction in the 1930s' in Apor et al. (eds), *Leader Cult*, pp. 83–101.

Benno Ennker and Heidi Hein-Kircher (eds), *Der Führer im Europa des 20. Jahrhunderts* (Marburg: Herder-Institut, 2010).

Orlando Figes and Boris Kolonitskii, *Interpreting the Russian Revolution. The language and symbols of 1917* (New Haven, CT: Yale University Press, 1999).

Philippe Forest, *Aragon* (Paris: Gallimard, 2015).

J. Arch Getty, *Practicing Stalinism. Bolsheviks, boyars and the persistence of tradition* (New Haven, CT: Yale University Press, 2013).

José Gotovitch, *Du communisme et des communistes en Belgique. Approches critiques* (Brussels: Editions Aden, n.d.).

José Gotovitch, 'Construction and deconstruction of a cult: Edgar Lalmand and the Communist Party of Belgium', *TCC*, 1 (2009), 129–52.

Jean-Marie Goulemot, *Pour l'amour de Staline. La face oubliée du communisme français* (Paris: CNRS, 2009 edn).

Stephen Gundle, 'The legacy of the prison notebooks: Gramsci, the PCI and Italian culture in the post-war period' in Christopher Duggan and Christopher Wagstaff (eds), *Italy in the Cold War. Politics, culture and society 1948–58* (Oxford: Berg, 1995), pp. 131–48.

Stephen Gundle, Christopher Duggan and Giuliana Peri (eds), *The Cult of the Duce. Mussolini and the Italians* (Manchester: Manchester University Press, 2013).

Anssi Halmesvirta, 'A foreign benefactor and a domestic liberator: the cults of Lenin and Mannerheim in Finland', *Scandinavian Journal of History* 34 (2009), 414–32.

Rolf Hellebust, 'Reflections on an absence: novelistic portraits of Stalin before 1953' in Nina Kolesnikoff and Walter Smyrniw (eds), *Socialist Realism Revisited. Selected papers from the McMaster conference* (Hamilton, Ontario: McMaster University, 1994), pp. 111–20.

Klaus Heller and Jan Plamper (eds), *Personality Cults in Stalinism – Personenkulte im Stalinismus* (Göttingen: V&R Unipress, 2004).

Gina Hermann, *Written in Red: the communist memoir in Spain*, 2010 (Urbana, Ill: University of Illinois Press, 2010).

Antony Howe, '"Our only ornament".Tom Mann and British communist "hagiography"', *TCC*, 1 (2009), 91–109.

Chang-tai Hung, *Mao's New World. Political culture in the early People's Republic* (Ithaca, NY: Cornell University Press, 2011).

Edward P. Johanningsmeier, *The Forging of American Communism. The life of William Z. Foster* (Princeton, NJ: Princeton University Press, 1994).

Polly Jones, *Myth, Memory and Trauma. Rethinking the stalinist past in the Soviet Union, 1953–70* (New Haven, CT: Yale University Press, 2013)

Pierre Juquin, *Aragon. Un destin français. 1: Le temps des rêves (1897–1939)* (Paris: Éditions de la Martinière, 2012); *2: L'Atlantide (1939–1982)* (Paris: Éditions de la Martinière, 2013).

Ian Kershaw, *The 'Hitler Myth'. Image and reality in the Third Reich* (Oxford: Oxford University Press, 1989 edn).

Ian Kershaw and Moshe Lewin (eds), *Stalinism and Nazism. Dictatorships in comparison* (Cambridge: Cambridge University Press, 1997),

David King, *The Commissar Vanishes. The falsification of photograph and art in Stalin's Russia* (Edinburgh: Canongate, 1997).

Stephen Kotkin, *Stalin: paradoxes of power 1897–1928* (London: Penguin, 2015 edn).

Annie Kriegel, 'Bureaucratie, culte de personnalité et charisme. Le cas français: Maurice Thorez, secrétaire général du PCF (1900–1964)' in idem, *Communisme au miroir français* (Paris: Gallimard, 1974), pp. 132–58.

Miklós Kun, *Stalin. An unknown portrait* (Budapest: Central European University Press, 2003).

Norman LaPorte, 'Ernst Thälmann: the making of a German communist, 1886-1921', *Moving the Social*, 51 (2014), 127–58.

Norman Laporte and Kevin Morgan, '"Kings among their subjects?" Ernst Thälmann, Harry Pollitt and the leadership cult as Stalinization' in LaPorte et al., *Bolshevism, Stalinism and the Comintern*, pp. 124–45.

Norman LaPorte, Kevin Morgan and Matthew Worley (eds), *Bolshevism, Stalinism and the Comintern: perspectives on Stalinization* (Basingstoke: Palgrave Macmillan, 2008).

Daniel Leese, *Mao Cult. Rhetoric and ritual in China's Cultural Revolution* (Cambridge: Cambridge University Press, 2011).

Matthew E. Lenoe, *The Kirov Murder and Soviet History* (New Haven, CT: Yale University Press, 2010)

Moshe Lewin, 'Stalin the mirror of the other' in Ian Kershaw and Moshe Lewin (eds), *Stalinism and Nazism: dictatorships in common* (Cambridge: Cambridge University Press, 1997), pp. 107–34.

Russel Lemmons, *Hitler's Rival. Ernst Thälmann in Myth and Memory* (Lexington, KY: University of Kentucky Press, 2013).

Robert Levy, *Ana Pauker. The rise and fall of a Jewish communist* (Berkeley, CA: University of California Press, 2001).

Lars T. Lih, *Lenin* (London: Reaktion Books, 2011).

Christine Lodder, 'Lenin's Plan for Monumental Propaganda' in Matthew Cullerne Bown and Brandon Taylor (eds), *Art of the Soviets. Painting, sculpture and architecture in a one-party state, 1917–1992* (Manchester: Manchester University Press, 1993), pp. 16–32.

Robert H. McNeal, *Bride of the Revolution. Krupskaya and Lenin* (Ann Arbor, MI: University of Michigan Press, 1972).

Robert H. McNeal, 'Krupskaya: the feminine subcult' in Bernard W. Eissenstat (ed.), *Lenin and Leninism. State, law, and society* (Lexington, KY: Lexington Books, 1971).

John Manley, '"Audacity, audacity, still more audacity: Tim Buck, the party, and the people, 1932-1939', *Labour/Le Travail*, 49 (2002), 9–41.

Marzia Marsili, 'De Gasperi and Togliatti: political leadership and personality cults in post-war Italy', *Modern Italy*, 3 (1998), 249–61.

Jamie Miller, 'Soviet politics and the Mezhrabpom studio in the Soviet Union during the 1920s and 1930s', *Historical Journal of Film, Radio and Television*, 32 (2012), 521–35.

Kevin Morgan, 'Ainsi pour Gallacher? Quelques regards sur la construction de la vie communiste modèle en Grande-Bretagne', *Communisme*, 87 (2006), 29–46.

Kevin Morgan, *Harry Pollitt* (Manchester: Manchester University Press, 1993).

Kevin Morgan, 'Harry Pollitt, Maurice Thorez and the writing of exemplary communist lives' in Julie Gottlieb and Richard Toye (eds), *Making Reputations: power, persuasion and the individual in British politics* (London: I.B. Tauris, 2005), pp. 56–69.

Kevin Morgan, Gidon Cohen and Andrew Flinn, *Agents of the Revolution. New biographical approaches to the history of international communism in the age of Lenin and Stalin* (Berne: Peter Lang, 2005).

Kevin Morgan, Gidon Cohen and Andrew Flinn, *Communists in British Society 1920–1991* (London: Rivers Oram, 2007).

J.P. Nettl, *Rosa Luxemburg* (Oxford: Oxford University Press, 2 vols, 1966).

Claude Pennetier, 'André Marty à l'épreuve des archives' in Paul Boulland et al. (eds), *André Marty: l'homme, l'affaire, l'archive* (Paris: Codhos, 2005), pp. 15–34.

Claude Pennetier, 'Thorez-Marty: Paris-Moscou, Moscou-Paris' in Mikhail Narimsky and Jürgen Rojahn (eds), *Centre and Periphery. The history of the Comintern in the light of new documents* (Amsterdam: Institute of Social History, 1996), pp. 203–17.

Claude Pennetier and Bernard Pudal (eds), *Autobiographies, autocritiques, aveux dans le monde communiste* (Paris: Belin, 2002).

Claude Pennetier and Bernard Pudal, 'Les autobiographies des "fils du peuple". De l'autobiographie édifiante à l'autobiographie auto-analytique' in idem, *Autobiographies, autocritiques, aveux*, pp. 215–46.

Claude Pennetier and Bernard Pudal, 'Deux générations de militants communistes français (1931–1951) en proie à des procès d'épurations internes' in José Gotovitch and Anne Morelli (eds), *Militantisme et militants* (Brussels, 2000).

Claude Pennetier and Bernard Pudal (trans. Kevin Morgan), 'Stalinism: workers' cult and cult of leaders, *TCC*, 1 (2009), 20–9.

Maureen Perrie, *The Cult of Ivan the Terrible in Stalin's Russia* (Basingstoke: Palgrave Macmillan, 2001).

Jan Plamper, *The Stalin Cult. A study in the alchemies of power* (New Haven, CT: Yale University Press, 2012).

Silvio Pons (trans. Allan Cameron), *The Global Revolution. A history of international communism 1917–1991* (Oxford: Oxford University Press, 2014).

Paul Preston, *The Last Stalinist. The life of Santiago Carrillo* (London: William Collins, 2015 edn).

David Priestland, *Stalinism and the Politics of Mass Mobilization. Ideas, power and terror in inter-war Russia* (Oxford: Oxford University Press, 2007).

Kimmo Rentola, 'Finnish communism, O.W. Kuusinen, and their two native countries' in Tauno Saarela and Kimmo Rentola (eds), *Communism: national and international* (Helsinki: Finnish Historical Society, 1998), pp. 159–81.

Lucy Riall, *Garibaldi; invention of a hero* (New Haven, CT: Yale University Press, 2008 edn).

Nicholas V. Riasanovsky, *The Image of Peter the Great in Russian History and Thought* (New York: Oxford University Press, 1985).

Alfred J. Rieber, 'Stalin, man of the borderlands', *American Historical Review*, 106 (2001), 1651–91.

Philippe Robrieux, *Maurice Thorez. Vie secrète et vie publique* (Paris: Fayard, 1975).

James G. Ryan, *Earl Browder. The failure of American communism* (Tuscaloose, AL: University of Alabama Press, 1997).

Tauno Saarela, 'Dead martyrs and living leaders: the cult of the individual within Finnish communism', *TCC*, 1 (2009), 30–49.

Marco Aurélio Santana, 'Re-imagining the Cavalier of Hope: the Brazilian Communist Party and the images of Luiz Carlos Prestes', *TCC*, 1 (2009), 110–28.

Donald Sassoon, 'Italian images of Russia, 1945-56' in Christopher Duggan and Christopher Wagstaff (eds), *Italy in the Cold War. Politics, culture and society 1948-58* (Oxford: Berg, 1995), pp. 189–202.

Robert Service, *Trotsky. A biography* (London: Pan edn, 2010).

Alexander Shklyaruk and Sergei Larkov, *Gustav Klutsis – Valentina Kulagina: posters, book graphic arts, magazine graphic arts, newsphotomontage 1922–1937* (Moscow: Contact-Cultura, 2010).

Karl Schlögel, *Moscow, 1937* (Cambridge: Polity, 2012).

Stéphane Sirot, *Maurice Thorez* (Paris: Presses de Sciences Po, 2000).

Paulo Spriano (trans. John Fraser), *Antonio Gramsci and the Party: the prison years* (London: Lawrence & Wishart, 1979).

Marietta Stankova, *Georgi Dimitrov. A biography* (London: Tauris, 2010).

Brigitte Studer, 'More autonomy for the national sections? The organisation of the ECCI after the Seventh World Congress' in Mikhail Narinsky and Jürgen Rojahn (eds), *Centre and Periphery. The history of the Comintern in the light of new documents* (Amsterdam: International Institute of Social History, 1996), pp.102–13.

Brigitte Studer, *The Transnational World of the Cominternians* (Basingstoke: Palgrave Macmillan, 2015).

Brigitte Studer and Heiko Haumann (eds), *Stalinistische Subjekte. Individuum und System in der Sowjetunion und Der Komintern 1929–1953* (Zurich: Chronos, 2006).

Ronald Grigor Suny, 'Stalin and his Stalinism: power and authority in the Soviet Union, 1930-53' in Kershaw and Lewin (eds), *Stalinism and Nazism*, pp. 26–52.

G.R. Swain, 'Tito: the formation of a disloyal Bolshevik', *International Review of Social History*, 34 (1989), 248–71.

Geoffrey Swain, *Tito. A biography* (London: Tauris, 2011).

Andrew Thorpe, 'Communist MP: Willie Gallacher and British communism' in Morgan et al., *Agents of the Revolution*, pp. 133–58.

Alexey Tikhomorov, 'The Stalin cult between center and periphery: the structures of the cult community in the empire of socialism, 1949–1956 – the case of GDR' in Ennker and Hein-Kircher, *Der Führer im Europa des 20*, pp. 297–324.

Robert C. Tucker, 'The rise of Stalin's personality cult', *American Historical Review*, 84 (1979), 347–66.

Robert C. Tucker, *Stalin in Power. The revolution from above 1928–1941* (New York: W.W. Norton, 1992 edn).

Nina Tumarkin, *Lenin Lives! The Lenin cult in Soviet Russia* (Cambridge, MA: Harvard University Press, 1983).

Tania Ünlüdag-Puschnerat, 'A German communist: Clara Zetkin (1857–1933)' in Morgan et al., *Agents of the Revolution*, pp. 93–110.

G.R. Utley, *Picasso: the communist years* (New Haven, CT: Yale University Press, 2000).

Erik van Ree, *The Political Thought of Joseph Stalin. A study in twentieth-century revolutionary patriotism* (London: Routledge Curzon, 2002).

Olga Velikanova, *Making of an Idol. On uses of Lenin* (Göttingen: Muster-Schmidt Verlag, 1996).

Eric D. Weitz, '"Rosa Luxemburg belongs to us!" German communism and the Luxemburg legacy', *Central European History*, 27 (1994), 27–64.

Annette Wieviorka, *Maurice et Jeannette: biographie du couple Thorez* (Paris: Fayard, 2010).

Annette Wieviorka, 'Picasso and Stalin' in Lynda Morris and Christoph Grunenberg (eds), *Picasso: peace and freedom* (London: Tate Publishing, 2010), pp. 26–33.

Serge Wolikow (ed.), *Pierre Semard. Engagements, discipline et fidelité* (Paris: Cherche Midi, 2007).

Rashit Yangorov, '*Onwards and Upwards!*: the origins of the Lenin cult in Soviet cinema' in Richard Taylor and Derek Spring (eds), *Stalinism and Soviet Cinema* (London: Routledge, 1993), pp. 15–33.

Tovah Yedlin, *Maxim Gorky. A political biography* (Westport, CT: Praeger, 1999).

INDEX

Note: Page numbers followed by "n" denote notes.

K. Morgan, *International Communism and the Cult of the Individual*, DOI 10.1057/978-1-137-55667-7

C

L

M

The manufacturer's authorised representative in the EU is Springer Nature Customer Service Centre GmbH, Europaplatz 3, 69115 Heidelberg, Germany. If you have any concerns regarding our products, please contact ProductSafety@springernature.com

Printed and bound by CPI Group (UK) Ltd, Croydon, CR0 4YY
12/08/2026
02194529-0001